The
New
Testament

Praise for *The New Testament: Methods and Meanings*

"This accessible and engaging book by two eminent New Testaments scholars is a welcome addition to the bookshelf of New Testament introductions. Carter and Levine bring their own particular interests to bear on their subject. Carter is particularly interested in the Roman context of the documents, and Levine focuses on their Jewish matrix. At the same time, they demonstrate the many different questions that can be addressed in the New Testament and show that answering these questions requires different reading strategies that will in turn result in different interpretations. The book provides a superb introduction to the New Testament books, as well as to the methods, approaches, and results of New Testament scholarship without glossing over the difficulties. It also conveys their profound respect for their readers, in all their diversity, and for the New Testament texts themselves. The clear and straightforward structure will make it easy to use for both formal and informal teaching situations."
—**Adele Reinhartz,** Professor and Director of Graduate Programs, Department of Classics and Religious Studies, University of Ottawa

"This book is a must read for all serious students of the New Testament. Teachers and preachers will also benefit greatly from the insightful treatment of texts that are often stumbling blocks. Carter, with his knowledge of the Roman imperial context of the NT and Levine, with her expertise in its Jewish matrix, make an extraordinary team. They not only show why the questions one asks about the Bible matter, but also demonstrate how to go about asking and answering questions in ways that produce meaning that is respectful toward all."
—**Barbara E. Reid**, Professor of New Testament Studies and Vice President and Academic Dean, Catholic Theological Union, Chicago

The New Testament

Methods and Meanings

Warren Carter & Amy-Jill Levine

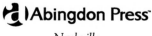

Abingdon Press

Nashville

THE NEW TESTAMENT:
METHODS AND MEANINGS

Copyright © 2013 by Abingdon Press

Library of Congress Cataloging-in-Publication Data

Carter, Warren, 1955-
  The New Testament : methods and meanings / Warren Carter, A.-J. Levine.
    pages cm
  Includes bibliographical references and index.
  ISBN 978-1-4267-4190-6 (pbk. : alk. paper) 1. Bible. New Testament—Criticism, interpretation, etc. I. Levine, Amy-Jill, 1956- II. Title.
  BS2341.52.C374 2013
  225.6—dc23

                                                                                          2013029534

13 14 15 16 17 18 19 20 21 22—10 9 8 7 6 5 4 3 2 1

MANUFACTURED IN THE UNITED STATES OF AMERICA

For those who ask, "What might Scripture mean?"

Contents

$\mathcal{T}$he Questions You Ask Shape the Answers You Get

W e wrote this book not only for college, divinity school, and seminary students—that is, the students we have taught, and who have taught us, over the past several decades—but also for any reader interested in how the New Testament (henceforth NT) has been, and can be, interpreted. We do not presuppose that all of our readers are Christians, let alone Christians of any particular type. Indeed, it is our hope that all readers will find themselves welcomed by our approach, challenged in places by our observations, and, most important, increasingly aware that how we interpret the Bible *matters*.

Regarding interpretation, we do have three major presuppositions:

First, we presuppose that any study of anyone's religious books should be undertaken with respect for those who hold those books sacred and for the interpretations that have accrued over the years. At the same time, we believe, to use the cliché, that the Bible should be a rock on which one stands, rather than a rock thrown to damage others.

Second, we recognize that the books comprising the NT were written in a time and culture very different from our own. Therefore, we seek to understand which comments are directed to a specific time and place and which have universal or timeless value; we attend to teachings in the text where even the most conservative of Christian commentators will prescind from promoting those teachings for today. Respect for a text, or a tradition, does not mean agreeing with all of its teaching. Rather, respect and love suggest thoughtful, critical engagement. Consequently, we foreground passages that have led to harmful stereotypes, or worse, and attempt to determine why they were written, how they were first understood, and how readers of Scripture today, both inside and outside of Christian contexts, might understand them. Passages that speak of Jews as children of the devil (John 8) or suggest that women are saved through childbearing (1 Tim 2) or that legitimate the institution of slavery (1 Pet 2) cannot be ignored or merely glossed over.

Third, we presuppose that the questions we ask of the text, and the reading strategies with which we approach it, will lead to different interpretations. Moreover, we also

1

recognize that our own subject positions, or social locations, will influence what questions we ask and what answers we find. On the simplest level, people interested in God, salvation, or church structure will ask different questions than people interested in Jesus' view of the Jerusalem Temple or Paul's view of women's leadership. Warren is particularly interested in the Roman context of the documents, and A.-J. focuses on their Jewish matrix. Thus, we attempt to bring into conversation both various reading strategies and the presuppositions of the readers.

Similarly, we think it important that interpreters be as honest as they can be about their own loyalties and contexts. Some interpreters present themselves with social markers that ostensibly influence the interpretation, for example, "I am a woman from Hong Kong" or "I am a white US male Protestant" or "I am a Mexican lesbian." Rarely, however, do these confessions speak to the concerns of the texts themselves or the discussion of history. It is usually more helpful when such self-identifications reflect on the meaning the biblical text has for the interpreter. Here we think it only fair that we acknowledge our interpretive stances.

Warren comes from the Christian tradition. He thinks that Christians must read these NT texts carefully, thoughtfully, and dialogically. He knows that interpretations of the NT writings can do—and have done—both enormous harm and enormous good among Christian communities and beyond. At their worst, they inspire hate, oppression, and exclusion. At their best, they witness to God's loving, liberating, and life-giving ways of working in our world and inspire people to worship and to perform consonant acts of justice and compassion.

A.-J. is a member of an Orthodox synagogue, although she is not Orthodox in terms of practice. She does not read the NT as authoritative for herself; she does not worship Jesus as Lord and Savior. However, she has spent over three decades studying the text and studying with people who hold it sacred. While she does not worship the messenger, she takes inspiration from much of Jesus' teachings, teachings that she recognizes as substantially reflecting her own Judaism. She has also seen, firsthand, the detrimental effects that unfortunate NT interpretations can have: she, and her children, have been accused of killing Jesus; she has been told by some of her students that, as a woman, she has no authority over them. And she has also seen the great good those who follow Jesus do.

We both recognize that the texts are products of human authors, with their own agenda, who wrote in a particular context. We also both insist on approaching the text generously. For example, one does not have to believe that Jesus literally rose from the dead after three days in a tomb to appreciate that many of his early followers, and many of his followers today, took this proclamation as literal and true. The same point holds for his miraculous conception and the miracles he is said to have performed. At the same time, we seek to press beyond the "what" of the events to the "so what?": How do these proclamations about Jesus relate to stories of other first-century miracle workers and heroes? What messages would his followers have derived from those stories, and what messages might people take today?

The use of the plural term "Meanings" in the title of this volume is, consequently, deliberate.

Making meaning is the task of every reader, and since all readers have their own questions, distinct experiences, and unique concerns, multiple and sometimes mutually exclusive interpretations are inevitable. As we detail, the NT texts have been interpreted in very different ways over the past 2,000 years.

That does not mean that all interpretations are equal, and it does not mean we can make these NT writings say anything we like. Some interpretations are better informed, more insightful, more articulate, more encompassing than others. Throughout the book, we will engage various interpretations, and we will offer our own. In cases where multiple and conflicting interpretations have claims to validity, we present the arguments and leave the decision to the reader.

In this way we will seek the meanings of each of the 27 writings that comprise the NT. In the individual chapters, we discuss some of the central ideas and perspectives of these writings, and we identify some of the important factors in the circumstances from which they originated. Throughout we follow the order in which the writings occur in the NT, with one exception. Because of constraints of space, we combine the discussion of 2 Peter and Jude. Our goal is to involve readers in this process of finding meanings in Scripture.

The other key word in the book's title is "Methods." Because *how* we read the NT shapes how we understand it, we discuss different reading strategies that facilitate the process of meaning making. The approaches, or the critical methods, that we use can be usefully grouped into three categories.

The first set focuses attention on what has been called "the worlds behind the text." By attending to historical-critical issues, we can make informed arguments about the circumstances in which a comment was formulated or a text was composed. Such concerns for history appear in each chapter. Whereas we do note that each generation has interpreted the text through its own concerns and for its own needs, we also want to respect the social location in which the composition arose.

It has also been said—by Henry Ford in 1916—that "history is more or less bunk. It's tradition. We don't want tradition. We want to live in the present, and the only history that is worth a tinker's damn is the history that we make today." To this we respond, "Bunk." To offer another saying in response, "A text without a context can be just a pretext for making it say anything the interpreter wants."

Historical approaches to the NT came under some suspicion especially with the rise in the 1970s of various literary-based types of biblical interpretation. The focus came to be on "what the text means to me" or "the worlds in front of the text" rather than on what the text might have meant to the people who first wrote and received it. To be sure, some early historical reconstruction was very much influenced by present-day concerns, and readings that had the guise of objective historical inquiry were really often attempts to reinforce present-day values. But the faults of past interpretive efforts should not erase the possibilities of doing history.

To deny the value of history, and so of historical-critical approaches to the NT, is to deny the peoples of antiquity their own culture and ultimately to center everything on our own experiences, our own values, and our own concerns. Further, to deny history is in a very pernicious way to deny multiculturalism; it is to promote the worst form of imperialism. To deny history is also, finally, theologically off track. If one takes the incarnation of Jesus seriously, then one should also take seriously the where and when of the biblical figures and events: the first- and early second-century worlds of Galilee and Judea, Asia Minor, Greece, and Rome. Jesus was not born in Nigeria or Nashville; Paul did not preach in the Falklands or Fort Worth.

Historical-critical approaches ask a cluster of seven related questions: who wrote what, to whom, when, where, why, and how? In each case, the biblical reader necessarily combines data with interpretation. For example, on the question "Who wrote the text?"—often, the answer is less clear than church tradition has suggested. The four gospels in the NT were originally anonymous texts; ascriptions to Matthew, Mark, Luke, and John are later additions, and none of the gospels actually claims to have been written by these men. Whereas 13 letters in the NT claim to have been authored by Paul, the majority of biblical scholars are confident that Paul wrote only seven of them, and even with those seven, good arguments can be made that the texts as we have them are not exactly the texts that Paul wrote. Editors have added, removed, and reorganized parts of these letters.

These observations lead to another point that should make us cautious when positing interpretations of Jesus or Paul or any of the other figures in the NT: we lack direct access to them. The Jesus we know is the one primarily attested in the four NT gospels: he spoke Aramaic, and the Gospels, like the rest of the NT, are written in Greek. He spoke to people who were unaware of claims regarding his resurrection, and the Gospels are written by people who proclaim him Lord; the Gospels are unlikely to have been composed by eyewitnesses, and they reveal evidence of having used other literary sources. Thus this book does not offer a chapter on the "historical Jesus"; it focuses rather on the *texts* of the NT.

A similar case holds for Paul. The documents we have in the NT are the texts the church chose to preserve, and those texts themselves underwent an editing process. We do not have complete and direct access to Paul; we have instead snapshots that his followers took and then put in their own album. We do not know if he changed his mind on certain issues, such as the proximity of the return of Jesus or the possibility of women's teaching or if his comments are church-specific or even utilitarian. Thus while historical inquiry is essential, it is always also tentative and partial.

Asking *what* was written is the focus of a field of inquiry known as "textual criticism." We do not have any "autographs," that is, any original manuscripts of any NT documents. The earliest scrap of text we have is a papyrus fragment of a few lines from John 18, dated by epigraphy (the study of handwriting) and papyrological analysis to the early second century. Conversely, we have thousands of later handwritten fragments of the NT, as well as citations from early Christian teachers; we have Greek texts as well as early translations into Latin, Syriac, Ethiopic, Armenian, Georgian, and Coptic. Text critics compare these various versions to determine, as best as possible, the earliest reading. For example, the famous story of the woman condemned for adultery, about whom Jesus said, "Let anyone among you who is without sin be the first to throw a stone at her" (John 8:7), appears in no early manuscripts; in some cases, it shows up in Luke's Gospel rather than John's. Thus text critics conclude that the earliest version of John lacked the story. For a more striking example, most scholars believe that the Gospel of Mark ends at 16:8, the report that the women who found Jesus' tomb empty "went out and fled from the tomb, for terror and amazement had seized them; and they said nothing to anyone, for they were afraid." Later scribes, finding this an incomplete account, added multiple endings, some talking about Jesus' appearances to his followers such as Mary Magdalene; others give new teaching about handling snakes and drinking poison. From studying different manuscripts, text critics have formulated a series of rules that help them decide the original wording among several versions.

Complicating this search for original manuscripts is that there may be no such original: the Gospels originated as oral compositions and were written down only after at least a generation. For likely another century or so, oral performance and written text influenced each other, until particular written versions came to be received as authoritative. We can draw a partial analogy to the classic stories of all cultures, whether of the Greek or Norse or Japanese gods or the folktales that mark all cultures: different people will tell the same story in different ways with different words. One can stress the multiple documents that do not agree and so call into question any truth claims to biblical accounts. We prefer to stress the consistency overall in the message.

The question "To whom?" seeks to identify the audience to which a text is addressed. At times, the answer seems obvious: Paul wrote the letter to the Romans to a church community or communities in Rome; the letter to the Ephesians went to the church at Ephesus. Yet in both these cases and others, the details are less clear than first appearances suggest. "To whom?" asks about more than an address. Concerning Romans, "To whom?" asks about the composition of the audience: Were they Jews, Gentiles, or a mixture? Rich or poor? Persecuted by the Roman government or living in a somewhat accommodated situation? Regarding the Ephesian correspondence, text criticism as well as the internal contents of the document question whether this letter was originally sent to Ephesus; good arguments can be made that it was a circular letter intended to accompany other letters of Paul and not addressed to any particular congregation.

Determining the audiences for the Gospels is even more precarious. We know the identity neither of the original author nor of the audience. Consequently, our best approach is to extrapolate possible identities cautiously from the text itself. That the Gospel of Matthew associates Jesus with numerous figures from the Scriptures of Israel (what the church will later call the "Old Testament") and seeks to preserve Jewish practices (for example, Jesus is quoted as saying in the Sermon on the Mount, "Do not think that I have come to abolish the law or the prophets; I have come not to abolish but to fulfill" [Matt 5:17]) leads to the thesis that the gospel originally addressed a Jewish community. But good arguments can also be made for a Gentile audience or an audience made up of both Jewish and Gentile followers of Jesus since Gentile believers certainly read Matthew as part of their Bible; even the "Old Testament" is part of the church's Bible, and some of Jesus' early Gentile followers adhered to the laws it mandates for Jews. Debated as well is whether the gospel was written for a single community or was designed to be read by multiple churches.

The "where?" question tries to identify the broader location within which a text was written and received. This question matters because the writings of the NT, like all writings, do not exist in social, ecclesial, or political vacuums. They are shaped not only by their audiences and by their writers' agenda but also by the circumstances, social structures, and historical events of the larger cultural and political worlds that they share: Jewish traditions, Hellenistic culture, and Roman imperial power. Archaeological exploration as well as other contemporaneous texts combined with sociological models tell us about these worlds; studies of ritual and myth (by which we mean not "imaginary" or "false" stories but narratives that convey cultural history) help us understand how people understood their place in the world.

For example, rituals of immersion and practices concerning eating are part of the first-century Mediterranean world. Knowing about the initiation rites of other religions and how table fellowship determined both insiders and outsiders helps us better understand practices such as baptism and the church's "love feasts." Studying myths and rituals is the purview of what is known as the *history-of-religion* approach. Or, for another example, understanding Roman culture helps the reader determine what parts of that culture Jesus and his followers imitated or rejected. That the term "gospel" itself (Greek: *euangelion*, literally "good message" or "good news") is a secular designation indicating the good news of an emperor's military victory or declaration of a tax holiday has implications for what the "good news" of the "kingdom of heaven" might be. *Roman history* and *archaeology* thus provide information on context.

Another aspect of the "where" can be answered in part by *social-science approaches*. These approaches inquire into the cultural values, practices, and structures that the texts assume and evoke. When NT documents use language of "father" or "honor" or "friend" or "tax collector," the terms find their meaning embedded in larger cultural structures and practices. Social science approaches ask what makes up these larger cultural structures to elaborate the values and practices that the texts assume. To pray, for example, "Our Father . . ." (Matt 6:9) invokes a host of connotations of the role of fatherhood (distant or intimate, disciplinarian or provider, specific fathers known in both Roman and Jewish traditions), of kinship structures, even of political loyalties given that the Roman emperors frequently presented themselves as "father" to the empire's population. When Paul speaks of refusing payment for his apostolic work in 2 Cor 11, what commentary is he making about the roles of patrons and clients? Would his refusal be seen as insulting to potential patrons, or inspirational to those who proclaim the gospel, or both?

To ask "why?" inquires about the purpose or function of the writing. Sometimes authors declare the purpose of their writing. For example, Luke 1:1-4 explains that many writers have attempted to compile an organized account of the life and teachings of Jesus and that the author of this gospel, "after investigating everything carefully from the very first," seeks to instruct the reader, an otherwise unknown person named Theophilus (appropriately, Greek for "friend of God"), that he may "know the truth" or "know security or assurance" (as the Greek can be translated) concerning the information in which he has been "catechized." Sometimes the purpose seems evident from the content; for example, Paul writes to the Galatians to correct what he perceives to be their misunderstanding of both biblical law and current practice. John, the author of the book of Revelation, writes to warn his readers against assimilation to Roman ideals and practices. Yet authors can have multiple agenda: Paul also writes to bolster his authority; John writes to combat rival teachers.

Finally, the question "how?" explores the processes by which a writing came into being. Identifying likely sources such as confessions or liturgical material, narratives, or collections of teaching that existed independently of the final writing is called *source criticism*. Scholars use *form criticism* to investigate the forms and particular ecclesial settings of this material where possible. For example, miracle stories and controversies between Jesus and several groups of interlocutors tend to follow particular literary conventions. These are recognizable "forms" just as today's romance novels, superhero comics, and cookbooks have familiar forms. To recognize the form helps us understand how the text might have been used.

When source material is included in the final form of a writing, it is edited or "redacted" to fit this new context. Asking questions about this editing is called *redaction criticism.* Sometimes the use of sources is explicit, such as most of the NT quotes or allusions to the Scriptures of Israel, usually not in their Hebrew form but in Greek translation. Scholars have also posited numerous sources behind the NT texts. For example, most scholars believe that the Gospels of Matthew and Luke used the Gospel of Mark as a source; redaction criticism indicates where, and seeks to explain why, Matthew or Luke made changes to that source. Many scholars also propose that Matthew and Luke had access to another source, designated Q (from the German *Quelle*, meaning "source"), composed primarily of Jesus' teachings, such as the famous prayer known as the "Our Father."

A second set of approaches focuses on "the world of the text" itself. These critical methods attend primarily to the text itself: What is its genre? How it is structured? How does its plot develop (if it has one)? How are characters presented? What role do settings play? How is its language used? To answer these questions, several moves prove helpful.

First, *rhetorical criticism* asks about how the NT writings communicate with their audiences. Just as today advertising agencies understand that effective marketing requires knowledge of and so appeal to the needs and interests of the target audience (campaigns promoting Medicare supplements do not typically use the same actors, music, or choreography as advertisements for beer), so writers in antiquity understood, even studied, how to produce effective arguments. Rhetorical treatises from Roman antiquity emphasize the point that persuasive communication must be appropriate to the particular situation being addressed. They also set out the sorts of topics or "proofs" that an argument might include and the techniques appropriate for expressing this material. Knowing how rhetoric functions, we can today get a sense of what the writer is trying to communicate. A missing "thanksgiving" section in a letter, for example, shows the writer's anger with the audience and conveys an urgency about the topic (so the letter to the Galatians). Further, understanding how a speech or a text seeks to manipulate its readers—and all writing, even this introduction, is a form of manipulation in that it attempts to engage readers, convince readers of the correctness of its arguments, dissuade readers from alternative views, and so on—helps us understand both what is at stake in the writing and, potentially, where the points of controversy are.

Narrative criticism, by attending to plot, characterizations, point of view, and setting, determines how the story is told. It indicates breaks in the narrative that might surprise or challenge or confuse; it helps readers to assess the characters (Do they remain constant, or change?) it provides guidance on *how* the story is told such that readers are led to accept or reject certain perspectives; it reveals the interaction of time and space, of center and periphery. The general narrative-critical approach will be familiar to anyone who has read literary theory, or for that matter a movie review.

A form of narrative criticism called *reader-response criticism* begins with the observation that plot, character, setting, and point of view do not exist in and of themselves. Whereas asking questions of plot and character can provide a partial answer to the question, "what does this text mean?" reader-response asks instead, "what does this text mean *to me?*" It can do so because it realizes that plot, character, and so on are "created" in the interaction between a reader and the writing. That is, there is no plot independent of the plot that a reader constructs in reading the work. Readers will inevitably fill in gaps, provide motives, and find relationships between events that the narrative itself does not detail. Characters are developed as a reader moves through a text and joins together the scattered traits that emerge at various points. Readers notice the significance of settings and evaluate actions and relationships according to the point of view that they construct. Reader-response criticism thus focuses on the reader's work in engaging a text. It recognizes, therefore, that multiple and different meanings will inevitably emerge.

It is through a reader-response approach that we determine, for example, our understanding of the disciples in the Gospel of Mark: Are they, at best, dolts who, after seeing Jesus twice feed thousands of people with just a few loaves of bread, lament that they have no food, or are they representative of human frailty and ignorance, people with whom readers can identify? Does Luke write off the Jewish community at the end of Acts, with the church's future focused only on Gentiles, or do Jews still have a positive role to play in salvation history? Reader response also explains how gaps are filled in: Do we attribute Mark's Judas with a motive—greed, politics, satanic possession—to explain his betrayal of Jesus? Do we invent the teachings of Paul's opponents in Colossae or Corinth in order to explain his invectives?

Readers also choose whether to accept the narrative presentation or to resist it. Resisting readers, for example, might find problematic narratives in which women are silenced or slavery promoted or vengeance celebrated. Other readers might seek to justify such teachings in light of their own presuppositions concerning biblical authority or apologetics. Does the depiction of the "whore of Babylon" in Revelation cause revulsion at Rome's imperialism and commercialism and thus a rejection of Roman values, or does John's apparent delight in her destruction cause us to question John's own sense of "love of neighbor" or depiction of women's bodies? Will the reader accept the NT's frequent, positive image of being a "slave" of God, or will the reader reject any positive attributes accorded to the institution of slavery?

Genre studies, which has some relation to form criticism, asks how we classify a document in relation to other writings. Knowing the genre of a text—gospel, letter, apocalypse, homily, prayer, paraensis (ethical instruction), satire, and others—is a necessary aid in interpretation. The identification of genre shapes readers' expectations for and experience in encountering the text. For a modern example, if we try to read a science fiction novel as if it were a historical treatise, we will miscue on a number of fronts.

The determination of genre, however, is not a science but an art. Scholars are still debating the genre of the gospels: biographies as that genre was understood in antiquity, histories as Seutonius or even Thucydides would have understood the term, a combination of multiple genres, something new? Nor do ancient "histories," let alone the Gospels of the NT, conform to the tenets of ideal reporting today: they are not even ostensibly objective accounts but partisan, insider literature. It was common for writers to compose speeches that main characters would give appropriate to the occasion: thus the numerous speeches in Acts—whether by Peter, Stephen, or Paul—are all Luke's compositions. It is unlikely that Jesus ever delivered the "Sermon on the Mount" (Matt 5–7); rather, the first evangelist has combined various individual statements from various sources into an opening discourse.

Generic concerns also apply to the "epistles" or "letters" of the NT. Several texts that have the name "letter" may not be: for example, the "Letter to the Hebrews" reads more like a sermon than a letter, and it lacks an epistolary beginning. Further, ancient writers were not obsessed with using only one genre or literary form: gospels contain apocalyptic elements, apocalypses contain epistolary forms, letters contain liturgical formulae, and so on.

Attention to genre along with rhetoric and narrative can also help us in distinguishing between what a text says and what it means. For example, when Jesus states in the Sermon on the Mount, "If your right hand causes you to sin, cut it off and throw it away" (Matt 5:30a), readers need to determine if he is speaking in the imperative or by exaggeration (one hopes for the latter). And is he is speaking about stealing—or masturbation? Such questions can be extended: Why is it that some interpreters will insist that 1 Pet 2:18 is no longer part of the Christian message: "Slaves, accept the authority of your masters with all deference, not only those who are kind and gentle but also those who are harsh," but find no problem with 1 Pet 3:1: "Wives, in the same way, accept the authority of your husbands, so that, even if some of them do not obey the word, they may be won over without a word by their wives' conduct"?

Genre criticism is not the only literary approach that looks at texts in relation to each other. *Intertextual* readings develop these connections by asking both how one text cites, alludes to, or evokes another, and what meanings are created when the texts are set into relationship. Sometimes an intertextual resonance is explicit; for example, in Acts 17:28:

> For "In him we live and move and have our being"; as even some of your own poets have said, "For we too are his offspring."

Luke depicts Paul as citing two Greek poets. The first is the sixth-century B.C.E. poet Epimenides; the second the third-century B.C.E. poet Aratus. Whether readers would know the original works and use them to interpret Paul's speech to the Athenians (a speech Luke likely composed), or whether the focus is simply to show that Paul is educated in Greek rhetoric and literature remains an open question.

Allusions to and quotations of the Scriptures of Israel, in their Greek translation, are much more prevalent. In some cases, the original contexts of the citations inform the NT uses. For example, Matt 2:18 comments on King Herod's slaughter of the children of Bethlehem by quoting Rachel's lament from Jer 31:15:

> A voice is heard in Ramah, lamentation and bitter weeping. Rachel is weeping for her children; she refuses to be comforted for her children, because they are no more.

Informed readers may know both that Jer 31 is the site of the prediction of a "new covenant," which Jesus can be seen as fulfilling and that Jeremiah provides an answer to Rachel:

> Thus says the LORD: Keep your voice from weeping, and your eyes from tears; for there is a reward for your work, says the LORD: they shall come back from the land of the enemy; there is hope for your future, says the LORD. (Jer 31:16-17)

Death is not the end of the story, for either Jeremiah or Matthew.

Similarly, in describing Jesus' entry into Jerusalem, Matthew sees the fulfillment of a prophecy:

Tell the daughter of Zion, Look, your king is coming to you, humble, and mounted on a donkey, and on a colt, the foal of a donkey. (Matt 21:5)

The citation is to Zech 9:9, but this earlier version actually reads:

Rejoice greatly, O daughter Zion! Shout aloud, O daughter Jerusalem! Behold, your king comes to you; triumphant and victorious is he, humble and riding on a donkey, on a colt, the foal of a donkey.

Matthew's readers may notice the omission of the claim of triumph and then may well fill it in.

In other cases, authors take the quotes out of context and apply them to completely different settings. Returning to Matt 2, we find that the evangelist applies Hos 11:1, "out of Egypt I have called my son"—a reference to the exodus of the Israelite slaves—to the "flight to Egypt" that Joseph, Mary, and Jesus took to escape Herod's slaughter and then to their return from Egypt to Nazareth in Galilee (Matt 2:14). In Gal 4, Paul offers an allegory of Hagar and Sarah, Abraham's wives, in which Hagar the slave comes to represent Mount Sinai, obedience to Torah, and slavery, and Sarah (whom Paul does not name) represents the heavenly Jerusalem. Hagar's eventual freedom is ignored, as is Sarah's earthly life.

Still other intertextual connections are allusive. Matthew 1–5 compares the story of Jesus fleeing to and returning from Egypt as well as his speaking from a mountain to that of Moses without ever mentioning Moses. When Jesus heals a man named "bar [Aramaic for "son of"] Timmaeus (Mark 10:46), might readers bring to their understanding of Jesus knowledge of Plato's "Timmaeus"? Will Luke's description of Paul and Barnabas's missionary work in Lystra (Acts 14), in which the evangelists are mistaken for gods, remind readers of Ovid's story of Baucis and Philemon (*Metamorphosis* 8.611-724)? Similarly, will Paul's heroism during and survival of shipwreck (Acts 27) recollect the story of Odysseus? When these intertextual connections are made, not only is the pleasure of the reading increased, but also new meanings can be obtained for both texts.

Canonical criticism asks questions about how individual NT writings interact with other NT texts as well as with the antecedent Scriptures of Israel as the Bible of the church. Attention to the canon foregrounds not the text's circumstances of origin or events behind the text but the text itself as part of a theological conversation with other canonical texts and as an authoritative text for communities of faith.

Frequently the canonical critic seeks to bring order to the canon's diverse voices by finding a central teaching, a "canon within the canon." The numerous options suggest that such a task is limited. Options include "justification by faith" with its center in Paul's Letters, or Jesus' "Great Commandment" (see Matt 22:36-40) combining "Love of God" (Deut 6) with "love of neighbor" (Lev 19), or Jesus' role as the "way and the life and the truth" (John 14). For some readers, usually those coming from Protestant perspectives, the letters of Paul are the primary guide for canonical understanding; for those in Roman Catholic and Eastern Orthodox communions, the Gospels are primary. In some churches today that have a strong eschatological focus, Revelation is the central book. Thus, even readers who have a very high view of biblical authority, and who will agree with 2 Tim 3:16 that "all Scripture is inspired by God [Greek: *theopneustos*, literally, "God breathed"] and is useful for teaching, for reproof, for correction, and for training in righteousness," can still recognize that some texts are valued more highly than others. Moreover, "useful for teaching and training" should not be confused with useful for making arguments about physics or astronomy. Here awareness of genre as well as diverse canonical voices becomes essential.

Attending to the order of the books in the canon is also helpful for NT interpretation. For example, the canon places Acts before the Pauline letters, and thus Acts provides the narrative by which we understand Paul's writing. Acts portrays Paul as a faithful, practicing Jew who worships in the Jerusalem Temple, begins his missionary work by preaching in synagogues, does miracles, and speaks in public brilliantly. This picture may not be the one those who begin with his letters develop. Or, for another example, the so-called catholic or universal letters—1 and 2 Peter; James; Jude; 1, 2, and 3 John—appear toward the end of the canonical collection; does this positioning relegate them to a less important role than the Pauline letters? Should it?

Canonical criticism also reveals, sometimes explicitly and sometimes indirectly, that the canonical list does more than determine what is authoritative for the churches who define the canon in question. The list also eliminates other volumes that may at one time have been recognized by Jesus' followers as authoritative. There were other gospels besides those that take the names of Matthew, Mark, Luke, and John. We have copies of the *Gospel of Thomas* and the *Gospel of Mary*, only recently was the *Gospel of Judas* restored and translated. There is a *3 Corinthians* ascribed to Paul and numerous Acts of various apostles. Ancient canonical collections sometimes included the *Letter of Barnabas*, *1 Clement*, and the *Shepherd of Hermas* while omitting Revelation and Hebrews. It was not until the Easter letter of 367 written by Athanasius, Bishop of Alexandria, that we actually have a list of the same books as our NT canon today. Thus attention to canon alerts us to the fact that what we come to recognize as the Bible of the church developed over several centuries. Consequently, we listen for the voices both of the historical winners whose views are represented in the canon and also seek to hear the voices of those who represented alternative or oppositional views.

Those critical methods that focus on the worlds in front of the text recognize that factors such as the reader's ethnicity, gender, social status, sexual orientation, nationality, and particular sociopolitical circumstances—what has been called "social location" but what might be better referred to as "subject position" (since individuals are not just products of their social setting but also bring distinct experiences to the act of reading)—influence the making of meanings. Several of the methods discussed previously under "the world of the text" anticipate this category. For example, both canonical criticism and reader-response criticism move beyond a focus on the text to highlight the contribution of interpreters.

Ideological criticism focuses on the political, social, economic, and theological commitments of the worlds in which the NT texts were written and which are inscribed in the texts. It seeks to make explicit the attitudes and structures that are oppressive, especially relating to women, Jews, slavery, sexual orientation, low social status, and disabilities. It asks questions about what contemporary interpreters should do with these oppressive practices and structures. Should messages be regarded as divinely inspired and eternally binding, or can the text be used to identify and critique their oppressive impact? In some cases, ideological critique meshes with reader-response criticism, especially when the reader chooses to interpret the text from a position of resistance.

NT writings do contain some disturbing content. For example, in places they sanction slavery, a basic institution of the Roman Empire. Generally, they reflect a patriarchal, androcentric world in which (free, adult) males are the norm and women, children, and slaves hold subordinate positions. For example, the famous "feeding of the five thousand" is actually underreported, because as Matt 14:21 reports, "And those who ate were about five thousand men, *besides women and children*" (emphasis added). On the other hand, we must be cautious both about pronouncements concerning the extent to which patriarchy impacted women's lives as well as the distinctive practices typically associated with Jesus and Paul.

Feminist criticism can entail the search for women's historical presence, but it does much more. It asks questions about how gender is constructed and presented in the NT books as well as in their interpretations. It recovers women who often go unmentioned in textbooks and sermons. It interrogates their literary representations as well as their social presence. It asks questions about NT teaching concerning marriage and childbirth, virginity and widowhood. For example, when Eph 5 compares the husband to Christ and the wife to the church, is this good news for women or bad? When Jesus forbids divorce (see Mark 10), is he protecting women's rights or condemning them to lives of despair—or neither? When 1 Pet 3:6 promotes the matriarch Sarah as an ideal role model because "she obeyed Abraham and called him lord," how is this verse to be understood today, given Sarah's own complicated personality and the context in which, according to the Greek version of Genesis, she uses this title?

Feminist analysis also encourages caution when we seek to understand the NT's

13

teachings regarding presentations of women. In the early years of feminist interpretation, Christian apologists typically described Jesus' relations to women as "radical" (the term has a popularity among NT scholars to this day): they regarded his speaking to women, healing them, and being accompanied by them as "radical" in his Jewish context, and they understood that context as epitomizing misogyny. The claims were not based on good history: they stemmed primarily from very select readings of post-NT Jewish sources coupled with an apologetic concern to use Jesus as leverage: if he could be seen as promoting women over and against the religious structures of his day, then he could be cited in appeals for women's ecclesial leadership in the modern era.

The idea was a good one, but not only does it fail the historical test, it also winds up promoting anti-Jewish views. It turns out that women at the time of Jesus had access to their own funds and served as patrons, had freedom of travel, frequented synagogues and the Jerusalem Temple, held leadership roles in synagogues, were teachers and prophets, and so on. The point is not that first-century Judaism was an egalitarian paradise; it wasn't. The point is, rather, that readings for liberation need to be cautious about how they understand the figures of the NT and the cultural context in which those figures lived.

Imperial-critical approaches, which are related to *postcolonial approaches,* focus on ways in which the NT intersects with Roman imperial power. Earlier imperial-critical approaches, like early feminist approaches, typically located Jesus and Paul in an anti-imperial stance and regarded Christian teaching as resisting the structures that marked the *Pax Romana* (Latin: "peace of Rome"): militarism, taxation, occupation, elite rule, public propaganda through coinage, statues and temples, games, and inscriptions that proclaimed Rome's might. The connection some academics drew between the *Pax Romana* and the *Pax Americana* allowed them to use NT scholarship to critique American policy. Today, scholars are more aware of the complexity of the NT texts and settings, for the ancient writers do not escape their own cultural contexts. At times the *Pax Romana* becomes the *Pax Christi* (the "peace of Christ") in the texts, where it is the followers of Jesus who rule, through divine might, and who condemn all who do not follow their teachings. Imitation, accommodation, and resistance coexist.

For example, when Revelation describes the divine throne room, replete with adoring worshipers, first-century readers may well have recognized a version of the imperial court. Whether the difference is taken to be qualitative, or merely quantitative, will depend on the stance of the reader. When in Mark 5, the demons who possess a man from the Decapolis announce, "My name is Legion; for we are many," are we to understand that Latinism "Legion" as a reference to the Roman legions, who destroy personal integrity through their militarism and psychological health through their imperial rule? In 1 Cor 6:1-2 Paul excoriates the members of the church in Corinth for suing each other:

When any of you has a grievance against another, do you dare to take it to court before the unrighteous, instead of taking it before the saints? Do you not know that the saints will judge the world? And if the world is to be judged by you, are you incompetent to try trivial cases?

His language both stereotypes all people outside the church community as evil and promotes the idea that people within the church will eventually hold the role of judge over the world. Imperial critical readings recognize that religion is not separated from political, economic, and social structures, and they recognize as well that the texts of the NT can be said both to contest Roman imperial rule and to imitate it.

Postcolonial criticism takes its initial cue from the experiences of people within contemporary colonial contexts, whether reflecting on British occupation of India, Japanese occupation of Korea, Spanish and Portuguese occupation of much of South America, or aspects of American foreign policy. The indigenous cultures accommodate to, resist, and mimic the cultures of the colonizers, and thereby they create a new situation of hybridity, with the colonized subject living in two worlds but at home in neither (sometimes called a "third space"). Questions of how this cultural negotiation works, and how it should be assessed, can inform our understandings of NT documents and of the people they address. For example, when Jas 1:1 addresses "the twelve tribes in the Dispersion" (Greek: *diaspora*) and 1 Pet 1:1 writes "to the exiles of the Dispersion in Pontus, Galatia, Cappadocia, Asia, and Bithynia," we can understand a readership that may see itself displaced from its home—whether the land of Israel or the kingdom of heaven. The extent to which these letters promote accommodation and resistance to their diasporic contexts not only informs our knowledge of the early followers of Jesus but also can serve to impact how followers of Jesus today understand their own social and political contexts, and values.

A final approach to the worlds in front of the text concerns *reception history.* For two millennia, the writings of the NT have functioned in diverse ways. For example, the famous parable of the Good Samaritan (Luke 10:30-37) has been understood variously as an allegory of Jesus' leaving his heavenly home, engaging the world of human degradation, and returning to God the Father; a moral tale about helping those in need; fiduciary advice that exhorts, "Take aid from whoever offers it, regardless of the donor's politics"; cultural criticism that sees in the presumed enemy a possible neighbor; and so on. The equally famous parable of the Prodigal Son (Luke 15:11-32) did not start out with this label. If we called it "the parable of the man who had two sons" (see Luke 15:11), we might arrive at a very different understanding of its message, one that includes the major role of the older brother. The beast whose "number is six hundred sixty-six" (Rev 13:18) has been connected with various popes and Martin Luther, Mikhail Gorbachev (via his birthmark), Ronald Wilson Reagan (via the six letters in each of his names) and Barney the Dinosaur (via grumpy adults).

Clearly the task of making meaning of NT texts is complex. Scholars continue to ask different questions of these texts and so develop and use new methods to read them. Limits of space mean we cannot in one volume engage every method used in NT studies. We do not offer, for example, examples of womanist interpretations, psychological approaches, minjung theology, mujerista readings, or disability studies, to name but some. Nor can any single interpretation ask all of the questions we may bring to the text. Limits of space also prevent us from using all of the methods for every NT document in every chapter of this book. So to make meanings of each NT writing, we have chosen either one or several critical methods that ask questions about some important dimensions of that particular writing. Every reading is partial and selective. Our goal throughout is to provide insights into both the meanings of the NT writings and into the methods or sets of questions that are often used to interpret them. At the same time, in each chapter we raise questions of application: "What are we to make of this material?" The answers will be as varied as there are readers, and so the conversations will continue.

CHAPTER 1
$\mathscr{M}$atthew

Interpretations of texts generally center on either the reader or the writer. The former highlights the experiences and situation of a person or group: What does this text mean *to us*? Do I accept its claims or resist them? The latter focuses on the identity of the author, the circumstances under which the text was written, its sources and intended audience.

However, there is often overlap between author and reader, origin and reception. Knowing a writer's cultural context and personal agenda can help readers understand what the writer is attempting to convey and why. Knowing the history can help in determining what the original audience might have understood. Knowing the author's concerns might help in determining what passages might speak to all readers and what are specific to the intended audience. Understanding a text's historical context can also help because it serves as a control on solipsism (i.e., "the text means what I want it to mean"). Understanding what a text meant to its first audience can also enhance what it might mean to readers today.

To understand Matthew's Gospel, in this chapter we focus on how the text came into being: who wrote what, to whom, when, where, and why? This cluster of interrelated questions comprises an approach called "historical criticism." The word "criticism" here does not indicate something negative or an attack. Rather, as with the phrase "critical thinking," criticism concerns identifying information, discerning meaning, and evaluating claims. Historical criticism takes seriously the text's circumstances of origin as part of this interpretive process.

Within "historical criticism" fall the subcategories of "source criticism" and "redaction criticism." The former looks at the sources, both oral and written, that the author used to construct the gospel. The latter looks at the author's editorial hand and asks: How were traditional materials reordered to tell a new story? What was added, or omitted, and why? In distinguishing tradition from redaction—that is, in distinguishing received materials from the author's own contributions—we can make good suggestions about the author's agenda.

17

Who, When, Where

Like the other canonical gospels, the text we call "Matthew" was originally anonymous. The first author to link the name Matthew with the gospel was the church father Irenaeus, who wrote ca. 180 C.E. (*Against Heresies* 3.1.1). Nor does the text commend Matthean authorship. The disciple Matthew plays no significant role (he appears eighth on the list of disciples in 10:3). He does not witness Jesus' baptism or transfiguration. He is not at Gethsemane.

Why the gospel was assigned to "Matthew" and not "Peter" or "Mary Magdalene" can only be answered, tentatively, through internal evidence. Perhaps the apostle Matthew provided the tradition on which the text rests, although he was probably dead by the time of composition. In Greek, "Matthew" (*Matthaios*) sounds like the word for "disciple" or "learner" (*mathētēs*), so perhaps the name signifies the gospel's ideal reader as one who learns from Jesus. Yet a third possibility: in Mark 2:14 and Luke 5:27, Jesus commissions a tax collector named "Levi," who becomes one of the Twelve Apostles. In Matthew's version of this account (9:9), the tax collector is "Matthew." Luke (6:15) and Mark (10:3) do note a "Matthew" among the Twelve, so the name was already associated with Jesus' disciples. Perhaps early copyists, noting the distinction in names of the tax collector, thought that "Matthew" had put in a correction.

Concerning dates, Matthew likely used Mark's Gospel as a source (90 percent of Mark appears in Matthew, often in the same words and same order) and so must postdate Mark. Both internal and external evidence commend a date toward the end of the first century. Matthew's parable of the Wedding Feast (22:1-14) states that the king sent troops to destroy the city of those who refused to attend, a response decidedly out of proportion to declining an invitation (22:7). Matthew may have added this reference to make a theological point: in the evangelist's view, Jerusalem was destroyed because its population refused Jesus' invitation to follow him. This redactional element suggests a date following 70 C.E., when Rome destroyed Jerusalem. Luke's version of this parable (Luke 14:15-24) lacks this detail. In turn, the earliest quotations of material in Matthew's gospel appear in Christian writings from around 100 C.E.: the *Didache* quotes Matthew's form of the Lord's Prayer, not Luke's, and Ignatius, a bishop from Antioch, refers in several letters to details that appear only in Matthew (for example, the star at Jesus' birth; Jesus' comment to John the Baptist at 3:15).

The location of composition is also a matter of speculation. Some scholars suggest Antioch-on-the-Orontes in Syria, since Ignatius of Antioch knows Matthew's Gospel. Antioch was also home to a large Diaspora Jewish community, and Matthew, as we will see, manifests several concerns that indicate connection to that community. Further, Matthew has a particular interest in Peter, who was active in Antioch (see Gal 2:11-14). Again, internal evidence supports the external: Matthew 4:24 refers to Jesus' fame

18

spreading "throughout all Syria," although the narrative has so far restricted him to Galilee (4:23, 25). This reference is Matthew's redaction (cf. Mark 3:7-8).

In determining provenance, date, and authorship, we inevitably risk a circular argument. We construct our conclusions substantially from evidence in the gospel, and then we interpret the gospel in light of the context we have determined. External support for conclusions about setting and authorship are helpful checks, but they cannot be determinative. In the end, doing history is often a matter of making the best argument; absolute proof can remain elusive.

Sources and Source Criticism

The Gospels of Matthew, Mark, and Luke have been known, since the work of David Friedrich Strauss in the nineteenth century, as Synoptic Gospels; the Greek term literally means to "see" (as in "optics") together ("syn" as in "synthesis" or "syncopation"). The three gospels are often very similar in wording and in the order in which they present material. Matthew contains all but some 55 of Mark's 661 verses, while Luke has just over half of Mark.

John's differences from the first three gospels are numerous. Instead of a Galilean ministry and then a final journey to Jerusalem, John's Jesus goes back and forth between the regions. John has distinctive characters (Nicodemus, the Samaritan woman), distinctive vocabulary and style (Jesus' long monologues), and distinctive themes (Jesus "coming down" from God; the relationship of Father and Son). We reserve discussion of John for chapter 4 and concentrate here on the relationship among the Synoptics.

Although they "see alike," the Synoptics have substantial differences. For example, Mark begins with the preaching of John the Baptist, Matthew with a genealogy, and Luke with the announcement of John the Baptist's conception. The challenge of determining the literary relationship among Matthew, Mark, and Luke—accounting for their similarities and differences—is known as the "Synoptic Problem."

Early Solutions to the Synoptic Problem: Matthean Priority

One theory, dating to Augustine (354–430 C.E.), was that Matthew was the first gospel written and that it rested on eyewitness testimony. For the early church, arguing for Matthean primacy made good sense. The gospel begins with a genealogy that anchors Jesus into the Scriptures of Israel. It is the only gospel to use the word "church" (Greek: *ekklēsia*). With Peter, it establishes a leadership system that helped the church in promoting doctrine and praxis. Only in Matthew does Jesus

---

respond to Peter's confession that he is "the Messiah, the Son of the living God" (16:16) by proclaiming, "You are Peter [Greek: *petros*], and on this rock [Greek: *petra*, a feminine noun] I will build my church. . . . I will give you the keys of the kingdom of heaven, and whatever you bind on earth will be bound in heaven, and whatever you loose on earth will be loosed in heaven" (16:18-19).

According to this first solution to the Synoptic Problem, Mark (regarded as the interpreter of Peter) used Matthew as a source, and Luke, regarded as the interpreter of Paul, used both Matthew's and Mark's Gospels. Yet this theory has several problems. For example, it fails to explain why Mark omits such important material as Matthew's Sermon on the Mount (Matt 5–7). The argument that Mark wanted to write a shorter gospel is not compelling, since most of Mark's individual pericopes (individual stories) are longer than the comparable versions in Matthew and Luke.

A second theory, popularized by Johann Jakob Griesbach (1745–1812) and today called the "Griesbach hypothesis," also proposes Matthean priority. In Griesbach's solution to the Synoptic Problem, Luke used Matthew's Gospel as a source along with uniquely Lucan traditions such as the parables of the Good Samaritan and the Prodigal Son. Finally Mark used both the Gospels of Matthew and Luke to produce an epitome of these earlier traditions. This theory has the merit of statistical support. Matthew and Mark sometimes agree against Luke in wording and order, and Luke and Mark sometimes agree against Matthew. But Matthew and Luke rarely agree against Mark when all three record the same story. The Griesbach hypothesis appropriately establishes Mark as the middle term—but not necessarily the latest gospel.

There are problems regarding Mark as the latest gospel. Both Matthew and Luke improve Mark's syntax. They smooth out the narrative by eliminating many instances of Mark's favorite expressions, such as "and immediately." They correct Mark's data. While Mark 6:14 refers to Herod Antipas as a "king," Matt 14:1 uses the correct title, "tetrarch." They omit confusing comments, such as Mark 9:49, "Everyone will be salted with fire." Matthew and Luke also provide a "higher Christology" or more exalted view of Jesus. For example, they both describe his miraculous conception, and they both provide resurrection appearances. According to Mark 6:5, Jesus could not do many miracles in Nazareth; in Matt 13:53-58, the issue becomes not capability but volition: Jesus *chooses* not to do miracles. Finally, both Matthew and Luke have a much more complimentary view of the disciples. None of these observations, alone or even together, clinches the argument against the Griesbach hypothesis: improvement of syntax is a matter of aesthetic judgment; Mark may have deliberately de-emphasized the miracles in favor of stressing Jesus' suffering, and so on.

Arguments against Matthean priority have prompted scholars to seek another solution to the Synoptic Problem. Today's dominant theory, called the "two source theory" or "four source theory," is that Mark's was the first gospel to be written. Subsequently, both Matthew and Luke made independent use of Mark's text, redacting and expanding it with additional sources. This view still makes Mark the middle term, but here Mark is the source rather than the summary of Matthew and Luke.

Positing Mark's primacy does not explain all the connections among the Synoptics. There are about 100 elements—many of them sayings of Jesus, such as the Beatitudes (for example, "Blessed are . . .") and the "Lord's Prayer"—shared by Matthew and Luke but absent from Mark. These elements suggest a second source, today known as either a "Sayings Source" or as "Q," probably after the German word for source, *Quelle.* No ancient copy of Q exists, but scholars have attempted to reconstruct it on the basis of the material common to Matthew and Luke. That we have the *Gospel of Thomas*, a collection of sayings attributed to Jesus, confirms that some of Jesus' followers collected sayings detached from any narrative frame. We saw earlier how Matthew and Luke both present the parable of the Wedding Feast, but with different details. The consensus is that Matthew "redacted Q" by adding the line about the troops burning the city. Thus, the "two source" theory indicates that Matthew and Luke are formed on the basis of two sources: Mark and Q.

About 20 percent of Matthew and 30 percent of Luke find no parallel in the other Synoptics. Scholars suggest therefore that Matthew had access to further material, which is designated as "M." Similarly, it is highly plausible that Luke used another source, known as "L." Examples of M and L material would be the nativity accounts, the genealogies, and the resurrection appearances. Hence there are four sources: Mark, Q, M, and L. Whether these sources were oral or written remains debated—as the question must, since M and L, like Q, are hypothetical.

Any solution to the Synoptic Problem has weaknesses. Among the many, here are three that need to be considered as we move to discuss Matthew's own agenda. First, we have to distinguish tradition (what the sources said) from redaction (how the evangelists edited those sources). Material that we think derives from M or L might actually be from Q, with either Matthew or Luke omitting it.

Second, material we assign to a source might actually come from the redactor's hand.

Third, the solutions all have ideological components to them. The argument for Matthean priority, already for Augustine, supported the needs of the church, with its emphasis on Peter's role and references to the "church" and church discipline (see Matt 18). But Marcan priority, a thesis developed in late eighteenth- / early nineteenth-century Germany, served that cultural setting. Mark's omission of the nativity accounts and consequent de-emphasizing of the Virgin Mary fit the needs of a country divided between Catholics and Protestants. All Christians could agree on the importance of Jesus, but Catholic Mariology was incompatible with the Protestant focus on Scripture alone. Further, Mark's downplaying of anti-Jewish polemic as compared to Matthew allowed for greater assimilation of Jews, even as Mark's comparative disinterest in Jewish ritual practices was more palatable to Germans unhappy with Jewish emancipation from the restrictions on residence and employment. German Protestants who embraced Marcan priority had the added benefit of Mark's not-always-complimentary picture of Peter, in contrast to Matthew's promotion of him. As is often the case, much biblical scholarship, whether recognized or not, is influenced by, and has implications for, religious confession and cultural concerns.

Matthew's Shaping of Sources: Redaction Criticism

Three sources—Mark's Gospel, a collection of sayings (Q), and a collection of other material (M)—most likely supply the building blocks for Matthew's Gospel. At times the author we call Matthew preserves the material unchanged; at times additions appear; this gospel also dispenses with 55 verses of Mark (that is, if we accept the idea that Matthew had more or less the same version of Mark that scholars have determined is close to an original). This process suggests that traditions about Jesus were not fixed. Changing circumstances needed new stories.

We can observe Matthean redaction by comparing Matthew's Gospel to Mark's Gospel and to (a reconstructed) Q. Redaction occurs in one of five ways: adding, omitting, reordering, abbreviating, and rephrasing. By attending to the changes, we see Matthew's nuances.

Additions, Expansions, and Omissions

Mark's Gospel begins with Jesus' baptism by John (1:2-8) and then his ministry (1:14-15). For Matthew, Jesus' public activity does not begin until 4:17. From 1:1 to 4:16 this gospel carefully defines who Jesus is and thus indicates the major themes to sound in the remainder of the narrative.

The Gospel of Matthew begins by describing Jesus as "Son of David" and "Son of Abraham" (1:1). This opening line, lacking any Marcan or Lucan parallel, links Jesus with the biblical accounts of God's promise to Abraham that through him all nations would be blessed (Gen 12:3) and of David's commission as king to manifest God's benevolent rule (Ps 72). For Matthew, Jesus is both in continuity with and the fulfillment of Israel's Scriptures.

22

While chapters 1 to 2 are sometimes called a "birth narrative," they actually give little attention to Jesus' birth (2:1a). The genealogy (1:1-17) locates Jesus within Israel's history; structured in three groups of 14 generations, which verse 17 summarizes as encompassing Abraham to David (1:2-6a), David to the deportation to Babylon (1:6b-11), and the return from exile to the coming of the Messiah (1:12-16), it suggests God's orderly arranging of history. In 1:18-25, Matthew shows how Jesus' conception is the result of divine activity; the description of a virgin birth, as opposed to a virginal conception, appears in extant written sources first in the post-NT text known as the *Protoevangelium* (that is, pre-gospel) *of James*. Matthew's second chapter displays Jesus' threat to Rome's ally, King Herod.

Matthean Mathematics

The genealogy's claim of three series of 14 generations is artificial on several fronts. First, to make the pattern of 14 generations fit, Matthew has to finagle history. In 1:5, for example, Matthew links Salmon the father of Boaz to Rahab, the prostitute from Jericho, even though Rahab predates Salmon by at least a century and neither Israel's Scriptures nor later Jewish literature gives any indication that they formed a pair. Naming Joram the father of Uzziah (1:8), the genealogy omits three kings and a queen and jumps some 60 years. Despite what 1:11 states, Jechoniah is Josiah's grandson, so a generation is missing. The third section, 1:12-16, identifies only 13 generations, despite the claim of 14. Confounding any attempt to find historicity in this genealogy, its details differ significantly from Luke 3:23-38, the NT's other genealogy.

While the claims of three series of 14 generations are not historically accurate, they nevertheless underscore two Matthean interests. First, the division of history into ages was conventional in Jewish literature. Daniel 2 and 7 present history in four eras, at the end of which God would intervene. The pseudepigraphical books of *1 Enoch* and *2 Baruch* employ 10 ages and 12 plus 2, respectively. This ordering demonstrates God's control especially when the world seems chaotic. Matthew presents three lots of 14 generations to show God's purposes will be fulfilled, despite exile and the world's ongoing evils. Perhaps that missing 14th generation in the last series indicates Matthew reading the period of the church into history. Since for Matthew, Jesus is "Emmanuel," "God with us" for eternity (1:21; 28:20), time has reached its culmination. And yet Matthew still can make time, as it were, for the *Parousia*, Jesus' return at the final judgment and the subsequent eternal period of peace and justice.

Second, although Matthew writes in Greek, the genealogy provides an example of Hebrew numerology (*gematria*). In the Hebrew language, letters double as numbers, with each consonant having a numerical value. The number 14 is the sum of the 3 consonants in the name David: D + V + D = 4 + 6 + 4 = 14. The focus on David in verse 1 is reinforced by references to him in 1:1, 6 (twice), and 17 (twice). David was Israel's most famous king, and 2 Sam 7 promises to him a dynasty; Matthew introduces Jesus as a king (2:2) and Matthew proclaims that Rome crucifies Jesus as a king (27:11, 37, 42). David's kingdom represents God's reign in terms of justice for the poor and defense of the needy (see Ps 72), and throughout the gospel, people in need of healing address Jesus as "Son of David" (9:27-28; 15:22; 20:30-31). Only in Matthew's Gospel do we have the detail that Judas Iscariot hanged himself (27:5); his death matches that of Ahithophel, David's advisor who betrayed him (2 Sam 17:23). Thus Matthew's Jesus is a new David, announcing a kingdom (4:17) manifested in actions and words.

Matthew's genealogy also signals redactional interests by including five women: Tamar (1:3a; see Gen 38), Rahab (1:5; see Josh 2), Ruth (1:5; see Ruth), the wife of Uriah (1:6, the unnamed Bathsheba, 2 Sam 11–12), and Mary (1:16). The inclusion of women in a genealogy is not unique, and in the book that bears her name, Judith herself is accorded a genealogy tracing her ancestry back to Jacob's son Simeon (see Gn 4), but it is uncommon in antiquity to record women in genealogies, for descent was typically traced through male lines.

We can eliminate one old explanation, namely, that the women are included because they are sinners, guilty especially of sexual sins. Women have no monopoly on sin; the inclusion of David and Manasseh makes that clear. Moreover, Rahab is a model of faith (Heb 11:31), Tamar of righteousness (Gen 38:26), and Tamar is positively linked with Ruth (Ruth 4:12).

There are more likely explanations for the women's presence. One centers on their *ethnic identity*. Rahab was a Canaanite, as probably was Tamar. Ruth was a Moabite. Bathsheba was married to Uriah the Hittite, and it is Uriah's name, not Bathsheba's, that Matthew records. Their inclusion shows the blessings promised through Abraham to all peoples. Abraham, a Gentile, was regarded as the first Hebrew, and so for Matthew's first-century readers, as the first Jew. Thus the women indicate that the message of God, for Matthew, is not restricted to Jews. However, since there is no evidence in Matthew (or history) that Mary was a Gentile, and since the Jewish tradition understood these women either to be Israelites or proselytes to Judaism, other explanations have been sought.

A second approach emphasizes what might be called *obstetrical irregularities*. Tamar tricked her father-in-law into thinking she was a prostitute and with him but out of wedlock, she conceives twins. Rahab was a prostitute. Ruth is a Moabite, a member of a people who, according to Gen 19, descended from the incestuous relationship of Lot and his daughter. David committed adultery with Bathsheba. Mary fits into this surprising list: Joseph had resolved to divorce her quietly because she became pregnant while they were engaged. Perhaps Matthew is responding to accusations that Jesus was of illegitimate birth. Just as Tamar, Rahab, Ruth, and Bathsheba conceived in unexpected ways, so the conception of Jesus initially suggested scandal but proved to be for the benefit of the covenant community. Whether the teaching of the virginal conception gave rise to accusations of illegitimacy or whether it responds to those accusations, or both, cannot be determined.

A variation on this second view is to see Tamar, Rahab, Ruth, and Uriah (the name mentioned) as exemplifying a *higher righteousness* than the figures with whom they are traditionally paired. Judah proclaims Tamar more righteous than he, in that he withheld his son from her (Gen 38:26); Rahab recites Israel's salvation history and is faithful to the spies Joshua sent to Jericho, while the Israelite Achan, in Josh 7, takes property dedicated to God; Ruth is the model of righteousness who leaves her homeland and her family out of loyalty to Naomi, while Naomi and her family forsook Bethlehem at the time of a famine. Finally, Uriah, the foreign mercenary, is faithful to Israel's God and his fellow soldiers by refusing to violate the rules of holy war, while the affairs David is minding are not the affairs of state. In these situations, outsiders to Israel show more fidelity than do insiders. The tradition of the "righteous Gentile" is already manifest in the Scriptures of Israel, and it continues through Jewish tradition into the present day.

Finally, all these figures anticipate the gospel's ethics. Although threatened with violence—Judah was prepared to execute Tamar for adultery; Rahab faced the destruction of Jericho; Ruth risked molestation in Boaz's fields; Uriah dies by David's order—none responds to violence with violence, and none abdicates personal dignity. Anticipating Jesus' ethic of turning the other cheek, stripping off the shirt as well as the cloak in the law court, and going the second mile, they find a way of living faithfully. Indeed, Tamar and Rahab, Canaanites, anticipate the Canaanite woman in Matthew 15:21-28, who responds to Jesus' insult not with verbal or physical violence, and not by abjection, but by insisting on her rights and those of her daughter to receive healing from the "son of David."

Joseph also models higher righteousness by accepting the angel's instruction that he marry his pregnant fiancée, Mary, about whom he is told: she "will bear a son, and you are to name him Jesus, for he will save his people from their sins" (1:21). Mark uses the name "Jesus," which comes from the Hebrew root meaning "to save" or "to deliver" (cognates are Hosea and Joshua) about 80 times while Matthew uses it at least 154 times. Matthew adds, "They shall name him Emmanuel, which means, 'God is with us'" (1:23). In the gospel's last line, the resurrected Jesus states, "Remember, I am with you always to the end of the age" (28:20). Unlike Mark, who offers no resurrection appearance, and unlike Luke, who depicts Jesus' ascending to heaven, Matthew ends with the assurance of Jesus' abiding presence.

In contrast to these models of higher righteousness, King Herod, who rules at Rome's pleasure, tries to kill Jesus (2:1-20). The hostile king, his slaughter of the children of Bethlehem, and the flight to Egypt, along with the later scenes of Jesus entering water at the baptism, facing temptation in the wilderness for a multiple of 40, ascending a mountain, and delivering instruction, echo the story of Moses. Thus another Matthean redactional theme, in harmony with the genealogy, begins: Jesus' story is the recapitulation of the story of Moses and Israel.

As in Mark, Matthew's Jesus begins his public mission by announcing the "kingdom/reign [Greek: *basileia*] of God" (cf. Mark 1:15; Matt 4:17) though Matthew rewords the phrase as "the kingdom of heaven." This phrase evokes the Scriptures of Israel, especially the psalms that depict God the king acting—often through Israel's king (Pss 45; 72; 89; 95). Matthew's use of "kingdom of heaven" in the context of Jesus' baptism (1:21-23) emphasizes that Jesus' rule involves manifesting God's ruling presence among humanity.

Following Mark, Matthew places the calling of the disciples in this context of heavenly rule (compare Mark 1:16-20 and Matt 4:18-22). God's reign claims human lives. But to live accordingly, people must learn what God's reign values and accomplishes. Mark's Gospel often presents Jesus teaching, but includes little of *the content* of that teaching. Matthew expands the details of the teaching. Often using Q and M material, Matthew creates five major teaching discourses: the Sermon on the Mount (chs. 5–7), the Mission Discourse (ch. 10), parables of the kingdom (ch. 13; cf. Mark 4), the Ecclesiastical or "Church" Community (ch. 18), and Eschatological teachings (chs. 24–25; cf. Mark 13).

The first block, the Sermon on the Mount, has no Marcan parallel in form or content. Matthew changes the setting of Mark's initial presentation of Jesus' teaching from a synagogue to a mountain; at the end of the sermon, Matthew picks up with Mark 1:22, the response of amazement at Jesus' teaching.

While the setting of the Sermon on the Mount likely alludes to Moses's receiving the Torah on Mount Sinai, the content shows that Matthew is not replacing or abrogating earlier material. Rather, like other Jewish teachers, Jesus explains how his followers are to practice the ancient laws. For example, Matthew includes several sayings that have come to be known as "antitheses" (5:21-48) but which should probably be called "extensions" in that they do not set up oppositions between Jesus and Torah as much as they show Jesus extending the original commandments. Whereas the Torah states, "You shall not murder," Jesus forbids anger; the Torah forbids adultery, and Jesus forbids a man looking at a woman with lust; the Torah forbids taking a false oath, and Jesus forbids swearing entirely. This is not making the Torah "easier" to follow; it is rather insisting that Jesus' followers "be perfect, therefore, as your heavenly Father is perfect" (5:48).

Best known among the antitheses is the following:

> You have heard that it was said, "An eye for an eye and a tooth for a tooth" [Exod 21:23-24; Lev 24:19-20; Deut 19:21]. But I say to you, Do not resist an evildoer. But if anyone strikes you on the right cheek, turn the other also; and if anyone wants to sue you and take your coat, give your cloak as well; and if anyone forces you to go one mile, go also the second mile. (5:38-41)

By suggesting that the law not be put into practice, Jesus is consistent with the teachings of his fellow Jews. Rabbinic commentary does not take the statement literally; neither do the Scriptures of Israel present it as ever carried out. Rabbinic sources (*m. Bava Kamma* 8.1; *B. Bava Kamma* 84a) understand the biblical law as a teaching about the worth of the human body and the need for compensation in case of injury; it is a legal principle and not a practice. In the rabbinic view, since no two eyes or limbs are equal, the party causing the injury must provide compensation for damages, pain, medical expenses, loss of work, and embarrassment.

Jesus also does not take the statement literally. To be struck on the "right" cheek presumes a backhanded slap. Jesus' advice to turn the other cheek suggests a response that is neither violent (the victim does not hit back) nor cowardly (the victim does not cringe or run) but one of self-respect: if you must hit me, hit me with the open palm. This response confronts the perpetrator with the violence of the act. Concerning the second teaching, regarding the coat: in circumstances where most people only had two garments, to sue for one is appalling. Jesus says, take off both, and lay bare (as it were) the injustice. Finally, in a situation where Roman soldiers could conscript locals to carry their gear for one mile, Jesus says, do not resist violently and do not strike back, but claim your own agency and dignity.

Parts of chapter 10, the Mission Discourse, parallel material in Mark and Q (Luke), but Matthew again shapes the material. For Mark, persecution is an eschatological sign; for Matthew, it is part of living in fidelity to Jesus and his teaching. Scholars debate whether Matthew is writing to a persecuted audience, or whether the remarks about persecution are historical memories. There was no empire-wide persecution of the followers of Jesus at the time the Gospels were written, and there would not be for another century and a half.

Yet unlike Mark (who recounts that the Twelve engaged in a successful mission and who contextualizes their mission in light of the death of John the Baptist in order to relate mission to suffering) and Luke (who describes the mission of 70 followers while keeping the Twelve with Jesus in order to serve as witnesses to his actions), Matthew presents no mission. Only with the "Great Commission" of the last four verses of the gospel are the disciples sent out.

Moreover, Matthew adds to the missionary instructions the unique command, "Go nowhere among the Gentiles, and enter no town of the Samaritans, but go rather to the lost sheep of the house of Israel" (10:5b-6). In his conversation with the Canaanite mother desperately seeking a healing for her demon-possessed daughter, Jesus repeats, again only in Matthew, "I was sent only to the lost sheep of the house of Israel" (15:24). The verses prove a fascinating test case for questions of source and redaction. Some critics suggest that Jesus must have restricted his mission: the refusal to engage Samaritans and Gentiles is so harsh (at least to modern ears familiar with Christian missions throughout the globe) that it could only have been preserved by Matthew if Jesus had actually said it. Still other critics suggest the line comes from the M source: regarding this source as stemming from a Jewish community, they see the restriction as a form of Jewish ethnocentrism if not anti-Gentile attitude; typically, they go on to show how the evangelist Matthew corrects this teaching with the "Great Commission."

Both views are problematic. First, had these sayings existed in the tradition, Matthew easily could have omitted them. As we have seen with other changes to Mark, Matthew is a creative editor. Moreover, had Matthew disagreed with the commandment, there is no reason to have repeated it. Nor have we evidence that Jesus' initial Jewish followers sought to restrict the mission: the issue for them was not could Gentiles be members of the church but under what rubrics—for example, following Jewish practices mandated in Torah, such as male circumcision; the avoidance of certain foods, such as pork; particular Sabbath practices—should they enter? Rather, the best explanation for the restriction in 10:5b-6 and 15:24 is that Matthew invented the saying: it explains why Jesus did not originally engage in a Gentile mission; it shows that the Jewish community had numerous chances to heed his message; and it shows that Jesus was faithful to the promises to Israel made by God to Abraham and his descendants.

Matthew's redactional hand can also be seen in pericopes addressing Christology (the understanding of Jesus) and discipleship. Concerning Christology, Matthew removes references to Jesus' emotions, particularly indications of anger (Mark 3:5 vs. Matt 12:12) or frustration (Mark 8:12 vs. Matt 12:39; 16:2). Mark sometimes presents Jesus as incapable of mighty works; Matthew often removes these references. The signal two-stage healing in Mark 8:23-25 does not appear in Matthew; in Mark 5:30 Jesus does not know what exactly happened when a hemorrhaging woman in the crowd touched him, but in Matthew, he has full knowledge (see Matt 9:21-22). In such comparisons as Mark 8:12//Matt 16:4 and 12:39; Mark 9:16//Matt 17:14; and Mark 9:33//Matt 18:1, Matthew offers a more exalted presentation of Jesus.

Matthew also presents, compared to Mark, a more complimentary picture of the Twelve. In Mark 4:13 Jesus rebukes the disciples for not understanding a parable. Matthew omits the rebuke and instead has Jesus bless them (Matt 13:18). Matthew changes Mark's description of the disciples as having no faith (Mark 4:40) into their having "little faith" (Matt 8:26; see also 14:31 vs. Mark 6:50-51; 16:8 vs. Mark 8:17). At the transfiguration, the disciples in Mark 9:6 are "terrified" and do not know what to say; Matthew (17:4-5) removes these features and has the disciples appropriately fall on their faces in awe (17:6). In Mark 9:10, responding to Jesus' comment about resurrection, the disciples wonder "what this rising from the dead could mean." Matthew (17:9) removes this nonunderstanding. In Mark 10:35-37, two disciples seek positions of honor; in Matthew's account (20:20-21), the request comes not from disciples but from their mother. With the increased focus on Jesus as teacher comes an increased level of comprehension by the disciples.

Biblical Citations

Along with Mark's gospel and Q, the Scriptures of Israel serve as a major source for Matthew, and a major site in which Matthean redaction is evident.

What Are the Scriptures of Israel?

"Tanakh" is an acronym referring to Judaism's Bible; the name derives from Torah (sometimes translated "law" but more accurately translated "instruction"; it refers to the first five books of the Bible; the Pentateuch); Nevi'im (Prophets), and Ketuvim (Writings). These books make up the "Old Testament" of Protestant churches, although the canons are in different orders. Catholic, Anglican, and Orthodox communions include in their "Old Testaments" additional material, written in Greek, such as the book of Judith, the books of the Maccabees, the Wisdom of Solomon, and the additions to Daniel and Esther. The different terms, Tanakh and Old Testament, indicate not only different canonical order but also different contents, and even different understandings of these books. Further, at the time of the composition of the New Testament, the canon of Israel's Scriptures had not yet become fully secure. The Torah was in place, as were the Prophets, but all the Writings, including the Psalms, were still in canonical flux. For example, the book of Esther does not appear among the Dead Sea Scrolls, although other books among the scrolls may well have been authoritative for the community that copied and preserved them. Also debated for their places in the canon of Scripture were the books of Ecclesiastes (in Hebrew: *Qohelet*), Ezekiel, and Song of Songs (Canticles).

Whereas Mark (7:19) suggests that Jesus "declared all foods clean" (the Greek literally says "cleansings all foods") and so abrogated the Bible's dietary regulations, Matthew not only omits that verse but also insists on Jesus' fidelity to Israel's Scriptures and traditions. In Matt 5:21-48, which has no parallel in the other gospels, Jesus quotes Scripture six times and then provides his interpretation (see also 9:13; 11:10; 12:1-8; 12:9-14; 13:14-17; 15:1-20; 19:3-12; 22:34-40; 22:41-46). The basis for his understanding is his assertion "Do not think that I have come to abolish the law [that is, Torah] or the prophets [that is, Nevi'im]; I have come not to abolish but to fulfill" (5:17).

In Matt 9:12-13, Jesus responds to criticism that he eats with "tax collectors and sinners" by declaring, "Those who are well have no need of a physician, but those who are sick." At this point Mark 2:17 continues, "I have come to call not the righteous but sinners." Matthew interrupts this sequence in 9:13 by having Jesus cite Hos 6:6, "Go and learn what this means, 'I desire mercy, not sacrifice.'" This addition provides God's sanction for Jesus' practice. He eats with sinners because God is merciful, and Jesus manifests that mercy in his action. Matthew reprises the same verse from Hosea at 12:7 to show that procuring food and healing on the Sabbath are also acts of mercy. In turn, mercy is to mark the disciples' lives (5:7; 18:33-35; 23:23).

In engaging in these actions, Jesus is not violating Jewish Law: there is no biblical law that forbids dining with sinners or specifically plucking heads of grain on the Sabbath; the Sabbath is to be a day of rest and a holiday of delight, not a time to go hungry. Jews at the times of Jesus and Matthew and to this day have varying views of how the Sabbath should be observed. The Pharisees' criticism of Jesus' table companions is not an issue of biblical law; it is a question of the company one keeps. The modern analogy would be the minister criticized by a congregation for eating with arms dealers, drug pushers, insider traders, and people who fix the college football schedules. Rabbinic teaching does prohibit "reaping" on the Sabbath (*b. Shabbat* 73b), which could be connected to what the disciples were doing. Matthew not only includes an exegetical justification for the disciples' actions, but the first gospel also adds to Mark's version the notice that the disciples were hungry. Since the Sabbath is to be a time of joy rather than of want, the notice accentuates Jesus' concern for its proper celebration.

Matthew frequently adds scriptural references to indicate that Jesus "fulfills" statements from the Prophets (1:22; 2:5-6, 15, 17, 23; 4:14; 8:17; 12:17; 21:4; 26:54; 27:9), even in cases where no one had earlier seen the material as predictive, and in one case (2:23), Matthew cites a prophecy that cannot be located in the Scriptures of Israel.

Such fulfillment citations are particularly prominent in the first two chapters and thus complement the genealogy in connecting Jesus to Israel's story. In 1:23, Matthew evokes Isa 7:14, the notice that a young woman would bear a child named Emmanuel, "God with us." Often Christian readers understand this and other fulfillment citations to mean that, centuries before Jesus, divinely inspired prophets predicted events in his life. This understanding sometimes comes with two accompanying messages: first, that Jesus fulfilled these predictions shows that what the church calls the "Old Testament" is reliable and second, that Jesus must be the Messiah because he fulfilled Old Testament messianic expectations.

Such conclusions require correction. First, prophets were much more forthtellers addressing their present circumstances than foretellers predicting the future. The prophets of Israel should be seen as "reliable" primarily because of their insistence on attending to God's will in their own contexts, not because of their ability to know events that will take place centuries after their time. Isaiah is addressing the circumstances of his own time in the 730s and 720s B.C.E: the threat of the Assyrian empire and an attempt by the kingdoms of Syria and Israel to coerce Judah into an alliance against Assyria created a crisis. Isaiah assures King Ahaz of Judah that Syria and Israel will be destroyed and that Ahaz should trust God rather than form an alliance with Assyria. As reassurance, God provides Ahaz the sign of a pregnant young woman whose child is to be called Immanuel,

God with us. The child signals that there will be a future, that Judah will not be destroyed (unlike the northern kingdom, Israel), that God is with the people and will protect them.

In his sign, Isaiah says nothing about a "virgin" conceiving. The Hebrew text describes the mother-to-be as an *almah*, a young woman, who is already pregnant. When the Hebrew is translated into Greek, in the Septuagint, the term *almah* is rendered *parthenos*. At the time, around the late third or second century B.C.E., *parthenos* meant "young woman," and not necessarily "virgin." In Gen 34, after Shechem has sexual relations with Jacob's daughter Dinah, he refers to her as a *parthenos*. However, by the first century, when Matthew is writing, *parthenos* had in some Greek-speaking circles taken on the more technical definition of "virgin." Thus, Matthew saw in his Greek Bible what could be regarded as a prediction of a virginal conception. Readers who believe that predictions of Jesus appear in the Old Testament will find confirmation of that view, because such readers will be encountering the text through what might be called Christian lenses. However, those who do not believe that Jesus is divine, or that Israel's Scriptures specifically refer to him, will see no such references. Theological belief provides the interpretation, and as we noted in the introduction, readers will respond to the same text in different ways.

Matthew Reads Isaiah 42 and 53: The Suffering Servant

Another example of reading through Christian lenses appears in Matthew's evocation of Isaiah's suffering servant in 8:17 (quoting Isa 53:4) and 12:18-21 (quoting Isa 42:1-4). Isaiah's servant figure is elusive. The servant references come from the sixth century B.C.E. when Judeans were in exile in Babylon. Isaiah's suffering servant—most likely originally to be identified with the covenant community exiled and then redeemed (see Isa 41:8, "Israel, my servant")—suffers the imperial violence of exile, understood by Israel's prophets to be punishment for the people's sins. The servant's redemption is Israel's restoration to its land. The result of the suffering and redemption is the salvation of the Gentile nations who witness God's power in restoring the people Israel to their homeland. For Matthew, Jesus is the suffering servant because "he took our infirmities and bore our diseases" (8:17; see also 12:17-21); thus Matthew connects the Servant passages with healings. For other early followers of Jesus, such as the author of 1 Peter, Jesus is the servant because he dies on behalf of humanity; he "bore our sins in his body on the cross" (1 Pet 2:24).

These instances are typical of the ways in which the Scriptures of Israel appear in the New Testament. Jesus' followers read these texts with christological glasses and found in them a reservoir of meaning from which to articulate their own beliefs. Nor were they the only ones engaging the Scriptures in this way. The community members at Qumran, with whom are associated the Dead Sea Scrolls, read the Scriptures through the lens of their experiences. For example, they interpreted the book of Habakkuk in terms of their community's history and conflicts. For all the heirs of the Scriptures of Israel—today, the various Jewish and Christian communities—the texts speak both to their own historical and social contexts and to the contexts in which their readers live.

From Redaction to Context

From determining Matthew's redactional concerns, we can offer a tentative reconstruction of Matthew's social setting, or *Sitz im Leben* (German for "setting in life"). That is, the redactor can be understood as shaping the tradition to address the needs of the gospel's audience.

Source criticism and redactional elements locate the date of Matthew sometime after 70 C.E., the time when many Jewish groups, especially in the land of Israel, redefined their identity in part in relation to the destruction of the Jerusalem Temple. The loss of the temple meant the decreased influence of the Sadducees and of the priests; the Romans wiped out the Qumran community in 68 as the troops marched from Galilee to Judea, and the last pocket of resistance ended on Masada in 73. Many Jews, already attracted to the Pharisees' teachings and way of life, sought increased meaning in the practice of Torah. Jews both in Israel and the Diaspora needed to assess their relation to the Roman state, given that Rome's army had destroyed Jerusalem. And some Jews, without giving up their Jewish identity, followed Jesus' disciples into what Matthew calls the "church."

The prevailing theory is that Matthew's Gospel emerges from and addresses a group of Jesus-followers, some of whom had probably been part of a synagogue community, perhaps in Antioch. The gospel affirms and refines their understandings of Jesus, and it defines them both in relation to the Jewish tradition and over and against the synagogue and its leaders.

Redaction critics find evidence for such a scenario. For example, Matthew changes Mark's phrase "the synagogue(s)" (1:21, 29; 3:1; 6:2, 6a; 12:39; 13:9; cf. Q (Luke) 11:49; 12:11) into "their synagogues" (4:23; 9:35; 10:17; 12:9; 13:54) or "your synagogue" (23:34); the phrasing distances Jesus and his followers from the synagogue, the "gathering place" (the Greek term comes from *syn* as in "synoptic" and *ago*, meaning to lead or come). In 10:17 Jesus warns disciples that they will be flogged in *their* synagogues. In 13:54-58 a synagogue rejects Jesus. In 6:2, 5 and 23:6 Matthew condemns the hypocrites "in the synagogues." In turn, Matthew omits favorable synagogue references. So Jairus, whose faith is commended, is a "leader" of the synagogue in Mark (5:22, 35, 36, 38), but Matthew calls him simply a "leader" (9:18, 23). Matthew omits from Mark an exorcism that Jesus performs in a synagogue (Mark 1:23-28), perhaps because it associated Jesus positively with a synagogue. The rhetoric serves to distance Matthew's readers from the Jewish community, whether to encourage them to leave or to keep them from affiliating.

Matthew also intensifies Mark's negative picture of the chief priest and Jewish community leaders such as the Pharisees. Already in chapter 2, Matthew allies "chief priests and scribes" with Herod; this group reappears as the prime factors in Jesus' execution (26:3, 14, 57; 27:1, 12). Some of the scribes declare Jesus' forgiveness of sin to be "blaspheming" (9:3) although, ironically, it would not be. Jesus does not say, "I forgive you" but rather, "Your sins are forgiven." The passive voice suggests that it is God who forgives sins, something all Jews would acknowledge. Some Pharisees attribute his actions to the devil (9:34; 10:25; 12:24). Others view his interpretation of Sabbath traditions as deserving death (12:14). The chief priests question his authority and its source (21:23-27) and accuse him of seeking to destroy the Temple (26:60-61). In turn, Matthew's Jesus condemns the chief priests for rejecting God's work (21:33-46), the Sadducees for knowing "neither the scriptures nor the power of God" (22:29), and the Pharisees for being "hypocrites" who "shut up" the reign of God (23:13).

Chapter 23 adds six references to hypocritical Pharisees, where Matthew alone describes them as "blind guides," "blind," and "blind fools" (23:16, 17, 19, 24, 26; cf. 15:14). Yet Matthew also appears to value what they teach, if not what they do. Before the diatribe against the Pharisees begins, the Matthean Jesus advises that followers "do what they teach and follow it" (23:2). In 21:45, Matthew concentrates Jesus' attack against the chief priests and Pharisees (not mentioned in Mark 12:12). Two times (21:43; 22:7) Matthew adds verses to Marcan (12:1-12 esp. v. 11) and Q (Luke 14:15-24, esp. v. 21) parables to underline God's punishment of Israel's leaders for rejecting Jesus.

Calling Jesus "Rabbi"

Twice in Mark's Gospel, Peter addresses Jesus as "Rabbi." Matthew replaces one instance with the title "Lord" (compare Mark 9:5 with Matt 17:4) and omits the other (Mark 11:21 with Matt 21:20). However, Matthew does retain Mark's third use of "rabbi," by Judas (Mark 14:45; Matt 26:49). In Matt 26:21-25 when Jesus announces that a disciple will betray him, the disciples ask, "Surely, not I Lord?" Matthew adds a verse in which Judas asks the same question, but Judas addresses Jesus not as "Lord" but "rabbi" (26:25). Finally, in 23:7 "rabbi" is a title that the self-seeking scribes and Pharisees prefer (23:2-7). Matthew's Jesus forbids his followers to use it (23:8). By associating the term with betrayal and hypocrisy, the gospel can threaten to inculcate prejudice against Jews who still use this title in reference to teachers and leaders.

Along with these and other additions in which Matthew condemns Jewish leaders, two more passages suggest conflict with and contempt for the Jewish community. First, only in Matthew's Gospel does Pontius Pilate call for a bowl of water, wash his hands before the crowd, and announce, "I am innocent of this man's blood; see to it yourselves" (27:24). Then, only in Matthew, do "the people as a whole" (the Greek literally says "all the people") respond, "His blood be on us and on our children!" (27:25). Many Christian interpreters presumed that this "blood cry," as it has come to be known, indicated that all Jews, for all time and in all places, should be held responsible for the death of Jesus. The verse has led not only to anti-Jewish prejudice, but to attacks on Jewish communities over the past two millennia. In 1965, the Roman Catholic Church officially rejected this theological view, and many Protestant churches similarly have denounced it. Yet the idea of Jews as "Christ-killers," and the prejudice that comes from it, continue in pockets of Christianity across the globe.

It is unlikely Matthew's initial readers understood this passage as condemning all Jews. Rather, Matthew's historical context may best explain the scene. The "children" of the people of Jerusalem at the time Jesus was executed—that is, sometime between 26 and 36 C.E., when Pontius Pilate was governor—would have witnessed the destruction of the city in 70. Matthew is indicating that Jerusalem was destroyed because the people refused to accept Jesus as their messiah. Matthew makes the same point in the parable of the Wedding Banquet (22:1-14).

Second, at the end of the gospel, Matthew distances his "church" from the Jewish community by strategically using the term "Jews." Until the last chapter, the gospel references groups of Jews in various combinations: "Chief priests and scribes" appear in Jerusalem in 2:4. Then "Pharisees and Sadducees" oppose John's baptism (3:7; again in 16:1-12). In 5:20 "scribes and Pharisees" are linked and in 21:45 "chief priests and Pharisees." Thereafter, various combinations of these figures appear, along with scribes (7:29), Pharisees (9:11), Sadducees (22:23, 34), and chief priests (26:14) appearing on their own. This mix-and-match approach links the groups together as opponents of Jesus and allies with the governor Pilate. But it also hides significant differences among these groups.

A scene unique to Matthew (27:62-66; 28:11-15) completes the erasure of any distinctions among Jewish groups and faults them all. The narrator describes how the priests and elders "gathered" and "devised a plan" to bribe the soldiers who had been guarding the tomb to explain that it is empty because "his disciples came by night and stole him away while we were asleep." The priests and elders would protect the soldiers from Pilate's wrath. Matthew 28:15 then reads, "So they took the money and did as they were directed. And this story is still told among the Jews [Greek: *Ioudaioi*] to this day." The story makes good sense for Matthew's redactional interest in distancing readers from the Jewish community, but little sense in terms of history. A Roman soldier who admitted to falling asleep on guard duty would be executed, not protected. Nor does it make sense for the soldiers both to be asleep and to know what the disciples purportedly did. Matthew includes the scene to distinguish "the Jews" from the church. Some scholars propose translating the Greek term *Ioudaioi* with "Judeans" and so giving it a national rather than a religious emphasis. The translation is viable, although the narrative flow of the gospel (literary criticism) coupled with what we know of the relations of the early followers of Jesus to the broader Jewish community (historical criticism) and how we understand sectarian movements (sociological or social-science criticism) all commend the translation "Jews."

Whether Matthew's Gospel is to be seen as "anti-Jewish" depends in part on how we understand the gospel setting. If we determine that Matthew is writing from within the Jewish community to Jesus-followers who themselves are part of that community, then we might declare the text to be an in-house polemic. A Baptist who criticizes Roman Catholic theology or practice, or a Methodist who criticizes Episcopalian theology or practice, would generally not be seen as "anti-Christian." However, we cannot with full confidence determine the composition of Matthew's community. It is likely there are Gentiles in the church, given Matthew's interest in Gentiles from the genealogy to the "Great Commission" in 28:19, "Go . . . make disciples of all the nations" (or "all the Gentiles": the Greek word *ethnē* can be translated either way). Whether the mission to the "lost sheep of the house of Israel" (10:6; 15:24) continues or not remains an open question: although the Great Commission is focused on the Gentiles, there is no formal rejection of the original charge.

Determining whether a text is anti-Jewish or not also depends on how "anti-Judaism" is defined and who is defining it. Therefore, rather than debate definitions, and recognizing that we cannot with full confidence determine either the authorship or *Sitz im Leben* of the gospel, the better approach is to acknowledge that the text has been interpreted in anti-Jewish ways and then to seek to avoid continuing the prejudice.

$\mathcal{M}$ark

To understand Mark's story, we use narrative criticism and reader-response criticism. Narrative criticism attends to matters such as the plot, characters, settings, and point of view. Reader-response criticism emphasizes the active, creative role that readers play in employing these categories to make meaning of a text.

Narrative critics sometimes talk about the "implied" or "ideal" reader, that is, the reader whom the narrative directly assumes, who knows most or all of the references, who agrees with the narrator's judgments of characters, who is sympathetic with the narrator's tone. Other readers however will resist the narrator's perspective.

To show how reader-response and narrative criticism work, and in order to uncover Mark's narrative clues, we begin with a very close reading of the gospel's first few verses, turn to several individual pericopes, and then summarize the overall impression the gospel makes.

Who? When? Where? Sources?

We have no original manuscripts or "autographs" of any NT documents. Our texts are composites based on scholarly analysis and editing of thousands of early manuscripts and citations from early Christian writings. Therefore, to determine the author, date of composition, and intended audience, we have to rely primarily on the information in the texts themselves.

Who? "Mark" came to be linked with the gospel in the second century. Some texts mention a "Mark" associated with Paul (Phlm 24; Col 4:10; 2 Tim 4:11; John Mark in Acts 12:12, 25; 15:37-39), and Mark's Gospel does share several Pauline interests, including a law-free mission (for example, 7:19 on declaring all foods clean), a stress on the redemptory aspect of Jesus' death (for example, 10:45, "For the Son of Man came . . . to give his life a ransom for many"), and an interest in Gentiles (for example, 13:10, proclaiming the gospel to "all nations"). But these concerns are sufficiently generic that a direct link between the gospel we call Mark and the Apostle Paul cannot be confirmed.

The fourth-century Christian historian Eusebius recounts that a second-century follower of Jesus named Papias learned from an earlier source called the "Elder" that Mark, seen as the author of the gospel, received his information from Peter (*Eccleciastical History* 3.39.15). The connection may have been prompted by 1 Pet 5:13, in which the author mentions "my son Mark." However it is doubtful, as we will see, that Peter wrote the two NT epistles in his name. Thus in attempting to understand Mark's Gospel, we are left with an originally anonymous text whose author remains unknown.

When? Most scholars suggest Mark was written just before or just after 70 C.E., when Jerusalem fell to Roman forces. Mark 13:1-2 and chapter 14 are usually seen as references to the city's (imminent or recent?) destruction. Also favoring this date is the widespread view that Mark was a source for the Gospels of Matthew and Luke.

Where? An older view locates Mark's composition in Rome; more recent arguments favor Galilee or southern Syria.

The link between Mark's Gospel and Rome dates at least from Papias. The narrative's themes of frail discipleship coupled with external persecution and internal betrayal (4:5, 16; 13:9-13, 19, 24; 14:66-72) could commend a Roman setting: There were earthquakes in Rome in 60 and 63 (cf. 13:8), and "wars and rumors of wars" (Roman troops were defeated by Parthia in 62; civil war after the Emperor Nero's death in 68; the Judean war in 66–70 [cf. 13:8]). Nero persecuted followers of Jesus in Rome after the fire of 64 for a short period of time (Tacitus, *Annals* 15.44). Other factors pointing to Rome in the late 60s include traditions linking Mark, Peter, and Rome (for example, the second-century church father Irenaeus of Lyon, *Adv. Haer* 3.1.2), perhaps the local reference to the Roman coin *kodrantes* ("penny") mentioned in 12:42 (though likely this value was also known outside Rome), and the description of a "palace" with the Latin term *praetorium* (15:16).

Those finding a Galilean or southern Syrian provenance observe both that Mark favors Galilee over Judea as the site for the resurrection (14:28; 16:7) and that the eschatological fervor of 13:24-37 complements traditions known in works from the land of Israel, such as *1 Enoch* 37–71 and some of the Dead Sea Scrolls. Yet Mark shows ignorance of some Jewish practices; for example, he states that all Jews wash their hands before eating. While this practice is attested in later rabbinic documents, no source in antiquity suggests it is a Jewish universal, and a negative attitude toward Jerusalem does not need to indicate Galilean or Syrian authorship. Finally, it remains unclear how determining the location of Mark's Gospel to be Galilee or Rome—whether of author or intended audience—will change how we understand the text.

Sources? The gospel does not claim to have been written by an eyewitness, and Papias's view that Mark was Peter's disciple cannot be confirmed. Scholars have attempted to isolate sources by studying material the gospel groups together, recurring vocabulary, common stylistic features, and tensions in the narrative flow. Possible sources include a collection of miracle stories underlying 2:1–3:6; a parable collection beneath chapter 4; a collection of eschatological teaching informing chapter 13; an account of Jesus' death, an early "passion narrative," may be the basis for chapters 14–15. Also relevant to determining sources is the larger question of the relationship between Mark's editorial hand and the material Mark received. Is Mark a conservative redactor, cautiously combining sources, or a creative interpreter making extensive and significant changes to the tradition?

One source, however, is known. Mark's narrative frequently cites the Scriptures of Israel—what Christians would come to call the "Old Testament" and Jews the "Tanakh"—especially Isaiah (1:2-3; 4:12; 7:6-7; 7:37; 11:17). Most of the citations draw on the Septuagint, the Greek translation of these texts, rather than on the original Hebrew. Mark reads these Scriptures through his own confessional lenses and uses them to tell a particular version of the story of Jesus.

Mark 1:1—"The beginning of the good news of Jesus Christ, the Son of God."

Mark's opening phrase—"the beginning of the good news"—introduces the good news to follow. Readers familiar with the Septuagint hear echoes of Genesis 1:1, where God creates the world, "In the beginning." The same Greek term, *archē* ("beginning," as in "archaeology" or "archaic") appears in the opening lines of both books. This intertextual echo suggests that with Jesus, God—whom Mark does not explicitly mention here—is creating a new world; it also intimates that the story of Jesus is in continuity with Israel's story.

The second part of the opening line—"of the good news"—reinforces the idea of something new. The Greek term is *eu-angelion*. "*Eu*" means "good" (as in "*eu*phemism" or "*eu*logy"), and *angelion* is a message ("angel," which has the same origin, originally meant "messenger"); it comes into medieval English as "gospel"—"good news" or "good story." In the Greek translation of Isaiah (40:9; 41:27; 52:7), *euangelion* denotes the good news of God liberating the people from Babylonian exile and restoring them to their land. Isaiah 40:9b reads:

Lift up your voice with strength, O Jerusalem, herald of *good news*, lift it up, do not fear; say to the cities of Judah, "Here is your God!" [emphasis added]

Mark's use of the word to introduce Jesus could evoke this anti-imperial tradition and suggest that God's purposes evidenced in Jesus are at odds with Rome's practices. Other readers, hearing the same echo, might find a stress on Jesus' divinity.

Mark's Greek-speaking readers would have brought yet another meaning to bear on this term. *Euangelion* also appears in imperial propaganda to announce events celebrating the beginning of an emperor's rule, his birthday, or a military victory. For example, an inscription from 9 B.C.E. from Priene in Asia praises the emperor Augustus because he has exceeded "all previous *good news*" and because his birthday was "the beginning of his *good news*." Mark and this inscription share the same language, but Mark defines that "good news" in terms of God's action, not the emperor's.

The narrative then names Jesus, but does not explain his name's meaning (contrast Matt 1:21). Some of Mark's readers may know the name relates to the Hebrew term for "salvation"; others will not. Two more descriptors follow. Jesus is "Christ" and "son of God." The use of these terms at the outset of the gospel, and their repetition—Christ six times (1:1; 8:29; 9:41; 12:35; 14:61; 15:32) and Son of God seven (1:1; 1:11; 3:11; 5:7; 9:7; 14:61; 15:39)—suggest their import.

Christ and Son of God

Both "Christ" and "son of God" had multiple connotations in the first century. "Christ" derives from the Greek *Christos*, which means "anointed." It is the Greek translation of the Hebrew term *mashiach*, which comes into English as "messiah." Thus a "messiah" is one who is "anointed." *Mashiach* in Israel's Scriptures refers to a person "anointed" or set apart for a particular task, such as a king (1 Sam 16:13; Pss 2:2; 18:50; 89:20, 38, 51), a priest (see Exod 30:30; Lev 4:3, 5, 16; cf. Sir 45:15), or a prophet (1 Kgs 19:16; cf. Sir 48:8). Isaiah calls Cyrus, the Persian ruler who conquered the Babylonian empire and released the people from exile, God's "messiah" (Isa 44:28–45:1).

In the first century, not every Jew was expecting a messiah, and those who were had diverse expectations: some were looking for a prophet like Elijah; others an angel like Michael. Some texts (*Psalms of Solomon* 17:32; *4 Ezra* 7:26-29; 12:31-34) anticipate a Davidic king who executes judgment on Rome and who conquers "by the word of his mouth" rather than by military might. *First Enoch* 46–48 speaks of a heavenly judge, also called the "son of man," who condemns "the kings, the landowners" who exploit the poor. The Dead Sea Scrolls speak of at least two messianic figures: one a priest and one a warrior; neither is divine. For Gentiles, however, "messiah" was not a familiar concept. Consequently, when Mark calls Jesus "Christ," readers will need to determine from the following narrative what sort of Christ, or messiah, Jesus will be.

Similarly, "Son of God" (which could also be translated "child of God") (1:1, 11) is open to multiple understandings. In the Tanakh, Israel's kings are God's sons (Ps 2:7), as is Israel as God's people (Hos 11:1). From the deuterocanonical books, Wisdom of Solomon 2:18 uses the title for righteous individuals who live faithfully amid opposition. The term also identifies angels (Job 38:7). The Gospel of Luke (3:38) identifies Adam, and thus all humanity, as a child of God. The connotation of "Son of God" as designating someone in intimate relation to God (or gods, given the pervasive polytheism of the Roman world) and as an agent of God's will is also evident in Hellenistic and Roman texts. Roman emperors were called "son of God" to indicate their connection with earlier emperors who had been deified (by senatorial vote) after their deaths. When Mark calls Jesus "Son of God," again readers need to ask: What does he do as God's agent?

Verse 1, then, functions as an invitation to continue reading. It makes assertions about Jesus even as it raises questions about his identity that will be answered in the reader's encounter with the subsequent narrative.

Mark 1:2—"As it is written in the prophet Isaiah"

Readers who know the Scriptures of Israel see Mark's interests at work in how the narrative interprets these sacred texts. Quoting Isaiah, Mark connects the prophet's writings with John the Baptist by, in effect, changing the punctuation.

Mark's second and third verses read:

As it is written in the prophet Isaiah, "See, I am sending my messenger ahead of you who will prepare your way; the voice of one crying out in the wilderness: 'Prepare the way of the Lord, make his paths straight.'"

The citation, which conflates Isa 40:3 with Mal 3:1 and Exod 23:20, is Mark's introduction of John the Baptist, the voice in the wilderness who tells people to prepare God's "way." That the Greek term for "way," *hodos* (as in "odometer"), is the initial self-designation of Jesus' followers (see Acts 9:2 and elsewhere) may be Mark's pun.

But this is not the message Isaiah's *initial* readers received. Isaiah (the so-called Second Isaiah) was writing in sixth-century B.C.E. Babylon to encourage the Jewish community: your exile is ending; you will return to your homeland. Isaiah's initial readers heard:

> A voice cries out: "In the wilderness prepare the way of the LORD; make straight in the desert a highway for our God." (Isa 40:3)

For Isaiah, the message is one of return from exile; Mark refocuses the text on John the Baptist and preparation for Jesus' "way."

Mark then introduces John. His designation "the Baptist" suggests a distinct activity: there was at the time no "Fred the Baptist" or "Susan the Baptist." The name comes from a Greek word meaning to "dip" or "dunk," with connotations of washing. Some commentators highlight the oddity of the epithet by referring to "John the Dipper."

John's appearance also evokes Israel's Scriptures. John resembles the prophet Elijah, who was taken up to heaven (hence the song "Swing Low, Sweet Chariot") according to 2 Kgs 2:11. The prophet Malachi states, "I will send you the prophet Elijah before the great and terrible day of the LORD" (4:5 in the Old Testament; 3:24 in the Tanakh); thus Elijah was expected to announce the messianic age (see Mark 6:15; 9:12-13). By connecting John with Elijah, Mark turns the one who announces the messianic age into the one who announces the messiah, even as his narrative prompts readers to see the "Old Testament" as imbued with the story of Jesus.

Mark 1:15—"The time is fulfilled, and the kingdom of God has come near; repent and believe in the good news."

Jesus' first activity as God's agent (Son and Christ) is proclaiming (1:14) "the good news of God," and 1:15 summarizes that news: God's purposes are being manifested ("the time is fulfilled"), God's reign is being asserted in Jesus' activity ("the kingdom of God has come near"), and people need to change their ways and participate in God's work ("repent, and believe in the good news").

The term "kingdom of God" is central to Mark's presentation, and it too requires a full reading of the gospel to understand its nuances. A "kingdom" (Greek: *basileia*) can suggest a place as well as a "reign," with an emphasis on activity; the reference to the "kingdom [or empire] of God" also establishes a contrast to all other kingdoms or empires, such as Rome's.

Israel's Scriptures regard God as king (see, for example, Pss 93:1; 97:1; 99:1; 145:1) and praise this divine rule's creative and ordering power, righteousness, goodness, mercy, and faithfulness to the people. Israel's kings, as God's representatives, were to model this rule. In Ps 72, for example, the king is to enact God's justice (72:1), defend the poor, resist the oppressor, deliver the needy (72:4, 12-14), and overcome enemies (72:8-11). When God's reign is enacted, it conveys benefits—or blessings— such as justice (72:1, 12-14), food and fertility (72:3, 6, 16), peace (72:7) and social harmony (72:8-11).

Mark's readers, familiar with the language of "kingdom," thus see a tension between their own world and that of the "kingdom of God." The kingdom Jesus proclaims presents him as a new authority, one better than the Roman emperor, as well as anyone else: Pharisees or chief priests, John the Baptist, even one's own mother and father (1:21-22, 39; 2:18-22, 23-27; 3:19-30; 4:1-34; 7:1-23; 8:14-21; 10:29). He further proclaims that rulers should act as servants, not lords (9:35). Thus the "kingdom" Jesus proclaims has political, familial, and practical implications. And the actions of Jesus, the son and Christ, show the workings of this rule in the conquest of Satan (1:21-28; 5:1-20), disease (1:29-31, 32-34, 40-45; 2:1-12; 3:1-6, 10, 53-56; 5:24a-34; 7:24-30, 31-37; 8:22-26), sin (2:1-12, 15-17), hunger (6:30-44; 8:1-10), chaos (4:35-41; 6:45-52), and death (5:21-43).

Mark 1:44—"See that you say nothing to anyone."

Throughout Mark's first eight chapters, Jesus performs numerous healings. However, in his hometown of Nazareth, he could "do no deed of power there, except that he laid his hands on a few sick people and cured them" (6:5). The people had taken offense at his claims to authority; they regard him only as "the builder [Greek: *tektōn*; "carpenter" is a viable translation; connotations range from handyman to skilled artisan], the son of Mary and brother of James and Joses and Judas and Simon, and are not his sisters here with us?" (6:3). Attentive readers notice the contradiction with the opening verse: for the narrative, Jesus is not just carpenter but Christ, not just the son of Mary but Son of God. They also recognize a connection between belief in Jesus and the reception of the kingdom: the kingdom cannot be seen if people are unwilling to believe in it, or in its messenger.

They also see that Mark's Jesus is neither omnipotent nor omniscient nor, apparently, sinless. Concerning his power, in 1:45 and 6:5 he is not able to do further works.

Concerning his knowledge, he does not know the demon's name (5:8). He does not know who touched him (5:30). He does not know if he has healed the blind man (8:23). In 9:16 he does not know the topic of conversation when he joins his disciples and the crowds (also 9:33). In 9:21 he does not know how long the child has been sick. Concerning sin: not only does Mark present, with no explanation, Jesus' participating in Mark's "baptism of repentance for the forgiveness of sins" (1:4) and thereby suggests that Jesus saw himself as needing this public testimony, but also the gospel never proclaims Jesus to be without sin. Such a depiction conflicts with Heb 4:15 and with many Christians' understanding of Christology or Jesus' identity. Readers may choose to resist these aspects of Marcan "low Christology," that is, Mark's understanding of Jesus' identity as limited.

Mark may also have sought to correct early Christologies that emphasized Jesus' miracles or supernatural attributes. Such works would not indicate Jesus was divine, or even necessarily messianic. Greek gods and heroes and emperors were also regarded as performing "miracles," as were figures in Israel's Scriptures, such as Elijah and Elisha. There were also rabbinic miracle workers, such as Honi the Circle-Drawer, who could control rain, and Haninah ben Dosa, who performed miraculous healings. Moreover, despite the prominence of "mighty works" (Greek *dynameis*, "dynamic"), especially in the first eight chapters, Jesus usually seeks to silence the news of both his identity and his abilities. He commands demons to be quiet, especially when they announce his identity (1:25, 34; 3:12). He orders people who have experienced his healing power not to speak about it (1:43-45; 5:43; 7:36; 8:26). And he gives a similar prohibition to disciples who have seen his power at work (8:30; 9:9).

Messianic Secret

From the Enlightenment until the start of the twentieth century, the dominant understanding of this "messianic secret" was that it served to correct the disciples' nationalist messianic expectations. On this view Jesus did not reveal his messianic identity because he feared that it might inspire people to revolt or that the news would draw the attention of the Roman authorities. A variant of this view notes that gathering crowds were already politically dangerous, and even more so if they proclaimed a healer to be a king (see John 6:15). In this reading, the secrecy claims are politically motivated.

In 1901, the German biblical scholar William Wrede, who coined the term "messianic secret," proposed an alternative interpretation. Wrede argued it was Mark, not Jesus, who created the commands to silence. In this reconstruction, Jesus never claimed to be the Messiah; it was his followers, after the crucifixion, who gave him this title. In order to explain why the majority of people did not recognize Jesus

---

as the Messiah, Mark reshaped the traditions to present Jesus as trying to hide his identity.

Still others proposed that the secrecy motif is designed to prevent the Jewish community from hearing the good news. This suggestion comes from a reading of 5:1-20, the story of the possessed man from whom Jesus exorcises the "legion" of demons. Rather than command that this Gentile man, in Gentile territory, keep silent, Jesus states, "Go home to your friends, and tell them how much the Lord has done for you" (5:19). However, because this man has no identifiable friends or family, perhaps the command is designed to provide him the means for finding "friends." Nor are the Gerasenes, who ask Jesus to leave their territory (the loss of the very large herd of pigs was a disincentive to extending hospitality), likely to create political danger by making him a king. Thus the man's commission can have several possible interpretations.

A reading sensitive to Mark's narrative may provide the best understanding of the messianic secret: the good news must include not only Jesus' power but also his suffering and *crucifixion* (16:6). Any other proclamation is inadequate.

The gospel not only emphasizes Jesus' suffering and death; it also establishes the integral relationship between discipleship and suffering/death. Mark 6:6-13 depicts the commission of the Twelve to teach and preach, cast out demons and anoint the sick. Then, 6:14-29 describes John's proclamation, Herod's retaliation, and John's death. In Mark 6:30, the disciples return to report their success to Jesus. The mission of the Twelve frames the death of John, and the two stories inform each other. Proclaim the "good news," suggests Mark, and you may be killed. This sandwiching technique, known as *intercalation,* appears other times: the accounts of the hemorrhaging woman and the dead girl in 5:25-43; the narrative of Jesus' trial and Peter's denial in 14:53-72.

Reinforcing this narrative insight about the importance of Jesus' suffering and death is the two-stage healing depicted in 8:22-25. The local people bring to Jesus a blind man and request a healing. Jesus takes the man out of the village, puts saliva on his eyes, lays his hands on him, and asks, "Can you see anything?" The man replies, "I can see people, but they look like trees, walking." That is, his sight is partial. Jesus touches the man again and, then, looking carefully, the man "saw everything clearly."

This healing anticipates Peter's confession at Caesarea Philippi in the next pericope (8:27-33). Peter correctly identifies Jesus as the "Messiah," but it becomes immediately apparent that he, like the blind man, has an incomplete sense of the term's connotations. Following the confession, Mark recounts that Jesus "began to teach them that the Son of Man must undergo great suffering, and be rejected by the elders, the chief priests, and the scribes, and be killed. . . . He said all this quite openly" (8:31-32b). Jesus' words summarize the remainder of the gospel's plot. Readers, having heard numerous commands to silence as well as obfuscating parables, need to determine how to understand this "open" statement, the passion prediction. So does Peter, who cannot imagine that the "Messiah" would suffer and die. He has the correct confession, but not the correct connotation. The rest of the narrative will raise the question of whether Peter ever gains full sight.

Readers also need to understand Jesus' self-designation here and elsewhere as "Son of Man" and to determine how this title relates to "Son of God."

Son of Man

God addresses the prophet Ezekiel as "son of man," translated as "mortal" in the NRSV (Ezek 2:1, 3, 4, 10; 3:1, 3, 4, 17). The term, which can also be translated "human being," denotes Ezekiel's identity as a human in contrast to God. But it also denotes Ezekiel's identity as God's prophetic agent: "Son of man, prophesy against the shepherds of Israel" (Ezek 34:2 KJV). According to Ps 144:3 (KJV), Son of Man indicates all human beings: "LORD, what is man, that thou takest knowledge of him! or the son of man, that thou makest account of him!" In Dan 7:13-14, the same term refers to a heavenly or angelic being, perhaps symbolizing the community of Israel, to whom God entrusts everlasting dominion in place of earthly empires. Similarly, in *1 Enoch* 37-71, a text likely contemporaneous with Mark's Gospel, "Son of Man" refers to a heavenly being who exercises God's judgment over the powerful and wealthy. Complicating the meaning even more, in first-century Aramaic, "son of man" could mean "I" or "someone."

Readers have to determine whether Jesus is speaking of himself as a human being or as a supernatural redeemer figure or both. Each time the title is used, new connotations may be added. In 2:10, 28, it suggests authority and power. In 8:38; 13:26; and 14:62 it suggests an eschatological judge; in 8:31; 9:9, 31; 10:33, 45; and 14:21, 41, it proclaims that Jesus will suffer and die. Complicating the term even more, at times it sounds as if Jesus is speaking of someone other than himself as "Son of Man." How or even whether he used the title, or used it with some connotations that his followers then embellished, remains an issue that continues to occupy New Testament scholars.

Mark 5:9—"My name is Legion; for we are many."

The Gospels are not "history" in the sense we use the term today. While they do contain historical elements—there was a man named Jesus; he died on a cross—they are not attempts at objective reporting. Rather, they are partisan, confessional documents designed to instruct readers about the "good news" of Jesus. Even when they are recounting historical events, they do so in a way that promotes their own agenda, just as does today's news media. Readers thus may ask whether Mark is presenting a description of what actually happened or symbolism or moral exemplar or a combination of these genres.

Our two test cases for this question of history and symbolism are accounts of exorcisms, one of a man and one of a little girl. Already readers today will need to assess their own worldviews: do they believe in demon-possession? Would they regard the afflicted individual as invaded by external forces of evil, by bacteria or a virus, or would they diagnose mental illness? Is Jesus an exorcist (as Mark suggests) or a psychotherapist or a "faith healer"?

In 5:1-20, Mark introduces a demon-possessed man who lives among the tombs; the connotations of death and impurity would be clear to all Mark's readers, Jewish and Gentile. The townspeople had attempted to restrain him with shackles and chains, but he was too powerful. The description suggests superhuman strength, a power that cannot be contained. Horrific descriptions continue: "He was always howling and bruising himself with stones" (5:5): he damages his own body; he is self-destructive.

Then comes Mark's christological focus. The possessed man not only recognizes Jesus as "Son of the Most High God"; he also "bowed down before him" and begged him not to torment. This man with superhuman strength cedes his authority to Jesus. Next, in many ancient exorcism accounts, the healer obtains power over the demon by gaining knowledge of his name. Jesus asks the man his name; the response, "My name is Legion; for we are many" (5:9), is more than a simple identification. Calling oneself "legion" is like calling oneself the "101st Airborne" or the "Sixth Fleet." The demon is comparable to a Roman army unit of 6,000 men, which also means that the Roman army is comparable to demonic possession: it is violent, destructive, and without Jesus' power, unstoppable. That the demonic "legion" then enters into a herd of pigs would have made great symbolic sense to a Jewish audience, for whom pigs represent impurity. Pigs do not stampede, but that the legion drowns in the sea would have, symbolically, been good news to any people suffering under Roman rule. And that the location of the event, Gerasa, is a cognate to the Hebrew term *gerash*, which means "to expel" (it is the term used for Adam and Eve's eviction from Eden), makes the scene all the more apt: Gerasa can mean something like "Exorcismville." Readers knowing that the symbol of the army legion, the 10th Fretensis, responsible for Jerusalem's destruction in 70 C.E., was the wild boar might find a delightful irony in a story suggesting the expulsion of Rome's demonic power.

The story may well have a historical kernel. There were numerous exorcists in antiquity, Jesus among them, and stories of exorcism were popular. But in this case, the account is more than just a possible historical report. For Mark's early readers, it would have functioned as a hidden transcript: it not only announces the authority of Jesus, but it also shows him in conflict with and ultimately defeating Roman military rule.

Mark 7:24-30—"Even the dogs under the table eat the children's crumbs."

In Mark 7, Jesus has withdrawn into the Gentile territory of Tyre and Sidon, north of Galilee. There a woman, "a Greek, of Syrophoenician origin" (7:26), kneels at his feet and begs him to exorcise her demon-possessed daughter. Jesus refuses: "Let the children be fed first, for it is not fair to take the children's food and throw it to the dogs" (7:27). Mark's initial readers would likely understand the "children" to be the children of Israel, the Jews. Although some commentators today take Jesus' comment as a gentle chiding, as if he spoke with a smile on his lips and a twinkle in his eye, the scene belies that interpretation. The mother begs for her daughter's recovery, and Jesus, instead of providing the healing, calls the woman a dog. To understand this story, readers do well both to understand the cultural repertoire of the time and to correct some common stereotypes of it.

One common interpretation, focusing on the woman's Gentile identity, suggests that the scene indicates Jesus overcoming Jewish xenophobia—here some commentators insist that "dog" is a Jewish insult for Gentiles. This explanation fails for several reasons. First, Jesus has already been involved with a Gentile in 5:1-20. Second, "dog" was a standard insult used by anyone, Jewish or Gentile, just as it is today. No evidence suggests that Jews thought the term connoted "Gentiles." Finally, Jews were not in general xenophobic. To the contrary, they welcomed Gentiles into synagogues, and the Jerusalem Temple's outer court, known as the court of the Gentiles, welcomed non-Jewish worshipers.

Another interpretation, focusing not on ethnicity but on gender, emphasizes Jesus learning that patriarchal conventions must not stand in the way of God's reign. However, there is no reason for Jesus to refuse the woman's petition because of her gender. Earlier Jesus healed a hemorrhaging woman and raised a dead girl, and he had women among his followers from the early days in Galilee.

Nor, contrary to numerous modern claims, should it be seen as unusual or shameful that the woman either makes the request of Jesus on her own (as opposed to having a male relative petition for her) or that she is not identified by a husband or father. The parent who asks for a favor on behalf of a child is a conventional image; Jairus, who seeks the healing for his little girl, is one of many examples. King Jeroboam's wife approaches the Prophet Ahijah in 1 Kings 14:1-14; the Shunammite woman appeals to Elisha in 2 Kgs 4:18-37. The widow of Zarepath seeks a healing for her son from Elijah in 1 Kings. And in his biography of Apollonius of Tyana—another story of a divine healer—Philostratus depicts "a little woman pleading for her boy . . . who had been possessed by a demon for the past two years" (*Life of Apollonius* III.38).

A fourth modern interpretation is that Jesus rejects the woman because of her socio-economic status and geographical location. Her identification as a "Gentile [literally a "Greek," *Hellēnis*], of Syrophoenician origin" suggests both an elite and a colonial status: she is a resident of the area traditionally assigned to the Israelite tribes of Asher, Dan, and Naphtali but colonized by the Phoenicians, then the Syrian-Greeks, and now Rome. Perhaps Jesus rejects her because she represents the people who took land from his people and who now exploit the Jewish residents of Galilee. If Mark was writing within a northern Galilean/Syrian context, the woman's designation and Jesus' initial response may have had particular resonances.

But Mark's initial readers may have seen something else entirely. In this story, there is a convention at play, one Mark's readers may have known but with which twenty-first-century readers have no familiarity. From antiquity, we have multiple accounts of people in positions of authority who refuse to provide service to the poor or the weak. In each case, the weaker person, through a clever word, changes the superior's mind.

Macrobius records (*Saturnalia* 2.4.27) how an old soldier who found himself in danger of losing a law case requested that the Emperor Augustus appear for him in court. Augustus chooses an attendant to act as counsel, but the soldier, stripping his sleeve and showing his scars, shouts, "When you were in danger at Actium, I didn't look for a substitute but I fought for you in person." As Macrobius puts it: "The Emperor blushed, and fearing to be thought both haughty and ungrateful, appeared in court on the man's behalf." Dio (*Roman History* 69.6.3) recounts that an old woman once made a request of Hadrian. When the emperor responds, "I haven't time," the woman cries out, "Cease, then, being the Emperor"; she gets her hearing. The Talmud (*B. Baba Batra* 8a) offers a similar story about Rabbi Judah the Prince, the man responsible for the codification of Mishnah, the initial compendium of Rabbinic Law. During a famine, Rabbi Judah offered food to scholars but not to the unlearned. R. Jonathan ben Amram, in disguise, demands, "Master, give me food." When Rabbi Judah learns that he has not studied the sacred texts, he demurs, but Jonathan responds, "Give me food, for even a dog and a raven are given food." Rabbi Judah acceded to the "beggar's" wish, but he is troubled. Another of his colleagues then advises him that the "beggar" was Jonathan ben Amran, "who all his life has refused to derive any perquisite from honor paid to the Torah." Hearing this, Rabbi Judah opens his storehouse to all. Not only do gospel and Talmud share a common convention, but also they both use imagery of "dogs" and "bread withheld."

Mark's story may well rest on historical memory, but for Mark, it is more. It shows a powerful person who comes to realize he must attend to the needs of all others. Thus the story is a lesson to church leaders. Moreover, this story instructs those lacking power. In Mark's story, the woman turns Jesus' insult back on him: "Even the dogs under the table eat the children's crumbs." She thus displays tenacity, a response that deflects violence, a response that maintains her dignity in outwitting him. In this, she becomes an example to all who require aid from social superiors.

Mark 10:45—"For the Son of Man came not to be served but to serve, and to give his life a ransom for many."

In 10:42-45, following his first passion prediction (8:31), Jesus interprets his mission and his death: to serve and to redeem. At stake here are both political and theological concerns. Politically, Jesus establishes his leadership in contrast to Roman rule and its society based on a "power-over" model: "Among the Gentiles those whom they recognize as their rulers lord it over them, and their great ones are tyrants over them. But it is not so among you; but whoever wishes to become great among you must be your servant, and whoever wishes to be first among you must be slave of all" (10:42-44).

Theologically, the idea of Jesus as ransom complements the depiction of the martyrs in 4 Macc 17:21, where their death becomes a means of freeing the nation from imperial oppression: "The tyrant was punished, and the homeland purified—they having become, as it were, a ransom for the sin of our nation." The idea behind Mark's language may be that the people are in captivity—To Rome? To Satan? To sin? To all?—and by dying, Jesus pays their penalty. But for Mark, this payment does not uniquely belong to Jesus. Disciples, too, are to "take up their cross"; that is, they must be prepared to suffer crucifixion as Jesus does, and suffering marks the time before Jesus' return (13:9-23).

The idea of the ransom finds a symbolic depiction in Mark's account of Barabbas, who "was in prison with the rebels who had committed murder during the insurrection" (15:7). When Jesus goes to the cross in place of the guilty Barabbas, he serves as Barabbas's ransom. That the name "Bar-abbas" is Aramaic for "son of the father" enhances the symbolism. On the one hand, Barabbas can represent every person; on the other, he is both connected to and contrasted with Jesus, the "Son of God [the Father]" and the "Son of Man."

This emphasis on suffering and ransom needs great care in its interpretation. Some readers conclude that those suffering from systemic oppression should not resist; some even find a warrant for martyrdom. Passages such as 3:13-15 indicate, however, that disciples are to engage oppression actively though not violently, and such passages make very clear that they are not to submit to it. To take up the cross does not mean to accept domestic violence or to seek death; it means to challenge evil, even at the risk of death.

Mark 16:8—"They said nothing to anyone, for they were afraid."

Of the numerous characters who populate Mark's narrative, some are named and others anonymous, some hold positions of authority and some need liberation. Readers find themselves identifying with some characters and condemning others. Attentive readers find in Mark's characterizations questions about who are the insiders and who are the outsiders, who are role models and whose behaviors should be rejected.

The ideal reader of the gospel is most likely already one of Jesus' followers and, as such, most likely identifies with Jesus' disciples, such as the Twelve. These male disciples begin on a positive note: Simon, Andrew, James, and John leave their homes, families, and businesses to join Jesus, even though they have heard no preaching and witnessed no miracle (1:16-20). Similarly, Levi leaves his toll booth (2:14). Jesus tells them, "To you has been given the secret [or mystery] of the kingdom of God" (4:10-12); the passive "it has been given" suggests divine revelation. They successfully carry out their mission (6:12-13, 30), and they express concern regarding the people's salvation (10:26) when Jesus states, "It is easier for a camel to go through the eye of a needle than for someone who is rich to enter the kingdom of God" (10:25). They knew that there was no "needle gate" through which camels passed with difficulty.

And yet, their characterization is not entirely positive. As early as 1:37 they interrupt Jesus, who was seeking solitude. Following the parable of the Sower (4:2-9), and after declaring that divine revelation grants them understanding (4:11), Jesus asks them, "Do you not understand this parable?" (4:13). After witnessing the disciples' fear, Jesus calms the storm and then excoriates his followers: "Why are you afraid? Have you still no faith?" Their response displays ignorance: "Who then is this, that even the wind and the sea obey him?" (4:41). In 5:31, the Twelve chide Jesus for asking who had touched him. When they are again caught in a boat in a storm, instead of trusting that Jesus will save them, they again choose fear, not faith (6:45-51). By 6:52, their depiction has deteriorated even more, "for they did not understand about the loaves, but their hearts were hardened." The verb "understand" recalls the division of insiders and outsiders that Jesus makes in 4:11-12. Here the so-called insiders do not understand. Worse, the last people who had "hardness of heart" were the Pharisees and Herodians, those seeking to kill Jesus (3:5-6). The phrase also echoes the description of Pharaoh in Exodus, the ruler who resisted God's purposes (though the language differs, Exod 7:3, 13, 14, 22; 8:15, 19, 32; 9:7; etc.).

Likewise in chapter 8. The disciples had seen Jesus feed over 5,000 people (6:30-44), but when another enormous crowd gathers, they ask, "How can one feed these people with bread here in the desert?" (8:4). After another miraculous feeding, Jesus and the disciples get into the boat (8:10-13). Readers recall the two previous scenes in boats where disciples manifested fear, not faith. Perhaps they anticipate that this time the disciples will sail through the test of faith. Jesus warns them about "the yeast of the Pharisees" and reminds them of the two previous bread scenes (8:21). But the disciples fail again. Not only do they take Jesus' comment about "yeast" to refer literally to bread rather than to the plot against them, but they lament, "We have no bread" (8:16).

The downward track continues as the disciples fail to understand Jesus' passion predictions (8:32-33; 9:32). Nor can they understand that following Jesus means they will also "take up their cross" (8:34-38). They rebuke parents and children for seeking Jesus' blessing (10:13-14). They have insufficient faith to heal an epileptic child (9:18-19 cf. 9:28-29); they reprove an exorcist who heals in Jesus' name (9:38-41). James and John, instead of recognizing Jesus' way of service and suffering, ask, "Grant us to sit, one at your right hand and one at your left, in your glory" (10:37). Readers may note the irony of Mark 15:27: "And with him they crucified two bandits, one on his right and one on his left." One disciple, Judas Iscariot, betrays Jesus (14:10-11, 20-21, 43-51). Peter, James, and John sleep as Jesus struggles in Gethsemane with God's will that he die (14:32-42). They all declare that they will not deny Jesus, but the last words any disciple utters is a tragic denial: Peter began to invoke a curse on himself and to swear, "I do not know this man of whom you speak" (14:71). They all flee (14:31, 50-51), a bitter contrast to the death of John the Baptist: while his disciples claimed his body, Jesus' corpse is interred by a stranger, Joseph of Arimathea. Finally, none of the Twelve is found awaiting the resurrection despite Jesus' threefold instruction (8:31; 9:31; 10:34).

Having encouraged readers to identify with the disciples as people called to follow Jesus, Mark complicates the identification. This characterization requires readers to think about their own discipleship. Some, perhaps those who failed to remain faithful themselves, would find in Peter a sympathetic figure. Some will know that Peter becomes the leader of the nascent community gathered in Jesus' name; thus they may regard Peter as a role model. If he could be forgiven, then there is a chance for everyone. Others might be prompted to (re)assess the leadership of the Jerusalem church that was founded on the authority of these failed followers. By raising such questions, readers continue the story past its final page and into their own lives.

This forward-looking thrust of the narrative is reinforced by the depiction of Jesus' women followers. In Mark 14:3-9 an unnamed woman anoints Jesus for burial. The male disciples object, but Jesus commends her: "She has performed a good service . . .

For you always have the poor with you" (14:7). Perhaps readers might see contributions they could make; one does not need to be an insider, or a leader, in order to follow Jesus. And others will query Jesus' statement about the eternity of poverty. Those who have attended to Mark's repeated challenges to the status quo realize that Jesus is not saying that systems cannot be challenged. Some readers may hear an echo of Deut 15:11, "Since there will never cease to be some in need on the earth, I therefore command you, 'Open your hand to the poor and needy neighbor in your land,' and so see Jesus as mandating care for the poor. Still others emphasize that the poor are "among" the followers of Jesus, and therefore insist on solidarity with them. Or perhaps the comment "among you" means that the disciples will be the ones who are poor (see here Mark 6:8). Thus the conversation continues as readers respond to Mark's narrative.

This unnamed anointing woman sets up Mark's introduction of the named women who have been with Jesus since the beginning. According to 15:40-41, "looking on from a distance" to the cross were

> Mary Magdalene, and Mary the mother of James the younger and of Joses, and Salome
> . . . [who] used to follow [Jesus] and provided for him when he was in Galilee; and there
> were many other women who had come up with him to Jerusalem.

Until this moment, just sentences before the end of the gospel, Mark has said nothing about women in Jesus' entourage or as serving in a patronage capacity. The Greek term the NRSV translates as "provided for him" is *diēkonoun*, which comes from the same word as "deacon" and which is normally translated "serve" or "minister." Attentive readers will reread the text and now see women together with the Twelve; they recognize women's ministerial roles, and perhaps they identify with the women.

Yet these insiders fail as well. After the Sabbath, Mary Magdalene, Mary, and Salome come to anoint Jesus' body, but they are too late. The unnamed woman had already "anointed [his] body beforehand for its burial" (14:8). Like the three named disciples—Peter, James, and John—who fail Jesus in Gethsemane, so the three named women fail him at the tomb: they come expecting to find a corpse, not new life. Similarly, in contrast to the named disciples in Gethsemane, an unnamed centurion, witnessing Jesus' death, proclaims him to be Son of God. This designation occurs seven times (1:1, 11; 3:11; 5:7; 9:7; 14:61; 15:39), by the narrator, by God, by the demons, and by the high priest. But no disciples use it. No human confesses Jesus to be Son of God—until the centurion, and until the moment of Jesus' death.

At the tomb, a young man—perhaps an angel—commissions the women to tell the disciples that Jesus will meet them in Galilee (16:7). They are to be the first apostles of the resurrection. But like the disciples, they choose fear, not faithfulness: "They said nothing to anyone for they were afraid" (16:8).

This is the gospel's original ending. There is no glorious resurrection appearance whereby disciples are commissioned to evangelize all nations as in Matthew, where a sequel narrates the expansion of the church as in Luke, or where the Holy Spirit descends on the disciples, as in John. The only people left at the end are the readers. They hear the same commission. They have the same options of faithfulness or fear. The narrative leaves them—and contemporary readers—with the same choice.

The Problem of Mark's Ending

Mark 16:18—"They will pick up snakes in their hands, and if they drink any deadly thing, it will not hurt them."

Text criticism undertakes the painstaking task of trying to establish from various manuscripts the earliest form of the NT writings. The task may already be partially doomed: there may have been multiple early versions of Mark's Gospel, created by different scribes who have listened to different oral performances of the gospel in different settings.

There are significant textual problems with the ending of Mark's Gospel. The earliest manuscripts indicate that the gospel originally ended with 16:8, the women's fear and silence. In terms of a narrative technique, this ending maximizes reader engagement with the story. Readers are called to continue the story.

Some early interpreters found Mark's unresolved conflict to be unsatisfactory. In one manuscript, an uplifting "shorter ending" appears after 16:8. "And all that had been commanded them they told briefly to those around Peter. And afterward Jesus himself sent out through them, from east to west, the sacred and imperishable proclamation of eternal salvation." Other scribes supplied an uplifting "longer reading," usually printed as verses 9-20. This account includes Jesus' appearance to Mary Magdalene and two other disciples, the commissioning of the 11, Jesus' ascension, and the obedience of the disciples. Influence from other gospels is evident here. Whether readers will recognize a disjunction between the gospel's de-emphasis on miracles in favor of suffering and the longer ending's celebration of the miraculous through the show of faith in picking up serpents will depend on their own literary and theological views.

CHAPTER 3

£uke

In this chapter, we first combine historical criticism with form criticism, the approach that attends to the literary forms or conventions of the units within the gospel (called "pericopes"). In asking questions about literary forms, we investigate both the purpose of the narration and the historical basis of the material narrated. We conclude by using feminist criticism to inquire into Luke's presentation of women.

Author, Date, Sources

As with the other gospels, we do not know who wrote the Gospel of Luke or its companion volume, Acts. Neither text identifies its author. Given the similar themes, literary style, and address, we can be confident that the same author wrote both texts.

Was Luke a Doctor and Companion of Paul?

The traditional identification of Luke as Paul's "fellow worker" (Phlm 24) and the "beloved physician" (Col 4:14; cf. 2 Tim 4:11) originates in the second century. The Muratorian Canon (ca. 170s C.E.) mentions "Luke that physician" (cf. Irenaeus's *Against Heresies* 3.1.1; 3.14.1). The author of Luke-Acts, however, is unlikely to have been a physician. The texts reflect no more medical language than that found in other Greek literature, such as the Septuagint and the works of Josephus. Even the connection of the author, whom we shall continue to call "Luke," to Paul is suspect, as we shall see in chapter 5, on the book of Acts.

Nor do we know where the text was written or much about its audience. Luke, whose Greek is of higher quality than Mark's, replaces Mark's Hebrew and Aramaic terms (for example, "rabbi" [Mark 9:5//Luke 9:33], "rabbouni" [Mark 10:51//Luke 10:41]) and omits others (for example, "Talitha cum" [Mark 5:41], "Abba" [Mark 14:36], and the cry of dereliction in Mark 15:34 where the dying Jesus quotes Ps 22:1, "My God, my God, why have you forsaken me?"). Thus Luke's target audience is not likely to include Aramaic speakers. Perhaps Luke omits these phrases because they sounded too "Jewish" or even, when used in healing narratives, suggested magical incantations.

Whether the author of Luke-Acts was Jewish or Gentile cannot be determined on the basis of internal content. Some scholars posit that Luke was a "God-fearer" (see, for example, Acts 13:16), a Gentile attracted by Judaism's theology, history, and ethical system. These Gentile God-fearers were affiliated with the social network of synagogue communities, but they usually did not observe the particular markers of Jewish identity, such as circumcision, food laws, and perhaps Sabbath observance.

We can, however, posit the gospel's sources: Mark's Gospel, the sayings collection Q, and material, whether oral, written, or both, from a third source, called "L." By one count, of the 1,150 verses in Luke, 320 are from Mark. Since Mark has about 600 verses, Luke uses about half of Mark. About 250 verses come from Q, and about 580 verses from "L." Luke generally follows Mark's order of events until Mark 9:50/Luke 9:50. Luke also omits two large sections of Mark (6:45–8:26; 9:41–10:12) along with some smaller sections. Whether Luke had narrative reasons for omitting this material (for example, Luke omits the "feeding of the four thousand" and the healing of the Syrophoenician woman's daughter because for Luke, the Gentile mission cannot begin until Acts), or Luke's copy of Mark lacked this material, or whether this solution to the Synoptic Problem (discussed earlier in the chapter on Matthew) is wrong and Mark in fact used Luke as a source, remain open questions.

After Mark 9:50/Luke 9:50, Luke departs from Mark's plot. In Mark, Jesus' journey from Galilee to Jerusalem takes one chapter (Mark 10). In Luke it takes 10 chapters (516 verses); Jesus does not arrive in the city until 19:37 (or possibly 19:41 or even 19:45). This journey, occupying about a third of the gospel, is known as Luke's Travel Narrative. Framed by passion predictions (9:21-22, 43-45, and 18:31-33) and emphasizing Jesus' destination and destiny in Jerusalem, the Travel Narrative contains a substantial amount of material unique to this gospel, including the parables of the Good Samaritan (10:29-37) and Prodigal Son (15:11-32).

With Jesus' entry into Jerusalem in 19:29-48, Luke returns to Mark's order of events, but again with several omissions, including the anointing at Bethany (Mark 14:3-9) and the mocking of Jesus as king (Mark 15:16-20). It is quite possible that Luke had a different version of the anointing story: Luke 7:36-50 describes a woman who anoints Jesus' feet. Luke's passion and resurrection narratives also have several additions, including the relation of Pilate and Herod (23:6-12), the Emmaus journey (24:13-35), and the appearance to the disciples (24:36-43). Thus, Luke freely reworks received materials, arranging them to create a new "orderly account" (1:3).

Given this use of sources, we can posit a date for the gospel in the last decade or two of the first century or in the early second century. Like Matthew (27:25), Luke interprets Jerusalem's destruction as resulting from the city's refusal to accept Jesus as God's agent:

> They will crush you to the ground, you and your children within you, and they will not leave within you one stone upon another; because you did not recognize the time of your visitation from God. (19:44)

Luke's Prologue: 1:1-4

Although it is often claimed that the gospel's opening four verses resemble the prologues of Greek and Roman historical writings and thereby indicate that Luke is writing "history," the resemblance is inexact and so the generic connection is not secure. First, Luke's prologue is much shorter than many historical prologues found, for example, in writings by Herodotus, Thucydides, Polybius, and Josephus. Moreover, Luke's prologue lacks the author's name and origin, a feature of the earlier Greek histories. It also lacks any moral reflection on the value of history that historians often included. Nor are prologues always indicative of historical works. Ancient medical treatises, writings on mathematics and engineering, rhetorical instructions and philosophical speculations, astrology and dream interpretations, even apologia (Josephus dedicates his *Against Apion* to "most excellent Epaphroditus") had prologues. These treatises more closely resemble Luke 1:1-4 in terms of length, dedication, and language. Thus, while the prologue does not indicate that Luke is writing "history," it does offer assurance that the gospel is a trustworthy account supported by careful research.

The content matches the form. First, Luke indicates that other accounts existed about Jesus (for example, Mark, Q) yet finds these accounts inadequate. Thus this gospel is meant as a corrective, or at least a supplement, to those earlier sources.

Second, the prologue suggests some years have passed between the time of Jesus (around 30) and the time of this writing. Stories about Jesus have been handed on through two generations by eyewitnesses, and by "servants" or "ministers of the word." Luke's point is that despite the passage of time, the sources are credible. Third, it underscores the gospel's reliability. The material is comprehensive ("investigating everything carefully"), appeals to the origins of the tradition ("from the very first"), and is clear ("an orderly account").

However, Luke is not a neutral narrator. By mentioning the "events that have been fulfilled" (1:1), the evangelist indicates God's activity in making something happen (4:21; 22:37; 24:44). By speaking of actions fulfilled "among *us*" and that were "handed on to *us*" (1:1-2, emphasis added), Luke indicates that only insiders, followers of Jesus, know what God has been doing. He identifies the accounts of God's activity in Jesus as "the word" (1:2), a term that in this gospel refers to God's promises made, enacted, and proclaimed

(1:38; 5:1; 8:11, 21; 11:28). This "word" is trustworthy, it connects the present and the past, and it is the means of encountering divine presence, faithfulness, and purposes.

The dedication to "most excellent Theophilus" suggests that Theophilus is Luke's patron, a high-status individual who supports the writer financially. Perhaps Theophilus was a patron of a house-church and supplied other benefactions for group members. Or, perhaps "Theophilus" is Luke's dedication to an ideal reader. The name "Theophilus" is Greek for "Friend of God" or "Lover of God," one who embodies Jesus' teaching to love God in Luke 10:27, quoting Deut 6:5. Luke 1:4 presents this reader as already having received Christian teaching. The verb usually translated "instructed" literally means "catechized" (Greek: *katēchēthēs*; cf. "catechism"), and in Acts 18:25, it refers to religious instruction.

Luke finally insists that the instruction will enable the reader to "know *asphaleia*" (1:4). The NRSV translation "truth" misleadingly suggests Luke is correcting false information. Rather, *asphaleia* is better translated "security," "assurance," or even "full confidence." Theophilus (and others like him) are followers of Jesus—they have been "catechized"—but they know doubt, uncertainty, confusion. Luke's account provides assurance and security. As we read through the gospel, we gain some idea of these uncertainties as well as Luke's assuring responses.

What is the Gospel's Genre?

Beyond the prologue, the gospel's genre becomes clear. The text exhibits features of ancient biographies that narrated the life of a significant figure—philosopher, emperor, general, politician. Ancient biographies described the birth, teaching, actions, and death of a worthy individual so that others might learn from them.

Luke 1:5–4:13—The Infancy Accounts

Unlike Mark, but like Matthew, Luke provides an account of Jesus' nativity. The gospel's first two chapters, likely a combination of traditional material ("L") and Luke's creative construction, provide alternating accounts of the conception and birth of John the Baptist and of Jesus. An angel announces first that John is to turn "many of the people of Israel to the Lord their God," (1:16) and then

> [Jesus] will be called the Son of the Most High, and the Lord God will give to him the throne of his ancestor David . . . and of his kingdom there will be no end. (1:32-33)

These annunciations follow a common literary pattern established in the Scriptures of Israel. A heavenly messenger (angel, voice from heaven, prophet) announces the birth of a child to an often infertile, menopausal, or otherwise unlikely-to-conceive woman or her husband. Luke's readers, likely familiar with the earlier Jewish stories, would recognize the convention and enjoy the literary play upon it through changes in characterization, timing, and setting. Genesis 16 presents an annunciation to Hagar, the pregnant Egyptian slave who is fleeing her mistress, Sarah. Then Sarah, well past child-bearing age, overhears the prediction that she will conceive (Gen 18). The previously infertile but now pregnant Rebekah learns from a heavenly messenger that the twins she carries represent two nations who will strive against each other (Gen 25). In Judg 13, the "wife of Manoah" encounters an angel who predicts she will conceive: the expected child is the mighty Samson. Second Kings 4 plays on the convention when the prophet Elisha seeks to provide a service for the "great woman" (4:8; the NRSV offers "wealthy woman") of Shunem; his servant Gehazi observes: "She has no son, and her husband is old" (4:14). Readers, knowing the convention, will know how the story ends.

Luke uses this literary form in depicting an "angel of the Lord" announcing to the priest Zechariah that his infertile, elderly wife, Elizabeth, will conceive (1:11). Like Sarah, Zechariah is incredulous. Unlike Sarah, he is punished for his disbelief by being rendered mute until his newborn son's circumcision (1:20, 62-64). Likewise, the angel Gabriel announces to Mary that she will conceive Jesus. Mary questions the angel: "How can this be, since I am a virgin?" (1:34). Instead of a rebuke, she receives reassurance. Luke does not explicitly state that Mary is a virgin when the child is conceived; this gospel does not cite Isa 7:14, as Matthew does. However, if we take Luke to be indicating a miraculous conception, then what God does with and through Mary, a virgin, is more astounding than the conceptions celebrated by previously infertile or postmenopausal women.

Luke presents another literary form, that of a genealogy (3:23-28). Matthew's version of Jesus' genealogy, as we have seen, emphasizes Abraham and David, traces the lineage through the royal line of King Solomon, presents an artificial structure of three sets of 14 generations, includes four women from Israel's Scriptures, and mentions "Jacob the father of Joseph" (Matt 1:16) to evoke the figures from Genesis and to anticipate the second Joseph's dreaming dreams and taking his family to Egypt (Matt 2).

Luke uses the genealogy to suggest different concerns important for his gospel. First, rather than mention "Solomon," Luke takes the genealogy through David's son "Nathan," thereby evoking the Davidic line but avoiding the royal prerogatives. This is part of Luke's political critique. Second, Luke begins with Jesus and works backward to "son of Seth, son of Adam, son of God" (3:38). For Luke, the title "son of God" encompasses all humanity, and connects Jesus to everyone.

Luke reinforces these political points by contrasting Jesus' context with that of John the Baptist. John appears in "the days of King Herod of Judea" (1:5), but Luke connects Jesus' birth to "those days [when] a decree went out from Emperor Augustus that all the world should be registered" (2:1). John's impact will be limited to the people of Israel; Jesus' will be empire-wide. Luke's hand is evident here. There was no empire-wide census in Roman antiquity. Nor did the Roman census require the empire's residents to return to their ancestral homes; people registered where they lived. Moreover, a census did take place in Israel, but in the year 6 C.E., well past the date of Herod's death. At that time, some Jews revolted against Rome; Acts 5:37 mentions "Judas the Galilean [who] rose up at the time of the census and got people to follow him; he also perished, and all who followed him were scattered." Luke's point is not historical, but political. Joseph and Mary, also residents of Galilee, comply with Rome's rule: the new kingdom that Jesus promotes will not be brought about by violent revolt.

The genealogy along with the infancy accounts provides another set of messages. These narratives first affirm that the Scriptures of Israel are part of divine revelation; the God associated with Adam, Abraham, and David is the same God whom Jesus calls "Father." Second, they insist that Jesus is of human flesh, indicated both by his birth and by his circumcision.

In the early second century, both of these claims were hotly contested. A follower of Jesus named Marcion argued that the Scriptures of Israel spoke of an inept and jealous deity, surely different than the one Jesus came to reveal. Marcion based his own canon on select writings of Paul as well as on the Gospel of Luke, but he stripped from the gospel any positive references to Israel's Scriptures and to Jewish practice. Marcion was also an ascetic, and he viewed the flesh as something to be overcome. Luke 1–2, with its evoking of annunciation scenes, its insistence on the goodness of conception, its references to the circumcisions of Jesus and John, and its depiction of Joseph and Mary's fidelity to Jewish custom, can be seen as responding to these concerns.

Another early group may have regarded John the Baptist rather than Jesus as the true prophet, as do Mandaeans to this day. Still others questioned why Jesus, if he were sinless, needed to submit to John's baptism. In Matt 3, John resists baptizing Jesus, but Jesus insists that it must be done to "fulfill all righteousness," a Matthean concern. In Luke's account, John acknowledges Jesus' superiority when in a short scene called the "Visitation" (1:39-45) the pregnant Mary visits her pregnant cousin Elizabeth. The older woman confirms the ranking when she exclaims to Mary, "And why has this happened to me, that the mother of my Lord comes to me?" (1:43).

Another conventional form present in the first two chapters is the "song of praise" or "hymn." Mary offers the Magnificat (1:46-56), Zechariah the Benedictus (1:67-80); the names come from the Latin for, respectively, "magnifies" (1:46) and "blessed" (1:67). The angels sing a brief song (2:13-14). Simeon, who greets the baby Jesus in the Jerusalem Temple, offers a prayer of thanksgiving, the "Nunc Dimittis," from the Latin translation of the opening line, "Now you are dismissing" (2:29-32). In addition, Zechariah offers praise after his muteness ends (1:64). The shepherds offer praise after encountering the angels and the newborn Jesus (2:20). These hymns sound several of the gospel's themes.

59

The Magnificat connects the conception and birth of Jesus with God's great reversal of unjust societal structures; it can be read as a celebration of divine power, but it also suggests a political manifesto anticipating social reversal:

He has brought down the powerful from their thrones, and lifted up the lowly. (1:52)

Zechariah celebrates God's faithfulness and mercy. The angels celebrate God's favor to all people. Simeon likewise declares the extent of God's salvation for Jew and Gentile and thereby anticipates the Gentile mission that the imperial context of Jesus' birth suggests and that Luke describes in Acts. The combination of form and content echoes throughout the gospel, as characters respond to Jesus with praise (see 5:25-26; 7:16; 13:13; 17:15; 18:43). Crowds from Jerusalem praise God for Jesus' deeds of power (19:37). And the gospel ends with the disciples praising God in the Jerusalem Temple (24:53). Readers notice hymnic forms and allusions, make connections among these pericopes, and quite likely connect the messages with their own liturgical practices.

Literary Forms and Historical Facts

The use of literary forms such as genealogies, annunciations, hymns, and scriptural allusions, especially when coupled with the quite different content in Matthew's infancy materials, can call into question the historicity of both accounts. For some readers, the gospels' discrepant details—such as the genealogies, the conventions and allusions, as well as the miraculous—aspects undermine their factual credibility. They regard the texts as recording not "what happened" but rather, like parables, as making theological claims: Jesus' continuity with the Scriptures of Israel; the incompatibility of the kingdom of Rome and the kingdom of heaven. They also see the evangelists' distinct concerns. Matthew connects the story of Jesus to that of Moses and Israel whereas Luke sets Jesus on the world stage. Matthew offers Magi, Gentile astrologers, who worship Jesus while the Jewish king, Herod, seeks to kill him and thus forces Jesus, Mary, and Joseph to become refugees in Egypt. Luke offers shepherds who respond not to a star but to an angelic annunciation. The Magi give expensive gifts of gold, frankincense, and myrrh whereas Luke emphasizes the humility of the nativity.

Other readers see some historical information in the shared material: Jesus' parents are Joseph and Mary (Matt 1:18; Luke 1:27, 34); the birth happens in Bethlehem (Matt 2:1; Luke 2:4-6) during Herod's reign (Matt 2:1; Luke 1:5); Jesus is raised in Nazareth (Matt 2:23; Luke 2:39). The typical "Christmas pageant" has little problem staging a crèche or "manger scene" (the tableaux was actually developed by Francis of Assisi in 1223) including Magi (usually transformed into "kings," although this is not what Matthew says) and shepherds, numerous animals, and a star six feet above the barn. On the other hand, popular stories about greedy Jewish innkeepers refusing to house a poor couple are the stuff of pernicious stereotype. Luke's point (2:7) is that there was no room *to have a baby.* The NIV translation of *kataluma* as "guest room" rather than "inn" (so the NRSV) thus moves in the right direction: Luke is describing not a motel but a single room (see also Luke 22:11). As for the "star" of Bethlehem, the common explanations that the star is a comet or planetary conjunction or supernova fail to note that people in antiquity did not realize either how large, or how hot, stars are. Nor could a star, in the modern sense of the term, stop "over the place where the child was" (Matt 2:9); if it did, the entire region would be incinerated. Rather, stars in antiquity were seen as living beings, not enormous masses of gas.

Those who assess the infancy accounts to be "history" take one message; those who see the chapters as "folktale" or "parable" or "mythology" take a different message. Yet even for the former group, history always requires interpretation. Readers of all perspectives should ask: "Why is the evangelist presenting this information? How do these stories help in understanding the rest of the gospel?" Addressing these questions, readers of various theological views may reach the same answers.

Luke 4:16-30—The Synagogue Sermon

All three Synoptic Gospels indicate that Jesus was not well received in his hometown. Mark 6:1-6 comments on the locals' unbelief, notes Jesus' inability to do mighty works, and records Jesus' comment, "Prophets are not without honor, except in their hometown, and among their own kin, and in their own house." Matthew 13:54-58 shortens the story, changes Jesus' inability to a matter of will, modifies Mark's identification of Jesus as a "builder" or "carpenter" to a "carpenter's son," and rewords Jesus' comment: "Prophets are not without honor except in their own country and in their own house."

In presenting the same story with different words, details, and emphases, evangelists are using a Greek rhetorical form called a *chreia.* As part of the art of writing and speaking, rhetoricians learned to expand and contract stories, to add or subtract detail, and to make the material relevant to the target audience. Not only was the content important, so was the means by which it was presented. Form worked together with function. We can see in these two examples a *chreia* in use. The basic data are (a) Jesus is rejected by his hometown community; (b) his family is identified; (c) he speaks of a prophet's lack of honor; (d) mighty deeds are mentioned.

Luke rewrites this entire scene (4:16-30). First Luke repositions it so that it becomes Jesus' first public act following his temptation by Satan. Then, he extends the scene by adding a synagogue sermon. Third, Luke replaces the comments about mighty works with narration of what Israel's prophets had done and for whom. Finally, Luke replaces Jesus' statement about lack of honor with the claim that the people of Nazareth sought to kill him. Thus Luke signals to readers a way of understanding Jesus' activity as well as responses to him. Indeed, many commentators take this pericope as Luke's signature scene summarizing the gospel's main points.

First, Luke establishes Jesus as a faithful Jew from a faithful family. The nativity accounts link him to the faithful, blameless, Temple-affiliated parents of John and to his own devout parents (2:21-38). This picture continues with 4:15-16 presenting the adult Jesus in "the synagogue on the sabbath day, as was his custom," where he "began to teach in their synagogues and was praised by everyone." Whether Nazareth had a "synagogue" in the sense of a separate building devoted to community worship and public gathering is unclear; no such archaeological structure has been found. But that historical detail does not impact Luke's narrative presentation. Handed a scroll of the book of Isaiah, Jesus finds a particular passage. Whether this was the passage expected to be read that Sabbath as part of the annual cycle of readings from the *haftarah* (a Hebrew word indicating the passage from the Prophetic corpus [Nevi'im] read on the Sabbath as an accompaniment to the reading from the Torah) or whether Jesus chose the passage is not stated. Had he searched for the passage, he might have taken a long time. A scroll of Isaiah, such as the one found at Qumran, runs about 24 feet long and 11 high, with 54 columns of text. Although Judaism continues the practice of reading every Sabbath a Torah passage and a passage from the Prophetic writings, the passage Jesus reads is not included in the cycle.

While Luke states that Jesus reads from Isaiah, the passage recorded is a composite of Isa 58:6 and 61:1-2. It provides, for Luke, the focus of Jesus' mission. First, Jesus reads, "The Spirit of the Lord is upon me, because he has anointed me . . ." (4:18). The reference to "anointed" (Greek: *echrisen*) reinforces Jesus' identity as the "anointed" one or "Christ." The Spirit has anointed or "christed" him to "proclaim good news [from the same Greek root as *euangelion*, gospel], to the poor." The verses belong to the justice tradition of the Jubilee year (for example, Lev 25) that envisions a societal transformation in which debts are forgiven, slaves released, and land returned. Luke displays considerable interest in economic reversal and insists the rich use their funds for the benefit of the poor. Jesus is also anointed to release captives (Acts depicts three scenes in which Jesus' followers escape from prison), to heal the blind (as both Jesus and his followers in Acts do), and to free the oppressed (as Jesus and his followers also do through exorcisms). Jesus' mission is in accord with the Scriptures. The synagogue members affirm him (4:22), although incorrectly identify him (only) as "Joseph's son."

But then Jesus goes on the offensive. Whereas in Mark and Matthew, the hometown people reject him, in Luke's version, Jesus rejects them. He references Elijah and Elisha, two of Israel's prophets who provided miracles for Gentiles. The people in the synagogue, enraged not at the implied extension of Jesus' miraculous gifts to Gentiles but at his refusal to manifest his powers for them, rise up. Luke states that they "led him to the brow of the hill on which their town was built, so that they might hurl him off the cliff" (4:29). The narrative exaggerates, given that Nazareth is not built on a cliff or even a hill. But Luke has established another thematic: synagogues are places of danger.

Throughout the gospel and onward through Acts, Luke depicts the rejection of Jesus and his followers by all but a small number of Jews. In the struggle for socioreligious self-definition, such depictions of enmity are common and indeed conventional, but they are never irenic.

Poverty and Wealth

Jesus' commissioning to "bring good news to the poor" highlights Luke's extensive commentary on economics. While it is commonly asserted that Luke is opposed to wealth—people do leave "everything" to follow Jesus (5:11, 28; 18:28)—the text is more subtle. References to abandoning wealth are often specific to particular individuals whose riches hinder the response to Jesus' call (see, for example, 18:18-30). Whereas Jesus prohibits disciples (9:1-6; 10:1-12) from taking supplies with them on their mission journey, thus forcing them to rely on hospitality, not all are called to this life. Indeed, Luke commends those who provide hospitality, such as Mary and Martha (10:38-42). If they renounced all, there would be no missionary support. Thus, Luke is less interested in condemning all wealth than in insisting on its appropriate use.

This concern begins when John instructs those who seek his baptism to share resources such as food and clothing, to act justly in transactions, and to avoid greed (3:10-14). Jesus' citation of the Jubilee traditions of "the Lord's favor" in Isaiah 58 and 61 in his synagogue sermon (4:18-19) underscores these norms, as do his instructions in the "Sermon on the Plain" about giving to those who beg without expecting reciprocity (6:29b-31; see also Matt 5:42). Jesus also commends the practice of almsgiving (12:32-34), a major concern in Judaism.

The theme continues in the sequence of four beatitudes and woes (6:20-26) that opens Luke's Sermon on the Plain (6:20-49). The "Beatitude" is a common literary form that begins "Blessed are . . ." or "Happy are . . ." It expresses God's favor toward certain people or situations. For example, Isa 30:18 notes, "The LORD is a God of justice; blessed are all those who wait for him"; Jer 17:7 adds, "Blessed are those who trust in the LORD." The Psalms as well as Proverbs and Ben Sirach are replete with the form: "Happy are those who consider the poor; the LORD delivers them in the day of trouble" (Ps 41:1; cf 94:12). Matt 5–7, the Sermon on the Mount, begins with a set of beatitudes (Matt

5:3-12), likely derived from Q, some of which Luke also records. Whether Matthew and Luke had variant copies of Q, or whether one or the other redacted an original, remains undecided.

We see in the first beatitude each gospel offers a theme repeated elsewhere in the gospel. The form stays the same, but the details are adapted to fit the needs of the broader narrative. In Matthew's setting, on a mountain that alludes to Moses receiving the Torah on Mount Sinai/Horeb, Jesus says to his disciples: "Blessed are the poor in spirit, for theirs is the kingdom of heaven" (5:3). Luke has a different focus. On a level plain, Luke presents Jesus as looking up (6:20) at his disciples and saying, "Blessed are you who are poor, for yours is the kingdom of God."

The beatitude form is the same in both; the nuances are different. While both name economic poverty, Matthew's focus includes interiority: the "poor in spirit" comprise those whose economic poverty crushes even their innermost being. Next, Matthew's statement is expansively general: the kingdom belongs to anyone who is poor in spirit; it is "theirs" and not just for the disciples. Luke's beatitude is in the second person: "You who are poor"; the focus is on economics and not attitude. Third, the Matthean signature phrase is "kingdom of heaven"; Luke uses "kingdom of God."

Differences continue. Luke alone complements the Beatitudes with a series of "Woes." The "Woe" is another common literary form found in Israel's Scriptures. Instead of "Blessed are . . ." or "Happy are . . ." the woe condemns: "But woe to you who are rich, for you have received your consolation" (Luke 6:24; other woes appear in 10:13-14; 11:42-52; 22:22).

Luke's focus is on how wealth is used, not on condemning the rich per se. Whereas Matthew uses the story of the centurion to contrast Gentile fidelity with Israel's lack (Matt 5:8-13), Luke (7:1-10) describes the centurion as loving the Jewish people and using his resources to build a synagogue. Again, same story, different emphases. For Matthew's parable of the Wedding Banquet, the rejection of the invitations results in destruction. For Luke, who describes not a wedding banquet but a "great dinner" hosted by a "someone" rather than a "king," the rejection results in invitations to the casualties of the Roman Empire, "the poor, the crippled, the blind, and the lame," people who cannot reciprocate the invitation (14:16-24).

After seeing Jesus, Zacchaeus, the rich, short, chief tax collector, states that he gives half his possessions to the poor and pays fourfold compensation to any he defrauds (19:1-10). The Greek verbs describing his actions are in the present rather than the future tense. His story could be seen not only as a conversion but also as a public witness to the people of Jericho. In this reading, he is to be compared to the tax collector in the parable of Luke 18:10-14, who unexpectedly repents of his sin and finds forgiveness. Jesus praises Zacchaeus's actions of doing justice through financial restoration: "Today salvation has come to this house, because he too is a son of Abraham" (19:9).

Sewn through Luke's Gospel is another thread that presents characters who exhibit greed rather than generosity. Parables beginning "There was a rich man who . . ." inevitably end badly for the rich man. The parables of the rich fool (12:17-21), the rich man and the dishonest steward (16:1-8), and the rich man and Lazarus (16:19-31) have quite different plots, but all convey a warning against greed. Luke even accuses the Pharisees of being "lovers of money" (16:14), a conventional insult. Josephus, in contrast, notes the Pharisees' simple lifestyles (*Antiquities* 18.12)

Through this material, the gospel articulates norms to guide disciples: generosity, acting justly, and resisting greed. It also provides some explanations for the damage to relationship with God and human beings that ignoring these practices causes. The gospel thus provides direction for ethical behavior as well as assumes a communal context of responsibility and hospitality, but Luke leaves it to disciples, and so to the readers, to work out the specifics.

Meals and Food

The references to food and meals that pervade Luke's Gospel highlight numerous important motifs: the problems of inadequate access to food; the role of hospitality in manifesting the kingdom of God; the ability to form less-stratified community in the context of a meal, especially with people who have put themselves out of the community, such as "tax collectors and sinners" (5:29-32; 7:34; 15:1-2). Such meals depict social inclusion and the breakdown of class-based divisions.

The parables of the rich men noted above present rich men who hoard or refuse to share food. The rich fool (12:31-21) builds more barns rather than distributes his excess grain to the poor. The rich man "feasted sumptuously every day" while Lazarus, who sat at his gate, "longed to satisfy his hunger with what fell from the rich man's table" (16:21-22). Failure to aid the poor and feed the hungry mark those in the narrative opposed to Jesus, a point Mary already announced in the Magnificat: he has filled the hungry with good things, and sent the rich away empty (1:53). Luke also adapts Q material to emphasize generosity in sharing food. In the Sermon on the Mount, Jesus instructs, "If anyone wants to sue you and take your coat, give your cloak as well" (Matt 5:40). In Luke 3:11, the legal setting disappears. The focus is not on injustice but on generosity: "Whoever has two coats must share with anyone who has none; and whoever has food must do likewise."

Several times, Pharisees invite Jesus to dinner (7:36; 11:37; 14:1). In each case, Jesus criticizes the host and uses the setting as an opportunity for teaching. With this "dinner plus teaching" format, Luke uses another conventional literary form, the *symposium* or banquet setting best known from Plato's work of the same name. Jesus critiques any host whose practices emphasize status-based reciprocity rather than inclusiveness and hierarchy rather than community. It is in this context that we should see the story of Mary and Martha (10:38-42; see discussion in later chapter).

Luke's infancy story depicts Mary as placing her newborn in a "manger," a feeding trough, a term repeated three times for emphasis (2:7, 12, 16). Attentive readers will recall this image when Luke describes the Last Supper, for in both settings Jesus' body is associated with food:

> Then he took a loaf of bread, and when he had given thanks, he broke it and gave it to them, saying, "This is my body, which is given for you." (22:19)

Similarly, the two travelers on the road to Emmaus recognize that their companion is Jesus in the breaking of bread (24:30-31). At the end of the gospel, Jesus commissions the disciples in the context of a simple meal (24:41-42).

The Delay of the Parousia

The Gospel of Mark offers a "little apocalypse" in chapter 13, where the manifestation of the kingdom of God is imminent. Mark conveys eschatological urgency by depicting Jesus as insisting,

> "Truly I tell you, there are some standing here who will not taste death until they see that the kingdom of God has come with power." (Mark 9:1)

Matthew makes a similar claim but redefines it in terms of Christology:

> Truly I tell you, there are some standing here who will not taste death before they see the Son of Man coming in his kingdom. (Matt 16:28)

For Matthew, the shift in wording anticipates not the eschaton, but Jesus' receiving "all authority" (see 28:18). Mark's focus on Jesus' return, the end of the world, and the final judgment shifts in Matthew to emphasize Jesus' abiding presence and the Gentile mission.

Luke offers another permutation on the same:

> Truly I tell you, there are some standing here who will not taste death before they see the kingdom of God. (9:27)

For Luke, the kingdom is both eschatological hope and present reality (17:21). Like the other Synoptics, this gospel's eschatological comments are related to a concern about

Jesus' return, what is sometimes called the "second coming" and, in Greek, the *parousia*. This Greek term, literally meaning "appearance," was used in imperial discourse to refer to the triumphant return of a conquering hero, emperor, or king. Luke's eschatological commentary may indicate that some among the gospel's readers were having doubts about the reliability of Jesus' words promising his return. Thus the eschatological material is part of the assurance given to Theophilus (1:4).

Like Mark, Luke affirms that the Parousia will happen and disciples must be ready for it. But Luke also acknowledges that Jesus' return will not be imminent. This shift is evident in Luke's redaction of the parable of the Pounds. A man entrusts his money to his slaves to use in his absence until his (delayed) return (Luke 19:11-27; cf. Matt 25:14). According to Luke (but not Matthew), Jesus tells the parable "because they [the identity of "they" is left unspecified] supposed that the kingdom of God was to appear immediately" (19:11). The parable corrects their mistaken perception. For Luke the parable is not about diminished eschatological hopes but about the opportunity for faithful action during that delay. Thus the delay represents not a time of disappointment but of opportunity and active faithfulness. Luke redacts other Q material, also depicting the faithful as slaves, to emphasize the certainty of Jesus' return rather than its immediacy. In 12:35-48 (cf. Matt 24:42-51), Luke frames the statement that "the Son of Man is coming at an unexpected hour" to stress that those who wait for the master's return must be faithful in their tasks.

Mark 14:62 depicts Jesus as saying, "'You will see the Son of Man seated at the right hand of the Power,' and '*coming with the clouds of heaven*'" (emphasis added). Luke (22:69) redacts the statement by omitting the italicized clause. The effect is to emphasize Jesus' current status ("seated at the right hand") rather than the expectation of his return. The ascension, depicted in Luke 24:51, reinforces this focus. Acts 1, which replays the ascension with more detail, presents the humorous image of the apostles staring into space, looking for Jesus. Angels appear and say to them:

> "Men of Galilee, why do you stand looking up toward heaven? This Jesus, who has been taken up from you into heaven, will come in the same way as you saw him go into heaven." (Acts 1:11)

In other words, go into Jerusalem, wait for the Holy Spirit, and fulfill your tasks. Your job is to look outward, not upward.

For Luke's Gospel and Acts, liturgical formulations reinforce the idea that the church's present action and Jesus' present exaltation work together. For instance, while Matthew offers the petition, "Give us today our daily bread" (6:11), Luke has, "Continue to give us our daily bread daily" (11:3). Luke reworks the tense of the verb "give" to indicate continuous time (a present tense instead of an aorist tense). "Daily," an adverb, emphasizes an ongoing regular occurrence. Luke even adds the same adverb to Jesus' invitation to discipleship in Luke 9:23, "If any want to become my followers, let them deny themselves, and take up their cross daily, and follow me" (cf. Mark 8:34).

The delay, yet certainty, of Jesus' Parousia does not, for Luke, mean that the kingdom is inaccessible. For Luke, it is already present: in preaching (4:43), lending money without repayment (6:35), healings (9:11), feeding the hungry (9:12-17), exorcisms (11:20), and breaking of bread. Luke states, "Once Jesus was asked by the Pharisees when the kingdom of God was coming." By placing the question on the lips of Pharisees, Luke signals to the readers that the question of doubt is one voiced by those on the outside, by "lovers of money," by those who would do Jesus harm. Jesus responds:

> "The kingdom of God is not coming with things that can be observed; nor will they say, 'Look, here it is!' or 'There it is!' For, in fact, the kingdom of God is among you." (17:20)

The Greek of the final phrase could even be read as "within you," and a double meaning may be possible.

Women in Luke and Feminist Criticism

Contemporary Lucan scholarship is divided over its assessment of Luke's presentation of women, and thus, by extension, on Luke's understanding of gender roles and social division. While the gospel continually speaks of reversals—the mighty brought down from the thrones and the poor elevated—study of gender in the gospel complicates the social message.

What is Feminist Criticism?

Although feminist criticism typically uses depictions of women and of gender roles (that is, the social codes that establish expectations for how men and women are to behave) as a starting point for analysis, its interests are broader: feminist criticism seeks to expose and resist all forms of domination whether social, sexual, political, economic, racial, religious, or ethnic.

Some feminist criticism is part of the historical-critical enterprise. It seeks to locate women's presence and their social roles. Other feminist criticism concentrates on women's literary depictions as role models, negative stereotypes, main or ancillary figures, representative norms or idiosyncratic figures, and so on. Both approaches will note systems in which men are the norm, women are marginal;

men are seen as rational, women are emotional; men exercise power, women submit. Feminist critics will also note the impact of language such as how descriptions of God in androcentric terms ("Father," "Lord," "He") relate to constructions of male and female identity. Other feminist criticism looks to the present construction of equal, just, and life-giving structures, practices, and interactions for women and men. And still other feminist critics welcome the personal voice of the reader and celebrate how the reader understands, from a personal subject position, the meaning of the text. No two feminists read the same way, and feminist scholarship on the Gospel of Luke provides an excellent exemplar.

For some readers, Luke is an ancient feminist seeking to enfranchise women and erase gender distinctions. Some scholars have even suggested that the Third Evangelist was a woman. The thesis has some supporting evidence. Luke does have more stories of women than the other canonical gospels, and Acts similarly has multiple references to women. Luke attributes to Mary the opening declaration about divine justice (the Magnificat) and recognizes women prophets such as Elizabeth, the mother of John the Baptist (1:5-7, 24-25, 39-45, 57-60) and Anna, the widow living in the Temple (2:36-38). The gospel depicts a woman exemplifying the gratitude of forgiveness (7:36-50), acknowledges women as patrons of Jesus' movement (8:1-3; 10:38-42), and uses women as major figures in parables, including the woman seeking her lost coin (15:8-10) and a very persistent widow (18:1-8). In a scene also unique to Luke, a woman from the crowd praises Jesus by blessing the womb that bore him and the breasts from which he nursed (11:27): Jesus' response speaks instead of praising those who hear and obey God's word. In a culture that accorded motherhood value, Jesus can be seen as saying that value should be found not in fertility, but in action.

Although Luke presents no woman explicitly commissioned by Jesus to teach or preach, nevertheless some feminist readers are inclined to see women among the 70 missionaries (10:1-12; the male plural in Greek can mask the presence of women), or understand Cleopas's companion on the road to Emmaus as a woman. They also note that Acts 9:36 uses the term "disciple" for Tabitha. Further, they observe correctly that absence of evidence is not the same thing as evidence of absence. Just because women are not explicitly mentioned at, for example, the Last Supper does not indicate that they were absent.

However, quantity of reference is not the same thing as quality of detail, and a patron is not necessarily the same thing as a leader. Less sanguine feminists note that while Luke often pairs male and female characters, the women appear less active. For example, while Anna and Simeon both acknowledge baby Jesus, Luke conveys Anna's words in a single phrase in the third person (2:38) while Simeon's prophecy is recorded in direct speech

(2:29-32). In redacting Mark 10:29, Luke adds "wife" among the relationships that disciples—clearly males—must leave (Luke 18:29). In Matthew and Mark, a woman performs a ritual action by anointing Jesus' head, and Jesus states she has anointed him for burial. Luke moves the scene, another chreia, out of the Passion narrative, characterizes the woman as a "sinner," erases the ritual aspect of her action, and describes the anointing as on Jesus' feet (Luke 7:36-50).

Nor are statistics definitive. By one analysis, there are 10 named women in the gospel compared with 39 named men (with another 94 mentioned). There are 10 unnamed women yet 40 unnamed men. There are references to 2 groups of women but 27 groups of men. Jesus' teaching refers to women 18 times but 158 times to men. Women speak 15 times with their words given 10 times. While women are spoken to 15 times, 9 of which are by Jesus, men are spoken to hundreds of times. Readers can draw their own conclusions about what the numbers signify.

The story of Mary and Martha (10:38-42) has been read as depicting an egalitarian Jesus who promotes women's right to theological education, something that Judaism would have forbidden, so it is claimed, because rabbis were not allowed to talk with women. This reading needs correction. While the point about theological education is valid, the claim that Jesus is here divorced from a misogynist Judaism that forbade rabbis from teaching women is Christian apologetic rather than historical argument. Luke's own writings show that Jewish men and women spoke together in public. Simeon speaks directly to Mary in the Temple in Jerusalem (Luke 2:34); Peter speaks to Sapphira (Acts 5:8); and Paul speaks to Lydia (Acts 16:14-15), and no scholar expresses surprise. The Talmud, the compendium of Jewish Law, frequently depicts women talking with rabbis; we know not only from Luke 8:1-3 but from other early sources that Jewish women served as patrons to men, and there would be no reason for a guest not to talk with a host or for friends not to converse with each other.

Conversely, the same story of Martha, Mary, and Jesus has been read as Jesus' approving of women as long as they are silent and at his feet: Martha, busy with "much serving" (the Greek verb is *diakonein*, from the same root as "deacon"), receives only criticism. Through this interpretation, Luke is understood to be instructing readers to prevent women from holding any formal role, such as "deacon," in the church; that Paul names Phoebe a deacon in Romans 16:2 may have been known to, and rejected by, the Third Evangelist.

Or perhaps we should understand the scene as another literary convention: with this interpretation, Martha as yet one more "host"—like Simon the Pharisee (7:36-50) and his fellow symposium hosts —who receives critique from Jesus the guest. In this case, Jesus insists that hospitality be focused on the guest, and that one has to listen to the gospel before it can be proclaimed. Indeed, perhaps Mary and Martha are a leadership couple, running a house-church. If this is the case, we still need to determine if the Lucan Jesus approves of Martha's ministry or not.

Whether readers of Luke find enfranchisement or marginalization for women is up to them. Indeed, whether readers celebrate Luke's emphasis on reversal, with the last being first and the first being last, or whether they note that the kingdom of God cannot be present as long as the categories of first and last are in place, again depends on their response. The Gospels do not always provide answers to the questions we pose to them, but they nevertheless provide the occasion to pose our questions and to engage those queries in conversation with other readers.

CHAPTER 4

*J*ohn

In John's Gospel, Jesus declares that he does God's will (5:19; 12:49-50), but he is more than a divine agent. Statements such as "The Father and I are one" (10:30) led some of his followers to conclude that Jesus shares God's very nature or being, what philosophers would call an "ontological oneness." Others, both from among those who regarded Jesus as the messiah and from among those who did not, saw this christological development as compromising the insistence in Israel's Scriptures that God is one; "Hear, Israel: The LORD is our God, the LORD alone" (or "the LORD is one" [Deut 6:4]). Debate over the gospel's claims about Jesus' relationship with the Father began in the first centuries of the church, and in some circles of Christianity, it continues to this day.

To understand John's Christology, one approach—and so the methodological focus of this chapter—is to see how John draws upon the Scriptures of Israel. In highlighting how John alludes to, quotes from, and retells Israel's story, we see how John understood and adapted Jewish traditions.

Who Wrote John's Gospel?

Since the second century, the gospel has been linked with John, the son of Zebedee, the "beloved disciple." Irenaeus of Lyon (*Against Heresies* 3.1.1) identifies John as the "beloved disciple" and claims that this identification came from Polycarp, bishop of Smyrna, who had known John personally. Hence Irenaeus could claim an unbroken chain of figures to guarantee the gospel's credibility. Yet other ancient authorities, including the North African church leader Tertullian, remark that, because of John's substantial differences from the Synoptics, the Fourth Gospel could not rest on apostolic authority. The gospel does not itself claim authorship by John the son of Zebedee, mentioned by name only in chapter 21, nor does it connect this John with the anonymous "disciple whom Jesus loved" (19:26; 21:7, 20).

Chapter 21, a likely addition to the original narrative, claims that the gospel's authority rests on the testimony of the "beloved disciple," an unnamed figure who first appears in chapter 13 at supper with Jesus (13:23-26). In the Passion Narrative, this disciple becomes increasingly prominent. John locates him at the cross with Jesus' (unnamed) mother, her sister Mary the wife of Clopas, and Mary Magdalene; Jesus entrusts his mother to him, and the beloved disciple to her (19:25-27). This disciple outpaces Peter to arrive at Jesus' empty tomb and he "believes" (20:2-10). According to the final chapter, the beloved disciple recognizes Jesus and identifies him for Peter (21:7). In the gospel's final verses, the narrator observes:

> The rumor spread in the community that this disciple would not die. Yet Jesus did not say to him that he would not die, but, "If it is my will that he remain until I come, what is that to you?" This is the disciple who is testifying to these things and has written them, and we know that his testimony is true. (21:23-24)

The identity of this beloved disciple, traditionally called "John," remains debated. The traditional identification could be correct, although other candidates for authors have been proposed. Some scholars suggest Lazarus, who is identified as loved by Jesus (11:3, 5, 11, 36). But the gospel never calls Lazarus a disciple, and if he is the "beloved disciple," then the narrative's reluctance to name him is inexplicable. Additional suggestions include Mary Magdalene, with the concomitant view that her authorship was masked because some followers of Jesus would not accept testimony from a woman. Others have suggested a figure well known to the Jerusalem establishment. The gospel's familiarity with the environs of Jerusalem commends this identification. However, the proposal that his identity is hidden to protect him and his family from local reprisals has its own problems: the gospel is a generation or two away from the actual date of events, so there would be little need to protect anyone's identity at this point; nor is there any indication that the gospel was written in Jerusalem; nor again does the gospel hesitate to name other figures, such as Mary, Martha, Lazarus, and Nicodemus. Perhaps like Luke's "Theophilus," the disciple may represent any faithful member of the community as a role model or, in a variation of this view: the disciple in the narrative is based on a real person whose testimony underlies the gospel, but the portrait is painted in such a way that readers can identify with this otherwise anonymous figure. The same point may hold for John's depiction of the mother of Jesus, the Samaritan woman, the royal official, and the other unnamed figures in the text.

Another approach concerning authorship is to think of John's Gospel as a community enterprise, since the narrative apparently went through several editions. The inclusion of chapter 21 after the likely ending of 20:30-31 is one indication. So too are chapters 15–17 in which Jesus continues to talk after he seems to have finished his teaching in 14:31 ("Rise, let us be on our way"). Throughout, the gospel displays numerous "aporias," or inconsistent content, rough sequences, and uneven style. For example, according to 3:22, Jesus was baptizing in the Judean countryside, but 4:2 insists that while his disciples were baptizing, he was not. In 7:8 Jesus says he is not going to Jerusalem to celebrate the Festival of Booths (known in Hebrew as Sukkot), but in 7:10 he goes, although secretly. The famous passage of the woman taken in adultery (8:1-11) is missing from the earliest and best manuscripts.

There are also theological inconsistencies. The content of 5:19-25 about Jesus' life-giving role and relationship with the Father is largely repeated in 5:26-30, but in the second section, the eschatological point of view changes from the present to the future. In 5:22 Jesus declares that "the Father . . . has given all judgment to the Son"; in 12:47 Jesus says he does "not judge anyone who hears my words."

These aporias and apparent inconsistencies need not suggest that the final editor of the gospel was inept, or even that the text is theologically confused. Rather, the gospel invites its readers to read again, to see new material each time, and with each encounter to deepen their knowledge of the mysteries being revealed in human flesh. Perhaps only the language of paradox or irony or poetry can most fully capture theological imagination. The authors of the Scriptures of Israel, with their various names for and depictions of the Deity, already knew this, and John's Gospel is heir to this tradition. When the subject is theology, often a "both/and" rather than an "either/or" approach to paradox is the better path.

The Tanakh/Septuagint/Old Testament as a Resource for NT Writers

Whatever we call them, the Scriptures of Israel—especially the Psalms and Isaiah—provided Jesus' followers with paradigms to express their experience of Jesus and their understanding of God in relation to him. Sometimes they quoted these writings directly, as Paul does by stringing quotes together for eight successive verses (Rom 3:10-18). Sometimes they borrowed language like "redemption" and "sacrifice of atonement" to express the significance of Jesus (Rom 3:24). Figures such as Abraham provided examples of faith and works (Rom 4; Jas 2). In emphasizing Jesus' miracles as well as his rejection, Luke suggests Jesus is a prophet like Moses (Deut 18:15; 34:10; Luke 7:11-17; 13:33-34; Acts 3:22; 7:35-38). Not only does Matthew depict Jesus as a new Moses and a new Israel, 12 times he insists that Jesus fulfilled the Scriptures: "These things happened to fulfill what was spoken by the prophet saying . . ." Reading what became their "Old Testament" through christological lenses allowed the followers of Jesus to show how Israel's story and understandings of Jesus were mutually informing. Those who were not followers of Jesus did not see the connections; they were reading through other lenses.

For John, the connection of Jesus to the Scriptures of Israel is accomplished more by allusion than by direct quote. Thus, if one does not know the earlier texts, one cannot pick up the richness of John's narrative. At the same time, John also draws upon images known in the broader Gentile world. To both Jewish and Gentile ideas, John provides new understandings.

The Fourth Gospel begins not with a genealogy (Matthew), or an eschatological prophet (Mark), or a dedication and conception stories (Luke), but with an 18-verse poetic prologue that opens with the majestic verse "In the beginning was the Word, the Word was with God, the Word was God" (1:1). Gentile and Jewish readers both would have recognized the term translated "word" (Greek: *logos*). For those schooled in Greek philosophy, especially Stoicism, the *logos* was the principal on which the order of the world rested. According to Jesus' contemporary, the Jewish philosopher Philo of Alexandria, the *logos* was the manifestation of the divine presence; Philo also referred to the *logos* as "the first-born of God" (*Dreams* 1.215). In the Aramaic paraphrases of the Scriptures of Israel (known as the *targumim* [singular: *targum*]), the term *memre*, Aramaic for "word," functions as a circumlocution for God.

Of all the evocations of the term, the Johannine *logos* finds its most immediate connection not in philosophy, but in the Wisdom Literature of Israel. The biblical Wisdom traditions span Job 28 and Prov 1–9 as well as the deuterocanonical books of Sir 24, Bar 3–4, and Wis 1–11. This tradition depicts Wisdom as the ordering principle of both creation and human interaction. Wisdom is simultaneously present with God at creation, active as God's agent who invites people into relationship with God, analogous to the Torah, and a manifestation of the Holy Spirit.

For John, Jesus is Wisdom incarnate: the manifestation of God in human flesh. Like Wisdom, Jesus the *logos* resides with God before creation and is active with God in creation (1:1-3). As Wisdom, Jesus dwells among humans and so reveals God's presence and will. He like Wisdom receives a mixed response: acceptance from some who thereby experience relationship with God, and rejection from others.

The Descent and Ascent of Wisdom

In Proverbs and subsequent literature, Wisdom is imaged as female, sometimes known as "Lady Wisdom." Language helps explain the image: both Hebrew (*chokhmah*) and Greek (*sophia*) words for wisdom are feminine. Wisdom is presented as a feminine manifestation of the divine, just as the Holy Spirit is understood in feminine terms or as female in some Jewish and early Christian writings. Indeed, when John describes the *logos* as "dwelling among us" (1:14), the term for "dwell" (Greek: *eskēnōsen*) can evoke the Hebrew term *shekinah*, a reference also to the Jewish mystical view of the feminine presence of the divine dwelling with humanity. The Hebrew term *mishkan*, "tabernacle," is a cognate. ~~We might regard the Johannine depiction of Jesus as embracing~~ this feminine ~~imagery;~~ alternatively, the Johannine Jesus may be understood as coopting or replacing Wisdom.

In personifying divine power and presence, Wisdom does not compromise the idea of one God. She is with God at creation, yet she is herself created. Wisdom states, "The LORD created me at the beginning of his work, the first of his acts of long ago" (Prov 8:22-23, 30). Sirach 24:3 quotes Wisdom: "I came forth from the mouth of the Most High, and covered the earth like a mist," and her description alludes to Gen 1:1-2:

> In the beginning when God created the heavens and the earth, the earth was a formless void and darkness covered the face of the deep, while a wind/breath/spirit [the Hebrew (*ruach*) and Greek (*pneuma*) terms convey all these meanings] from God swept over the face of the waters.

Wisdom is immanent in creation: "Because of her pureness she pervades and penetrates all things" (Wis 7:24). Proverbs 8:35 connects Wisdom with life and divine approval: "Whoever finds me finds life and obtains favor from the LORD."

Early readers of John's Gospel would have understood Jesus the Logos in much the same way, although whereas Wisdom is clearly created by God, John's Gospel offers both an eternal Logos who is God as well as a separate figure who is with God and subordinate to God. Being with God from the beginning in intimate loving relationship (5:20) is the basis for Jesus' revelation (3:32; 8:38-40; 12:50). He has listened to (8:40) and watched the Father (5:20). He is the only one to have seen God (1:18; 6:46; these assertions create some tension with the earlier Scriptures, since Gen 32:30 states that Jacob sees God "face to face" and God speaks "face to face" with Moses according to Exod 33:11; also Num 12:8; Deut 5:4; 34:10). Thus John's readers will have to reassess how they understand not only Jesus, but also the Scriptures that undergird the gospel. According to John, Jesus has one will with God: "The Father and I are one" (10:30; 14:11). To honor Jesus (5:23), to hear Jesus (12:50), to see Jesus (14:9) is to honor, hear, and see God. ~~To deny Jesus is to deny God~~ (5:23). ~~Yet Jesus also declares that "the Son can do nothing on his own"~~ (5:19) ~~and that "the Father is greater than I"~~ (14:28).

The Johannine Logos, like Wisdom, comes from God (3:34; 8:42), descends to earth from heaven (3:32; 6:38; 8:23), and dwells among humans to manifest divine will and presence. However, the Logos also returns to the Father (cf. Phil 2:6-11). Keeping Wisdom's presence, and so the presence of the Logos, amid the community is the Holy Spirit, another figure associated with the biblical Wisdom tradition as well as with Jesus.

Having come from heaven to earth, Jesus departs to God (13:1-3). Whereas in the ~~Synoptics the death of Jesus is humiliating, agonizing, and tragic,~~ for John it is indicative of his victory. As paradoxical as is the idea of a divine being incarnated in human flesh, so is the idea that crucifixion could be a sign of glorification. John develops the idea of Jesus' departure as victorious ascent by depicting him as "lifted up" in three ways: by crucifixion, when he is raised up on the cross; by resurrection, when he is raised from the dead; and by ascension, when he is taken up into heaven. In these depictions, images of Sophia/Wisdom combine with other images from Israel's Scriptures. For example, John 3:14-15 states:

Just as Moses lifted up the serpent in the wilderness, so must the Son of Man be lifted up, that whoever believes in him may have eternal life.

The allusion is to Num 21:8, where God commands Moses, "Make a poisonous serpent, and set it on a pole; and everyone who is bitten shall look at it and live." This apotropaic symbol (that is, an image of evil used to ward off evil, much as gargoyles were thought to protect churches from evil spirits) preserves the lives of the Israelites, just as the crucified Jesus gives life.

Here the gospel's irony is evident: those who crucify Jesus believe they have conquered him, but in his being lifted up, he is victorious.

In one of its eschatological statements, rare compared to the Synoptics, John's Gospel links Jesus' ascension to his subsequent return. Jesus states:

In my Father's house there are many dwelling places. If it were not so, would I have told you that I go to prepare a place for you? And if I go and prepare a place for you, I will come again and will take you to myself, so that where I am, there you may be also. (John 14:2-3)

Similarly, Jesus affirms:

The hour is coming when all who are in their graves will hear his voice and will come out—those who have done good, to the resurrection of life, and those who have done evil, to the resurrection of condemnation. (John 5:28-29)

Thus the assurance of the second coming, with attendant rewards and punishments, is in place. The Johannine Jesus here talks about his return (14:3; 21:3) and a general resurrection (5:28-29; 6:39-40; 11:23-24; 12:48). However, John is much more interested in how Jesus' followers will experience the abundant life Jesus promised them. Rather than concentrate on eschatological rewards, and at the same time dispelling any concern about the delay of the Parousia, John makes two major moves. First, the Fourth Gospel links Jesus' ascension with giving the Holy Spirit; second, Jesus reveals that events expected to take place in the future are already happening in his ministry.

Concerning the Spirit, Jesus tells his followers, "It is to your advantage that I go away, for if I do not go away, the [*Paraclete*] will not come to you; but if I go, I will send it to you" (16:7). This Greek term *paraclete* literally means "called alongside." English translations include "advocate," "comforter," "counselor," and "helper." The *Paraclete* in secular Greek is comparable to a defense attorney who pleads a case before a judge. "Advocate" and "counselor," both with forensic connections, are helpful translations. Jesus defines the *Paraclete's* role:

> The Holy Spirit, whom the Father will send in my name, will teach you everything, and remind you of all that I have said to you. (14:26)

The Spirit represents Jesus in his absence.

Jesus' promise of the *Paraclete* comes to fruition in John 20:22. Jesus "breathed on" (again that connotation of "breath" or "spirit") his disciples and said, "Receive the Holy Spirit." Occurring one week after Jesus' crucifixion, this scene differs from Luke's description of the Spirit falling upon Jesus' followers at Pentecost (Acts 2), 50 days after. In both cases, however, the Spirit provides comfort until Jesus' Parousia while maintaining divine presence amid his followers.

This ongoing divine presence relates to what is called "realized eschatology." For John, the experience of eschatological benefits or punishment is available already, now, in the present, when one decides whether to follow Jesus or not. One does not have to wait until either personal death or the Parousia to "realize" or experience the fullness of blessing or the verdict of condemnation.

John's prologue declares, "In him was life, and the life was the light of all people" (1:4). Jesus states, "I came that they may have life, and have it abundantly" (10:10). The phrase translated "life abundantly" literally denotes "life of the age." So John records:

> For God so loved the world that he gave his only Son, so that everyone who believes in him may not perish but have eternal life. (3:16).

John goes on in this chapter to quote Jesus as saying: "Those who believe in him are not condemned; but those who do not believe are condemned already" (3:18). Similarly, eternal life is already present for those who believe in the Son (3:36), for the one who believes "has passed from death to life" (5:24).

The gospel thus offers comfort for the followers of Jesus: although he has not returned in glory, the *Paraclete* is present to guide them. Although they will experience death, and John is very clear about the reality of death, they are already, through their relationship to Jesus and so to God, "saved." At the same time, their opponents are already damned.

The Rejection of Wisdom, Johannine Dualism, and John's Worldview

In Israel's traditions, the figure of Wisdom is personified as a woman, sometimes known as "Lady Wisdom." She also has a personified opposite, Lady Folly or Foolishness, who attempts to divert people from discerning God's ways. Those whom Lady Folly entices are trapped: "They do not know that the dead are there, that her guests are in the depths of Sheol" (Prov 9:18). John intensifies this distinction by constructing a dualistic worldview between those who follow Wisdom/Jesus to life, and those who follow Folly/Satan to sin and death. While "God so loved the world" (3:16), the "world" rejects this love and God's purposes (1:10). Thus Jesus condemns those who reject him as having their origin in, and their allegiance to, the world rather than the Word: "You are from below, I am from above; you are of this world, I am not of this world" (8:23). The little word "of" could be translated "from" to designate origin and allegiance.

Such dualism leads easily into a predestinarian understanding, in which some people are fated to believe and be saved while others are fated to reject Jesus' claims and be damned. John presents other passages that support this understanding. Jesus states, "No one can come to me unless drawn by the Father who sent me" (6:44) and "I am the way, the truth and the life; no one comes to the Father except through me" (14:6; see also 6:53; 15:6). Yet elsewhere the Fourth Gospel emphasizes human responses to God sending Jesus in "receiving" (1:12) or "accepting" (3:33) or "hearing" (5:24) or "believing" Jesus.

Whether because of a predestined plan or because of personal choice—or for John's Gospel, likely both—in the narrative's dualistic scheme, people are fundamentally allied either with God or with the devil (8:42-47), so much so that John literally demonizes those on the outside. Outsiders to John's claims love "human glory more than the glory that comes from God" (12:43). They love "darkness rather than light because their deeds were evil" (3:19). The culmination of this demonizing rhetoric appears in John 8, where Jesus tells "the Jews," who represent "the world" that does not accept the claims of and by Jesus:

> You are from your father the devil, and you choose to do your father's desires. He was a murderer from the beginning and does not stand in the truth, because there is no truth in him. When he lies, he speaks according to his own nature, for he is a liar and the father of lies. (8:44)

John offers no mandate to love enemies as in Matthew (Matt 5:38-48; 22:37-39; see also Luke 6:35). Instead of promoting a universal mission, as in the Synoptics, John's Jesus restricts the "love commandment" to his followers. In John 15:12 he states, "This is my commandment, that you love *one another* as I have loved you" (emphasis added).

Jesus says about his followers: they "do not belong to the world, just as I do not belong to the world" (17:16).

Conflict Situations

To explain John's dualistic language, scholars frequently propose an underlying conflict to which John reacts. For example, competition with other Jesus-followers may lie behind the verse claiming that salvation is only through Jesus. The disciple Thomas asks Jesus, "Lord, we do not know where you are going. How can we know the way?" (14:5). Jesus responds, "I am the way . . ." Thomas also initially refuses the claim of the resurrection, but when Jesus invites him, "Put your finger here and see my hands. Reach out your hand and put it in my side," Thomas responds, "My Lord and my God!" (20:27-28).

The figure of Thomas may well symbolize rival groups who also claim allegiance to Jesus' teaching. Late first- and early second-century Christian texts associated with Thomas—the *Gospel of Thomas*, the *Acts of Thomas*—focus not on the cross but on the possession of theological knowledge (Greek: *gnōsis*) as the means to salvation. They also regard the body or flesh as a prison preventing the spirit from uniting with the divine. By stressing Jesus' incarnation, death, and physical resurrection, John shows Thomas, and those who would follow him, "the way."

Competition might also explain the presentations of Peter and the Beloved Disciple. Whereas in the Synoptics, Peter is the principal apostle, in John's Gospel, the Beloved Disciple is preeminent. He reclines next to Jesus at the last supper (13:23). He is beloved by Jesus (13:23; 20:2; 21:7, 20). He outraces Peter to the tomb and believes (20:8).

If Thomas, Peter, and other characters in the gospel represent external constituencies—and this is a big "if" because John does not say so explicitly—then we can see John's recognition of other churches and his attempt to control their teaching. Although NT scholars continue to debate whether John had access to the Synoptic Gospels, and whether the *Gospel of Thomas* antedates or postdates the canonical texts, we can be fairly certain that John knew the traditions reflected in these texts. For John, these other followers of Jesus represented by the Synoptic and Thomasine traditions have incorrect or incomplete views that can be corrected, but they are not demonized.

The same cannot be said for the conflict the gospel depicts between Jesus and the *Ioudaioi*. This Greek word, which John uses over 70 times, can be translated as both "Jews" and "Judeans." The connotations of *Ioudaioi* in John's Gospel are, like much else in the gospel, multivalent. Positively, *Ioudaioi* comfort Martha and Mary, the sisters of Lazarus (11:19-37). Some *Ioudaioi* believe in Jesus (11:45). In his conversation with the Samaritan woman at the well, Jesus states that "salvation is from the [*Ioudaioi*]" and therefore not with the Samaritan tradition associated with Mount Gerizim (4:22). Yet most often, the term is used in negative ways. While Jesus is clearly a *Ioudaios* (4:2)—that is, a "Jew" although not a Judean in that he is from Galilee—John depicts Jesus in intense conflict with the *Ioudaioi.*

John depicts the *Ioudaioi* as resisting Jesus' teaching (6:41, 52), not understanding it (8:22, 48), and intimidating his followers (7:13; 9:22). Jesus accuses them of not hearing God's words (5:37-38), not believing (5:38b), not knowing how to interpret the Scriptures (5:39), not loving God (5:42), not observing the law (7:19), not knowing God (7:28; 8:19), having the devil as their father (8:44), and hating the Father and Jesus (15:24). Falsely, according to the gospel, they maintain that descent from Abraham, rather than imitating Abraham's actions, defines the covenant community (8:39-59). They think Jesus is a false prophet who leads the people astray (7:12-13). They reject central claims about Jesus: his origin from God (6:41-42; 9:16), his authority from God (7:29-30), his unity with God (10:31-33), his identity as God's agent (8:25), his revelation of God (8:26-27) and God's purposes (7:16-24). They are, as we have seen, children of the devil (8:44).

Such harsh rhetoric, conventional in antiquity, serves several purposes. It affirms one group's identity by denigrating another's. It discourages group members from affiliating with the outside group. It explains why the vast majority of Jesus' own people chose not to follow him—according to John, the *Ioudaioi* were predestined to damnation.

To explain John's invective, multiple theories have been proffered. Some interpreters proposed that the negative uses of *Ioudaioi* refer not to all "Jews," but only to the Jerusalem-based leaders, including the "priests and Levites from Jerusalem" (1:19). These leaders persecute Jesus because they rejected his healing on the Sabbath and claims for himself (5:16-18; 6:41). They seek to kill him (7:1; also 10:31-33). In this scenario, John's invective is restricted. Others insist that the term does not refer to the Jewish people but to any who would oppose Jesus; here the *Ioudaioi* are synonymous with the "world" that God "so loved" but that rejected God's message. Here the invective is universal and so not specifically or entirely about Jews. Still others prefer the translation "Judean" and thereby restrict the opponents to a particular group of Jewish people associated with Judea as opposed to Galilee and Samaria. One suggestion is to translate *Ioudaioi* as "Judean" rather than Jew. This approach works in a number of cases. In a number of others, such as 6:41, where Jesus seems to be talking to Galileans, this translation is not appropriate. The move by some biblical scholars always to translate *Ioudaioi as* "Judean" also creates a NT that has no "Jews"—and thus the translation severs the common root of Judaism and Christianity. Leaving *Ioudaioi* untranslated is another option. None of these suggestions, though, removes the sting of John's demonization.

Some scholars propose that the Fourth Evangelist represents a community expelled from and persecuted by a synagogue. In response, John presented a two-stage drama. Onto the story of Jesus, John mapped the experiences of Jesus' followers.

This approach rests on three major pillars, each shaky. First, it appeals to John's three uses of the rare term *aposynagōgos*, meaning "out of the synagogue" (9:22; 12:42; 16:2) to indicate that the Jesus-believers had been expelled from the Jewish community. In this scenario, the man born blind depicted in John 9 as "driven out" (9:34) represents the group put "out of the synagogue." Second, it claims that most synagogue members regarded christological assertions about Jesus as lacking scriptural support, challenging the authority of Moses, and blasphemous (5:18; 10:33; 19:7). Third, it suggests that the synagogue used a post-70 benediction (known as the *birkat ha-minim*) to expel Jesus-believers.

While this proposed scenario is fascinating, each pillar turns out to be constructed on sand. First, the gospel's polemical tone cautions against interpreting the references to being expelled from the synagogue as providing objective data. We have no evidence that first-century synagogues expelled people who confessed Jesus. To the contrary, Paul indicates that he was disciplined *within* the synagogue (see 2 Cor 11:24). Nor did synagogues then, or now, have any centralized system for creating such policy. Synagogues are community-based, not centrally controlled. Moreover, no definitive break existed between Jesus-believers and synagogues at the end of the first century. From the second-century writer Ignatius to John Chrysostom in the fourth century, we have evidence of Christians preaching sermons designed to *discourage* the followers of Jesus from attending synagogues where they were welcomed. John's references to expulsion may reflect conflict between two opposing groups, or they may attempt to create division and conflict.

Second, in early Judaism, messianic proclamations are not heretical. Josephus identifies several sign-prophets who presented themselves, or were understood by others, as salvific figures. The book of Acts mentions two of them: Theudas (5:36) and the Egyptian (21:38). The great Rabbi Akiva, martyred by the Romans around 135 C.E., spoke of Bar Kokhba, a Jewish general who led the Second Revolt against Rome (132–135), as the Messiah. Akiva was wrong, but he was not expelled from the community. Indeed, the figure of Wisdom, which Jesus evokes, shows that exalted claims for Jesus as the agent of God in creation and God's revealer among people fit into a first-century Jewish theological context.

Third, the idea that Jews instituted, circa 90, a prayer designed to weed out Jesus' followers from the community is not well supported by the evidence. We do find, in rabbinic texts, reference to a "benediction against heretics," the *birkat ha-minim*, to which proponents of this theory usually appeal. However, *min* (plural: *minim*) is a generic term for "sectarian." Some medieval versions of the prayer do include the term "Nazoreans," which is likely a reference to the followers of Jesus (the prayer is said in no synagogues today, and the extent to which it was said anywhere in antiquity remains unclear). However, the manuscript evidence does not support the conception that the benediction would have been directed at the followers of Jesus as early as the first century. The earliest evidence for the prayer in rabbinic literature dates it around 90 C.E., but in its original context, it has no formal, let alone generally distributed use. Nor does the story in John 9 reflect a liturgical process for excommunication. The man is "driven out" in 9:34, but from where or what is not clear. He is driven out *before* his confession about Jesus in 9:38, without any formal proceedings, cursing, or prayer.

Positing an expulsion from the synagogue as the situation from which the gospel emerges is not convincing. It invents an evil Judaism seen to be responsible for the condemnations John hurls at its members. Perhaps the ready coexistence of Jesus-believers and synagogue members concerns the writer or writers of the gospel, as such coexistence later concerned Ignatius and Chrysostom. Perhaps there were escalating conflicts in a synagogue over various claims Jesus' followers did make. Had they suggested that Jesus replaced Torah, or that all who did not follow Jesus were children of the devil, they may well have been made unwelcome. Moreover, they may have been perceived to be political liabilities in proclaiming a crucified Jew as Lord and Savior. Perhaps they poached from the synagogue the Gentile affiliates (God-fearers) who served as a buffer to protect the Jewish minority. As is often the case with attempting to locate the Gospels historically, we have more questions than answers.

Reading and Preaching John

The gospel's polemical language has often shaped preaching and teaching that leads to hatred of Jews. There is a tragic history of Jewish-Christian relations over the past 2,000 years. Christians forced Jews into ghettos—the term is an Italian word, used for the area in Venice where Jews were permitted to live and where they were locked in every night. Christians expelled Jews from various countries (England, Spain, Portugal, German states, and so on) and killed them in crusades and in pogroms. It is important not to forget this history, and it is important that prejudice not be communicated in proclaiming John's Gospel.

Readers will need to determine if substituting language of "leaders" or "Judeans" for "Jews" fits their understanding of the gospel, and whether notes in church bulletins, congregational education, or direct comment would be effective.

Jesus' Public Ministry

John's Gospel presents Jesus' public ministry from 1:19 to the end of chapter 12, chapters marked by vivid characterization combined with allusions to scenes from Israel's Scriptures. For example, in 3:1, Jesus encounters "a Pharisee named Nicodemus, a leader of the Jews" (3:1). Readers aware of John's generally negative use of "the Jews" may be predisposed to regard Nicodemus negatively; readers sensitive to the mystery of how some people come to believe particular religious views and others struggle with the same beliefs may regard Nicodemus as a sympathetic figure. Those who know Greek will find his name, which is not uncommon in antiquity, ironic: *Nico* means "to conquer" (as in the term Nike); *demos* means "people" (as in "democracy"). But Nicodemus is hardly the conquering hero, and when he finally speaks out against the "chief priests and the Pharisees" (7:45) who want to condemn Jesus, he is ignored. (7:51-52).

To inquire about Jesus' teachings, Nicodemus comes to Jesus at night (3:1-2). By setting the scene "at night," John suggests Nicodemus is "in the dark." He does not walk in the light (3:19-21), and he has not grasped that Jesus/Wisdom is the "light of the world" (8:12; 9:5). Whether he ever understands Jesus remains unclear. When he, together with Joseph of Arimathea, entombs Jesus with "a hundred pounds" of myrrh and aloes (19:39), he does not seem to expect resurrection.

Jesus tells Nicodemus, "No one can see the kingdom of God without being born from above" (3:3). The Greek word *anōthen*, here translated "from above," can mean variously "anew," "from above," or "again." Deriving from this word is the phrase "born again" used by some Christians to express their new life in a personal experience of Jesus as Lord. Ironically, "born again" is not quite the right expression for those who speak of this religious experience. Nicodemus, who interprets the Greek *incorrectly*, asks:

> "How can anyone be born after having grown old? Can one enter a second time into the mother's womb and be born?" (3:4)

John's point is not about being born *again*; it is about being born both *anew* and *from above* (3:7). Accepting Jesus, like accepting Wisdom, reveals one's origin as being "from above," from God, like Jesus. That the pun works only in Greek and not in Hebrew or Aramaic suggests that the conversation was developed by the gospel writer or an earlier Greek-speaking follower of Jesus; whether Jesus knew Greek, or enough Greek to make sophisticated puns, remains an open question.

John's Jesus goes on to tell Nicodemus that "no one can enter the kingdom of God without being born of water and Spirit" (3:5). The same images reappear when the spear pierces Jesus' side while he hangs on the cross (19:34). For John, Jesus' death is the necessary act of salvation. Nicodemus does not understand Jesus' cryptic language, but the reader of John's Gospel does.

In contrast to Nicodemus stands the Samaritan woman at the well, another figure unique to John's Gospel. Because she meets Jesus not at night but at noon (4:6), readers familiar with John's use of light and dark realize that she will be a faithful follower who walks in the light (3:19-21). Jesus draws the Samaritan woman into belief in him through encouraging her questions (4:7-26). Like Wisdom he responds to those who seek him (Prov 8:17) and "makes them friends of God" (Wis 7:27). Unlike Nicodemus, who is rendered speechless and confused, the woman continues to engage Jesus.

Jesus opens the conversation by saying, "Give me a drink" (4:7), and the image of drinking and thirst will continue to mark the scene. As the conversation progresses, he tells her, "Those who drink of the water that I will give them will never be thirsty" (4:14). On the cross, "when Jesus knew that all was now finished," he says, only in John's Gospel, "I am thirsty" (19:28). Symbolically, he yearns to provide living water to those who would follow him. His words and actions echo Wisdom's, who says, "Those who eat of me will hunger for more, and those who drink of me will thirst for more" (Sir 24:21).

Although numerous interpreters have understood the woman as a five-time "loser" because of her multiple marriages (4:16-19), that is not how John portrays her. She is, rather, a match for Jesus. Like the man born blind in John 9, she is led by incarnate Wisdom to belief. She then becomes a successful evangelist in bringing the people of her village into relationship with Jesus (4:28-30, 39-42). That they are willing to listen to her when she tells them, "He cannot be the Messiah, can he?" (4:29) indicates that they respect her rather than dismiss her. Claims that the woman went to the well at noon because the townspeople shunned her hold no basis. Indeed, not only does the noon meeting symbolize the woman's gaining of Wisdom and walking in the light, but also the timing evokes the meeting of Jacob and Rachel at the well (Gen 29:7). That the woman asks Jesus, "Are you greater than our ancestor Jacob, who gave us the well, and with his sons and his flocks drank from it?" (4:12) reinforces the connection between Jesus and Israel's patriarch.

The meeting of Jesus and the woman at a well does more than recapitulate the meeting of Jacob and Rachel. That earlier scene is part of a literary convention from Israel's Scriptures comparable to the annunciation scenes in Luke's Gospel. Four times, Israel's Scriptures depict a man and woman meeting at a well. Three times marriages result: Rebecca and Isaac (Gen 24); Jacob and Rachel (Gen 29); Moses and Zipporah (Exod 2). The fourth time (1 Sam 9), Saul meets a group of women at a well, but he fails to marry any of them. Attentive readers realize that just as he does not fulfill the convention, so he will not fulfill the promise of his kingship. In John 4, Jesus and the woman at a well discuss marriage. A union of sorts occurs in that the woman brings the Samaritan community into relationship with Jesus. Thus John recalls Israel's Scriptures and in the process both reinterprets them and adds richness and nuance to the story of Jesus.

John and the Synoptic Gospels

These scenes and others within the first half of John raise questions about the relationship of John's Gospel to the Synoptic Gospels.

Plot and Characters

John shares some scenes with the Synoptic Gospels: Jesus' healing of the official's son/ servant, feeding the 5,000, anointing by a woman, entry to Jerusalem, the temple incident, trial before Pilate, crucifixion, and resurrection. Yet there are significant differences. John begins with John the Baptist, but John does not baptize Jesus nor does Satan tempt Jesus. The Temple incident appears immediately after the first sign of turning water into wine at Cana (2:13-22) and not at the beginning of Jesus' last week as in Mark 11:1-11; in the Synoptics, Jesus quotes Isaiah and Jeremiah to explain his actions; in John, he alludes to Zech 14:21. Whereas in the Synoptics, the Temple incident is the immediate cause of the priests' enmity and so Jesus' arrest, the raising of Lazarus has this role in the Fourth Gospel. Caiaphas the high priest, being told that the people's belief in Jesus will lead to Roman reprisals, suggests, with typical Johannine irony, that "it is better for you to have one man die for the people than to have the whole nation destroyed" (11:50). In the Synoptics, Jesus' public activity takes place in Galilee and he travels at the end to Jerusalem (Mark 11:1; Matt 19:1-2; Luke 9:51). In John, Jesus travels back and forth from Galilee to Jerusalem throughout the gospel (John 2, 5, 7–11, and 12–19). Johannine references to the Passover (2:13, 23; 6:4; 11:55; 12:1; 13:1; 18:28; 19:14) suggest his activity lasted at least three years, not the one year as the Synoptics suggest. Much of John is structured around Jewish holidays (5:1; ch. 7, Tabernacles [Sukkot] or Booths; 10:22, Dedication or Hanukkah; 5:1-47; 7:14-24; 9:1-41, Sabbath). And rather than present Jesus as teaching in parables, the Johannine Jesus offers lengthy monologues or dialogue. These scenes include the conversations with Nicodemus (ch. 3), the Samaritan woman (ch. 4), the man born blind (ch. 9) and Lazarus (ch. 11). In John 5:1-18, another chapter marked by a lengthy conversation, Jesus encounters a paralyzed man at the pool of Beth-zatha in Jerusalem. To the man, who has been ill for 38 years, Jesus commands, "Stand up, take your mat and walk" (5:8). The same exhortation appears in the Synoptics, but there it concerns the paralyzed man whose friends dig through a roof in a home in Capernaum (Mark 2:9).

Along with healing the paralyzed man, John's Jesus performs no exorcisms and only six other mighty works, which John calls "signs": turning water into wine (2:1-12), healing the son (4:46-54), feeding the crowd (6:1-14), walking on water (6:16-21), healing the blind man (9:1-17), and raising Lazarus (ch. 11). In the Synoptics, Jesus' "mighty works" usually require faith. In John, these "signs" reveal Jesus' identity and lead people to faith.

Mary and Martha provide another example of John's distinct style. Whereas in both the Gospels of John and Luke, Martha is active, even forceful, and Mary comparably quiet and situated at Jesus' feet, there the connections end. According to John 11, the women are the sisters of Lazarus, whom Jesus raises from the dead. In Luke 10:38-42, Jesus responds to Martha's demand that he ask Mary to help with her "service" by insisting that Mary, hearing his teaching, has chosen the better part. In John, Martha is the one to voice the correct christological confession, "I believe that you are the Messiah, the Son of God, the one coming into the world" (11:27). Then Mary, rather than an anonymous woman, anoints Jesus' feet in 12:1-8 before his Passion. Lazarus does not appear in Luke's scene, but Luke does record the parable of the Rich Man and Lazarus, which speaks of someone rising "from the dead" (Luke 16:31). Whether John turned a parable into a sign, or Luke turned a sign into a parable, or an early redactor, knowing John's story, named the figure in Luke's parable "Lazarus" (the only figure in a parable to have a name) remains undetermined.

Peter is an important disciple in John's Gospel, but others, such as Andrew (1:40-44; 6:8; 12:22), Philip, and Nathanael (1:43-49; 6:5-7; 12:21-22; 14:8-9; 21:2), get comparably more attention. Jesus' mother appears at Cana and at the cross (2:1-12; 19:25-27), but she is never named. John also enhances the portrait of Mary Magdalene. Mary finds Jesus' tomb empty, as she does in the Synoptics, but then John extends the story. Convinced that the body has been stolen and seeing a figure she supposes to be the gardener, Mary inquires about the body's location. When the figure calls her by name, she recognizes her teacher (20:11-18). Here John alludes not to the Scriptures of Israel, but to another literary convention associated with the "Hellenistic romance." These novels, whose legacy is best known today in the plots of many of Shakespeare's comedies, involved separated lovers, mistaken identity, the belief of one lover that the other is dead, recognition (often at a tomb), and marriage. Like the use of the "woman at a well" scene in chapter 4, John takes a familiar plot line and adapts it: the conventions are present, but the end of the story is, in John, decidedly unconventional.

Following the narratives in chapters 1–12, John presents a five-chapter section called the "Farewell Discourse" (chs. 13–17). This section, in which Jesus instructs his disciples about how to live in his absence, lacks any Synoptic parallel. At a last supper, Jesus assumes the role of a slave and washes the disciples' feet. There is no institution of the Eucharist at this meal, which is not, as it is in the Synoptics, set on the first night of Passover. Instead, John 6 presents the "Bread of Life Discourse" where Jesus speaks of eating his body and drinking his blood.

Jesus and God

Throughout, John's portrait of Jesus differs substantially from that of the Synoptics. In the first three gospels, Jesus preaches the "kingdom of heaven/God." John uses the term "kingdom" only three times (3:3, 5; 19:36). Instead, in John, Jesus proclaims himself. Eight times he uses the formula of divine revelation "I am" (Exod 3:14; Isa 43:25) as a self-reference (John 4:26; 6:20; 8:24, 48). Twelve times he uses "I am" with an image from Israel's Scripture to express his revelatory and salvific role. He is the bread of life (6:35, 51); the light (8:12; 9:5); the gate (10:7, 9); the good shepherd (10:11, 14); the resurrection and life (11:25-26); the way, truth, and life (14:6); and the true vine (15:1,

5). All the complements of these revealing "I am" statements—with one exception—are also associated with wisdom: bread (Sir 24:21), vine (Sir 24:17, 19), way (Prov 3:17; 8:32; Sir 6:26), light (Wis 7:26; 18:34), truth (Prov 8:7; Wis 6:22), life (Prov 3:18; 8:38), gate/door (Prov 8:34-35). The one exception concerns "good shepherd," which is an image for the divine in both Israel's Scriptures (Ps 23:1) and pagan contexts.

The gospel has two dominant images for God. One identifies God as the one who sends Jesus. The other identifies God as Father some 120 times. As Father, God rules the world (1:1-5), gives life (5:21), judges (1:17; 8:16), and creates and shapes a community of children (1:12; 6:44-45). This presentation of God as Father interfaces competitively with the Roman emperor, who was known as *Pater Patriae*, "Father of the Fatherland," and is ascribed similar roles.

Jesus' Death

Unlike the Synoptics, John depicts no trial before a full Sanhedrin. Instead, there is a nighttime hearing before Annas, the father-in-law of the high priest Caiaphas, after which Jesus is taken to Pilate. According to John, Jesus dies on the day before Passover (18:28), not on the first day of the festival, as in the Synoptics (Matt 26:17; 27:1). John's Jesus, the "Lamb of God" (John 1:29, 36), dies on the cross at the same time the Passover lambs are being sacrificed in the Temple. For John, Jesus *is* the Passover offering. Despite the heavy symbolism, John's depiction of Jesus' last week makes more historical sense than does the Synoptic version. Although the Synoptics appear to confirm the events and chronology, in the sense of three witnesses against one, this appearance is incorrect. Rather, given their interrelationship, the Synoptics present three takes on the same story. For example, a hearing before the full Sanhedrin on the first night of Passover is not only illegal according to Jewish law, but it is also illogical.

All four canonical accounts of Jesus' crucifixion offer different emphases. For Mark, Jesus cries out in the words of Ps 22, "My God, my God, why have you forsaken me?" He dies, deserted by his followers. Matthew retains these images, but emphasizes that Jesus' death gives new life to others: "The tombs also were opened, and many bodies of the saints who had fallen asleep were raised" (27:52). Some versions of Luke depict Jesus praying, "Father, forgive them; for they do not know what they are doing," and all depict him promising a crucified criminal, "Today you will be with me in Paradise." In all three Synoptics, Jesus cedes authority to those who oppose him and dies a suffering victim.

Conversely, in John's Gospel Jesus appears to orchestrate his Passion. Jesus lays down his life (10:17-18; 15:13). He lets himself be arrested even though all the soldiers collapse (18:6).

John's version of Jesus' trial includes several exchanges between Pilate and the *Ioudaioi*. In a power game, Pilate taunts his allies, the Jerusalem leaders, in threatening not to crucify Jesus. The *Ioudaioi* respond:

"If you release this man, you are no friend of the emperor. Everyone who claims to be a king sets himself against the emperor." (19:12)

Jesus' identity as a king who represents God's reign but is not sanctioned by Rome puts him at odds with the emperor. Pilate responds, "Shall I crucify your King?" The chief priests answered, "We have no king but the emperor" (19:15). Thus they ironically renounce their covenant relationship with God as King and declare their loyalty to the emperor. When Pilate later asks Jesus, "I am not a Jew [*Ioudaios*], am I?" (18:35), the attentive reader, recognizing how the term has been developed to indicate anyone opposed to Jesus, might answer, "Yes, Pilate, you have proved yourself to be one."

John also includes a scene in which the dying Jesus speaks from the cross to his mother and the Beloved Disciple. He says to his mother, "Woman, here is your son" and to the disciple, "Here is your mother" (19:26-27). Interpretations are numerous: Jesus provides for his mother and so models the care the church should provide. The Beloved Disciple and not one of Jesus' own brothers, such as James, represents the continuity of the tradition. Fictive kinship groups in which nonbiologically or nonmaritally related individuals treat each other as family will comprise the community founded in Jesus' name. Whereas the scene can be interpreted as emphasizing the disciple's care for Jesus' mother, the care works both ways: she is also support, as mother, to him.

Distinctions from the Synoptic account continue. John observes that "the Jews" are concerned that bodies not be left on the cross on the Sabbath—again, Johannine irony: they do not hesitate to crucify God's agent, but they are concerned with transgressing the Sabbath—and so "they asked Pilate to have the legs of the crucified men broken" (19:31). The point was not to add to the torture but to speed their dying. Crucifixion kills by asphyxiation. Victims would push up by the legs to get air into the lungs, and breaking the legs prevented their gaining breath and so hastened death.

When the soldiers come to Jesus, they find he has already died. One of the men pierces Jesus' side with a spear, "and at once blood and water came out" (19:34). John explicitly notes the scene is a fulfillment of prophecy: "These things occurred so that the scripture might be fulfilled, 'None of his bones shall be broken'; and . . . 'They will look on the one whom they have pierced'" (19:36-37). The first verse alludes to Ps 34:20; the second to Zech 12:10.

The image has been understood through Christian history and art in various ways. Some have seen the blood and water as suggesting the image of parturition, as if Jesus is giving birth to the church. Some have seen it as evoking the sacraments of baptism and Eucharist. Some have seen it in terms of lactation. Medieval art frequently compares Jesus' pointing to his wounded side with Mary pointing to her breast. This gender-bending can fit with the image of Jesus, here as feminine Wisdom.

John's resurrection chapters also contain material not paralleled in the Synoptics. This material includes not only the conversation between Jesus and Mary Magdalene (20:11-18), but also the encounter between Jesus and "doubting" Thomas (20:24-29), Jesus' breakfast with seven disciples by the sea of Tiberias (21:1-14), and conversations with both Peter and the Beloved Disciple (21:15-23).

Whether John wrote with knowledge of the Synoptics (a view gaining increasing popularity among New Testament scholars) or not remains debated. Moreover, if John does know the Synoptic texts, then what John expected readers to do with these other gospels creates another problem: Did John write to supplement, correct, or replace? Did John consider them "Sacred Scripture" or templates on which to build? These same questions can be posed to Luke, who speaks of other attempts to recount the story of Jesus, and to Matthew, who likely used the Gospel of Mark as a source.

cts

O ur largely narrative approach to Acts will focus on its plot, major characters, and themes. In addition, using text criticism, we look at a version of Acts known as the "Codex Bezae," or the "D" manuscript.

Acts: What and How Are We Reading?

The opening verse—"In the first book, Theophilus, I wrote about all that Jesus did and taught from the beginning"—establishes Acts as a companion volume to Luke's Gospel. Although scholars frequently refer to "Luke-Acts" and suggest that the two volumes comprise one coherent narrative, the precise relationship between the two books remains debated: Is Acts a continuation of the gospel, or does it also serve to clarify and correct? As we proceed through Acts, and as the focus of the church's mission expands from Jerusalem to Asia and Europe, we attend to four changes in subject: (1) from Jesus the proclaimer of the kingdom of God to the proclamation of Jesus as resurrected Lord; (2) the establishment of and challenges to apostolic authority; (3) the Gentile mission and presentation of Jews and Judaism; and (4) Roman imperial justice.

These questions focus more on literary presentation than historical detail. Like Luke's Gospel, Acts contains historical references. For example, L. Junius Gallio Annaeanus, mentioned in 18:12, was proconsul in Achaia circa 51–52. The procurators Felix and Festus (ch. 24) are historical figures, as are the Jewish kings Herod Agrippa I (ch. 12) and Agrippa II and his sister Berenice (chs. 25–26), as well as their sister Drusilla, Felix's wife. References to Roman law (ch. 24) and sailing routes (see 27:9-44) create the impression of verisimilitude.

The Death of Agrippa

According to Acts 12:1-5, Herod Agrippa, the grandson of Herod the Great and brother-in-law of Herod Antipas, killed the apostle James, brother of John, and

---

imprisoned Peter. Shortly after, Acts recounts how the king in royal robes delivered a speech. Despite Luke's interest in writing speeches, he does not grant Agrippa one. Instead, Luke emphasizes the impression Herod made on the people, who exclaimed: "The voice of a god, and not of a mortal!" (12:22). This is not good, and Luke's readers would have known it. "And immediately, because he had not given the glory to God, an angel of the Lord struck him down, and he was eaten by worms and died" (12:23; contrast Peter's response, 10:20). The Jewish historian Josephus (*Antiquities*, 19.343-52) mentions that in 44 C.E., Agrippa was acclaimed as a god at a public spectacle in Caesarea and almost immediately thereafter died. This connection, with several others, suggests that Luke knew Josephus's writing. For Luke, only Jesus, and so his followers, are to be recognized as speaking for the divine.

The term "history," though, claims for Acts an unsustainable comprehensiveness. Historical information is enhanced by legendary details and presented in service to theological claims. Acts includes features of a wide range of genres including sermons, apologetic speeches, and conventions from Hellenistic novels. Although called "Acts of the Apostles," the volume limits its focus primarily to Peter and Paul, and to Europe, not Africa or South and East Asia. Later Apocryphal Acts recount other stories, such as Thomas's evangelization of India and Paul's encounters with the female ascetic Thecla.

While comparing gospels can be profitable in identifying particular emphases and for attempting to get behind the narrative accounts to a picture of the life of Jesus not influenced by understandings of his death, comparing Acts with other texts is possible only in parts. The early accounts of the Jerusalem church—its communal lifestyle, the descent of the Holy Spirit at Pentecost, Stephen's stoning—are unique to Acts. The speeches that recur throughout share the same syntax and vocabulary and are likely Lucan compositions. In ancient historiography, writers commonly composed speeches appropriate to an occasion.

When the narrative turns to Paul, however, comparative work is possible. Four passages—16:10-17; 20:5-15; 21:8-18; 27:1–28:16—suddenly use "we" language and thereby give the impression that the author is an eyewitness to the events, or at least is using eyewitness testimony. Luke may have had access to an itinerary of Paul's travels that underlies Acts 13–21. Another theory explains the "we" language in terms of narrative technique, especially since the material does not differ in style from the rest of Luke's narrative. The first-person plural creates the impression that the narrator offers a reliable account; in terms of narrative effect, it makes readers present at the action.

Comparison of Acts' presentation of Paul with the apostle's own letters proves frustrating. Attempts to reconcile Acts 15 (the Jerusalem Council) and Paul's autobiographical comments in Gal 2 about his relationship with the Jerusalem church remain at best spec-ulative. According to Acts, James, the leader of the Jerusalem church, issues a letter "to the believers of Gentile origin in Antioch and Syria and Cilicia" (15:23), declaring that the Gentile followers of Jesus must observe four requirements: "abstain from what has been sacrificed to idols and from blood and from what is strangled and from fornication" (15:29). These four requirements are most likely intended to keep Gentile believers out of pagan temples. They also have a possible connection to laws concerning the resident alien as recorded in Lev 17–18 and reflect the Noahide laws, guides given to Noah and all humanity according to several postbiblical Jewish texts. They do not, however, presup-pose that Gentiles would adhere to Jewish dietary regulations: a pig that is slaughtered in a kosher manner and drained of blood is still a pig.

Conversely, Paul declares that the Jerusalem leaders "contributed nothing" (Gal 2:6) to his mission. He makes no mention of this letter in his own letters, even in 1 Cor 8–10, where he discusses eating food offered to idols. He insists that his meeting with the Jerusalem leaders about his Gentile mission was a private audience, not the full church gathering of Acts 15. And he says the Jerusalem authorities required of the Gentile churches "only one thing, that we remember the poor," which he was "eager to do" (Gal 2:10). If James sent a letter to the churches, Paul either doesn't know about it or ignores it.

Nor do Paul's speeches in Acts reflect the theological emphases found in his letters. Paul's letters teach that God accomplishes justification "for us" through Jesus' death (Rom 3:24-26; 5:6-11; 2 Cor 5:18-20). But Jesus' death receives scant attention in Paul's speeches in Acts. The two references lack the "for us" dimension (13:27-29; 20:28). Likewise, Paul anticipates the triumph of God's purposes in the return of Jesus (1 Thess 4:13–5:11; 1 Cor 15:20-27; Rom 5:8-11; 8:18-25). The Paul of Acts mentions the future establishment of God's reign once (Acts 14:22) and Jesus' future role as judge once (17:31). One could argue that the emphases arise from different audiences—Acts presents missionary speeches; the letters are pastoral in addressing church members. Nevertheless, the differences seem to outweigh an appeal to diverse audiences.

These and other distinctions between the Paul depicted in Acts and the Paul derived from the seven letters most scholars think he wrote (Romans, 1 and 2 Corinthians, Galatians, Philippians, 1 Thessalonians, Philemon) suggest that Acts, written perhaps 50 years or more after Paul's death, constructs a picture of the apostle appropriate for the early second-century church. This Paul works in harmony with the Jerusalem leaders, and so Acts suggests a church marked by mutuality and harmony. This Paul is educated by Gamaliel, a famous Jewish teacher mentioned in rabbinic works and by Josephus, and so is appropriately trained in the interpretation of Torah. This Paul speaks positively of Israel's Torah, worships in the Jerusalem Temple, and begins his mission with visits to synagogues. Acts thereby establishes continuity among Israel, Jesus, and the Pauline church. Countering Marcionite claims, it proclaims the followers of Jesus—not their Jewish opponents—as the true heirs of Israel's Scripture and covenant.

From Proclaimer to Proclaimed

Luke's Gospel ends with Jesus commanding his apostles to remain in Jerusalem until they receive heavenly power. Blessing them, "he withdrew . . . and was carried up into heaven" (24:51). This narrated *ascension,* unique to Luke and Acts although suggested by the Johannine concern for the departure of Jesus and the descent of the *Paraclete,* marks Jesus' transition from proclaimer of the kingdom of God to the resurrected one whose lordship is proclaimed. Luke marks this change in status by announcing that the apostles "worshiped him" while they "were continually in the temple, blessing God" (24:51-53).

This shift of focus from kingdom to Christology can be seen in Acts' diminished use of "kingdom" language. While Acts 1:3 presents Jesus "speaking about the kingdom" to the apostles, thereafter the focus on Jesus becomes more prominent. Peter evangelizes fellow Jews: "Repent, and be baptized every one of you in the name of Jesus Christ so that your sins may be forgiven" (2:38). In Samaria, Philip proclaimed "the good news about the kingdom of God and the name of Jesus Christ" (8:12). Paul, under house arrest in Rome, testified "to the kingdom of God . . . *trying to convince them about Jesus* both from the law of Moses and from the prophets" (28:23, emphasis added). Acts ends with Paul "proclaiming the kingdom of God and *teaching about the Lord Jesus Christ* with all boldness" (28:31, emphasis added).

In the opening verse, Luke speaks of having addressed in the first volume "all that Jesus began to do and teach" (Acts 1:1). What Jesus began, the apostles continue. Just as the Holy Spirit is present at Jesus' conception and the outset of the ministry (Luke 1:35; 4:18), so the Spirit launches the church at Pentecost (Acts 2). Just as Jesus preaches in Jewish settings and is rejected, so are Peter and Paul. Just as he taught, healed, exorcised, and confronted political authorities, so do they. Continuity of message complements continuity of actions and character.

Jesus' Continuing Presence

All four gospels provide assurance of Jesus' continuing presence despite his physical absence. Matthew presents Jesus as Emmanuel, "God with us" (1:23) among gathered disciples (18:20), by his words (24:35), and in mission (28:19-20). Mark expects Jesus' return very soon, so the absence is only temporary. Both Luke-Acts and John present the Spirit as the continuing presence of Jesus (Acts 2; John 14–16).

Related to Jesus' followers continuing his mission is the question of the Parousia. In Acts 1:6, the apostles ask Jesus, "Lord, is this the time when you will restore the kingdom to Israel?" The use of "kingdom" reminds readers that Israel, land and people, remains under Roman domination. Jesus deflects the question: "It is not for you to know the times or periods that the Father has set by his own authority" (1:7). The Parousia will happen, but in God's timing. Peter assures the Jews in Jerusalem that their appointed messiah "must remain in heaven until the time of universal restoration that God announced long ago through his holy prophets" (3:20-21). Jesus will return, says Peter, as "the one ordained by God as judge of the living and the dead" (Acts 10:42). And Paul tells the Athenians that God

> has fixed a day on which he will have the world judged in righteousness by a man whom he has appointed, and of this he has given assurance to all by raising him from the dead. (17:31)

The proclamation of Jesus' resurrection stands as surety that a general resurrection and final judgment will occur.

The church's focus in the meantime is on proclaiming not God's "kingdom" but God's messenger, Jesus the Christ. Jesus' next comment to the apostles, "But you will receive power when the Holy Spirit has come upon you; and you will be my witnesses in Jerusalem, in all Judea and Samaria, and to the ends of the earth" (1:8), establishes Acts' plot.

To reinforce Jesus' lordship, Acts develops another theme from Luke's Gospel: the appeal to Israel's Scriptures. Peter compares Jesus to the prophet promised by Moses (3:22; Deut 18:15) and announces him as the one to whom the prophets pointed (3:24). Stephen asserts the same, "It is Moses who said to the Israelites, 'God will raise up a prophet for you from your own people as he raised me up'" (7:37). So does Philip, a Hellenist dispersed from Jerusalem after Stephen's martyrdom and one of the seven appointed to serve at table. He first brings the message of Jesus to the Samaritans (ch. 8) and so unites to the church the Samaritans, descendants of the population of the northern kingdom of Israel. Then on the road from Jerusalem to Gaza, Philip encounters "an Ethiopian eunuch, a court official of Candace, queen of the Ethiopians, in charge of her entire treasury" (8:27).

The official, who may be understood to be a God-fearer, a Gentile attracted to Jewish practices, ethics, and theology, is returning home from worship in Jerusalem. He is reading a scroll of the prophet Isaiah, and he asks Philip for help in scriptural interpretation (8:27-28): "How can I [understand], unless someone guides me?" The passage under discussion is Isa 53:7, "Like a sheep he was led to slaughter . . ." It is not insignificant that several chapters later Isa 56:4-5 declares that Israel's God promises:

> The eunuchs who keep my sabbaths, who choose the things that please me, and hold fast my covenant, I will give, in my house and within my walls, a monument [literally,

"hand"] and a name better than sons and daughters; I will give them an everlasting name that shall not be cut off.

Philip, "starting with this Scripture [Isa 53:7], proclaimed to him the good news about Jesus" (8:35). The eunuch is baptized and travels out of the narrative, presumably to Ethiopia, which Luke's initial readers may well have thought of as "the ends of the earth."

As is typical with NT claims that Israel's Scriptures predict Jesus' ministry, the argument that Jesus is the sheep led to slaughter described by Isaiah is more assertion than demonstration. The issue here is not the "obviousness" of a "prediction." Rather, it is recognition in the light of preexisting convictions. Luke describes the same process in the account of the two disciples on the road to Emmaus: "Then he opened their minds to understand the scriptures" (Luke 24:45). Had not the intervention of the risen Jesus given them a certain perspective, they would not have "seen" the passages as predictions of Jesus.

Apostolic Authority and Cautionary Tales

Luke's Gospel (6:13) presents Jesus choosing twelve disciples as *apostles* (Greek: "ones sent out") to be witnesses to his actions and special bearers of his teaching. Acts names them: "Peter, and John, and James, and Andrew, Philip and Thomas, Bartholomew and Matthew, James son of Alphaeus, and Simon the Zealot, and Judas son of James" (1:13). Their "witnessing" (Greek: *martyrion*, origin of the term "martyr") to Jesus' ministry guarantees their apostolic authority. However, the term "apostle" is not limited to the Twelve. Acts 14:14 names Barnabas and Paul as "apostles." In his letters, Paul accords the title to himself (1 Cor 9:1), Andronicus and Junia (Rom 16:7), Apollos (1 Cor 4:6, 9; Acts 18:24-28; 19:1), Barnabas (1 Cor 9:5-6), Epaphroditus (Phil 2:25), Silvanus and Timothy (1 Thess 1:1; 2:7), and James, Jesus' brother (Gal 1:19).

As the story of Judas proves, being an apostle does not guarantee fidelity. Luke's account of Judas's death provides a cautionary tale for church members about the dangers of apostasy. Mark and John narrate only Judas betraying Jesus. Matthew and Luke present quite different accounts of Judas's death. In Matthew, Judas recognizes his "betraying innocent blood," throws down the thirty pieces of silver in the temple, and hangs himself. The priests reject his money from the temple treasury and buy a "Field of Blood" in which to bury foreigners (Matt 27:3-10).

Acts has Peter describe how Judas (described as possessed by Satan in Luke 22:3) acquired a field with the money he earned in betraying Jesus; the motif of the field is the same as that of Matthew, but its description is distinct. Rather than recount a hanging, Peter details how Judas "falling headlong, burst open in the middle and all his bowels gushed out." This death explains why the place was called "Field of Blood" (Acts 1:19). The larger point is clear. Betray Jesus, Acts declares, and suffer the consequences.

Acts provides further commentary on Judas's actions. Fulfillment citations assure readers that Judas's betrayal of Jesus was in accord with God's purposes: "The scripture had to be fulfilled, which the Holy Spirit through David foretold concerning Judas . . ." (1:16). Peter explains:

> For it is written in the book of Psalms, "Let his homestead become a desert, and let there be no one to live in it"; and "Let another take his position of overseer." (1:20-21)

The first reference is to Ps 69:25. The psalm was a favorite early proof-text used by Jesus' followers to support their claims of his appearance in Israel's Scriptures. The second is Ps 109:8. Both quotations say nothing about Judas in their original contexts but are "reread" to interpret his actions.

Next, Peter proposes a replacement apostle for Judas. He must be "one of the men [Greek *andrōn*; the reference is gender-specific] who have accompanied us during all the time that the Lord Jesus went in and out among us, beginning from the baptism of John until the day when he was taken up away from us—one of these must become a witness with us to his resurrection" (Acts 1:21-22).

The apostles then cast lots (today the equivalent would be to "shoot dice") to decide between "Joseph called Barsabbas . . . and Matthias" (1:23). Matthias "was added to the eleven apostles" (1:26). The important factor is not the person, but the concerns of eyewitnessing. However, when James is killed by Herod Agrippa I (12:2), he is not replaced. The tradition has been secured. The church will move on to new leaders and new practices. Unlike the letters of Paul, Luke does not mention the offices of either deacon (see Rom 16:1; Phil 1:1; 1 Tim 3:8-13) or bishop (Phil 1:1; 1 Tim 3:1-2; Titus 1:7).

Peter is clearly the leader of this early group, as we would expect from Matt 16 and as Paul confirms in his own letters (for example, Gal 2:9, where he calls Peter "Cephas," a Greek version of the Aramaic word for "rock"). He oversees this replacement process (Acts 1), preaches at Pentecost (Acts 2), is in the Temple in chapter 3, and oversees the communitarian lifestyle of the followers of Jesus in Jerusalem (4:32-37). According to 5:1-11, a married couple, Ananias and Sapphira, pretend to place all the funds from their property sale "at the apostles' feet." Peter, aware they had offered only part of the proceeds, accuses Ananias of being in Satan's control and of lying to the Holy Spirit and to God. Hearing the apostle's words, Ananias drops dead. Three hours later, Sapphira suffers the same fate (5:1-11). This type of communitarian living, commended in the writings of Aristotle and Cicero and practiced by the Qumran covenanters, is not attested in Paul's letters. For Luke, the ideal of sharing property was part of the golden age of the church; for readers, Ananias and Sapphira serve as another cautionary tale: do not be false to the concerns of the church.

A further breakdown of the communitarian ethos emerges in Acts 6, which recounts a dispute between the Aramaic-speaking "Hebrews" and the Greek-speaking "Hellenists" (perhaps Jews from the Diaspora who had settled in Jerusalem) over the Hellenistic widows being overlooked in the daily food allotment. The apostles, busy with preaching, advise the Hellenists to select "seven men [the term is gender-specific: 6:3 names "brothers" (Greek: *adelphoi*) and "men" (*andras*)] of good standing" to correct the oversight. Traditionally called "deacons" (from the Greek *diakonos*, "servant")—although this is not a title Acts gives them—the seven are commissioned by the apostles, "who prayed and laid their hands on them" (6:6).

The subsequent narrative shows this division of roles to be quite fluid. The "deacons" do what the Twelve do in terms of preaching and even performing mighty works, but they are never shown overseeing table fellowship. One Hellenist, "Stephen, full of grace and power, did great wonders and signs among the people" (6:8). The portrait of Stephen evokes that of Jesus: the righteous witness persecuted by Jewish authorities. According to Acts, Jews belonging to several synagogues in Jerusalem that associated with Diaspora communities "secretly instigated some men to say, 'We have heard him [Stephen] speak blasphemous words against Moses and God'" (6:11), as well as against the Temple and the Torah, that is, the instructions given by Moses (6:13-14; cf. the charges against Jesus in Luke 21:6).

Stephen's impassioned speech, in which he condemns the Temple and charges his Jewish audience with murder past and present, is Luke's composition, and it shows the Lucan theme of the general Jewish rejection of Jesus and his followers. For both the gospel and Acts, the true heirs of Israel are Jesus and his followers. Readers who recall Luke 4, the events in the synagogue in Nazareth, will find the scene of Acts 7 evocative.

> "Which of the prophets did your ancestors not persecute? They killed those who foretold the coming of the Righteous One, and now you have become his betrayers and murderers." (7:52)

About to suffer martyrdom for his "witness," Stephen announces: "I see the heavens opened and the Son of Man standing at the right hand of God!" (7:56). The Jewish mob drags him outside the city and stones him. He dies as Jesus dies in Luke, with the plea that the Lord receive his spirit, and "not hold this sin against them" (7:60; see Luke 23:34a, 46).

A good case can be made that Luke has composed the entire story. Although the first "martyr" in the Christian tradition, Stephen is not mentioned by the early church fathers, or by any other New Testament writing, even those that speak of martyrdom. That his name means "crown" in Greek—and the image of the crown of martyrdom was known in second-century contexts—may be more than coincidence. Nor does the speech suggest historical reporting. As a speech defending himself against false charges, it is off-topic and ineffective. As a speech presenting Lucan themes and driving the plot forward, it is brilliant.

Stephen's stoning leads to a general persecution of the church, with all but the apostles dispersed to areas outside Jerusalem (8:2-4). Luke is certainly exaggerating. Paul attests to "the poor" in Jerusalem for whom he is collecting funds: he means more than twelve apostles. Nor does Paul speak about this general persecution that decimated the Jerusalem church. Indeed, Acts 15, the Jerusalem Council, indicates the local community is in place. The persecution, though, fulfills Jesus' promise, and the Lucan motif, that his followers witness to the ends of the earth (1:8). Although Paul is first mentioned in Acts as a witness to Stephen's stoning, and as approving of it, Luke defers discussion of Paul for two chapters. Acts 8 depicts the movement of the church to Samaria, the area populated by the descendants of Israel's ten northern tribes.

Another of the Hellenists appointed to wait tables, Philip, leaves Jerusalem and finds himself in Samaria, where he converts the population (8:5-8). However, despite their belief, they do not receive the Holy Spirit until Peter and John arrive from Jerusalem. Luke again insists on apostolic authority. In Samaria, the apostles encounter Simon Magus (magus is a title, the singular of the term "magi" [see Matt 2]), whose magical feats had convinced the local population that he had "the power of God that is called Great" (8:10). Witnessing the power of the Spirit, Simon offers Peter and John money and exhorts them, "Give me also this power so that anyone on whom I lay my hands may receive the Holy Spirit" (8:19). Peter curses Simon for what the church will later call *simony*, the sin of purchasing church office. The last we hear of Simon is his plea to Peter for prayer that the curse be lifted. Acts does not describe Simon's fate; later Christian texts portray Simon as an arch-heretic.

Philip then converts the Ethiopian chamberlain, a man who already has some affiliation with the Jewish community in that he has been worshiping in Jerusalem and he is reading from the scroll of Isaiah. Perhaps his condition of being a eunuch compromised his converting to Judaism (see Deut 23:1); perhaps he came from a family of proselytes; likely he is understood to be a God-fearer. Acts regards Cornelius the centurion, whose story is told in chapter 10, as the first Gentile "convert" who enters the church apart from prior affiliation with Judaism. The conversion of the Samaritans and then of the Ethiopian shows the movement of the mission beyond the traditional borders of Israel and anticipates the Gentile mission begun by Peter and then fulfilled by Paul.

The apostle to the Gentiles, Acts' major character, is introduced in the context of Stephen's martyrdom:

> Then they dragged [Stephen] out of the city and began to stone him; and the witnesses laid their coats at the feet of a young man named Saul. . . . And Saul approved of their killing him. (7:58–8:1)

By 8:3, Saul is dragging the followers of Jesus, men and women, to prison. Luke does not, however, explain why. As we saw in the chapter on John's Gospel, there were several reasons why Jewish communities might find members who confessed Jesus as Lord to be dangerous or unwelcome.

Following the two stories of Philip, which indicate that despite or even because of persecution the message continues, Acts depicts Paul (still called "Saul"; readers might be reminded of King Saul, who struggled against David, just as here Saul of Tarsus struggles against the followers of the "son of David") "breathing threats and murder against the disciples of the Lord" and with letters from the high priest authorizing him to arrest Jesus-followers in Damascus and extradite them to Jerusalem (9:1-2). But on his way, Saul/Paul has a visionary experience of the risen Jesus on the road to Damascus. Blinded, he is led to the city, where he fasts for three days. The risen Jesus tells Ananias, a follower in Damascus:

> [Paul] is an instrument whom I have chosen to bring my name before Gentiles and kings and before the people of Israel; I myself will show him how much he must suffer for the sake of my name. (9:15-16)

The comment establishes the plot for the rest of Acts. Paul recovers his sight, is filled with the Spirit, is baptized, joins "the way" (9:17-18), and will face numerous persecutions in his mission to proclaim the gospel of Jesus.

In his subsequent ministry, Paul recapitulates Peter's role: they both preach, heal and exorcise, counter false teachers, raise the dead, and are delivered from prison. Similarly, the pattern of punishing opponents, epitomized by the deaths of Ananias and Sapphira and of Herod after killing James, continues in relation to Paul. For example, on Cyprus, Paul encounters a "Jewish false prophet, named Bar-Jesus" (13:6), who opposes Paul's influence on the Roman proconsul, Sergius Paulus. Paul attacks him, and Bar-Jesus becomes an anti-type to Paul, blinded on the road to Damascus. Paul's reaction to his opponent is typical of ancient invective:

> "You son of the devil, you enemy of all righteousness, full of all deceit and villainy . . .
> the hand of the Lord is against you, and you will be blind for a while, unable to see the sun." (13:10-11)

Again, Luke issues a cautionary tale: oppose the apostles of Jesus at your own risk. Readers, who are likely already to be followers of Jesus, might take no small pleasure in the defeat of the church's enemies.

In Ephesus Paul encounters competitors doing signs and wonders. Acts presents Paul's own "extraordinary miracles," to the extent that when the handkerchiefs or aprons that had touched his skin were brought to the sick, their diseases left them, and the evil spirits came out of them. (19:11-12)

Paul's competitors here are seven sons of an otherwise unknown Jewish high priest named Sceva. As itinerant exorcists, they "tried to use the name of the Lord Jesus" in their activities (19:13). In this case, an "evil spirit," not the apostle, responds, "Jesus I know, and Paul I know; but who are you?" (19:15). The man with the spirit beats them up and, like the possessed man in Gerasa (Luke 8:27), they flee naked. The result is not only the spread of the gospel (19:17) and a humorous example of *schadenfreude* for Luke's readers, but also an expensive renouncing of magic:

A number of those who practiced magic collected their books and burned them publicly; when the value of these books was calculated, it was found to come to fifty thousand silver coins. (19:19)

Acts' warnings are again clear: Oppose an apostle; suffer the consequences. Readers are entertained while being cautioned about apostasy, simony, and lying to church leaders. The cursing and blinding of opponents, beating of the exorcists, economic loss to the magicians through book burning, and the humiliation and suffering of the opponents all serve Luke's rhetorical purposes of promoting the church and dishonoring anyone who would challenge its claims. Today's readers, perhaps more aware of the power of stories and the dangers of stereotype, might understand Luke's purposes even as they might criticize his approach.

Jewish Rejection and Gentile Response

Luke anticipates the Gentile mission through several scenes, each set in relation to Jesus' Jewish context. Jesus' birth occurs during the time of the Roman census impacting "all the world" (Luke 2:1). The genealogy stretches back to Adam, showing his connection to all of humanity (Luke 3:38). Simeon foretells that Jesus will be "a light for revelation to the Gentiles and for glory to your people Israel" (Luke 2:32). But who this "people Israel" will be is an open question. John announces to the Pharisees and Sadducees, "Do not begin to say to yourselves, 'We have Abraham as our ancestor'; for I tell you, God is able from these stones to raise up children to Abraham" (Luke 3:8). In his synagogue sermon at Nazareth, Jesus announces that the missions of the prophets Elijah and Elisha were not to their own people but, respectively, to the (Gentile) widow of Zarephath and Naaman the Syrian (Luke 4:26-27). Enraged, the synagogue congregation attempts to hurl Jesus off a cliff. The scene is set for Acts. For the most part, Gentiles receive Jesus; most Jews, after some initial acceptance, reject him. Only a remnant, represented by the Jerusalem apostles and Paul, maintain the connection to ethnic Israel.

Throughout Acts, the Jewish base of the movement—Galilean apostles; Jerusalem home; Temple focus—gradually recedes in favor of a Gentile emphasis away from Jerusalem. In Acts 2, Jews and proselytes to Judaism "from every nation" (2:5) gather in Jerusalem for the pilgrimage festival of Shavuot (the Hebrew term for "weeks"), known in Greek as Pentecost ("50," indicating seven weeks plus one day after Passover; Tob 2:1; 2 Macc 12:32). Originally Shavuot celebrated the spring harvest when pilgrims brought first fruits to Jerusalem as a thanksgiving offering (see Exod 23:16; 34:22; Lev 23:15-21; Num 28:26; Deut 16:9-12). Marked by joy and feasting, it encompassed both Israelites and sojourners, or what we might call "resident aliens":

> Rejoice before the LORD your God—you and your sons and your daughters, your male and female slaves, the Levites resident in your towns, as well as the strangers, the orphans, and the widows who are among you. (Deut 16:11)

By the Second Temple period, the festival was associated with the giving of Torah to Moses at Mount Sinai (see Exod 19:16 and *Jubilees* 6:17-21).

During this festival as Acts describes it, "suddenly from heaven there came a sound like the rush of a violent wind" and "divided tongues, as of fire" rested on Jesus' followers (2:2-3). "All of them were filled with the Holy Spirit, and they began to speak in other languages" (2:4), a phenomenon known as *xenoglossia* (Greek for "foreign speech"). This is not the same phenomenon Paul describes in 1 Cor 14. There "speaking in tongues," or *glossolalia*, is speaking in syllables that do not have semantic coherence, the type of speaking Paul describes that is found today in Pentecostal and other charismatic congregations. The scene attracts a crowd of devout Jews gathered for the festival:

> Parthians, Medes, Elamites, and residents of Mesopotamia, Judea and Cappadocia, Pontus and Asia, Phrygia and Pamphylia, Egypt and the parts of Libya belonging to Cyrene, and visitors from Rome . . . Cretans and Arabs. (2:9-11)

From this group come the next followers of Jesus. Peter explains the miracle as fulfilling Joel's prophesy that God's Spirit will be poured out on all "in the last days" (2:17). Acts thereby links the delayed Parousia with Pentecost. The followers of Jesus *are* in the last days; the messianic kingdom is arriving.

Some from the crowd do not see a miracle; rather, they conclude that Jesus' followers are drunk, "filled with new wine" (2:13). Peter discounts this explanation by declaring that "these are not drunk, as you suppose, for it is only nine o'clock in the morning" (2:15).

The bars are not open yet. Plutarch associates wine and prophetic speech, so the bystanders might be drawing a reasonable conclusion (*Oracles at Delphi* 406B). But given Luke's negative depiction of Jews who reject the gospel message, this reading would be optimistic.

Peter's speech highlights both Jewish opposition and acceptance. He announces to his "Israelite" audience that *they* were the ones who "crucified and killed" Jesus (2:23).

> Therefore let the entire house of Israel know with certainty that God has made him both Lord and Messiah, this Jesus whom you crucified. (Acts 2:36)

Roman involvement goes unmentioned. The only option for the people is to "Repent, and be baptized every one of you in the name of Jesus Christ so that your sins may be forgiven" (2:38). Acts presents Jews as either killers of Jesus, or his followers. The scene ends with the notice that about 3,000 Jews were baptized (2:41).

The Pentecost scene can be read as an interpretation of the Jewish pilgrimage festival. Along with celebrating the Feast of Weeks and the giving of the Torah, Jesus' followers celebrate the giving of the spirit to the church. The scene may also be interpreted in light of a midrash, an early Jewish interpretation of the Sinai narrative, which explains that God offered the Torah to other nations, but each refused it. One rejected the commandment not to murder; others rejected commandments forbidding stealing or committing adultery. Only Israel exclaimed, "We will listen and we will do" (Deut 5:27), and hence the Torah is in Hebrew, not Moabite or Hittite. Now, at Pentecost, the other nations can hear the word of God in their own languages. In Acts 20:16, Paul eagerly travels to Jerusalem for Shavuot. There is no indication that he comes to celebrate the descent of the Spirit. Most likely, he celebrates the giving of the Torah.

Jewish opposition and affiliation continue as the movement expands. In Acts 3, Peter again accuses his Jewish audience of having "rejected the Holy and Righteous One and asked to have a murderer given to you" and having "killed the Author of life, whom God raised from the dead" (3:14-15). He concedes that they "acted in ignorance" (3:17), but their only option is to repent and believe. Five thousand (4:4) join the church.

Yet "the priests, the captain of the Temple, and the Sadducees" arrest Peter and John for "proclaiming that in Jesus there is the resurrection of the dead" (4:1-2). The Sadducees did not accept the idea of resurrection, but this was hardly a reason to prompt arrest. If belief in resurrection were illegal, they would have to arrest Pharisees as well. But the scene does support one of Luke's themes: later, Paul will establish his Pharisaic credentials by appealing to the concept of resurrection (24:21). Peter and John are freed by an angelic prison break (the first of several in Acts), which is a convention in Greek and Roman literature generally associated with the story of Dionysius (Bacchus) and known as well from Hellenistic romances and Philostratus's *Life of Apollonius of Tyana*. Luke's readers would be entertained by these "baptized" versions of familiar plot lines.

The apostles continue their preaching but are arrested again. The cycle continues. In

Acts 5, the increasingly exasperated Sanhedrin and high priest—whose ineptitude should be taken as humorous—accuse Peter and John:

> "We gave you strict orders not to teach in this name, and yet here you have filled Jerusalem with your teaching and you are determined to bring this man's blood on us."
> (5:28)

Their charge might remind readers of Matt 27:25, the infamous cry of "all the people": "His blood be on our heads and on our children."

At this point, Gamaliel, a Sanhedrin member and a Pharisee known from rabbinic texts (for example, *m. Sota* 9.15), supports the release of the apostles from prison. He mentions the defunct movements associated with Theudas and Judas the Galilean "at the time of the census" (5:37; the reference reminds readers of Luke 2: the obedience of Joseph and Mary to the census and their travel from Galilee to Bethlehem). Jesus is not like these two failed figures, Theudas and Judas. Gamaliel concludes that the apostles should be released and their fate left to God (5:38-39).

In Acts, Gamaliel is an ambivalent character. He favors releasing the prisoners and thereby permits the church's growth. Yet he does not join the movement. Later, Paul testifies to a hostile Jerusalem crowd:

> I am a Jew, born in Tarsus in Cilicia, but brought up in this city at the feet of Gamaliel, educated strictly according to our ancestral law, being zealous for God, just as all of you are today. (22:3)

Given that Paul starts as a persecutor of Jesus' followers, one wonders what he learned from Gamaliel, or even if he did: in his letters, Paul mentions neither being brought up in Jerusalem nor having studied with Gamaliel.

Stephen's martyrdom and the subsequent persecution (7:54–8:1) end conversions in Jerusalem. But the persecution facilitates the mission outward (8:1): to Samaritans (8:4-25), to the Ethiopian officer who had worshiped in Jerusalem and was reading Isaiah (8:26-40), and finally to the Roman centurion Cornelius, an undisputed Gentile with no association to the Scriptures of Israel, synagogues, or the Jerusalem Temple (10:1–11:18). Predictably, Cornelius's conversion occurs in the context of Jewish opposition, although ironically that opposition comes from Pharisaic members within the church. Ironically as well, it is not Paul—the evangelist to the Gentiles—who facilitates the conversion, but Peter.

The scene opens with Peter, asleep on the roof at the home of Simon the tanner in Joppa. Peter receives a vision of a large sheet, descending from heaven and filled with nonkosher food. Despite being told three times to "kill and eat," Peter refuses. Then a voice from heaven responds, "What God has made clean, you must not call profane"

(10:15). There may be some humor in the scene: tanners cure leather by boiling it in urine; the smell is not pleasant. Peter's dream could be seen as a nightmare brought on by the combination of his hunger (which 10:10 makes explicit) and the odors wafting up to the roof. For Acts, the dream also has theological import: it turns out not to be a reference to dietary regulations, but to the entry of Gentiles into the church.

Summoned to Cornelius's house, Peter announces to the centurion, his family, and guests:

> You yourselves know that it is unlawful for a Jew to associate with or to visit a Gentile; but God has shown me that I should not call anyone profane or unclean. (10:28)

There is no such law, and numerous examples of associations between Jews and Gentiles belie its historicity. Jews were not culturally isolationist but participated in all sorts of cultural and civic practices. They received Gentile "God-fearers" as participants in their communities (see Acts 10:22; 13:16; 16:14; 17:4, 12; 18:7). The Jerusalem Temple's Court of the Gentiles welcomed foreign worshipers. Luke's Gospel mentions a centurion who built a synagogue and on whose behalf the Jewish elders sought Jesus' help (7:1-10). The line speaks not to historical accuracy, but to Luke's agenda.

God as Main Character?

The story of Cornelius's conversion greatly emphasizes divine intervention: vision (10:3), angel (10:3), trance and vision (10:10-16), voice (10:13), the Spirit (10:19), angel (10:22), God (10:28), angel (10:30), Holy Spirit (10:44). These interventions sanction Gentile inclusion.

Who is the main character of Acts' narrative? The most obvious candidates are Peter (the first part) and Paul (the second part). Hence the title "Acts of the Apostles." But there is a case to be made for thinking of God and the Spirit as the main characters. They are continually at work shaping the plot. Their purposes and goals are constantly disclosed in the plot, characters, and settings.

Peter's assertion in 10:28 frames Jewish law as a problem. The point is reinforced when, at the Jerusalem Council, Peter justifies the inclusion of the Gentiles apart from Torah to his fellow Jews. He asks:

> Why are you putting God to the test by placing on the neck of the disciples a yoke that neither our ancestors nor we have been able to bear? On the contrary, we believe that we will be saved through the grace of the Lord Jesus, just as they will. (15:10-11)

This contrast of law and grace, and the assertion of Torah as an impossible burden, does not express what Jews thought, then or now. Had the Law been impossible to bear, Judaism then, and to the present, could not have continued. The Law for Jews was not a burden but a delight, a means by which they expressed their identity amid Roman pressures to assimilate, a system which today we might think of as an expression of multiculturalism, a lifestyle by which they could sanctify their bodies, time, and space. For Luke, likely addressing a Gentile audience for whom Jewish practices such as dietary regulations and circumcision would have been odd at best, if not abhorrent, the description may well have seemed correct.

Acts again redefines what it means to be a member of Israel, this time by setting up an opposition between law and grace, the followers of Jesus and the (majority of) the descendants of Abraham. Abraham's true heirs are those who follow Jesus, not those who persecute him and his followers. Peter secures this point by suggesting that the Jews—but not Jesus' followers—killed Jesus: "They put him to death by hanging him on a tree" (10:39). Peter speaks on behalf of Gentiles joining the movement, but the "circumcised believers" (11:2) criticize him. Even within the movement, Jewish opposition seeks to thwart divine purposes.

According to Acts 12, Herod Agrippa kills James, and "after he saw that it pleased the Jews," he proceeded to arrest Peter also" during the festival of Unleavened Bread, that is, Passover (12:3). Parallels to Jesus' arrest cannot be missed, nor can the distancing of the apostles from "the Jews." Reinforcing this distance is the new name introduced for Jesus-followers, "Christians" (11:26).

The pattern of general Jewish rejection and Gentile acceptance continues. In Acts 13, Paul and Barnabas speak in a synagogue in Pisidian Antioch. While many Jews and proselytes are initially attracted to their message, "when the Jews saw the crowds, they were filled with jealousy; and blaspheming, they contradicted what was spoken by Paul" (13:45). The mission turns to the Gentiles (13:46). The Gentiles, predictably, convert, and the Jews, predictably, "stirred up persecution against Paul and Barnabas, and drove them out of their region" (13:51). Similar scenes repeat in Lystra (14:19), Thessalonica (17:5), Beroea (17:13), Corinth (18:6), Macedonia (20:3), and Jerusalem (21:27; 24:19). Acts recounts that rumors had been spread that Paul advised fellow Jews not to circumcise their sons or observe the teachings given in the Torah (21:21). Such a rumor might well have developed in light of the teachings found in Paul's letters, especially his correspondence with the churches in Galatia. Controlling Paul's legacy by insisting on his fidelity to Jewish practice, Acts depicts him as participating in a Temple ritual of purification (21:23-26).

Although the Jerusalem church celebrates with Paul the "many thousands of believers there are among the Jews, and they are all zealous for the Law" (21:20), by the end of Acts, this Jewish contingent disappears. When Paul is finally arrested in Jerusalem, they offer no support. Instead, Luke frames Paul's fate as a recollection of Jesus' passion.

Both men are persecuted by Jews, handed over to Gentiles (Luke 18:32; Acts 21:11), and speak to a member of the Herodian household (Luke 23:6-12; Acts 25:23-27).

Acts' closing verses replay the convention. Paul, under house arrest in Rome, proclaims the resurrected Lord. Some Jews are convinced; others refuse to believe. Paul announces to those who reject his claims:

> The Holy Spirit was right in saying to your ancestors through the prophet Isaiah, "Go to this people and say, You will indeed listen, but never understand, and you will indeed look, but never perceive." (28:25-26)

Paul's last words underscore Gentile inclusion, "Let it be known to you then that this salvation of God has been sent to the Gentiles; they will listen" (28:28). Whether Luke holds out any hope for Jews, or whether they and Jerusalem are relegated to extinction, with the Gentile church being heir to the name and traditions of Israel, remains a debated issue.

Roman Imperial Justice

Acts mentions Rome or Roman about 16 times. The narrative references the emperor, including his title Sebastos or "Revered One" (the Latin is "Augustus"), in 25:21, 25. The exemplary Gentile convert is the Roman army officer, Cornelius (10–11). Other Roman officials, such as Sergius Paulus (Acts 13) and centurions who encounter Paul (22:25-26; 24:23; 27:43), are portrayed sympathetically. Paul is presented as a Roman citizen (16:37; 22:24-29; in his letters, Paul never makes this claim) who exercises his right of appeal to have his case heard before Caesar (25:12); it is this appeal that brings Paul to Rome. But the Roman authorities find no viable charge about which they can inform Caesar (25:24-27).

Acts has often been understood as a literary defense or apology written to assure the empire that the church poses no threat. But this view is inadequate. First, the portrayal of the empire is not always complimentary. For example, in Corinth, Paul is accused before Gallio, the proconsul of Achaia, of persuading people to worship in unlawful ways. Gallio dismisses the charges, but he does not intervene when the synagogue leader, Sosthenes, is beaten (18:12-17). In Jerusalem, Paul escapes a flogging from the tribune Claudius Lysias only when he reveals he is a Roman citizen (22:22-29); Roman justice appears arbitrary. The same tribune subsequently rescues Paul from the Jerusalem leaders and takes him to the corrupt governor Felix in Caesarea (23:23–24:26). Felix turns Paul over to the next governor, the equally inadequate Festus. Rome cannot be trusted.

Moreover, the church in Acts can be seen as subversive. Paul is accused of promoting "customs that are not lawful for . . . Romans to adopt or observe" (16:21) and "acting contrary to the decrees of the emperor, saying that there is another king named Jesus" (17:7). Although often understood as false charges, they have some credibility. The charges may suggest that Paul advocated withdrawal from honoring civic and imperial deities and leaders, an action that, while not illegal, was perceived by some as jeopardizing divine and imperial favor. The same charge could underlie anyone who followed the apostolic decree promulgated by James of avoiding blood, meat from a strangled animal, meat offered to idols, and *porneia,* if these regulations mean eschewing contact with pagan temples. Riots break out in Ephesus because Paul's preaching damages the business of those making silver shrines of the goddess Artemis. Urging calm, the city clerk reminds those inciting the turmoil both that they risk Roman retaliation for rioting and that the courts and the proconsuls are available for complaints (19:21-41). But the justice of the proconsuls is not dependable. Indeed, by noting that Paul's preaching prompted a riot, the narrative can be read as suggesting that Christian claims are economically and politically threatening. Just as Acts depicts Paul as a faithful Jew and attempts to correct the view that he stood against Torah and Temple, so Acts insists that while Paul's evangelism could be seen as a challenge to the empire, it is not Paul but his opponents who are the real troublemakers.

The narrative ends with Paul under house arrest in Rome. If Paul were executed in Rome, as some tradition suggests, and if Acts' initial audience knew this story, then it also knew that the empire is antithetical to God's messengers. Acts is clearly not interested in the violent overthrow of the Roman government, but it is very much interested in promoting the lordship of Christ over the lordship of Caesar. Numerous references to Jesus as the Lord exalted in the heavens as the reigning son of king David (1:3-11; 2:25-26, 36; 3:20-21; 5:31; 10:42; 13:22-23; 14:22; 15:11; 17:7, 31; 24:25) proclaim an alternative power structure. Perhaps Acts adopts an accommodationist stance so as to protect Jesus-believers while they continue their mission work. Perhaps it disguises in places both the dangerous nature of Roman power and the threatening implications of the gospel message, though insiders know both threats exist. There is no "God and country/empire" alliance.

Text Criticism

We do not have the original manuscript of any New Testament writing. Consequently, the NT writings have to be constituted on the basis of thousands of handwritten copies. These copies of copies of copies almost always show some disagreements. The work of text criticism (sometimes called textual criticism) examines these copies in order to reconstruct what the original or at least the earliest copies most likely said.

Textual Criticism

More than 5,000 Greek manuscripts contain parts or all of the NT. The earliest, from the second to fifth centuries, are usually written on papyrus. There are also majuscules (large letter writing) dating from the fourth to the ninth century approximately, written on vellum or parchment in uncial, or capital letters. Minuscules (small letter writing), also vellum or parchment, date to the ninth century or later. In addition, there are translations from Greek into languages such as Syriac, Latin, Coptic, Georgian, Ethiopic, Armenian, and Old Church Slavonic. Finally, there are NT quotations in Patristic sources (the writings of the church fathers) dating from the second century and later, as well as NT allusions in noncanonical Christian texts, such as Infancy Gospels, Apocryphal Acts, and Gnostic materials.

Text critics often begin by determining families of texts. For example the Alexandrian grouping or family often includes the earliest and best copies. There is a Western grouping featuring Codex D. A Byzantine grouping of latter copies is often regarded as less reliable. Having located the manuscript in its textual tradition, the text critic typically asks questions to determine earlier and later readings. One starting point asks, "How many copies support a reading?" But quantity of manuscripts does not necessarily indicate quality of text. There may be many copies of a flawed text. Next, "how old are these copies?" Errors may have been introduced and then copied, whereas an earlier text with fewer copies might offer the more original reading; conversely, the "error" might have been early and then corrected by later scribes. Third, "where does the text originate?" A cluster of copies from one particular area containing the same form may reflect the influence of a particular scribe, whereas copies from widely scattered geographical locations containing the same form are more likely to contain earlier readings.

The text critic then investigates features of the variant readings themselves. Some variants are readily identified as spelling mistakes or omissions and repetitions caused by weary scribes. Text critics often work with the rubric known as the *lectio difficilior*: a more difficult reading is more likely to be the original. That is, we can more easily posit why a scribe would have smoothed over a difficulty than introduced one. But even here, guesswork is involved: what might seem difficult or confusing to us might not have been to a text's author. Sometimes a scribe will conform a passage in one gospel with the parallel passage in another gospel. Or a scribe might make the text cohere with developing Christology or ecclesiology. It is this last dimension of deliberate changes, especially related to the church's identity, that brings us to a manuscript form of Acts.

The manuscript known today as the Western text, Codex Bezae, or Codex D offers a version of Acts that is 10 percent longer than the versions of the Alexandrian grouping. Codex D emerges from the fifth or sixth centuries, though it may represent an earlier tradition, perhaps from the second century.

This Western version has distinct features that suggest not random copying errors but intentional scribal changes. These features include stylistic preferences (expanded stories and added details) and a distinctive theological-ecclesial agenda. Four features of the scribe's agenda are particularly prominent.

First, Codex D frequently reduces the roles of women. Acts 1:14 refers to "certain women" who pray with the apostles. Codex D domesticates this independent group using the phrase "wives and children" to present them as spouses and mothers of the apostles. The reference in 17:4 to some "leading women" becomes in Codex D "wives of leading men." Codex D omits the reference in 17:34 to a convert in Athens, a "woman named Damaris." In 18:26 the order of the names of the wife and husband, Priscilla and Aquila, is reversed to give the husband prominence. These changes suggest a domesticating of independent women and a possible reduction of women's authority in the churches that used this manuscript.

Second, Codex D consistently expands references to "Lord Jesus" or "Jesus Christ" or "Christ Jesus" to the fullest form, "Lord Jesus Christ" (1:21; 2:38; 4:33; 5:42; 8:16; 10:48; 11:20; 13:33; 15:11; 16:31; 18:5; 19:5; 20:21; 21:13). Likewise, the phrase "in the name of the Lord Jesus Christ" is added to miracle references to make explicit the source of the miracle (6:8; 14:10; 18:10). It is also added to clarify the object of the belief (18:8). This addition shows greater christological reverence.

A third feature of Codex D's theological agenda is its heightened attention to the Spirit (pneumatology). The codex adds references to the Spirit helping Stephen (6:10) and Peter (15:7). In 8:39, the Holy Spirit comes on the newly baptized Ethiopian chamberlain, thereby linking the Spirit with baptism. In 19:1, it adds a reference to the Spirit directing Paul to Asia. In Acts 20:3, an added reference in Codex D has the Spirit intervene to protect Paul from a plot and direct him to Macedonia.

The fourth ecclesial-theological commitment complements the second and third by exaggerating anti-Jewish references. In 3:13 Codex D adds "Christ" to "Jesus": "the God of our ancestors has glorified his servant [Christ] Jesus, whom you handed over and rejected." The addition stresses that the Jerusalemite crowd had not recognized Jesus as Messiah. Codex D heightens Jewish responsibility for Jesus' death, Jewish opposition to the apostles, and the Gentile identity of the church. For example, Peter mitigates the charge that the Jews crucified Jesus by stating, "And now, brothers ["friends" in NRSV], I know that you acted in ignorance, as did also your rulers" (Acts 3:17). Codex D makes three changes. First, Peter's "I know" becomes "we know." The plural heightens the contrast between the apostles as representatives of the church, and the Jews. Second, after the verb translated "acted," Codex D adds the word "evil" so that Peter says, "We know that you did evil," heightening Jewish responsibility for Jesus' death. And third, Codex D adds a small Greek particle (*men*) after "you." This word, which has the sense of "on the one hand . . . on the other hand," contrasts 3:17 and 3:18: "We know that you did evil, in ignorance, as did your rulers, on the one hand, but on the other, this way God fulfilled what he had foretold through all the prophets, that his Messiah would suffer."

Another example appears in 13:27. The Alexandrian text offers:

> Because the residents of Jerusalem and their leaders *did not recognize him* or understand the words of the prophets that are read every sabbath, they fulfilled those words by condemning him.

Codex D omits "did not recognize him" and thereby erases any appeal to ignorance and heightens the Jews' failure to understand the Scriptures.

Finally, Codex D heightens the presentation of the church as a distinct, superior, and universal community marked by doing God's will. Additions in Codex D emphasize the church's commission to preach the gospel (1:2; 13:43; 14:4, 7, 25; 16:4). In Acts 2:17, Codex D reinforces this Gentile identity with several small but significant alterations to Joel's prophecy:

> I will pour out my Spirit upon all flesh, and your sons and your daughters shall prophesy, and your young men shall see visions, and your old men shall dream dreams.

Codex D has the Spirit given to "all fleshes" (rather than "all flesh") and it removes "your" before "young men" and "old men" to erase their specific Jewish referent.

The text-critical questions show us that for the first several centuries, the wording of the books that would become the New Testament was in flux. Indeed, the wording continues today to be less than secure, both as new arguments are made for earlier readings and as new translations are made for later readers. Some scholars will concentrate on the discrepancies in the manuscript tradition and so call into question the legitimacy of the New Testament's witness; others will concentrate on the overall coherence of the message if not the actual wording. Readers today thus have to choose not only what text to read but also how to interpret it.

Romans

P aul's Letter to the Romans has exerted enormous influence throughout Christian history. In his late fourth-century autobiography, *Confessions*, the great theologian Augustine notes the converting power of Rom 13:14: "Put on the Lord Jesus Christ and make no provision for the flesh to gratify these desires." While lecturing on Romans in 1517, Martin Luther came to clarity about God's justifying grace encountered through faith. In his *Institutes*, published in 1536, John Calvin appealed to Rom 9 in explaining what has come to be known as "predestination," the idea that divine will, rather than human action, determines who is saved and damned: "Even before they had been born or had done anything good or bad (so that God's purpose of election might continue, not by works but by his call) she was told, 'The elder shall serve the younger'" (Rom 9:11-12, in reference to Gen 25:23; Calvin also cites Rom 9:13, 16, 18, 21). While listening to a reading from Luther's writing on Romans in 1738, the founder of the Methodist movement, John Wesley, felt his heart "strangely warmed" and experienced assurance that God had forgiven his sin.

In *The Women's Bible* of 1895, Elizabeth Cady Stanton highlights references to Phoebe, Mary, Priscilla, and others in Rom 16 to argue that "one who uses unbiased common sense in regard to the New Testament records [realizes that] there can be no question of women's activity and prominence in the early ministry." Paul calls Phoebe a "deacon" (the Greek uses the masculine form) to indicate her authoritative role. The 1965 Declaration on the Relation of the Church with Non-Christian Religions of the Second Vatican Council, *Nostra Aetate* (Latin for "In Our Time"), cites extensively from Romans to repair and promote good relations between the Roman Catholic Church and the Jewish community: "The Church keeps ever in mind the words of the Apostle about his kinsmen: 'theirs is the sonship and the glory and the covenants and the law and the worship and the promises; theirs are the fathers and from them is Christ according to the flesh' (Rom 9:4-5)." In South Africa, Paul's injunction in Rom 13:1, "Let every person be subject to the governing authorities; for there is no authority except from God, and those authorities that exist have been instituted by God," gave theological legitimacy to apartheid even as opponents of apartheid read Rom 13 in relation to Rev 13 to show its cultural contingency rather than its timeless mandate.

Romans continues to inspire and challenge as it speaks to each generation anew about subjects as diverse as morality, theology, ecclesiology, politics, gender roles, and interfaith relations. Fundamental to understanding it or any text are the decisions we make about genre or, more broadly, purpose. For example, the Protestant reformer Melanchthon (1497–1560) called Romans a "Compendium of Christian Doctrine" and thereby named an approach that emphasizes the letter's theological nature. Finding in Romans a comprehensive, timeless theological system, he relegated to the background hints about its address to any particular or contingent situation. Recent interpreters, taking a more nuanced approach, look also to the occasion of the letter to ask questions such as why Paul wrote, to whom he wrote, and even if his views might have changed over time. Romans clearly begins (1:1-15) and ends like a letter (15:14–16:27) and thus at least addresses a specific community in specific circumstances.

In this chapter, we investigate the implications of these different understandings of Paul's letter. We look at select passages both as components of a theological treatise, the summation of Paul's understanding of God's work in Christ, and thus as decontextualized from any specific setting, as well as at the letter as a response to the concerns of a specific church community. The first approach emphasizes matters of theology (the depiction of God), Christology (the depiction of Christ), and soteriology (the salvific work of Christ in relation to humanity and the created order). The second approach takes a more sociological and pastoral focus. To look at one reading strategy and ignore the other will necessarily present an incomplete picture: readers continue to debate, however, which approach should be placed in sharp focus and foregrounded. The various approaches of this chapter—historical, genre, theological reading, ideological, and the multiple interpretations they produce—reflect and foreground the diverse interests of readers; consequently, we might identify the general approach throughout as a type of reader-response criticism.

Romans 1 and Same-Sex Relations

The starting and centering point for Paul's theological thinking in Romans is God in relation to creation. In the opening verse Paul refers to the "gospel of God"; he addresses his audience as "beloved of God" (1:7a) and blesses them with "grace and peace from God our Father" (1:7). The opening chapters then explain that both Gentiles and Jews exist in a broken relationship with their Creator and that God has acted in Christ to reconcile both Jews and Gentiles to God and to each other. As he states in 1:16-17, citing Hab 2:4:

> For I am not ashamed of the gospel; it is the power of God for salvation to everyone who has faith: to the Jew first, and also to the Greek. For in it the righteousness of God

is revealed through faith for faith, as it is written, "The one who is righteous will live by faith."

In Rom 1, Paul argues that the Gentiles, failing to recognize and worship God, have turned to worship idols. The failure is not God's fault, but human error, for

> ever since the creation of the world his eternal power and divine nature, invisible though they are, have been understood and seen through the things he has made. So they [the Gentiles] are without excuse; for though they knew God, they did not honor him as God or give thanks to him. (1:20-23)

God's response to those who fail to heed both the evidence of creation and their own consciences is to hand them over to the power of sin: "God gave them up in the lusts of their hearts to impurity, to the degrading of their bodies among themselves" (1:24).

It is in this context that Paul references what most readers take to be same-sex relations:

> For this reason God gave them up to degrading passions. Their women exchanged natural intercourse for unnatural [Greek: "against nature," *para physin*], and in the same way also the men, giving up natural intercourse with women, were consumed with passion for one another. Men committed shameless acts with men and received in their own persons the due penalty for their error. (1:26-27; see also 1 Cor 6:9-10; 1 Tim 1:9-10)

Given the culture wars over the general question of "the Bible and homosexuality"—and given the enormous personal suffering these wars have created—we take the time to address how Paul's words have been understood from a theological perspective, how from a contextual one the words take on different nuances, and how people might choose to understand these words today.

If we consider Paul is writing a theological treatise of universal, timeless truths, we may conclude that same-sex attraction serves as punishment for idolatry. This reading would then potentially lead to the conclusion that any person who turns from idols to Christ, and who worships the Creator rather than the created, would also turn from "unnatural" to "natural" intercourse. We might also choose to read Rom 1 in the context of Gen 1–3, given Paul's concern for proper creation. In this intertextual approach, Paul affirms the created order, in which human beings were paired "male and female," with the woman as the "helper" and "partner" of the man (Gen 2:18). Such an allusion to Genesis would not be out of place: Rom 5 adduces Adam in order to understand the role of Christ. Finally, those who see Paul's concern for the "natural" will argue that it is "natural" for men and women to engage in intercourse, but it is unnatural for two men or two women to do so, since such relations cannot lead to pregnancy and so are sterile.

Contrary to some claims we have heard, individuals who hold such views should not be automatically seen as bigots, superstitious, or uncaring. The issue comprises that person's view of biblical authority coupled with how the individual understands the prohibitions in Lev 18 and 20, the few other NT passages that refer to same-sex relations, and the wording as well as the argument of Romans.

For many in churches today, any prohibition of the expression of love by two people of the same sex is contrary to their understanding of the good news of Jesus. The experiences of countless gay and lesbian Christians, including those who have undergone "reparation therapy"—a discredited psychological attempt to "fix" gay people—testify both that homosexuality is not the result of idolatry and that belief in Christ will not convert an individual into being heterosexual. For like-minded readers, the appeal to Genesis also does not convince, since they take Genesis not as a universal truth, but as a culturally contingent story. Those who hold such views should not be understood, as we have also heard, as liberal yahoos or as dismissing the Bible. The issue comprises a different understanding of how the Bible is to be interpreted. Nor does the argument that equates a "sterile" act with what is "natural" hold for all such readers, since they see non-procreative sexual intercourse (for example, between a postmenopausal woman, or *yes* a woman who has had a hysterectomy, and her husband) as something to be celebrated rather than condemned.

Readers who approach Rom 1 as theological truth will sometimes confirm Paul's condemnation of same-sex relations by appealing to Lev 18:22: "You [masculine singular] shall not lie with a male as with a woman; it is an abomination" (see also Lev 20:13). This view continued in first-century Jewish circles. Philo writes, "Not only did they [the men of Sodom] go mad after women, and defile the marriage bed of others, but also those who were men lusted after one another" (*On Abraham* 26.133–37). He also condemns those "who, being accustomed to bearing the affliction of being treated like women, waste away as to both their souls and bodies, not bearing about them a single spark of a manly character to be kindled into a flame" (*Special Laws* 3.37–42).

Josephus declares: "That Law owns no other mixture of sexes but that which nature has appointed, of a man with his wife, and that this be used only for the procreation of children. But it abhors the mixture of a male with a male; and if anyone do that, death is its punishment" (*Against Apion* 2.25).

The view that same-sex relations are "naturally" aberrant finds some confirmation among Roman moralists. Juvenal, the first-century satirist, implores, "Father of our city, whence came such wickedness among your Latin shepherds? How did such a lust possess your grandchildren, O Gradivus? Behold! Here you have a man of high birth and wealth being handed over in marriage to a man" (*Satires* 2).

Others regarded such relations as "unnatural": first, they do not lead to procreation; second, it was regarded as shameful both for a man to be penetrated "like a woman" and for a woman to take the "man's role" (the Roman, male, moralists perceived lesbian sexuality to be mimicking).

Readers who take a contextual approach are likely to foreground the fact that the Roman world had a much different view of sexuality, gender, and human nature than we do today. Pederasty (sexual contact between an adult male and a non-adult male—usually between the ages of 14 and 17) was culturally sanctioned in the Gentile world. The younger man became the beneficiary of his partner's patronage through his gifts as well as his political and social influence. Prostitution and brothels were also legal in the Roman Empire; there men as well as women, often slaves, provided customers sexual services. Masters had the legal right to their slaves' bodies, both male and female, which included sexual use.

Finally, for the Roman world, men were to be dominant and active; women were to be subordinate and passive, because that was the "natural" order (see 1 Cor 11:2-16). Today, many would disagree with this configuration as being "natural." Across history, "nature" or "natural" is often used when the better term would be "cultural." For example, for generations it was considered "unnatural" for women to work in higher education or seek political office. Three generations ago, in the United States, elementary school teachers would sometimes insist that left-handed children write with their right hands, because to be left-handed was unnatural. First Corinthians 11:14 asks: "Does not nature itself teach you that if a man wears long hair, it is degrading to him?" Many people, having looked at lions and peacocks, would respond today, "No, it does not." Arguments based on "nature" thus need to be carefully analyzed to determine if they are based on science or on culture. Nor does "unnatural" then—or now—necessarily mean something wrong. It is not "natural" by most definitions today to operate on a fetus in the womb, and yet we typically praise the physician who thereby saves a life. In Rom 11:24, Paul explains that Gentiles receive membership in Israel by a manner "contrary to nature": "For if you have been cut from what is by nature a wild olive tree and grafted, contrary to nature [Greek: *para physin*], into a cultivated olive tree, how much more will these natural branches be grafted back into their own olive tree."

Paul can be understood as issuing a universal, timeless truth about same-sex relations, or as reflecting the values of his own culture. Readers can choose whether recent studies of sexuality, or the experiences of gay and lesbian individuals, should inform biblical interpretation. Essential in these discussions is to avoid demonizing those who hold either perspective. Essential as well is the consideration that this discussion is not merely an academic or even theological one: it is one that has implications for people's lives.

116

Romans 2–4 and
Jewish-Gentile Relations

In chapter 1, Paul explains that the Gentiles are alienated from God. Rather than recognizing God's presence in creation and in their own conscience, they chose to worship incorrectly and experience the consequences. The question Paul next addresses is why the Jews, who have the Law and the Prophets—and who have multiple covenants that God established with Abraham and Moses—are also in need of Christ's redemption.

The theological perspective begins with the concepts of God and sin. For Paul, both Jews and Gentiles require justification—that is, being in a "right relationship," with God/being reconciled with God—since "all, both Jews and Greeks, are under the power of sin" (3:9). He alludes to Ps 143:2 in his claim that "there is no one who is righteous," and, by implication, everyone requires reconciliation with God.

Paul then redefines "Jews" (Greek: *Ioudaioi*) not as people whose Torah obedience is attested in external markings, such as circumcision for males, or who are descended from Jewish parents, but as those who do "instinctively what the law requires" (2:14, suggesting their conscience is informing them), for "they show that what the law requires is written on their hearts" (2:15). Paul concludes that "a person is not a Jew who is one outwardly, nor is true circumcision something external and physical. Rather, a person is a Jew who is one inwardly, and real circumcision is a matter of the heart—it is spiritual and not literal" (2:28-29).

At this point, one might suspect that Paul has replaced the Jewish community with Jesus-followers in terms of being the heirs to Torah and covenant. This is not the case. Romans 3:1 begins with the rhetorical question, "Then what advantage has the Jew? Or what is the value of circumcision?" Instead of answering, "None at all," Paul insists, "Much in every way" (3:2). First, the Jews were entrusted with God's earlier teachings. Second, returning to his theological basis, Paul observes that even if some Jews are unfaithful to their part of the covenant, God will not be.

Third, Paul teaches that the "righteousness of God," which is evident in the Law and the Prophets, is now disclosed "through faith in Jesus Christ for all who believe" (3:22); therefore both Jews and Gentiles have the same access to reconciliation. As we further discuss in our analysis of Paul's Letter to the Galatians, the phrase "faith in Jesus Christ" is controverted. Literally, the Greek is a genitive, "faith of Jesus Christ." The grammatical construction could mean either "through faith directed toward or placed in Jesus" (where Jesus is the object) or "faith [fullness] expressed by Jesus" (where Jesus is the subject). Several factors promote the second view, known as the "subjective genitive" reading. For example, in 3:22 immediately after "through faith of Jesus Christ," Paul uses the phrase "for all who believe." If he meant "faith in or directed toward Jesus Christ," the reference to "all who believe" would be redundant: both phrases would refer to people putting faith in Jesus. But if the first phrase refers to Jesus' expression of the "righteousness of God," if Jesus' death expresses his faithfulness to God's saving purposes, then the second phrase provides the complement. It indicates that people participate in Jesus' faithfulness by also living faithfully.

Moreover, Paul explains that reconciliation occurs "through the redemption that is in Christ Jesus, whom God put forward as a sacrifice of atonement (Greek: *hilastērion*) by his blood" (3:24-25). The Greek term beneath the phrase "sacrifice of atonement" actually means "mercy seat" (so the NRSV translation of Heb 9:5). That is, Jesus displayed his own fidelity by going to the cross, and that fidelity elicits faith from his followers.

Sacrifice of Atonement

The word translated "sacrifice of atonement" (*hilastērion*) to denote Jesus' faithfulness in his crucifixion alludes to Lev 16 which describes ancient Israel's sacrificial system in relation to the Day of Atonement (Hebrew: *Yom haKippurim*; see Lev 23:27-28; 25:9). The same image of *hilastērion* or mercy seat appears in 4 Macc 17:21-22 (in the Apocrypha/deuterocanonical literature) to refer to the deaths of martyrs at the hands of the Seleucid tyrant Antiochus Epiphanes. Their spilled blood is said to have atoning properties.

Paul concludes in 3:29-30 by asserting the unity of Jews and Gentiles in the soteriological plan:

> Or is God the God of Jews only? Is he not the God of Gentiles also? Yes, of Gentiles also, since God is one; and he will justify the circumcised on the ground of faith and the uncircumcised through that same faith.

Justification (which we also discuss in more detail in the chapter on Galatians) is what God accomplishes for humanity; it is something "deeds prescribed by the law" (3:20) cannot do, and were never intended to do.

The theological reading emphasizes the universal human condition of alienation created by sin, understands sacrifice as an effective means of passing over sin, and regards faith—whether the faith Jesus shows in his actions or the faith people have in his atoning death or a combination of both (see discussion of "faith" pp. 174-75)—to be what facilitates justification. Yet this reading also typically takes a generally negative view of Torah and those who follow it. Traditionally, Paul gospel's of "faith in Jesus Christ" as the means of relationship with God has been seen as a contrast to and rejection of Jewish striving for or earning God's favor.

Scholarly work on what is called "a new perspective on Paul" has questioned this interpretation, and it no longer seems sustainable. In this new understanding, "works of the law" signifies actions that the law required as expressions of faithful living, not striving for something that God had already granted. Certain "works of the law" came to be seen as especially significant in marking Israel's covenant identity: circumcision, which indicated membership of the covenant (Gen 17:9-14); Sabbath observance, which honored the covenant relationship with God and distinguished Israel from the nations (Exod 20:8-11; 31:12-17); and dietary regulations (Lev 20:22-26), which were understood as both a distinguishing characteristic and a means of sanctification of the body. The "new perspective" argues that Paul's problem with "works of the law" lay not with their performance but with their significance as markers of identity and with the heightened emphasis on them as indicators of Israel's privileged place in God's purposes. Such "works" came to be seen, so the argument goes, as indicating Israel's *uniquely exclusive* place on God's favor. And, as Paul himself notes, following them can lead to "boasting" (Rom 2:17, 23, and elsewhere).

This use of the works of the law as identity markers, or badges, may have been a problem in the congregation Paul addresses in Romans. Thus, for some scholars, understanding the community to which Paul addresses his remarks helps us understand both what Paul is saying, and why. The problem here, as with all Paul's letters, is that we have only the letter itself to help in reconstructing the audience. Even more problematic, Paul addresses this letter to a church he neither founded nor visited. Thus his knowledge of its internal workings is at best secondhand.

Nevertheless, some clues in the letter, coupled with external data, allow us to posit a possible scenario concerning uniting Jewish and Gentile believers. Paul's much more positive view of these "works of the Law" in Romans compared to Galatians can be seen as resulting from the change in audience. In Galatians, Paul writes to a predominantly Gentile congregation. In Romans, perhaps addressed to a congregation consisting of both Jews and Gentiles, a different approach is needed.

The writings of Josephus and Philo as well as several references among Roman historians and satirists indicate that in the early first century C.E., there was a large Jewish population in Rome. In his *Lives of the Twelve Caesars,* the historian Suetonius (69–122) remarks: "As the Jews were making constant disturbances at the instigation of Chrestus, he expelled them from Rome" (*Life of Claudius,* 25.4). The year is circa 49, and the edict would be rescinded upon Claudius's death in 54. Acts 18:2 refers to this same event: "a Jew named Aquila, a native of Pontus, who had recently come from Italy with his wife Priscilla, because Claudius had ordered all Jews to leave Rome." "Chrestus" may be Suetonius's version of "Christ"; if so, the Roman historian may be suggesting that the proclamation of the crucified messiah created such tension within Rome's Jewish community that imperial action was needed. However, "Chrestus" can be a Greek name, and so Suetonius's reference could be to a local teacher. In either case, the expulsion suggests a possible scenario for the letter's emphasis on the unity of Jew and Gentile. Romans may be written within the context of a church, originally comprising mainly Jews, becoming almost entirely Gentile in 49, and, after 51, witnessing the return of the original members. This scenario also explains Rom 16, wherein Paul sends greetings to 26 people, including Prisca and Aquila. He may have met them while they were in exile from Rome.

If the church is divided between Jewish and Gentile members, or between those who celebrate the identity markers of "works of the law" and those who dismiss them, then Paul is offering a pastoral message emphasizing unity. He needs to emphasize that God's gracious purposes extend to all people. At the same, perhaps to protect the church's Jewish minority, he ensures that their covenantal claims are honored, not rejected.

Thus, in Rom 4, Paul appeals to Abraham, the "father of many nations" (4:17), as the model for both Jews and Gentiles. The "work" of circumcision is honored, but faith takes priority:

> He received the sign of circumcision as a seal of the righteousness that he had by faith while he was still uncircumcised. The purpose was to make him the ancestor of all who believe without being circumcised and who thus have righteousness reckoned to them. (4:11)

In 4:16 Paul refers to the "faith of Abraham." This phrase cannot mean "faith directed toward or placed in Abraham" because Paul emphasizes Abraham's obedience to God's promise. For Paul, then, "faith" is not passive inactivity, but lived faithfulness to God's faithful purposes (3:1-3). This is the same faithfulness to and obedience for God's purposes that Jesus exhibits. Paul demonstrates how faith and obedience connect when he begins by referring to his own commission to "bring about the obedience of faith among all the Gentiles" (1:5; also 16:26).

Romans 5–8: Adam, Sin, and the Groaning of Creation

For Paul, the opportunity Jews and Gentiles have for justification is anticipated by Abraham, and the reason they require such reconciliation, Paul explains, is the initial breach in the relationship between humanity and divinity that Adam's disobedience created in the garden of Eden. Paul says, "Yet death exercised dominion from Adam to Moses, even over those whose sins were not like the transgression of Adam, who is a type of the one who was to come" (5:14). Just as through "one man's trespass" sin entered the world (5:15), so "the free gift in the grace of one man, Jesus Christ, abounded for the many" (5:15). In 5:18, he reiterates:

Therefore just as one man's trespass led to condemnation for all, so one man's act of righteousness leads to justification and life for all.

Theologically, Paul's explanation requires that readers accept Gen 3 as historical: a real man in the garden of Eden ate forbidden fruit and, because of his disobedience, condemned the world to sin and death. Had Adam not sinned, then the sacrifice of Christ would have been unnecessary. This theological interpretation also follows from Paul's sense of Scripture: he reads the sacred texts of Israel as speaking to his own generation as well as offering eternal truths. Paul needs to show how Genesis speaks to his own time and to his own concerns about Jewish and Gentile unity. By appealing to Abraham and then Adam, Paul shows divine concern for all people, regardless of nationality or ethnicity. By positing that Adam is a "type" of Christ—by which he means a model or stamp, what we might think of as a "first draft"—he demonstrates the unity of the biblical story. Finally, Paul's appeals to Abraham and Adam move the discussion from a focus on Mosaic law and so from the division between Jews and Gentiles to creation and thus anticipate the division between humanity living in the sphere of Adam and humanity living in the sphere of Christ. The human condition is, for Paul, more central than distinct identity markers.

This theological view underlies some of the interest today in the more extreme forms of what is known as "creationism." The argument goes as follows: if Adam's sin did not plunge humanity into a broken relationship with God, and if death did not enter the world because of the events in Eden, then Christian claims about Christ's saving people from alienation, sin, and death can also be called into question. Bluntly put: if Adam is not the cause of sin and death, then Christ is not the remedy. Therefore, because the accounts of the garden of Eden in Gen 2 and 3 must be literally true, the theory of evolution cannot be. Other readers who regard the Genesis accounts as narrative reflections on the human condition may nevertheless regard the sacrifice of the Christ as having redemptory value. It effects the reconciliation of humanity and divinity presently separated by the sin of all people. It also displays the faith(fulness) of the Christ in enacting the divine purposes.

According to the letter, humanity, held in the power of sin and the reign of death, makes its transition into grace and life via the act of baptism, which Paul describes in Rom 6. For Paul, baptism does not just wash away the stain of sin. Nor is it simply an initiation symbolizing being "born again" as if the follower of Jesus emerges from the womb of the church. Baptism is a participation in the death of Jesus and an anticipation of his resurrection:

> Do you not know that all of us who have been baptized into Christ Jesus were baptized into his death? Therefore we have been buried with him by baptism into death, so that, just as Christ was raised from the dead by the glory of the Father, so we too might

walk in newness of life. For if we have been united with him in a death like his, we will certainly be united with him in a resurrection like his. We know that our old self was crucified with him so that the body of sin might be destroyed, and we might no longer be enslaved to sin. For whoever has died is freed from sin. (6:3-7)

Notable here are the verb tenses. "We were buried" employs a past tense; that is, the congregation died to sin. The realm of Adam, the sphere of sin and death, no longer has power over them. However, the clause "we will certainly be united with him in a resurrection like his" employs a future tense. The future is open; salvation is reserved for the future. The follower of Christ is "justified" but not yet "saved." For example, 5:9-10 states, "Now that we have been justified . . . we will be saved." This distinction will disappear in the Deutero-Pauline writings. Such delay in the granting of salvation allows Paul to insert his theological observations, and pastoral and ethical concerns. His teachings include how the person, now justified, is to act, to "walk in newness of life." The tenses also preclude the view that the followers of Jesus are "saved" in the present, a view that, as we shall see, some of the members of the churches in Corinth held. Salvation for Paul includes the transition from the physical body to the resurrected body; the perfection of the individual, the community, and the world has not yet happened. Unlike John's Gospel, which emphasizes a realized eschatology in which the judgments of salvation and damnation are already present, Paul, like the Synoptic Gospels, presents an eschatology that speaks of temptation and suffering in the present and rewards at the Parousia.

In Rom 7, Paul addresses the practical problems of living in the interim between baptism and salvation. Just because one is justified, temptation to sin remains active. Paul states in 7:15, "I do not understand my own actions, for I do not do what I want, but I do the very thing I hate." Biblical scholars have long puzzled over this line. Some suggest that Paul is not speaking of his present condition, but is speaking in the voice of Adam, since the narrator also states "I was once alive apart from the law" (7:9). Adam, who has already been mentioned in Rom 5, lived prior to the time when the Torah was given on Mount Sinai. The idea is possible but unlikely, since the earlier part of the chapter leaves Eden and returns to the role of the Law in pointing out sin. Others suggest that Paul is speaking of his own self-perception prior to his Damascus Road experience. The idea, popular in some theological circles, that Paul was neurotically unable to fulfill all the commandments and then had a psychological break on the Damascus Road, is modern myth, not biblical history. It runs counter to everything Paul tells us about himself. In all other places Paul speaks to his robust faith in Jewish practice (see Phil 3:4-6, "If anyone else has reason to be confident in the flesh, I have more . . . as to righteousness under the law, blameless").

Most likely, Paul's first-person agony, speaking in the present tense, is meant to reflect the struggles of humanity still caught between the realms of Adam and Christ. Paul, the pastor, understands that life on earth still remains a cosmic battleground between sin and grace, death and life. Sin is both part of the general human situation and a human responsibility. It is a "transgression" or an infringing (5:14) of God's command. In 5:15-20 Paul refers to "trespass," suggesting the breaking of a relationship; in 5:19 sin is an act of disobedience; in 7:7-13, sin works through the law to stir up misdirected desire. It is through divine grace, manifested in the faith of and sacrifice of Christ, that humanity escapes the prison of sin.

In Rom 8:15 Paul employs a legal metaphor, "adoption," to denote transfer of status from alienation to justification, Adam to Christ, the slavery of sin to freedom in Christ. Adoption was a process often used whereby slaves or orphans were adopted as the heirs of a master. For Paul, God frees people from the slavery of sin and "adopts" them into a new relationship. To be a child of God is to be an heir with Christ in inheriting or participating in the completion of God's good purposes (8:17).

This participation is not, however, restricted only to humans; it has a cosmic dimension, for creation has also been caught up in the power of sin (8:19-22; see Gen 3:17). Instead of being that which reveals God (1:20), creation has become the object of human worship. For Paul, both humans and creation fail to live out their God-given identity. A fundamental solidarity exists between human beings and creation under the power of sin, and that power still has effect. On the one hand, "the law of the Spirit of life in Christ Jesus has set you free from the law of sin and of death" (8:2); on the other, humanity and creation both still groan for the complete freedom that comes with the full in-breaking of God's kingdom:

> For the creation waits with eager longing for the revealing of the children of God; for the creation was subjected to futility, not of its own will but by the will of the one who subjected it, in hope that the creation itself will be set free from its bondage to decay and will obtain the freedom of the glory of the children of God. We know that the whole creation has been groaning in labor pains until now. (8:19-21)

Christians who understand ecological degradation—the groaning of the earth—to be the result of human sin might determine that just as humanity set free from sin's power still needs to fight its temptations, so humanity might help the earth in recovering from the effects of human sin. Others, convinced that those "labor pains" are about to end by the imminent in-breaking of God's kingdom, or adopting a predestinarian view that suggests that global destruction is part of the divine plan, or taking literally the idea that there will be a "new heaven and a new earth" (Rev 21:1), may have less concern about environmental protection.

Romans 9–11, Reconciling Jews and Gentiles

In the next three chapters, Paul returns to the question of the Jews. He has several reasons for doing so. First is a personal concern, for they are his "kindred according to the flesh" (9:3). That is, he and they are members of the same people, what we today would call an "ethnic group." Second, returning to a point he made in Rom 3, they are the recipients of God's grace and so they have the "adoption, the glory, the covenants, the giving of the law, the worship, and the promises" (9:4). All these gifts are valuable, although all also for Paul are secondary to the Christ. Third, he realizes their priority in receiving the divine word and responding to it, given the phrase "to the Jew first and also to the Greek" (1:16; see also 2:9-10). Thus Paul needs to address the implications of this priority for God's soteriological plan. Fourth, because he insists on divine fidelity, he must insist that this fidelity includes Israel.

In assessing Paul's view of these kindred, readers may be misled by the NRSV's translation of Rom 11:28-29:

> As regards the gospel they are enemies of God for your sake; but as regards election they are beloved, for the sake of their ancestors; for the gifts and the calling of God are irrevocable.

The Greek, however, says nothing about being enemies "of God"; the words "of God" are the NRSV editors' insertion. Rather, Paul suggests that the Jews are presently enemies of, that is, opposed to, the gospel. They have not at present accepted the "good news" of Jesus. The term translated "enemies" is actually an adjective, and it may be translated "hostile" or even, to use a neologism, "enemied." Paul therefore may be saying that they have been made hostile to the gospel *for the sake of the Gentiles*. In this interpretation, it is the initial Jewish "no" to the gospel that prompted the message to go to the Gentiles. Paul will later explain that the Gentile "yes" in turn will have salvific import for the Jewish majority that refused the initial call.

Finally, Paul repeats his theme of God's covenantal fidelity. To the question, "Has the word of God failed?" (9:6) he answers with a resounding "By no means." Paul then needs to explain why the vast majority of Jews have not accepted the proclamation of Jesus as Lord. As he does in Galatians, he piles up proof-texts from the Septuagint to make his various arguments.

First, he claims that the true heirs of Abraham are those who accept the lordship of Christ. Thus because "not all Israelites truly belong to Israel" (9:6), God's promises to Abraham have not failed. Second, he claims that divine election proceeds not according to caprice, but according to mercy, "So then he has mercy on whomever he chooses, and he hardens the heart of whomever he chooses" (9:18). Third, using the analogy of the olive tree, he describes how the natural branches (that is, Jews) were broken off of the root of Israel *so that* the Gentiles could be grafted on "contrary to nature" (11:24). Yet he holds out the assurance that these natural branches will be grafted back on. How this happens he describes as a "mystery" (11:25).

In Paul's soteriological program, "a hardening has come upon part of Israel until the full number of the Gentiles has come in" (11:25). It is through Israel's rejection of the message, their "stumbling" or hostility to the gospel, that "salvation has come to the Gentiles." According to Paul, the Gentile reception of God's mercy—with its attendant worship of the God of Israel—will "make Israel jealous" (11:11, 14). The Jewish refusal of the gospel resulted in the preaching of Christ to the Gentiles. The Gentile acceptance will ultimately prompt the salvation of the Jews. As Paul finally proclaims, "so all Israel will be saved" (11:26). Paul explains this "mystery" (11:25) as divine will, beyond human comprehension but providing hope nonetheless:

> O the depths of the riches and wisdom and knowledge of God! How unsearchable are his judgments and how inscrutable his ways! For who has known the mind of the Lord, or who has been his counselor? (11:33-34)

Sociological prompts along with a theological program may have influenced Paul's presentation. If the Roman church is strained by a new Gentile majority that regards the Jews as holding on to outdated practices, or punished by God through their banishment from Rome and now minority status, or as representative of a people who, for the most part, refuse to accept Jesus as Lord and so are doomed, then Paul does well to promote positive views toward his fellow Jews. By intimating that the majority of Jews, who have rejected the proclamation of the church, do so as part of a divine plan, Paul lessens the possible condemnation members of the church might have of these Jewish neighbors. The point may also lessen conversionary efforts, which may have prompted the expulsion of the Jews from Rome and which were likely to have created tension between Jewish followers of Jesus and their non-messianic counterparts in local synagogues. That Paul notes frequently that the Gentiles should not boast in their justification (for example, 11:18) suggests concern for community relations.

Paul's insistence on divine covenantal fidelity to "Israel according to the flesh" has led to various mutually exclusive understandings of Rom 9–11. For some readers, Paul promotes the idea of two covenants: one with the Jews and one with the Gentile nations. Thus, the Jews will be saved because of God's fidelity to the covenant and the Gentiles by the sacrifice of Christ. The problem with this argument is that it takes away the universal implications of the cross and Paul's understanding of Adam's disobedience. For some, all are saved by Christ's sacrifice, but Jews are not to be evangelized because their present hardness is a result of God's mysterious action. For some, the promises of Israel pass over to the followers of Jesus and the Jews, because of their infidelity to Christ as well as their insistence on continuing to follow Torah, are disinherited; this view is called "supersessionism" or "replacement theology." For others, the promises to "Israel according to the flesh" remain since the divine promises are "irrevocable." And for yet another group, these promises include the land of Israel, and thus their understanding of Romans has deep implications not only for Jewish-Christian relations and evangelism but also Middle Eastern politics. All these concerns bear more discussion than these pages can contain; that is, of course, the case for each verse of the New Testament.

Romans 13: Obedience to the Governing Authorities

Romans 12–15 move to practical issues: How is the follower of Jesus to live in a world where redemption is incomplete, and where Rome holds political power? In 13:1, Paul begins, "Let every person be subject to the governing authorities; for there is no authority except from God, and those authorities that exist have been instituted by God." Here begin major exegetical debates.

The predominant theological reading has been that Paul, writing to a congregation at the heart of the empire, mandates compliance with the empire. Yet readers who take Romans as a summation of Paul's views, not dependent on the situation of the audience, also wrestle with this mandate. Some, recognizing that empires are often unjust, read the exhortation in light of Paul's call to love (Greek: *agapē*) in 13:8, "Owe no one anything, except to love one another; for the one who loves another has fulfilled the law." Others limit Paul's pronouncement to good rulers, for Paul classifies the ruler as "the servant of God to exercise his wrath on the wrongdoer" (13:4), or see Paul as speaking pragmatically only about tax payment (13:7): pay your taxes and avoid persecution so that you can live to proclaim the gospel. Still others suggest that Paul is not speaking of Roman rulers at all, but of synagogue rulers, and that taxes and tribute refer to the half-shekel Temple tax as well as local support for upkeep of the institution. Yet others recognize that the canon has various views of governing authorities, with Revelation describing the Roman system as a "great whore." And still another set of readers understand Paul's comments within an eschatological context: be obedient to the government now, no matter how unjust, for this system is about to end: "the night is far gone, the day is near" (13:12).

Putting Paul into conversation with Jesus does not resolve the problem, since Jesus' own view of Roman rule is ambivalent. When Jesus states, "Give to the emperor the things that are the emperor's, and to God the things that are God's" (Mark 12:17) he does not actually answer his opponents' question about whether they should pay taxes to Caesar. The question is meant to trap Jesus, and he turns the trap back on the interlocutors: give to Caesar what you think Caesar deserves. Paul does not quote Jesus on paying taxes, although he does echo several ideas found in the gospel tradition. For example, Rom 12:14 relates to Matt 5:44//Luke 6:27-28 in the concern for blessing those who persecute. Romans 12:17, 21 (cf. 1 Thess 5:15) resembles Luke 6:27-36//Matt 5:38-48 in insisting that evil cannot repay evil. Romans 14:14 sounds much like Mark 7:15 in insisting that nothing is unclean. Like Jesus, Paul understands the kingdom to be present and future; there is a "now" and "not yet" about God's reign. Paul awaits its eschatological establishment in full when Jesus returns.

Whether Paul is compliant with the Roman system, resistant to it, or caught in between as is often the case with the colonial subject, he ultimately promotes the rule of Christ over the rule of Caesar. Roman propaganda made much of the empire's divinely given mission to establish justice and law and order throughout the world. Rome is to "rule the nations . . . and crown peace with law" (Virgil, *Aeneid* 6.851–53). But the justice resulting from Roman rule is primarily punitive; it is based on intimidating submission and punishing those who transgress Roman policy. Divine rule, in Paul's view, is based in mercy and love, and therefore Jesus' followers should base their lives on these virtues.

Romans 14–15: Factionalism

In chapters 14 and 15, Paul speaks to the question of factionalism in the Roman church. He describes the weak as those who eat only vegetables and who observe fast days, and the strong as omnivorous and resisting ascetic practice. Typically, the weak have been understood as Jews within the community who, because they do not have access to kosher meat, limit their diet; they observe the fast days (for example, the Day of Atonement) that Torah prescribes. However, given Paul's promotion of Jewish concerns and his interest in preventing the Gentiles from "boasting" in their justification, the label of this Jewish practice as "weak" is at best inconsistent. The problem may be one of Jewish-Gentile relations, but it could also be one of internal Christian practice unrelated to ethnic or cultural concerns. Some followers of Jesus did fast (see, for example, Matt 6:16-17, "And whenever you fast, do not look dismal, like the hypocrites, for they disfigure their faces so as to show others . . . But when you fast, put oil on your head and wash your face"). The concern could also be an internal one about avoiding meat offered to idols (see 1 Cor 8–10), which was the major way people obtained meat in urban areas.

The conflict is destructive, marked by despising and judging (14:3, 10, 13). The various terms concerning "judging" denote not just negative opinion, but the calling down of eschatological judgment. The strong are in effect telling the weak to "go to hell."

Paul resolves the problem, or at least seeks to, in 15:7, not by condemning or promoting fasting, but by stressing hospitality: "Welcome one another, therefore, just as Christ has welcomed you." The rest of the paraenesis or exhortation in these chapters supports this conclusion. In 12:5, echoing 1 Cor 12, Paul speaks of the community as one body comprised of many members, all interrelated. Each member has "gifts that differ according to the grace given" to them (12:6), with gifts including not only ministering and teaching, but also compassion and cheerfulness.

Romans 15: The Collection

At the end of the letter, Paul elaborates his plans. He plans to evangelize Spain after his visit to Rome (15:24, 28), and he intimates that he wants the Roman community's financial support for the mission. But before going to Spain, Paul plans another trip. He is going to Jerusalem with a collection of funds from his churches in Achaia and Macedonia to give to the "poor," the followers of Jesus in Jerusalem (15:25-27). This is a gift from Gentile churches to their Jewish brothers and sisters (15:25-32). Paul apparently wants the Roman church to use its influence in encouraging the Jerusalem church to receive the collection (15:30-32). Were they to do so, they would indicate their recognition of his Gentile converts. The extent to which Paul's statements throughout the letter are rhetorically designed to gain the Roman congregation's support, and the extent to which they are simply summaries of Paul's theological views, will remain a subject for debate.

It is not clear that the collection was received: the NT offers no record of its reception. Nor does the NT depict Paul's evangelizing of Spain. Romans thus ends with an unfinished story, with Paul's legacy to be carried on through his preserved and edited letters, through Acts, and through letters written in his name and legends told about him.

1 Corinthians

If they ever heard Paul, many residents of the cities of the Roman Empire would have found his message strange, if not absurd. As he says:

We proclaim Christ crucified, a stumbling block to Jews and foolishness to Gentiles. (1 Cor 1:23)

The term "stumbling block" (Greek: *skandalon*, "scandal") is appropriate. Despite diverse Jewish views concerning the Messiah's identity and tasks, death on a cross was not expected; a final judgment, peace on earth, and the ingathering of Jews forced into exile were. "Foolishness" (Greek: *mōrian*, "moronic") is also appropriate. Many Greeks (Gentiles) would have ridiculed the idea of a crucified Jewish carpenter as savior of the world. Yet, for Paul, and those who accepted his teaching, this scandalous, foolish message was "good news," gospel.

For Paul and his followers, questions of their relationship to the broader society inevitably arose. They sought to convince others of their claims, and yet they knew how foolish the message seemed. They sought to preserve their teachings and the practices they shaped, yet they lived as a suspect minority in the Roman Empire. Their lives were thus necessarily forms of negotiation—establishing social and confessional boundaries yet securing work and food, redefining relations with natal and marital families, and determining how much to participate in and/or distance themselves from their wider society. These issues of how much and in what ways the church should be in the world, and its corollary question, how much and in what ways the world should be in the church, drive the discussion in 1 Corinthians.

Rather than engage these issues with an abstract theological treatise, Paul addresses them specifically and contingently. In order to understand the questions the Corinthians posed to Paul in their letters to him, and Paul's instructions to them in response, we investigate the cultural assumptions operative in this urban Roman setting, which are different from our own. Therefore, in this chapter, we employ social-science criticism, an approach that arose out of historical-critical work, to identify some of the systems that the letter assumes and engages.

Social-Scientific Criticism

Paul's language of "scandal" and "folly" fits within a broader form of social discourse that scholars today call "honor/shame." Honor refers to the public recognition of a person's conformity to and embodying of society's central values. Shame denotes the verdict on a person's lack of conformity. Honor and shame were either attained or ascribed. Honor was ascribed based on one's family, ethnicity, or status. Honor is not self-ascribed; it is not the same as "self-esteem." It is attained through the approval of others and continually refreshed through a complex of culturally acceptable behaviors, commitments, and attitudes understood to protect and enhance the public good. Shame or disgrace comes from public disapproval for failing to adhere to those values.

A second cultural code concerning participation in the broader society is in play in 1 Corinthians. *Patron-client relationships* constituted much of Roman social interaction. In the dominant worldview of the empire, the gods chose and blessed the emperor who ensured honor was returned to the gods. In turn, emperors blessed elite associates and provincial cities with various material and personal benefits, like gifts of land and cash, appointments, and political access. Elites and cities reciprocated these honors in various ways, such as providing temples and statues of the emperor in their cities and staging festivals with games, meals, and processions to honor him. In turn, elites blessed lower-status clients or subordinates with benefits such as gifts of material goods, employment, political appointments, and connections within a system that today we would call "networking." These clients were both obligated to return honor to their patrons, as well as to benefit their own clients beneath them. Patron-client relationships formed through household connections, voluntary and funerary associations, trade guilds, and around law courts. One patronage ritual comprised the morning *salutatio* in which clients—the more the better—appeared at the elite person's house to honor him or her and attend to any matters that furthered his interests and reputation (honor). The relationship, which could be exploitative, was often a part of what society considered "friendship" interactions. For a modern, though somewhat imprecise, analogy of how this "friendship" worked between patrons and clients, we might consider the relationship between contractors and employees, or homeowners and domestic workers.

Elites and patrons competed with each other to exercise influence and gain honor. This competitive quest for social status constituted an *agonistic society*. In what might be considered society's zero-sum game, the honor gained by one member of the elite represented the loss of honor to another. Thus, competition for honor drove elite economics. One major form of elite competition involved civic benefactions or euergetism (good works), such as building fountains, sponsoring games, functioning as a priest or priestess of the imperial cult, supplying food handouts. The more clients such benefactions produced, the higher the patron's honor and status.

Although reinforcing societal hierarchies, this system did give subordinates some leverage. All patrons need clients to mark their status, to sing their praises, and to support their causes. And clients benefited from the patronage.

Social-scientific criticism therefore identifies first-century cultural practices and social codes assumed by and evident in NT writings. This approach reminds us of the vastly different presuppositions and structures of first-century life. It also helps us here to understand how Jesus-believers negotiated their dominant culture.

Negotiations around the concepts of honor and shame and around patron-client structures offer insight into ways in which the church defined itself. Like the Cynics, another group that challenged cultural conventions concerning honor and patronage by refusing both, Paul and his churches redefined social codes. Paul plays down the ascribed and attained markers of honor, such as noble birth, wealth, education, and rhetorical skill, to emphasize commitment to a crucified Lord and the divine preference for the weak, the foolish, and the powerless (1:18-30). Similarly, he attempts to avoid the patronage system by insisting on his independence from the financial support of wealthy church members.

Social-scientific criticism often constructs models to map social realities at work in diverse social conditions and apply them cross-culturally. We should, however, not be misled by the term "scientific," which suggests objective inquiry and replicated results; that is not the case with any method of biblical interpretation. Precision is elusive in discussing human interactions and societies, especially across cultures and time periods. Deriving models from twentieth-century field work—in the Andalusian hills or among Bedouin populations—and applying them to the ancient world without utilizing ancient sources and without taking into consideration particularities based on the cultural ethos, political situation, geography, weather, and so on, would not only incorrectly assume that cultures remain unchanged, but would also threaten to impose an anachronistic essentialist view of "the other" onto New Testament texts and the societies they disclose. Models of society or social interactions can at best be a heuristic, that is, a general, guide.

Thus, in this chapter, we cautiously employ the social-science heuristics of honor/shame and patron/client relationships to understand the "what?" and "how?" of the problems among the Corinthian believers and Paul's responses to them. Granting the distinctions between first-century Corinth and our twenty-first-century readers, we address the question along the way of "and now?" If Paul's teachings in 1 Corinthians engage cultural values no longer operative today, to what extent are these teachings relevant for contemporary Christians?

Paul's Contingent Address

First Corinthians opens with a letter's standard elements (1:1-9). Paul uses this common literary form but adapts it by introducing issues important for the specific occasion of the audience. For example, he defines himself by asserting his apostolic identity: "called to be an apostle of Christ Jesus by the will of God" (1:1). This introduction identifies him in relation to Jesus and God and thereby secures his own honorable position. Paul's opening therefore challenges his readers: Were the Corinthians to reject Paul, they would also be rejecting God's will. Paul's claim to be the authoritative voice in the community, though, is contested by competing voices. The Corinthians, it seems, have divided into factions around various teachers:

> Each of you says, "I belong to Paul," or "I belong to Apollos," or "I belong to Cephas," or "I belong to Christ." (1:12)

Paul's assertion of his divine commissioning and attendant authority and honor seeks to unite this fractured church.

Paul greets the Corinthians as "sanctified in Christ Jesus" (Greek: *hagiadzō*, literally, "made holy" [1:2]). The notion of "sanctified" or "made holy" denotes their being set apart for divine service. He thereby constructs for them a special or honorable identity. Were they to fail to behave in this "set apart" manner, they would be dishonored and would dishonor the God who called them.

The thanksgiving section (1:4-9) reminds them of their eschatological accountability as well as of God's faithfulness to them (1:7-9). Paul here prepares the Corinthians for the critique to follow. He seems to commend them in giving thanks "for in every way you have been enriched in him, in speech and knowledge of every kind" (1:5). Yet his sarcasm will become evident when he counters those who promote speaking in tongues (glossolalia) as a major spiritual gift, and who promote "knowledge" (Greek: *gnōsis*) over faith (chs. 12–14). Because Paul's letters were read aloud to the congregation, the reader may well have signaled through vocal inflection Paul's dismay if not disgust with the congregational members who promoted *gnōsis* and its presumed honor over faith and community solidarity.

That the congregation has "divisions among you" (1:10) is in part explicable by the church's context. Corinth, largely destroyed in 146 B.C.E. in a war with Rome, was rebuilt as a Roman colony in 44 B.C.E. It was the provincial capital of Achaia, an area of modern-day Greece, and an important trade center. Situated approximately 40 miles south of Athens with the port of Cenchreae about 6 miles to the east, its population included sizable groups from Asia Minor, Syria, Judea, and Egypt, veterans of the Roman army, migrant workers, artisans, and merchants. The slave population may have been as high as 30 percent.

Another substantial part of the population comprised manumitted slaves (*liberti*), many of whom retained relations with their former masters in a patron-client relationship. Inscriptions identify freedmen called the *Augustales* who expressed loyalty to the emperor with monuments, statues, and inscriptions. Other inscriptions indicate that several times in the mid-40s to mid-50s—the time of Paul's writing—elite figures were appointed *curator annonae* ("guardian of the grain supply") to purchase (with their own money and that of other elites) extra grain for the city during famines. With this form of benefaction, the elites gained honor for themselves even as they both provided service for and pacified the population.

The city's political organization consisted of a lawmaking council including *aediles*, who oversaw markets, public buildings, roads, and finances; *duoviri* (judges); and *agonothetes* (in charge of the Isthmian games, regional competitions named after the isthmus of Corinth). This structure was oligarchic and hierarchical, agonistic, and closed to most except elites who used patronage structures of wealth, family connections, and benefactions to secure their base among clients. Inscriptions show that this elite group, perhaps 2 to 3 percent of the population, remained relatively stable over the first centuries B.C.E. and C.E.

Most Corinthians lived just above or around subsistence level, with perhaps some 25 to 30 percent below that. Most lived in *insulae*: multistoried tenement buildings with shops and workshops on the ground floor and cramped living space above. Sewage disposal, disease, fire risk, violent and petty crime, overcrowding, and periodic food shortages made urban life dangerous. Death rates for newborns and young children may have been as high as 50 percent.

Religiously, Corinth was very diverse. Temples to various gods were pervasive and prominent. Most popular, at least in terms of architectural remains, were Roman gods, especially Aphrodite/Venus and Poseidon/Neptune (god of the sea), the latter crucial for Corinth's mercantile economy. Other gods worshiped included Apollo, Asclepius, Jupiter Capitolinus (the god who oversaw the Roman Empire), Ephesian Artemis, and Isis and Serapis from Egypt. Worship of the emperor (the Roman imperial cult) was observed with elites often taking the role of priest or priestess, sponsoring observances, and funding temples, sacrifices, feasts, and games. Thus Paul, and the Jesus-followers to whom he wrote, had to negotiate a multicultural city replete with competing religious opportunities, extensive social networks, poverty, and various social ills.

The Corinthian church reflected this social diversity as well as this religious competition. Some were Jews or possibly Samaritans (9:20; 12:13). Some others, Gentiles by birth, appear to have wanted to become circumcised. Paul cautions, given his own eschatological orientation,

Was anyone at the time of his call already circumcised? Let him not seek to remove the marks of circumcision. Was anyone at the time of his call uncircumcised? Let him not seek circumcision. (7:18)

Most were "Greeks," that is, Gentiles (1:24), whose religious expressions included honoring idols (8:1-13; 12:2). Some have Greek names (Chloe, 1:11 [assuming she is a member of the church and not just the owner or patron of several members]; Stephanas, 1:16; 16:15); others have Roman names (Crispus and Gaius, 1:14; Fortunatus and Achaicus, 16:17). Some of these individuals may have been Jews, for Jews then, as now, took names that were popular in the dominant culture.

Socially, most church members were nonelite (1:26), poor (11:22), and slaves (7:21-22). A few had some resources (1:26), including Crispus (1:14, identified in Acts 18:8 as a former "head or ruler of the synagogue"), Stephanas (16:17), those involved in court actions (6:1), likely Chloe, and the unnamed man having sexual relations with his father's wife (5:1). These individuals, with resources but not clear status, may have sought to promote themselves in the church. Becoming a benefactor of a group was a means of gaining honor and so social status, just as it is today. Paul explains that the normal ways of gaining honor and status—benefactions through patronage—are not to be the way the church works. He attempts to unite this diverse group by insisting both on their relation to him as apostle and parent (patron) and that they recognize their unity: "in the one Spirit we were all baptized into one body—Jews or Greeks, slaves or free—and we were all made to drink of one Spirit" (12:13). By declaring himself the "father" of the congregation (4:14-16), Paul uses kinship language to establish his authority as their patron and founder. Social-science studies emphasize the importance of family values in antiquity. Honoring one's parents was not only a commandment in Judaism (for example, Exod 20:12); it was also a moral virtue in Roman culture. Thus, Paul's kinship language indicates the Corinthians' obligations to be loyal to him.

The Corinthian Church in Social Context

After establishing the church in Corinth, Paul wrote a letter to the congregation, which he mentions in 5:9-11. In it, he advised his new converts "not to associate with sexually immoral persons"; apparently some recipients thought he meant people outside the church. But Paul does not separate church members from their external friends, patrons and clients, or relations. Throughout 1 Corinthians, he recognizes these relationships (5:11-13; 7:12-16; 10:27-29). Instead, Paul advises disassociation from sexually immoral or greedy church members. "Do not even eat with such a one" (5:11). Thereby, Paul encourages congregants to shame members of the church who are not behaving in a manner Paul finds to be morally upright, or honorable.

The Corinthians responded to Paul's letter with visits from "Chloe's people" (1:11; perhaps 5:1) and from Stephanas, Fortunatus, and Achaicus (16:17-18). Some congregants, though precisely who is not specified, have also written to him with questions (7:1). Somewhere in this sequence, Paul sent his coworker Timothy to visit the Corinthians. Although he was acting on Paul's behalf, Timothy was ill received by some of the congregation, much to Paul's disappointment (4:17-18). By dismissing Timothy, they dismissed

Paul. Conversely, some Corinthian church members apparently welcomed Apollos, another missionary (1:12), who had contact with Paul (16:12; see also Acts 18:24–19:1). These comings and goings form the context for writing what we know as 1 Corinthians, dated probably in the mid-50s.

As with all of Paul's letters, we lack surety in reconstructing the particular concerns of the recipients. We do not know what exactly was reported to Paul, or whether the information was accurate or complete. We do not know the extent to which Paul has reinterpreted the information he received. Several times he refers to what he has been told (7:1), "Now concerning the matters about which you wrote . . ." The same "now concerning" phrase introduces topics at 8:1; 12:1; 16:1. From these details, we can tentatively reconstruct three specific Corinthian issues: factionalism and internal community relations, sexual ethics, and relations with people outside the church. Each topic is informed by categories social-science criticism investigates: honor and shame, patron/ client relations, group dynamics. And each topic finds its corollaries in contemporary church discussions over sexual behavior and the church's relationship to broader society on subjects ranging from public education to home schooling, gender roles, and participation in political and economic systems.

Factionalism and Community Relations

Factionalism in the Corinthian community takes several forms: people appeal to their own leaders or teachers; socioeconomic issues divide rich and poor; and different christological and eschatological views and related practices impact how members view their bodies and each other. Thus personal relations, economics, and theology combine to create not unity but discord.

Despite the factions, the church has not yet splintered. They still gather as one group:

> When you come together as a church, I hear that there are divisions among you; and to some extent I believe it. (11:18)

Paul's pastoral concern is to prevent the community from breaking further apart and to bring it into unity:

> Be in agreement and that there be no divisions among you, but that you be united in the same mind and the same purpose. For it has been reported to me by Chloe's people that there are quarrels among you, my brothers. (1:10-13a; see also 3:2-9)

Thus one form of division seems to be based on rival teachers, authorities, or patrons.

What Are They Fighting About?

Paul says one group has allegiance to Cephas. This name is the Greek transliteration of the Aramaic word *kēpha*, meaning "rock." The translation is "Peter." It is possible this Petrine group promoted adherence to Torah, such as dietary regulations (see Gal 2). Apollos is Paul's coworker in Corinth: "I planted, Apollos watered, but God gave the growth" (3:6). If Acts is helpful, perhaps Apollos from Alexandria took a more allegorical approach to Scripture, or a more text-critical one, than did Paul. Allegory and text-criticism were both major forms of literary interpretation in Alexandria, known not only from the writings of the Jewish philosopher Philo, but also from contemporaneous criticisms of Homer. In Acts, Luke makes it clear that Apollos had a faulty gospel and required instruction from Paul's friends, Priscilla and Aquila. Perhaps Luke is responding to ongoing divisions in the Corinthian church and wants to secure Paul's legitimacy for the late first- and early second-century churches. The Christ party might have stressed personal revelation or a greater eschatological orientation.

A pristine church in which everyone agreed fully with each other (as Acts 1–4 present) never existed. Congregants in Thessalonica disagreed on eschatological issues. In Galatia they disagreed on the extent to which Torah should inform practice. The Gospels present different Christologies. First Peter and Revelation disagree on how Jesus-believers might negotiate Roman power. The NT, like the Scriptures of Israel, offers different views and at the same time, stresses internal relations marked by love.

In addition to appeals to different authorities or patrons, the Corinthian church's factionalism includes a socioeconomic divide. Paul addresses abuses that occur during the celebration of the "Lord's Supper," the fellowship meal that should have united the congregation (11:23-34): Some wealthier members imitate the meal practices of the broader society by displaying their greater wealth and status with plentiful food while not caring that the low-status members go hungry. The practice replicates the socioeconomic inequities of Corinthian society. Paul harshly expresses his disdain for such practices: "Do you show contempt for the church of God and humiliate those who have nothing?" (11:22).

The meal should promote not status-based divisions, but concern for one another (11:33), recollect the "new covenant," and "proclaim the Lord's death until he comes" (11:26).

In his effort to heal the factionalism, Paul questions the typical form of patronage that governed social relations in Corinth and offers an alternative. In 1 Cor 9, he presents himself as one who, by virtue of his apostolic role, is entitled to the church's financial support. However, by not accepting support from any potential patron in the church, Paul retains his independence. He can establish equal relations with all in the community. Instead of taking their money to finance his own mission, he encourages the Corinthians to contribute funds for the collection he will bring to the Jerusalem church (16:1-2).

A second place where division occurs in worship concerns "spiritual gifts" (Greek: *charismata*; see 12:1-8), such as prophecy, healing, miracle working, and glossolalia. Rather than rank the gifts as some seem to be doing, Paul insists that all gifts come from the same Spirit and exist for the common good. Paul spends much of 12:12-26 using the analogy of the human body to underline the diversity, interdependence, and equal importance of every member of the body. In chapter 14 he emphasizes that prophecy is more beneficial than glossolalia because it builds up the group (14:3, 12, 26).

Anchoring these discussions is Paul's emphasis on love (ch. 13), to which all other spiritual gifts are subordinate. His emphases on diversity, not superiority; on the common good, not individualistic glory; on love, not self-serving benefit; on the Spirit's workings among all, preclude the use of worship as an opportunity to demonstrate or enhance anyone's status.

Some social-science readings posit a correlation between economic status and theological assertions, with those in Corinth who have greater resources more likely to stress spiritual exaltation. Those who are rich, in this construct, regard themselves as more spiritually aware, and "wiser," than other congregants. Certain members seem to think that they already share the fullness of God's reign. Believing they have completely experienced the eschatological benefits of salvation now in the present and disregarding future divine purposes, they boast in this knowledge.

Paul's disdain for this extreme view of realized eschatology is clear, and his invective connects the markers of wealth with incorrect theology:

> Already you have all you want! Already you have become rich! Quite apart from us you have become kings! Indeed, I wish that you had become kings, so that we might be kings with you! . . . We are fools for the sake of Christ, but you are wise in Christ. We are weak, but you are strong. You are held in honor, but we in disrepute. (4:8, 10)

His complaint is not simply that these congregants dismiss and dishonor him. Paul is also concerned that their eschatological views lead to sinful behaviors that dishonor the church. Some who believed they have experienced full eschatological blessing also believed, if Paul has correctly presented their view, that they are already resurrected and so free from bodily constraints. They have taken Paul's teaching that to be in Christ does not require adherence to Israel's markers and concluded that "all things are lawful" (6:12; 10:23). Hence, they believe they can, with impunity, practice behaviors that Paul judges to be sinful, such as having sexual relations with a stepparent (5:1-13), visiting prostitutes, and having other extramarital affairs (6:9). Paul affirms the importance of bodies in God's eschatological purposes in chapter 15.

Worse yet, others among the congregation tolerate these behaviors. The church's failure to rebuke the man living with his father's wife may suggest he has some status in the congregation as a patron. These elite members further display a pride that excuses sin and alienates others. Paul complains they have become "arrogant" (Greek: *physioō*, literally, "puffed up") in not removing the man "living with his father's wife" (5:1) just as they have become arrogant against one another (4:6), and against Paul (4:18-19). They are arrogant in their knowledge about idols (8:1) and so by eating food offered to idols risk misleading weaker members of the congregation to think that worship of the gods is permissible. In Paul's view, they do not love because "arrogance" is not part of love (13:4).

Trying to correct these attitudes, Paul seeks to replace factionalism with a concern for mutual good. His approach consists not of erasing differences but emphasizing that all need to work together to build up the body of Christ. He affirms the view that "all things are lawful"—there is, for example, nothing inherently wrong in eating food offered to idols in pagan temples—but he immediately observes, "not all things are beneficial" (6:12; 10:23). In acknowledging all *charismata*—apostles, prophets, teachers, miracle workers, healers, helpers, administrators, speakers in tongues (12:27-28)—Paul develops the metaphor of the parts of the body working together. He insists, "The members of the body that seem to be weaker are indispensable, and those members of the body that we think less honorable we clothe with greater honor, and our less respectable members are treated with greater respect" (12:22-23).

Sexuality and Gender

Theology and corporeality are inevitably related, and "religion" however defined is never a matter simply of belief. Belief impacts actions, and actions impact one's view of both physical and societal bodies. Paul's concerns with the very human act of eating—celebrating the Lord's Supper, eating food offered to idols—show the interconnection of the body (in both senses) and theological issues. For some Corinthians, belief that they had already been raised from the dead and that "all things are lawful" led to the view that their bodies were beyond the power of sin (4:8-10). The redeemed body was free to do anything. Others took the opposite approach. Seeing the body as a problem or as the locus of sin, they attempted to model eschatological existence by denying physical concerns. Their slogan was not "All things are lawful" but "It is well for a man not to touch a woman" (7:1), a euphemism for abstaining for sex.

Concerns for disciplining and monitoring the body were commonplace in the first century. Indulgence was seen as decadent, and lack of physical training for men was seen as a weakness. Maleness and femaleness were less determined by anatomical differences than constructed by behaviors. A man who indulged his senses risked being dishonored as feminine. For women to behave as men was regarded as even more dishonorable. Gender roles were seen as fixed and natural rather than as culturally constructed. Paul is consistent with this cultural ethos in insisting,

> Does not nature itself teach you that if a man wears long hair, it is degrading to him, but if a woman has long hair, it is her glory? For her hair is given to her for a covering. (11:14-15)

For the Corinthians, theological questions involved sexual ones, and Paul's responses present sexual instruction in theological terms. The discussion begins in chapter 6 where Paul establishes that the body is not to be dismissed. It cannot be, for it is "a temple of the Holy Spirit" (6:19). Therefore, church members are not to engage in fornication [i.e., sexual relations outside of marriage], for "the body is meant not for fornication but for the Lord, and the Lord for the body" (6:13). Since their "bodies are members of Christ" they cannot be made "members of a prostitute" (6:15).

Responding to one Corinthian view that "it is well for a man not to touch a woman" (7:1), Paul acknowledges that sexual relations in marriage are not sinful. Consistent with views of marriage in Roman thought, he acknowledges that husbands and wives have authority over the bodies of their spouses and that both have conjugal rights. To those couples who practice celibacy, he advises that they "deprive one another" only by mutual agreement and only for a set time, since "lack of self-control" could damage their relationship (7:5).

But Paul's acknowledgment of marital relations is more "concession" (7:6) than endorsement. Paul would prefer all were celibate, as he is, but not all can practice "self-control" (7:9) and not all have the spiritual gift (7:7) allowing them to do so. In Paul's view, "it is better to marry than to be aflame with passion" (7:9); that is, if one must have intercourse, do so within a matrimonial relation. For slaves, who were not legally permitted to marry, Paul offers no advice.

Paul knows the tradition of Jesus forbidding divorce and remarriage (7:10), but he glosses the commandment with a different teaching for couples in which only one is a Jesus-believer. He prefers that these marriages remain intact:

> For the unbelieving husband is made holy through his wife, and the unbelieving wife is made holy through her husband. Otherwise, your children would be unclean, but as it is, they are holy. (7:14)

Yet he permits divorce if the "unbelieving partner separates" (7:15a). The bottom line for Paul is not enforcing marriage on those who do not want it; as he concludes, "It is to peace that God has called you" (7:15b).

Church-based sexual teachings today are typically promoted as a means of anchoring society, upholding marriage, and advocating a fulfilling sexual relationship in the context of marital love. For Paul, in a different social context, sexual behavior does not ground society. "He who marries his fiancée does well; and he who refrains from marriage will do better" (7:38). Even within marriage, celibacy is the better state (7:5), and the relation of sexual expression to marital love he leaves unaddressed.

One rationale for Paul's view is a practical one: In 1 Cor 7:32-33, he speaks of the "anxieties" that the married man has concerning the "affairs of the world" and "how to please his wife." Paul would prefer that the followers of Jesus remain unmarried, because then their "anxieties" would be directed toward "how to please the Lord." However, the principal rationale for Paul's views is an eschatological one:

> I think that, *in view of the impending crisis*, it is well for you to remain as you are. Are you bound to a wife? Do not seek to be free. Are you free from a wife? Do not seek a wife . . . Those who marry will experience distress in this life, and I would spare you that . . . *The appointed time has grown short;* from now on, let even those who have wives be as though they had none . . . For the *present form of this world is passing away.* (7:26-28; see also 1:18–2:8; 4:5; 11:26, 32; 15:20-28; emphasis added)

Slave Bodies?

Paul takes the same approach to slavery as he does to virginity and marriage: remain in the state in which you are called (7:24), for the world is passing away. Whether he encourages slaves to take advantage of the possibility of freedom is debated. In 7:21, Paul writes:

> Were you a slave when called? Do not be concerned about it. Even if you can gain your freedom, *make use of your present condition now more than ever.* (emphasis added)

Behind the words in italics are two Greek terms: *mallon*, an adverb meaning "more" or "rather," and *chrēsai*, an aorist (single action) imperative verb meaning "use" or "make use of." Thus a literal translation is, "Even if you can gain your freedom, rather, make use." Missing is the verb's direct object.

Three possible direct objects, and thus three possible readings, have been proposed: make use of (1) slavery, (2) calling, or (3) freedom. Paul may be saying, "But if you can indeed become free . . ." either "use instead slavery" or "by all means live/

use your calling as a free person" or "use instead freedom." These different translations are impacted by one's understandings of first-century slavery, Paul's attitudes
to slavery, the context of chapter 7, and the syntax.

The first option instructs slaves to remain in slavery even if offered freedom.
This option is supported by the context of 7:21-24, where Paul urges believers to
"lead the life that the Lord has assigned" (7:17) and "Let each of you remain in the
condition in which you were called" (7:20). Paul then offers slavery as one of two
examples of remaining in one's current assignment (the other being circumcision).
The choice to remain in slavery can also be supported by the contrastive force of
the word *mallon*—instead of freedom remain in slavery. Finally, Paul's eschatological expectation in 7:31 is that all oppressive structures will end soon, so there is no
need to do anything about slavery now. In Paul's view, slavery, like marriage, is not
only a social, but also an eschatological issue.

Against this option is the observation that Paul is not consistently opposed to
people changing their status. He says that spouses can separate (7:11). He says that
a single person can marry (7:28). The second and third options see Paul supporting
a transition to freedom if manumission becomes a possibility.

In chapter 11, Paul turns to questions of gender. He insists that gender roles, as
understood in his first-century context, be maintained. For Paul, a product of his time,
men were the norm and women the exception. Men were to rule and women were to be
ruled. God was male, as was Christ. The world was established according to a hierarchical
system, and the church was part of that establishment. Thus "Christ is the head of every
man, and the husband is the head of his wife, and God is the head of Christ" (11:3).

Given this system, it was "natural" in Paul's view for men and women to pray differently. Men were to pray without a head covering and women with a veil: "For a man
ought not to have his head veiled, since he is the image and reflection of God; but woman
is the reflection of man" (11:7). He then insists that the veil is a "symbol of authority,"
since woman was created "for the sake of man" (11:9). While the discussion ends with a
note of mutuality—"in the Lord woman is not independent of man or man independent
of woman" (11:11)—the hierarchical model prevails.

Perhaps some women in the congregation had taken literally Paul's teaching that in
Christ there is one body and no longer male or female. Perhaps they claimed equal rights,
and rites, with men (cf. 12:13; Gal 3:28). Perhaps some, believing that the fullness of
God's purposes was already established (4:8-9), found a freedom in the body that ignored
and even subverted cultural gender roles. Paul rejects such views. Church members are
to subscribe to normative gender roles, because the fullness of time has not yet arrived.

Controversial is 1 Cor 14:34-36, which circumscribes women's roles even more:

Women [Greek: *gynē*, also "wives"] should keep silent in the churches. For they are not permitted to speak, but should be subordinate, as the law also says. If there is anything they desire to know, let them ask their husbands at home. For it is shameful for a woman to speak in church.

This restriction is consistent with Paul's insistence on maintaining gender standards and hierarchy, and with the category of shame for transgressing what Paul and his contemporaries considered "natural" behavior.

Despite this consistency, many scholars see the passage as an interpolation or addition made to 1 Corinthians, perhaps by the writer of the Pastorals (1–2 Timothy, Titus), who shares a similar view of gender (see, for example, 1 Tim 2:11-14; Titus 2:5). The NRSV places the verses in parentheses to signal a possible interpolation.

The interpolation argument has some merit. First, the verses can be read as disrupting the argument beginning in 14:30-33 and continuing in verses 36-37. Second, in some early manuscripts, they appear in different locations. This text-critical observation, though, does not prove that they are interpolations. It may indicate that scribes felt that the verses would be better placed elsewhere. Third, the verses contradict 11:5, 13, where Paul recognizes that women speak by praying and prophesying in church. Fourth, in other letters, Paul acknowledges women's teaching and leadership roles. He describes Phoebe the deacon (Rom 16:1-2) as a *prostatis*, which is best translated as "benefactor" or "patron." Among his coworkers are Prisca and Aquila (Rom 16:3; 1 Cor 16:19). Fifth, the reference to the "law" makes no sense as a Pauline comment, since Paul says that "all things are lawful" (1 Cor 6:12), and as one schooled in the Scriptures of Israel, Paul knows that the Torah contains no such law against women speaking in churches.

Others have seen the verses as original to the letter but not expressing *Paul's* opinion. Rather, they see him quoting the view of one of the factions, as he does elsewhere in 1 Corinthians (7:1). On this reading, some in the church claimed that women should not teach. Paul opposes this view with irony: "Or did the word of God originate with you? Or are you the only ones it has reached?" (14:36).

Still others see the verses as original to Paul and intended to stop women's speech. This view appeals to the context. Paul had been discussing glossolalia, so the topic of women's speaking would be a plausible segue. Perhaps women in Corinth had been among those exhibiting the gifts of tongues and prophecy. Perhaps Paul, aware of opposition within and suspicion from without, sought to prevent the practice. That first-century Roman culture had encounters with, and in some settings a distaste for, other women's religious rites, such as Bacchic practices, might influence Paul's comments. Taking the verses as addressed specifically to the Corinthian church, perhaps only to wives and only concerning glossolalia, suggests that the verses do not apply in other contexts or churches.

Paul's various comments on gender and sexuality demonstrate the relationship between theological belief and bodily action. They also show that both theological proclamations and issues of sexuality and gender are related to the cultural circumstances in which they are formulated. These observations are confirmed in chapter 15 when Paul explains how and why the eschatological enthusiasm of those who think they are already resurrected and therefore free to do with their bodies as they will, is wrong.

In 1 Cor 15, Paul declares that Jesus' resurrection guarantees a general resurrection and the establishment of God's empire (15:20-28). As the new Adam (see also Rom 5), Jesus will finally and fully rectify the breach that initial disobedience created between humanity and divinity:

> For since death came through a human being, the resurrection of the dead has also come through a human being; for as all die in Adam, so all will be made alive in Christ. (15:21-22)

Paul's comments are contextually understandable. He took Gen 3 literally. He understood that Adam and Eve's actions impacted all their descendants. Jesus' resurrection began to reverse these consequences. Already the process is under way, but it will be completed at his return (15:20-28).

The completion of this process includes a transformation of the body. According to Paul, there is a difference between the bodies people presently inhabit and those in which they will dwell in the resurrection.

> [The body] is sown in dishonor, it is raised in glory. It is sown in weakness, it is raised in power. It is sown a physical body; it is raised a spiritual body . . . flesh and blood cannot inherit the kingdom of God. (15:43-50)

Paul does not specify what this "resurrection body" looks like save to affirm it is under the Spirit's power. But his point is clear. Since God's purposes embrace life in the body that God created from dust (Gen 2), the Corinthians must live now in ways that honor their bodies and those of others, whether in personal or societal interactions.

Jesus' Resurrection Body?

Paul's other accounts of Jesus' resurrection do not clarify what sort of body Jesus came to possess. His description of the "road to Damascus" incident states only that "God . . . was pleased to reveal his Son to me" (Gal 1:15-16). That revelation could have been an audition, vision, or a blinding light. It need not have been a body. The same point holds for Paul's claim that Jesus "appeared to more than five hundred brothers at one time, most of whom are still alive, though some have died"

(15:6). This claim, along with the notice that Jesus appeared to Peter (Cephas), to James, and to the other apostles is what Paul "received" (15:3) from others. Paul did not see the events, and he never describes the form Jesus took. For the Gospels, Jesus' resurrected body could be considered "flesh and blood": he can be touched; he eats. Further, the Gospels insist that the tomb was empty: thus the body in which Jesus died is the same body in which he rose. Whether Paul thought the same—he mentions neither the empty tomb nor Mary Magdalene nor the details of his experience of the risen Christ—remains debatable.

Broader Society

The extent to which the followers of Jesus should engage the world—Evangelize it? Fully participate in it? Withdraw from it? Condemn it? Imitate it? Expect its imminent end or adapt to its ongoing existence?—occupies many New Testament texts. The question occupied the members of the church in Corinth. Some recognized that idols are not gods and that eating meat offered to the gods and then sold in the market did not compromise their theological views (1 Cor 8). They continued the practices that marked their lives prior to their baptism. Others condemned such actions. Paul therefore has to address two major issues: Can followers of Jesus eat food in a pagan temple (8:8-12; 10:14-22), and can they eat food that had been sacrificed to idols (10:23–11:1)?

He forbids the first and permits the second. The elite are not to participate in meals in a pagan temple (10:14-22), but they can eat anything sold in the market (10:25) and attend meals in the houses of those who do not share their theological views (10:27-30). The instructions are both theological and pastoral. Paul recognizes, as do the Corinthians who seek to participate in such activities, that "no idol in the world really exists" (8:4). But he also recognizes that

> not everyone, however . . . has this knowledge. Since some have become so accustomed to idols until now, they still think of the food they eat as food offered to an idol; and their conscience, being weak, is defiled. (8:7)

Therefore, for the sake of weaker members of the congregation, he advises against eating this meat or participating in the pagan rites.

But the Corinthian situation entails more than matters of religious knowledge. For people participating in Corinth's patronage system, eating meat offered to idols and frequenting pagan temples were part of daily life. If patrons—and clients—wanted to display and extend their social status, they needed to be active participants in Corinth's civic life and networks. Temples are places of seeing and being seen. Participation in temple rites would span social occasions such as marriages and funerals, business opportunities, and the imperial cult celebrations. To bar the followers of Jesus from temples was to force them out of the patronage system.

In 6:1-11 Paul addresses a related social question: Should followers of Jesus sue fellow congregants in Corinth's courts? Should they participate in the court system at all? Since going to court was expensive, Paul addresses wealthier, higher-status believers, possibly patrons in the Corinthian community. He finds this type of civic participation appalling:

> When any of you has a grievance against another, do you dare to take it to court before the unrighteous, instead of taking it before the saints? (6:1)

Then he again grounds his instruction in an eschatological reality:

> Do you not know that the saints will judge the world? And if the world is to be judged by you, are you incompetent to try trivial cases? (6:2)

Third, he employs the discourse of honor and shame:

> I say this to your shame. Can it be that there is no one among you wise enough to decide between one believer and another? (6:5)

To avoid the law court means being absent from an arena where conventional patron/client relationships and elite agonistic interactions were on display.

Today, litigation is not restricted to the rich, and courts are at least expected to proceed in a just manner. With social circumstances having changed, followers of Jesus must determine if avoiding courts is appropriate because they will soon be judging the world, and because it is shameful publicly to display internal discord. The issue is more than a hypothetical one. For example, some congregants in Christian churches today have been instructed that bringing charges of child molestation against a church member to the attention of a court is not permitted, because Paul says that saints should be judging the outsiders and that it is shameful to involve outside authorities. This shielding of a child molester is illegal in the United States. It is also, in the view of many Christians today, immoral.

Social context matters in assessing biblical practice, whether in the first century or in its appropriation and application today.

CHAPTER 8

2 Corinthians

As a missionary, church founder, pastor, theologian, and ethicist, Paul writes to his churches for numerous purposes:

to defend his gospel against competing teachings and his role against rival missionaries;

to promote harmony in congregations where class, ethnicity, and gender issues create conflicts;

to encourage ethical behavior as they await Jesus' return;

to ease doubts about the date of the Parousia;

to help congregations locate themselves in relation to Israel and the Scriptures;

to provide instruction on how to live within the Roman imperial context; and

to thank congregations for their support and their steadfastness.

In all cases, Paul has to communicate his ideas effectively, to convince his audiences of the correctness of his views, and to counter alternative claims. The means by which he does so fall into the category of rhetoric, the art of verbal persuasion.

In this chapter, we employ rhetorical criticism and ask *how* Paul goes about constructing his address to the followers of Jesus in Corinth.

Rhetorical Criticism

Aristotle understood "rhetoric" as a means of persuasion (*Rhetorica* 1.2.1). Quintillian called it "the art of speaking well" (*Institutes of Oratory* 2.17.37). In numerous treatises or "handbooks" about how to make a convincing argument, Greek and Roman rhetoricians identified four key dimensions of effective communication: the situation, the argument's structure, its content, and its execution.

Rhetoric assumes, as well as creates, a *rhetorical situation* from which the communication originates and to which it is addressed. The rhetorical situation is not the same as the historical setting since the speaker determines what aspects of the situation to highlight, marginalize, caricature, ridicule, or ignore. Understanding the rhetorical situation requires we know something about the relationship between the speaker and the intended audience. Does the speaker compete with others for the addressees' loyalty? Does the audience perceive the speaker to be trustworthy or authoritative, or does it resent some previous actions? Perhaps the speaker is disappointed with or proud of the audience, or perhaps the speaker seeks to motivate the audience to perform certain actions or to cease from doing others.

In seeking answers to such questions from Paul's letters, we are hampered by limited data. We have only Paul's perspective as the basis for (re)constructing the rhetorical situation. Yet the Pauline letters do indicate that much was happening in these communities apart from his instruction. His was one voice among many.

Complicating rhetorical analysis further is our limited access to Paul himself. The canon presents to us a picture of Paul based on the collection and preservation of letters certain early churches found to be authoritative. Some of his letters, including the first he wrote to the Corinthian church, have been lost; others have been edited or had interpolations (text added) or were written in his name. The Paul we have is a constructed Paul, the Paul that his early followers wanted to preserve.

The *rhetorical structure* concerns the way the argument is organized. *How* an argument is made greatly impacts its effectiveness. In the ancient world, different types of communications take set forms. Similar to "form criticism," analysis of rhetorical structure illuminates how the writer or speaker adopts and adapts recognizable structures: diatribe (a dialogue with an imagined opponent), encomium (praising an individual or group), flattery and name-calling, and so on.

Moving from *how* the argument is presented to *what* constitutes the argument takes us to the *rhetorical content*. In ancient rhetoric, arguments often comprised conventional "topics" or *topoi* considered appropriate to the subject matter. Aristotle identified three kinds of "proofs": *logos* referred to rational arguments; *ethos* appealed to matters of character, and *pathos* concerned manipulating emotions.

Finally, the study of *rhetorical execution* asks about the techniques and style employed to make the argument. Does the speaker use repetition or contrasts, key words or personal illustrations? Does the speech quote from opponents, or from sources that the audience is likely to respect? Is the argument developed by passionate language or by detached details? Does the speaker use techniques to appeal to the audience's aesthetic tastes, such as puns or alliteration? Does the speaker's self-identification promote sympathy or garner respect?

In attending to these four dimensions, rhetorical criticism helps us assess how language is used to communicate effectively. Rhetorical criticism helps us to identify the agenda and techniques of a speaker and to assess the effectiveness of the strategy. It can also offer insight into the dynamics at work among the parties involved.

Yet like all approaches, rhetorical criticism has limitations. One problem in asking rhetorical-critical questions of Paul's letters concerns whether Paul himself was trained in rhetoric. While numerous handbooks on rhetoric trained elite young men and some women for civic roles, it is not clear that Paul had such training. Paul does not explicitly appeal to an elite education, and we cannot assume that he had formal rhetorical training.

The matter, though, may be more subtle. Even if Paul were not trained in rhetoric, he had numerous opportunities to hear people trained in rhetoric give public speeches. He could have been self-educated. Further, he may have learned effective communication through practice and experience, of which Paul had plenty. Finally, Paul worked with scribes (1 Cor 16:22; Gal 6:11; Rom 16:22), and he generally dictated his letters rather than wrote out drafts. Perhaps a scribe, called an "amanuensis," edited the letters for better communication by using classical rhetorical techniques.

A more significant caution concerns the analysis of rhetorical techniques and arguments intended for public speaking to assess letters. Rhetorical handbooks focused on speeches, not written texts. There are several tricky questions here. For example, how can we assess the role of tone in reading letters, given the inevitable slippage between assessing a written text and hearing it read? One limitation in studying a written document intended to be performed is that we do not encounter it in the oral-aural situation of its delivery. Consequently, we can only speculate on its impact. With Paul's letters, some positive impact is likely. Otherwise the letter would not have been preserved, copied, and eventually canonized. However, the extent of the letter's impact is difficult to gauge: that Paul had to continue to write to the Corinthians suggests that the earlier letters may have been of limited impact.

A third problem in the application of rhetorical criticism to the New Testament is that occasionally in scholarship, identification of the rhetorical forms becomes a rote exercise. Analyzing forms, though, needs to move to their impact: Why might Paul have used this form in this context? Is he mimicking his opponents? Is he angry? Does he seek support from his audience? In other words, rhetorical analysis also asks about the relationship of form to function, of medium to message.

With these caveats, we turn to a rhetorical-critical reading of 2 Corinthians. Our approach consists of four steps: (1) identifying the *rhetorical situation* from which the text emerges and which it addresses; (2) determining the letter's *rhetorical structure*; (3) explaining the *rhetorical content* or kinds of arguments (*topoi*) and appeals Paul makes; and (4) assessing the *rhetorical execution* or skill in employing rhetorical techniques.

Rhetorical Situation

The central issue in 2 Corinthians concerns Paul's apostolic legitimacy. Controversy about Paul is the rhetorical situation he constructs and engages. Already in 1 Corinthians, Paul alludes to doubts some Corinthian Jesus-believers had about his apostleship:

Am I not free? Am I not an apostle? Have I not seen Jesus our Lord? Are you not my work in the Lord? (1 Cor 9:1)

Last of all, as to one untimely born, he appeared also to me. For I am the least of the apostles, unfit to be called an apostle, because I persecuted the church of God. But by the grace of God I am what I am, and his grace toward me has not been in vain. On the contrary, I worked harder than any of them—though it was not I, but the grace of God that is with me. (1 Cor 15:8-10)

It appears that since Paul wrote 1 Corinthians, the situation in Corinth had deteriorated. In 2 Corinthians, his own apostolic authority has become the preeminent topic. Paul now has to work even harder to demonstrate both his apostolic qualifications and his integrity.

The signs of a true apostle were performed among you with utmost patience. (12:12)

Since you desire proof that Christ is speaking in me. (13:3)

The two letters give some hints as to what happened between 1 Corinthians (ca. 56–57) and the composition of 2 Corinthians. According to 1 Cor 16:1-4, Paul, writing from Ephesus, states that when he visits Corinth again, he plans to collect the funds that the congregants have been donating weekly for the church in Jerusalem. In 1 Cor 16:5-7 Paul describes a planned lengthy visit to Corinth after "passing through" Macedonia, where he would reconnect with churches he founded in Philippi and Thessalonica. First, though, he will stay in Ephesus "until Pentecost" (16:8), send Timothy to visit the Corinthians (16:10-11), and perhaps send Apollos later (16:12).

The Collection

In 1 Cor 16 and 2 Cor 8–9, Paul refers to funds he is gathering from his Gentile churches for the "saints" (1 Cor 16:1) in Jerusalem. The collection appears to be more than a charitable donation: there are people in need throughout the Roman Empire, including in the local Corinthian church. Thus the concern for the church *in Jerusalem* needs to be explained.

In Galatians, Paul recounts that James, Cephas, and John, the leaders of the Jerusalem church, asked him to "remember the poor" (2:10). The concern is not only for economic aid. Such donations also served to solidify the relationship between the Jewish apostles and Paul's Gentile congregations. Jerusalem's acceptance of the collection would also legitimate Paul's apostolic role. Were Peter and his colleagues to accept the money Paul collected, they would also be accepting Paul and those he had brought into the church. The underlying cultural system concerns mutual benefaction. Just as Gentiles have received the benefit of participating in Israel's spiritual blessings, so Gentiles should provide material blessings for the Jerusalem church. Whether the term "poor" is a generic descriptor or whether it designates destitute folks—who have donated all their funds to the church that has exhausted its budget; or who have given up their livelihoods, such as fishing and tax collecting, to relocate to Jerusalem; or who have given away all they had in order to earn "treasures in heaven" (Matt 6:20); or who ceased working in anticipation of the Parousia—is not clear.

In 1 Cor 16:1-4 Paul suggests that the Corinthians imitate the Galatian churches in making regular weekly offerings that representatives, including Paul, will take to Jerusalem. In 2 Cor 8–9, Paul renews his appeal for contributions. Were the Corinthians to contribute to this collection, they would tangibly display their loyalty to Paul and to his gospel, and not to the ministry of rival teachers. Thus the collection represents interrelated issues of authority and relationship. That Paul devotes two chapters—2 Cor 8–9—to the collection suggests the importance of his vision of the unity and mutuality of the Jerusalem/Jewish church and the Gentile congregations.

In Rom 15:25-26, Paul announces that he is going "to Jerusalem in a ministry to the saints; for Macedonia and Achaia have been pleased to share their resources with the poor among the saints at Jerusalem." He does not mention the Galatians; perhaps they refused to support him. In Rom 15:30-31, Paul asks the congregation to pray that the collection will be acceptable. Were the Jerusalem leaders to refuse the collection, the unity of Jewish and Gentile Jesus-believers that it represents will be undermined. Members of the church, such as the people mentioned in chapter 16, may well have connections with the Jerusalem community. Likely Paul is asking not only for their prayers but also for their influence.

The book of Acts does not mention the collection. Some have suggested Acts 24:17 might refer to it: "Now after some years I came to bring alms to my nation and to offer sacrifices." If so, it is an odd reference, since Paul says nothing about the recipients of the funds. Given Luke's emphasis on both the legitimacy of the Gentile mission and the harmony by which the leaders of the movement work together in fostering this mission, the lack of reference might indicate a failed mission.

Some scholars have seen another function for the collection. They locate it in the understanding that Paul was leading not just a religious movement but an international societal alternative to the Roman imperial order. The collection was an economic practice that moved resources from the provinces not to Rome (as with imperial taxation and tribute) but away from Rome and to Jerusalem. It also redistributed resources not vertically from the poor to the rich to make them richer (as with imperial practices), but horizontally, from the poor to the poor. The collection functioned to secure solidarity across considerable distances, ethnicities, and social experience.

For reasons that remain unclear, Paul was unable to fulfill his plans to visit Corinth. In 2 Cor 1:3-11 he mentions without elaboration, "the affliction we experienced in Asia; for we were so utterly, unbearably crushed that we despaired of life itself."

As a result, Paul changes his plans. He journeyed to Macedonia but did not return to Corinth. As he explains at the beginning of 2 Corinthians:

I wanted to visit you on my way to Macedonia, and to come back to you from Macedonia and have you send me on to Judea. (1:16)

Paul's failure to make good on his promise resulted in his being charged with being unreliable (1:16-22), a charge Paul's rhetoric suggests he deeply resents:

Was I vacillating when I wanted to do this? Do I make my plans according to ordinary human standards, ready to say "Yes, yes" and "No, no" at the same time? As surely as God is faithful, our word to you has not been "Yes" and "No." (1:17)

Summoning God as a witness against himself, Paul explains that he did not visit Corinth because he wanted to "spare" them another painful visit (1:23–2:2). He does not elaborate this "painful" visit, so we can only speculate: Was he accused of misappropriating funds for the Jerusalem church? Were his apostolic credentials questioned? Were his ethical teachings about mutuality versus patron/client relations or about conforming to certain gender roles or about sexuality or redefined "honor" rejected? His language echoes the Jesus tradition: "Let your word be 'Yes, Yes' or 'No, No'; anything more than this comes from the evil one" (Matt 5:37). Rhetorically, Paul may be reminding the congregation of what he had originally taught them, even as he is allying himself with what Jesus commended. Whatever the situation, the visit to Corinth did not go well.

Thereafter, Paul wrote the congregation a letter "out of much distress and anguish of heart" (2:3-4). Titus delivered it and then reported to Paul in Troas that the letter prompted some "repentance" (7:5-16). That is, it was rhetorically effective and served to reconcile some of the Corinthian believers to Paul. Paul then writes 2 Corinthians, it seems, to secure this reconciliation with the Corinthian congregants.

Meanwhile, a small group of teachers has become influential in Corinth. Second Corinthians suggests that they have aligned themselves with church members already unhappy with Paul. They proclaim a gospel different from his (11:4-5) and raise questions about his apostolic legitimacy (12:12; 13:3). Issues of legitimacy had plagued the movement since its beginnings. The early church congregations had primarily a charismatic rather than institutional structure (1 Cor 12–14). There were no divinity schools or seminaries or ordination boards to provide clerical credentials. There was no "New Testament" to quote. There were competing stories about Jesus coupled with claims of ongoing revelation through visionary appearances, prophecy, and new understandings of the Scriptures of Israel. For some, Paul's recounting of his Damascus Road experience may have seemed a weak basis for authority compared to that of Peter and John and others who had followed Jesus initially, or James, who was his brother. For others, working wonders and the ability to use rhetorical flourish (style) may have trumped the daily work (substance) in which other teachers were engaged. How, then, was the church to recognize "the signs of a true apostle"?

Paul, away from Corinth, has to make his case rhetorically that he has apostolic legitimacy. For example, he insists that he does not peddle God's word, since he is a person "of sincerity" (2:17). He has "renounced shameful things" (4:2), tries to conduct his ministry without fault (6:3), and denies he has corrupted or taken advantage of anyone (7:2). He also goes on the offensive by attacking the teachers who seek to discredit him (chs. 10–13). He describes them as "boasters . . . false apostles, deceitful workers, disguising themselves as apostles of Christ" and compares them to the devil, for "even Satan disguises himself as an angel of light" (11:13-14).

Identifying these opponents only through Paul's description presents numerous risks (on the technique of mirror-reading, see the chapter on 1–3 John). How much direct access Paul has to their teaching and the situation is not clear. Nor is he objective in his presentation, as his vilification indicates. He may be exacerbating an already caricatured description of their teaching. Although the inclusion of Paul's letter in the canon gives the impression that Paul's perspective was objectively right, that determination was not clear when 2 Corinthians was written. Ironically, while we might think of Paul's opponents as "outsiders," they seem to have become "insiders" for some (many?) members of the church in Corinth. Paul's voice was by no means the determinative one among Corinthian believers.

Despite the challenge of reconstructing an oppositional view from a polemic response to it, 2 Cor 10–13 suggest at least five likely features that mark Paul's opponents.

First, they, or their Corinthian followers, value rhetorical ability and consequently they devalue Paul's personal presentations: "For they say, 'His letters are weighty and strong, but his bodily presence is weak, and his speech contemptible'" (10:10). Paul, ironically, seems to agree with their assessment. Whether he is being honest or falsely modest cannot be determined. He then attempts to counter their charge rhetorically by promoting knowledge over rhetoric in a nicely contrasting statement: "I may be untrained in speech, but not in knowledge; certainly in every way and in all things we have made this evident to you" (11:6). In the competition between rhetoric and knowledge, knowledge wins. That some within the Corinthian church value knowledge (*gnōsis*) over faith, a concern Paul addresses several times in 1 Corinthians, heightens the effectiveness of Paul's language. Here rather than dismiss *gnōsis*, Paul claims that he has more than his opponents.

Second, these opponents claim Jewish heritage, and thus, by implication, a closer understanding of Jesus than Gentiles can claim. Paul trots out his own credentials:

Are they Hebrews? So am I. Are they Israelites? So am I. Are they descendants of Abraham? So am I. (11:22)

His point is not only that he can match them but also, as we will see, that he thinks they appeal to inappropriate criteria.

Third, the opponents appear to value works of power, visions, and other manifestations of the supernatural. As Paul states in 12:11-12:

I have been a fool! You forced me to it. Indeed you should have been the ones commending me, for I am not at all inferior to these super-apostles, even though I am nothing. The signs of a true apostle were performed among you with utmost patience, signs and wonders and mighty works.

Paul even describes "the exceptional character of the revelations" he has personally experienced (12:7). At the same time, he indicates that he has not put forward his abilities and experiences; rather, the Corinthians have "forced" him toward this self-recommendation. By calling himself "fool" he is actually setting up those in Corinth who doubt him as the real fools. Finally, Paul claims that he has supernatural credentials not only equal to but better than his rivals', but again these criteria are inappropriate for determining a "true apostle."

Fourth, the content of the rivals' teaching, albeit difficult to determine, may have emphasized Jesus' resurrection and exaltation over his suffering. First Corinthians 4:8-10 indicates that some Jesus-believers had embraced an extreme form of realized eschatology, and these congregants would find this teaching appealing.

Fifth, Paul indicates that these rivals take financial support from the Corinthians, something Paul refuses to do. Perhaps some members of the Corinthian church appreciated these apostles' involvement in the conventional patronage system. The obligations related to accepting support would have solidified relations between the rival apostles and those in the Corinthian church who provided the financial support. Moreover, the church members providing patronage would have gained authority and honor through their contacts with the so-called super-apostles. Paul's independence broke convention and seems to have raised suspicion. While it was common for teachers to receive support from patrons and students, Paul's argument is that conforming to cultural expectations and practices does not identify a "true apostle."

Against these opponents, with their eloquence and education, Jewish connections, miracles, appealing Christology, and formalized relationship through financial arrangements with members of the Corinthian church, Paul makes his case for recognizing their falseness and his own legitimacy as an apostle. He makes his case not with direct speech, but with the written word.

Rhetorical Structure

Immediately we run into difficulties, for it is not clear that Paul wrote 2 Corinthians in the form in which the NT presents it. For centuries, readers have noted seams in the letter. For example, after two fairly peaceful chapters about the collection (8–9), chapters 10–13 introduce a new focus on the "super-apostles." A new tone, both sarcastic and combative, emerges. And the sequence is not good. Chapter 9 ends with what sounds like a closing benediction: "Thanks be to God for his indescribable gift!" (9:15). Chapter 10 begins with an apparent non sequitur:

> I myself, Paul, appeal to you by the meekness and gentleness of Christ—I who am humble when face to face with you, but bold toward you when I am away! (10:1)

Some scholars see 2 Corinthians comprising two letters joined together (ch. 1–9 and 10–13), though not necessarily composed in that order. Some identify chapters 10–13 with the letter Paul mentions in 2:3-4, a letter written "with many tears" (sometimes called the "tearful letter"). Others suggest that 2:12-13 was originally followed by 7:5. In 2:13, Paul talks about going to Macedonia, and in 7:5 he picks up the same thread:

For even when we came into Macedonia, our bodies had no rest, but we were afflicted in every way—disputes without and fears within.

On this reading, 2:14–7:4 was spliced into an earlier letter.

Not all scholars find such theories convincing. Some think that too much has been made of the supposed seams and non sequiturs. No manuscript evidence indicates that sections of 2 Corinthians circulated independently. What we do know is that Paul wrote to the Corinthians at least four times: the letter mentioned in 1 Cor 5:9; 1 Corinthians; the tearful letter of 2 Cor 2:3-4; and the letter (or part of it) that we know as 2 Corinthians. Here we discuss 2 Corinthians in its present, canonical form.

Rhetorical-critical approaches identify the structure of 2 Corinthians section by section, with each section contributing to Paul's argument. The *Exordium* (1:1-7) introduces speaker and audience and seeks to gain the audience's attention and goodwill. A "thanksgiving" is typical. Then comes the *Narratio* (1:8–2:16 or perhaps just 1:8-11), which sets out the events to which the letter responds.

The *Propositio* asserts the letter's central argument. However, determining the *Propositio* is not always easy, especially if a letter has multiple functions. If we misidentify the *Propositio*, we will likely misinterpret the letter. Some scholars locate the *Propositio* in 2:17, where Paul insists, "I am not at all inferior to these super-apostles." Others place it at 1:12-14:

Indeed, this is our boast, the testimony of our conscience: we have behaved in the world with frankness and godly sincerity, not by earthly wisdom but by the grace of God—and all the more toward you. For we write you nothing other than what you can read and also understand; I hope you will understand until the end—as you have already understood us in part—that on the day of the Lord Jesus we are your boast even as you are our boast.

The choice of 2:17 as the *Propositio* highlights more the competitive interaction between Paul and the other apostles. The choice of 1:12-14 highlights more Paul's defense of his own apostleship.

The *Probatio*, the major section (3:1–13:4, or even 1:15–9:15), presents proofs supporting the central argument. The *Peroratio* restates the main arguments and attempts to gain the audience's support often through an emotional appeal (13:5-14 10:1–13:14). The *Closing* offers a final appeal and a benediction (13:11-14). The different chapters and verses offered for each section show that rhetorical analysis is as much a matter of aesthetic taste as obvious division. People in the Corinthian church, upon listening to the letter read aloud, might not have heard the same *Propositio*. The different outlines reflect the role interpreters, rather than authors, play in determining rhetorical structure.

Rhetorical Content: *Topoi*

Paul employs a number of conventional "topics" or *topoi* to argue for his legitimacy as an apostle. In 2 Corinthians, three appeals are prominent: affliction and consolation; self-commendation; and motifs concerning friendship, boldness, and sincerity.

First, by appealing to his sufferings, Paul seeks to gain the audience's sympathy. By noting the consolation he received, he seeks to legitimize his authority. We might classify his approach as a "win/win" situation. Suffering shows his strength of character; consolation shows divine approval.

Paul begins by acknowledging his present and past affliction, including that unspecified experience in Asia. There he experienced God's consolation (1:3-11; 7:5-16). He then speaks of the affliction of church members in Corinth (2:5-11). He mitigates his criticism of them, though, by acknowledging that they also experienced consolation. Thereby, Paul establishes a common bond with his audience:

> If we are being afflicted, it is for your consolation and salvation; if we are being consoled, it is for your consolation, which you experience when you patiently endure the same sufferings that we are also suffering. (1:6; see also 7:4)

He acknowledges that his "painful" letter caused them suffering (2:5-11; 7:8) as well as caused them to discipline an offender (2:6: "This punishment by the majority is enough for such a person"). Immediately he turns to consolation by exhorting his audience to forgive the offender (2:7). Interestingly, this conciliatory approach differs from his response to the Corinthians' lack of action over the man living with his stepmother in 1 Cor 5. There Paul rebukes them, urges them to remove him "from among you," and tells them to "hand this man over to Satan" (1 Cor 5:2, 5). Different circumstances call for different actions.

Paul also connects the suffering he experienced in his dealings with the Corinthians to the sufferings he experiences as an apostle. He boasts of being "afflicted," "perplexed," "persecuted," and "struck down" (4:8-9), as well as of "hardships, calamities, beatings, imprisonments, riots, labors, sleepless nights, hunger" (6:4).

Several times he details his difficulties, until they sound like a litany of the "perils of Paul."

> Five times I have received from the Jews the forty lashes minus one. Three times I was beaten with rods. Once I received a stoning. Three times I was shipwrecked; for a night and a day I was adrift at sea; on frequent journeys, in danger from rivers, danger from bandits, danger from my own people, danger from Gentiles, danger in the city, danger in the wilderness, danger at sea, danger from false brothers and sisters; in toil and

hardship, through many a sleepless night, hungry and thirsty, often without food, cold and naked. And, besides other things, I am under daily pressure because of my anxiety for all the churches. . . . In Damascus, the governor under King Aretas guarded the city of Damascus in order to seize me, but I was let down in a basket through a window in the wall, and escaped from his hands. (2 Cor 11:24-33)

In delineating his extensive suffering, Paul evokes common cultural understandings of human afflictions to secure the Corinthians' loyalty and to refute the influence of the competing apostles. One conventional notion was that shared suffering secures friendship. Hence Paul underlines his solidarity with the Corinthians. He and they share their suffering with the crucified Christ. The opposing apostles, with their eloquence and signs, do not. Further, given the details of his suffering, Paul is indicating to his audience the enormous strength of his own character and at the same time undermining charges that he is weak.

Paul also utilizes a cluster of three *topoi* concerning suffering: suffering reveals character, causing affliction for the sake of discipline or rebuke is a sign of love, and affliction can lead to reconciliation. So in 7:8-10 Paul acknowledges the pain he caused the congregation and celebrates its repentance:

For even if I made you sorry with my letter, I do not regret it (though I did regret it, for I see that I grieved you with that letter, though only briefly). Now I rejoice, not because you were grieved, but because your grief led to repentance; for you felt a godly grief, so that you were not harmed in any way by us. For godly grief produces a repentance that leads to salvation and brings no regret.

To demonstrate his integrity as an apostle, Paul admits his distress over his afflictions, and he affirms the divine grace he experienced in them.

Three times I appealed to the Lord about this [affliction], that it would leave me, but he said to me, "My grace is sufficient for you, for power is made perfect in weakness." So, I will boast all the more gladly of my weaknesses, so that the power of Christ may dwell in me. (12:8-9)

Here again, Paul establishes his credentials over those of the rival apostles. He may appear weak, but that weakness testifies to his strength, which comprises the power of the risen Christ. They may have visions, but he has direct empowerment by Christ. They may perform signs, but Paul has Christ indwelling within him. He reframes his apparent weaknesses as occasions for manifestations of divine power:

We have this treasure in clay jars so it may be clear that this extraordinary power belongs to God and does not come from us. (4:7; see also 3:5-6; 12:9)

His claim is that his life embodies the gospel of death and resurrection. He walks the talk.

Along with suffering and consolation, Paul's second appeal or *topos* concerns "boasting" (12:9) or self-commendation. In ancient rhetoric, boasting was regarded as an appropriate means of gaining an audience's attention, mounting a defense, and promoting a greater good. Self-commendation also worked with exhortations to imitation (*mimesis*). The person to be imitated had to display impeccable credentials, and rhetorically those credentials were demonstrated through self-promotion.

In 1:12, Paul appeals to a standard *topos* but gives it a distinctive christocentric quality:

Indeed, this is our boast, the testimony of our conscience: we have behaved in the world with frankness and godly sincerity, not by earthly wisdom but by the grace of God—and all the more toward you.

Within two verses, he brings the Corinthians into this praise:

As you have already understood us in part—that on the day of the Lord Jesus we are your boast even as you are our boast. (1:14)

Continuing this rhetorical self-promotion, Paul presents his sufferings in terms of participation in the sufferings of Christ; his sufferings thus serve to validate his ministry. Just as God was at work in the resurrection of Jesus, so God is at work through Paul in the same pattern of death and new life, weakness and divine power. Paul carries "in the body the death of Jesus, so that the life of Jesus may also be made visible in our bodies . . . death is at work in us, but life in you" (4:10-12).

In 10:8 he boasts again, with false modesty:

Now, even if I boast a little too much of our authority, which the Lord gave for building you up and not for tearing you down, I will not be ashamed of it.

The more he promotes himself, the more he denies doing it:

We, however, will not boast beyond limits, but will keep within the field that God has assigned to us, to reach out even as far as you. (10:13; see vv. 15-16)

Paul goes on to boast of not taking the Corinthians' patronage (11:7-11), of his visions and revelations (12:1), and of his actions that are not in accord with human standards (11:18). He wants the Corinthians to boast of him (5:12) as he boasts of them (7:4, 14; 8:24; 9:2).

The language of "commending ourselves" has the same function. Paul offers legitimate (self-)commendation in doing God's work:

> Are we beginning to commend ourselves again? Surely we do not need, as some do, letters of recommendation to you or from you, do we? (3:1; see also 4:2; 5:12; 6:4; 10:18)

Letters of commendation were common for itinerant teachers. His opponents probably displayed them. Paul dismisses them as validating true apostleship. In his view, the super-apostles "commend themselves" apart from God's working (10:12, 18).

Paul's consistent boasting and self-commendation regarding suffering and weakness also speak to matters of eschatology. If the rival apostles were promoting a type of realized eschatology, Paul's emphases correct the view. According to Paul, his ministry constantly participates in "weakness" (the present evil age) so that the resurrecting power of God (the new age) might be manifested (6:4-10; also 11:23-33; 12:9; 13:3-4). Underlying this claim is Paul's conviction that he lives in the overlap of the ages. The old age marked by sin and death has *not yet* ended, but the new age, the new creation (5:17), has begun with the resurrection of Jesus. He therefore presents himself as demonstrating in his life and ministry the gospel message of death and life, weakness and power, judgment and transformation. Presenting himself as the model that church members are to follow, he describes himself as incarnating the gospel of Jesus' death and resurrection (4:7-15).

A third *topos* counters the charge that Paul might be exaggerating. Along with appeals to his suffering, consolation, and self-commendation, Paul appeals to a cluster of *topoi* concerning friendship, boldness, and sincerity.

Writers on rhetoric recognized that speakers could make their argument in several ways. Flattery was one form of appeal. They could argue indirectly by analogy or directly with boldness. Frankness or boldness, seen in explicit expressions of sincerity, was expected. Paul utilizes the *topos* of frankness in relation to his friendship with the Corinthians. "Friendship" itself was a conventional rhetorical subject. Friends were responsible for stimulating self-reflection, correcting each other's behavior, and maintaining goodwill. (See the discussion of Philippians and friendship.)

Paul defends his ministry as a demonstration of the boldness or frankness appropriate to his friendship with the Corinthians. His "tearful" or "sorrowful" letter exemplified "frank" or "bold" speech in causing them pain:

For if I cause you pain, who is there to make me glad but the one whom I have pained? And I wrote as I did, so that when I came, I might not suffer pain from those who should have made me rejoice; for I am confident about all of you, that my joy would be the joy of all of you. (2:2-3)

This approach presumes friendship and loyalty between Paul and the Corinthians, even though the relationship was fragile.

References in 1:1–2:17 to his previous relationships with the congregation underline their friendship. Paul enhances the appeal both by distinguishing his own frankness from the presumed duplicity of his rivals and by equating his sincerity with that of Christ:

For we are not peddlers of God's word like so many; but in Christ we speak as persons of sincerity, as persons sent from God and standing in his presence. (2:17; also 4:1-2; 6:3)

After reinforcing his claims of sincerity by evoking God as his witness (5:11), Paul moves from language of friendship to language of kinship to create a parental relationship with his audience:

We have spoken frankly to you Corinthians; our heart is wide open to you. There is no restriction in our affections, but only in yours. In return—I speak as to children—open wide your hearts also. (6:11-13; see also 7:2-4)

In chapters 10–13, Paul's frankness intensifies. After again asserting his consistency (10:1-11; 11:12) and integrity (11:20; 12:14; 13:8), he demands from the Corinthians their self-evaluation and loyalty to Jesus and to himself (10:7; 13:5). He asserts his authority by claiming twice the power to build up and to tear down (10:8; 13:10), and the second time he threatens them if they refuse his appeals:

So I write these things while I am away from you, so that when I come, I may not have to be severe in using the authority that the Lord has given me for building up and not for tearing down. (13:10)

The threat is not empty: Paul had already told the Corinthians that his own teaching—his rhetoric—would destroy anything contrary to his version of the gospel:

We do not wage war according to human standards; for the weapons of our warfare are not merely human, but they have divine power to destroy strongholds. We destroy arguments and every proud obstacle raised up against the knowledge of God, and we take every thought captive to obey Christ. We are ready to punish every disobedience when your obedience is complete. (10:3-6; see also 1:3-4)

Words have power.

Rhetorical Execution: Techniques

Among the techniques rhetorical handbooks recommend, and that Paul uses effectively in 2 Corinthians, are comparisons and contrasts, irony, and the evocation of emotions, especially pity. These techniques served to attract and maintain the audience's attention.

Comparison can take various forms, from evaluating alternative plans to juxtaposing good and bad qualities for purposes of praising or invective. Paul presents his ministry as "a ministry of a new covenant" (3:5), in contrast with the "old covenant" (3:14). In 3:7-18 he compares his ministry and message with those of Moses and aligns himself with his (Gentile) followers over against those who follow Torah, whether Jews not in the church or, more likely, the rival "super-apostles" who may be accentuating their "Israelite" credentials.

The comparison is stark. Paul speaks of being "ministers of a new covenant, not of letter but of spirit; for the letter kills, but the Spirit gives life" (3:6). He refers to Mosaic law as "the ministry of death, chiseled in letters on stone tablets" (3:7). Finally, Paul provides the Corinthians a visual image by which they can contrast Torah with his gospel. Again appealing to his sincerity, he begins:

> Since, then, we have such a hope, we act with great boldness, not like Moses, who put a veil over his face to keep the people of Israel from gazing at the end of the glory that was being set aside. But their minds were hardened. Indeed, to this very day, when they hear the reading of the old covenant, that same veil is still there, since only in Christ is it set aside. Indeed, to this very day whenever Moses is read, a veil lies over their minds; but when one turns to the Lord, the veil is removed. (3:12-16)

With this image, Paul unites himself and the Corinthians in their interpretation of Israel's Scriptures, in triumphant solidarity against Jews who do not follow Jesus, and who, in Paul's view, lack ability to understand God's purposes. The rhetorical point also condemns any Gentiles in Paul's audience who propose to follow the practices designed to keep Jews distinct among the nations, such as circumcision and the dietary regulations.

Paul's claim is a theological view, not a historical fact. It expresses the rhetoric of religious rivalry and apologetics. Rhetoric can be nasty and harmful as well as inspirational and consoling.

Elsewhere, Paul's comparisons have an ironic quality. Irony, a technique of indirect communication, involves saying what we mean by saying the opposite. It engages an audience in discerning proper meaning. For example, Paul states that he will not use the rhetorical technique of comparison against his opponents, because this is what the opponents do:

> We do not dare to classify or compare ourselves with some of those who commend themselves. But when they measure themselves by one another, and compare themselves with one another, they do not show good sense. (10:12)

He then goes on to do precisely this, by boasting of his own abilities in contrast to theirs.

After asserting that he is not inferior to the "super-apostles" (11:5), he sets out in 11:21–12:10 a lengthy comparison between his ministry and theirs. Taking the form of a parody, this speech—sometimes called the "fool's speech"— establishes Paul's credentials. In the opening section (11:16-21), Paul announces six times that he will boast like a fool:

> Let no one think that I am a fool; but if you do, then accept me as a fool, so that I too may boast a little. What I am saying in regard to this boastful confidence, I am saying not with the Lord's authority, but as a fool . . . For you gladly put up with fools, being wise yourselves! . . . But whatever anyone dares to boast of—I am speaking as a fool—I also dare to boast of that.

The irony is clear and sarcastic. Paul is no fool, and the Corinthians know this. If he were, they would not have believed him or accepted his message in the first place. Second, by calling the Corinthians "wise" in putting up with "fools," Paul suggests that they are the fools. Indeed, Paul says his acting the fool is necessary because the Corinthians have responded to the "foolish" outsiders. If he acts and talks like a fool (the rival apostles), perhaps the Corinthians will accept him also.

Paul then launches into a lengthy boast about suffering, claiming to beat the outsiders at their own game of self-commendation. He suffers more than anyone (11:23). And he has better visions and revelations. He expresses his claim indirectly, as if he were talking about someone else:

> I know a person in Christ who fourteen years ago was caught up to the third heaven—whether in the body or out of the body I do not know; God knows—was

caught up into Paradise and heard things that are not to be told, that no mortal is permitted to repeat. On behalf of such a one I will boast, but on my own behalf I will not boast, except of my weaknesses. (12:2-5)

Irony continues. His visions are so stupendous that he cannot repeat them! That of course is the point of "revelations." They should be revealed. The reference to "third heaven" may express modesty or perhaps a failed ascent, since some traditions spoke of at least seven heavens. If so, the irony continues: Paul made it to the third heaven; the super-apostles, by implication, remain on earth. More, by failing to progress farther into the heavens, Paul is showing his weakness. That is his point, for it is in weakness that Christ is manifest in Paul, and it is in his weakness that Paul boasts. Finally, Paul secures his point by stating that he is no fool (the congregation should have already realized this); instead, "But if I wish to boast, I will not be a fool, for I will be speaking the truth" (12:6a).

Together with creative use of comparison/contrast and of irony, Paul makes several appeals to the emotions. Some rhetoricians saw appealing to or manipulating the audience's emotions (*pathos*; "passion" or "emotion") as especially important in opening and closing sections. Reflecting on the earlier, somewhat successful, sorrowful or tearful letter, Paul names a number of his own emotions: "much distress," "anguish of heart," "many tears," "abundant love" (2:4). He recognizes that he caused the Corinthians pain (2:4; 7:8), but he celebrates that it resulted in "godly grief" (7:9) as well as "earnestness . . . eagerness . . . indignation . . . alarm . . . longing . . . zeal . . . punishment" (7:11). In reporting these emotions, he presents himself as deeply troubled by what has happened in Corinth, genuinely concerned for the Corinthians, and eager to rectify the situation.

Paul seeks to arouse their emotions in order to secure or solidify their reconciliation. *Pity* is the dominant emotion to which he appeals, especially in the opening section. He tries to arouse the Corinthians' pity for him by naming his suffering and theirs (1:3-7), his own serious affliction and reliance on God for rescue (1:8-11), his suffering from his opponents (2:5-11; 7:12), his anxiety in waiting for his coworker Titus to return to him in Troas (2:12-13; 7:5), and his ill treatment by the rival apostles (chs. 10–13). Concurrently, Paul seeks to provoke his audience to anger directed at any who have offended him, an unnamed congregant (2:5-11; 7:12) and the super-apostles whom he mocks as agents of Satan (11:3, 13-15).

That 2 Corinthians has been preserved suggests that some within the Corinthian congregation were persuaded by Paul's rhetoric. A late first-century letter known as *1 Clement*, which appears in some early Christian canons, indicates, however, that the Corinthian church remained wracked by factionalism well past the time of Paul. Despite the church's difficulties, 2 Corinthians remains a testimony to the power of words, to unite as well as to separate; to commend as well as to demonize; to manipulate, to please, to provoke, and to inspire with a vision of "the signs of a true apostle."

$\mathcal{G}$alatians

To study Paul's Letter to the Galatians, we focus on its history of interpretation. This approach shows how the setting from which the interpreter speaks profoundly impacts understandings of the text and reconstructions of the situation it addresses. It also shows how decisions about the interpretation of Galatians have had far-reaching, even destructive, consequences across the church's history. Then we employ historical criticism to formulate a reconstruction of the circumstances the letter addresses, a reconstruction informed by recent research into first-century Judaism. In this context, we track the arguments concerning three major concepts in the letter: works of the law, justification/righteousness, and faith in/of Christ. We end by noting something of Galatians' contemporary challenge.

History of Interpretation: A Reformation Reconstruction and Reading

---

Martin Luther (1483–1596) offered an understanding of Galatians that influenced the church for some 500 years. We outline the circumstances in which he formulated his interpretation, some of its features, and some of its consequences.

Luther, initially a Roman Catholic priest, had become disillusioned by church practices such as recognizing the authority of post-canonical doctrines rather than the teachings of Scripture alone (Latin: *Sola Scriptura*), priestly celibacy, and selling indulgences that assured the remission of postmortem punishments for sins. During Luther's time, some abused this system by collecting indulgences to rebuild St. Peter's basilica in Rome or by promising that the faithful could buy their way out of Purgatory. His Ninety-Five Theses, translated into German from Latin and distributed widely by the recently invented printing press, formed the basis of the Protestant Reformation.

Central to Luther's theology was the concept of justification by faith. Luther and other self-designated "reformers" of Roman Catholic teachings and practices believed that faith in Jesus restored the relation to God that had been broken by Adam's sin in the garden of

Eden. In their view, people could not do anything to restore this relationship. No good works or following any rite or law would earn or merit God's favor. Rather, only God's gracious and freely given love restores the relationship. God declares the sinner in "right relationship with God" when the sinner accepts Jesus as Lord by faith. This declaration is known as "justification by faith" (compare the term "justified margins," in which alignment is correct). For Luther, faith alone makes a person just.

Galatians, sometimes called "Luther's Book," provides the Reformation's central verse:

> Yet we know that a person is justified not by the works of the law but through faith in Jesus Christ. And we have come to believe in Christ Jesus, so that we might be justified by faith in Christ, and not by doing the works of the law, because no one will be justified by the works of the law. (2:16)

Luther and other reformers read this contrast between "justification by faith" and "justification by works" in terms of their disagreement with Catholic theology and practice. They saw buying and selling indulgences and participation in other good works as efforts that tried—unsuccessfully—to buy God's favor, and they understood Paul as speaking to their own reformation interests in terms of justification by faith. That is, they determined that Paul addressed an ecclesial situation in Galatia that paralleled their own. They viewed Paul as struggling against Jews, who taught that one propitiated an angry, violent, distant God and earned divine love by practicing works such as circumcision, Sabbath observance, and dietary regulations. The idea that one is made righteous through specific actions or works became known as "legalism" (always a negative term) or "works righteousness." The reformers then made a second move to interpret this contrast between Christianity and Judaism for their own context. They equated their *invented* monolithic, legalistic, dead Judaism with the medieval Roman Catholic Church. They argued that just as Paul opposed a works-based, legalistic Judaism by means of proclaiming justification by faith, so they opposed a works-based, legalistic Roman Catholic Church.

These two interpretive moves had several consequences. One was the formulation of an interpretation of Galatians that has continued to this day. It pits Paul against his fellow Jews, grace against law, faith against works, salvation by faith in Christ against works righteousness, Christianity against Judaism.

Another consequence was a massive rift in the Christian tradition between Protestant and Roman Catholic churches, with continuing prejudice on both sides. To this day, anti-Catholic attitudes surface among certain Protestant groups that incorrectly regard the Roman Catholic Church as Satan's agent, view any pope as the antichrist (see commentary on 1–2 John), and misunderstand Catholicism as based entirely on works, with little concern for faith. Misunderstandings of Protestant traditions by Roman Catholics occur also, and these misunderstandings become exacerbated by nationalist, political, cultural, and extremist views expressed by individual Protestants, Catholics, and some ecclesial bodies.

A further consequence has been a lengthy tradition of anti-Jewish attitudes and practices promulgated by various churches and their representatives. To be sure, this tradition began well before the reformers; anti-Jewish (*adversos Ioudaios*) literature also appears in the works of the church fathers. Luther and his contemporaries tapped into what was already a component of Christian thought. To this day, preachers continue, erroneously, to present Judaism as a religion devoid of God's grace and presence and marked by the futile pursuit of God's favor through good works.

Changing Location and the Interpretation: Toward a Different Reconstruction

The second half of the twentieth century saw a changing historical context shaped by several major events: the Shoah; the discovery of the Dead Sea Scrolls and the resultant new attention to the literature of Second Temple Judaism; and the change in the way biblical and related Jewish and Christian texts are studied in the academy. This new context has challenged the view of first-century Judaism in terms of legalism and justification by works that the reformers constructed from Galatians.

The first event was the horror of the Shoah (a biblical Hebrew term for "calamity" or "catastrophe"), also known as the "Holocaust," the killing of millions of Jews during the Nazi period. In the aftermath of World War II, many Catholics and Protestants became increasingly aware that their teachings about Jews and Judaism in sermons, Sunday schools, and textbooks, contributed to and were complicit in that horror.

A second factor involved the discovery of a collection of Jewish documents at Qumran, east of Jerusalem by the Dead Sea, in the late 1940s. These documents are known as the Dead Sea Scrolls. Among the scrolls are the earliest known manuscripts of every book in the Tanakh except Esther. About 25 percent of the Dead Sea Scrolls are nonbiblical. These documents include community rules that move between ideal visions and regulations for everyday life, scriptural interpretations (such as "Pesher Habakkuk," which interprets Hab 1–2 in terms of events that the community has experienced), and liturgical texts, such as hymns. The remaining scrolls include rewritings of Scripture (for example, the Genesis Apocryphon; the Temple Scroll) and apocalyptic, wisdom, and calendrical materials.

Subsequent work on the nearly 1,000 manuscripts found in 11 caves stimulated a massive rethinking of our understanding of Jewish theology and practice from the third century B.C.E. through to the destruction of the Second Temple in 70 C.E. Scholars did not find works righteousness, attempts to earn God's favor, and a sense of God's wrath and distance in these documents.

Connections between The Dead Sea Scrolls and the New Testament?

Some scholars have suggested that John the Baptist had connections with the Qumran community given their shared eschatological emphases and concern with ritual washing. Early Christian writings and the Dead Sea Scrolls also share interests in interpreting the Scriptures of Israel as speaking directly to their own historical setting, and messianic expectations (the scrolls identify at least two messianic figures—one a priest and the other a king, a descendant of David). Both sets of writings reflected as well as shaped community life and worship. In particular, several scrolls and the Gospel of John share motifs such as contrasts between light and darkness, "truth" and error, hints at predestination, internal community love (as opposed to proselytizing or evangelizing), water symbolism and rejuvenation, and priestly concerns extended to the community. However, no distinctly Christian texts appear among these scrolls. They do not mention Jesus, John the Baptist, Paul, James, and so forth. The commonalities found between the scrolls and the NT may indicate direct borrowing or influence, but more likely they result from common interests that marked many sectors of Second Temple Jewish life.

The discovery of the scrolls prompted a fresh investigation of other Jewish texts from the Hellenistic and early Roman periods. These texts include the writings of Josephus and Philo as well as books such as *1 Enoch, 2 Baruch,* and *Jubilees,* and over 50 others known under the collective title of Pseudepigrapha. This study has also contributed enormously to changing perceptions of Judaism.

Scholarly investigation has shown that the reformers' understanding of Judaism was substantially incorrect. What has emerged is a picture of Jewish culture marked by diversity and vibrancy, a living religion in which worshipers celebrate God's gracious faithfulness and in which repentant sinners are reconciled apart from Temple sacrifice or the shedding of blood. The Prayer of Manasseh, for example, from the deuterocanonical (OT Apocrypha) literature, celebrates God's "immeasurable and unsearchable . . . promised mercy" (v. 6) and "forgiveness to those who have sinned against you, and in the multitude of your mercies you have appointed repentance for sinners, so that they may be saved" (v. 9).

As understandings of Jewish practice and belief changed, terminology also changed.

Scholars used to speak of first-century Judaism as "late Judaism" (the German original of the term, *Spätjudentum*, appears in some academic literature) with "late" carrying a negative connotation of decline from the high point of the prophets, such as Amos and Isaiah. If first-century Judaism was "late," what place was there for present-day Judaism, 2,000 years later? Scholars now speak of "early Judaism" (and "early Christianity") or sometimes of "Middle Judaism." Rather than discuss a "normative" Judaism, terms such as "formative Judaism" or even "Judaisms" (the plural) now appear.

Amidst this vibrant diversity of first-century Jewish life, scholars have also looked for its center. Suggestions include the Jerusalem Temple, the land, the covenant, and the sense of peoplehood (that is, Jews knew they were Jews and not Gentiles). E. P. Sanders proposed "covenantal nomism," with the center of Judaism being God's gracious, loving gift of the covenant. In this understanding, Israel does not follow the Torah to earn God's love. That love is already freely given in Israel's election. Israel follows the Torah because that is how one lives faithfully in the covenant. Sin does not exclude one from the covenant, since the merciful God reconciles the repentant sinner. Simply put, in this "new" understanding of early Judaism, one "gets in" not because of human effort but because of God's grace in establishing the covenant with Israel. One "stays in" by retaining community affiliation, by obeying the teaching, and through atonement. First-century Judaism was not based in justification by works, was not ignorant of God's grace, and was not obsessed with legalism. We can no longer read Galatians over and against this false and negative stereotype.

A third factor prompting a new understanding of both early Judaism and Christian origins was the change in academics. Until the 1960s and 1970s, the Bible and other texts regarded as authoritative for religious communities, including rabbinic literature, were studied and taught primarily in confessional settings (this is the case to this day in Germany). When the Bible (always both New and Old Testaments) was compulsory reading for primary and secondary education, in U.S. schools and elsewhere, the texts again were taught from a confessional perspective. With the opening of non-seminary-based PhD programs in Bible and the related founding of religion departments in secular colleges and universities, biblical study became detached from confessional issues. Similarly, confessional biblical studies in primary and secondary schools became elective programs, and the focus shifted from theology to either history or "religion and literature." For the new secular academic programs, the theological focus—if it was retained at all—became enhanced by the application of new approaches to the text: literary and sociological criticism, social sciences and archaeology, ideological and post-colonial criticisms, and so on. This new academic atmosphere allowed old views to be reconsidered, and it prompted the recognition that much of what we thought was secure was rather a projection of our own biases.

Historical Criticism

In discussing the circumstances Galatians addresses, it might seem reasonable to expect the Letter to the Galatians to be the best source. However, this "reasonable" approach sets up an interpretive circle or circular argument whereby we construct a text's context by internal evidence and then interpret the text in light of the reconstruction. This situation, problematic as it is, may be unavoidable. We have little external evidence for any reconstruction of the Galatian situation. Paul provides no information on how he learned about the struggle in the local church (5:15). We have no texts or direct testimony from the opponents Paul addresses. This letter, like all his letters, responds to a situation as he understands it—subjectively, partially, and perhaps incorrectly.

Nor is Paul always transparent. People have long known that in his letters "there are some things in them hard to understand" (2 Pet 3:16). Paul's style can be cryptic, compact, and complex. Moreover, he employs common and numerous rhetorical tools to make his argument—hyperbole, polemic, invective, allusions to other texts, and others. It is the interpreter's challenge to try to reconstruct both Paul's argument and the circumstances to which that argument is addressed.

Even the letter's name creates difficulty in determining the audience. "Galatia" can denote both an area settled by an ethnic group and a Roman province. The area of ethnic settlement comprised western and central Asia Minor, where Celtic tribes lived. Its major cities were Ancyra, Tavium, and Pessinus. The Roman province came into being in 25 B.C.E. According to Acts 13–14, Paul established churches in cities in the province's southern part: Pisidian Antioch, Iconium, Lystra, and Derbe. Acts 16:6 and 18:23 suggest journeys that point to a northern or ethnic Galatian area.

Scholars often support the "Roman province" or "south Galatia" option in determining the audience of the letter. First, Paul typically refers to Roman provinces in locating his churches. He mentions Asia (Rom 16:5; 1 Cor 16:19; 2 Cor 1:8), Macedonia (Rom 15:26; 1 Cor 16:5; 2 Cor 8:1), and Achaia (Rom 15:26; 1 Thess 1:8). Second, the southern area had a larger Jewish population, which might explain the letter's concern with circumcision, Abraham, and Mosaic Law. But these factors are not probative. Concerns for the ritual, the patriarch, and the Torah may well have occupied any reader of the Septuagint, which was the Bible of the early church, and such concerns would be enhanced by any missionary who insisted that the followers of Jesus attend to them.

In terms of ethnicity, the letter's audience appears to be primarily Gentile. By describing them as "people who did not know God" (4:8), Paul employs scriptural language for outsiders to Israel's covenant (for example, Ps 79:6; Jer 10:25). Moreover, Paul's recounting of their previous religious observances suggests idolatry: "enslaved to beings that by nature are not gods" (4:8). It is possible that the Galatians Paul addresses were first "God-fearers" attracted to synagogues, but again, we have no definitive case for this claim.

Exactly when Paul wrote Galatians remains unclear. Because using Acts to establish a chronology of Paul's life has proved at best problematic, scholars have tried to derive a chronology from Paul's autobiographical comments in Gal 1–2. According to 1:13-17, following his encounter with the risen Jesus on the Damascus Road, Paul spent some time in Damascus and also Arabia, an area perhaps near the Syrian desert or in Transjordan. However, he offers no fixed dates. According to 1:18, "after three years," he went to Jerusalem, then Syria and Cilicia (1:21), then "after fourteen years," to Jerusalem (2:1), and on to Antioch, where he and Peter disagreed over table fellowship with Gentiles (2:11-14). But Paul does not say how much time passed after the Antioch incident until he wrote Galatians. The consensus dating of the letter to circa 50–53, remains speculative.

A Different Reconstruction

Any reconstruction of the situation Paul addresses in Galatians is partial and hypothetical. We must remember that as much as Paul accused the Galatians of "so quickly deserting the one who called you" (1:6) and of being "bewitched" (3:1), the rival teachers and teaching they were embracing made sense to them (4:17-18). It does not help to think of the Galatians as deliberately faithless, willfully disobedient, or witless. Nor does it help to dismiss these rival teachers as heretics who tried to "pervert the gospel of Christ" (1:7). They most likely saw themselves as faithful members of this new movement. At the time Paul was founding churches, there was no established orthodoxy, no NT canon, no single leadership structure. Heretics are recognized only in retrospect.

In talking about the opposing teachers in relation to "the grace of Christ," "turning to a different gospel," and "gospel of Christ" (1:6-9), Paul indicates that he understands them to be Jesus' followers, albeit mistaken ones. They disagree over how Gentile members of the church are to act. Thus the conflict depicted in the letter is not between Judaism and Christianity, as the reformers thought. Nor is it about earning salvation. It is a dispute among Jesus-believers over orthopraxy, the correct understandings and practices for Gentiles in the church.

That the letter regularly refers to the circumcision of male followers (5:2-3; 6:12) suggests that these teachers may have been Jewish followers of Jesus who saw this initiation rite as requisite for membership in the *church*'s covenant community. A possible comparison would be the role some Christian groups accord to baptism: without it, one is not fully a member. Given Paul's emphasis in the letter on Abraham as "justified by faith" and not by "works of the law," it is possible that these teachers also appealed to Abraham as the model for Gentile converts. The argument that all members of the church should follow Abraham's example of being circumcised so as to be members in the covenant people has some scriptural warrant. Genesis 17:14 quotes God saying:

Any uncircumcised male who is not circumcised in the flesh of his foreskin shall be cut off from his people; he has broken my covenant.

These teachers in Galatia, then, may have been teaching a "Christ-plus" gospel comprising acceptance of his gospel of Christ plus circumcision to confirm membership in God's covenant people. They may also have advised "observing special days, and months, and seasons, and years" (4:10) based on Israel's Scriptures.

A historical understanding of early Judaism as rooted in God's gracious covenant prohibits the notion that Paul's opponents were teaching the Galatians to relate to God on the basis of earning divine favor. Abraham did not "earn" anything through circumcision; nor do Jews. Rather, circumcision is a sign of his, and their, belonging in and commitment to God's covenant. It expresses an existing identity rather than works righteousness.

Paul judges that in insisting on faith-plus-circumcision, these teachers "pervert" the gospel and "proclaim . . . a gospel contrary to what we proclaimed" (1:8-9). For Paul, "works of the law," like circumcision, are not necessary for Gentile Jesus-believers. He emphasizes that Abraham is established in right relationship with God, "justified," through faith. Gentiles become righteous in the same way, by faith (3:7): "Just as Abraham 'believed God, and it was reckoned to him as righteousness'" (Gal 3:6, citing Gen 15:6 [LXX]). In this way, the Galatians participate in God's promise to Abraham that "all the Gentiles shall be blessed in you" (3:8).

Works of the Law and Justification by Faith in/of Jesus

To make his argument that Gentiles in the church need not be circumcised, Paul opposes "works of the law" to "justification by faith in Christ." All these words are crucial for Galatians.

The key verse employs the phrase "works of the law" (emphasis added) three times:

We know that a person is justified not by the *works of the law* but through faith in Jesus Christ. And we have come to believe in Christ Jesus, so that we might be justified by faith in Christ [or "of Christ"], and not by doing the *works of the law*, because no one will be justified by the *works of the law*. (2:16)

The phrase also appears in 3:2, 5, 10, and 12.

By "works of the law," Paul is not talking about earning God's favor. We saw earlier that such an understanding of "works" did not exist given the covenant God initiated with Israel. There was nothing to earn. Rather, Paul understands "works of the law" to refer to a cluster of actions that Torah outlines by which Jews *respond* to God's covenant. These actions include circumcision, observance of Sabbath and festivals, giving alms, and following purity laws concerning diet and sexual practice. They are what sociologists call "identity markers." They distinguish Israel from the nations, celebrate their distinct identity, and proclaim their covenantal relationship to their God.

Works of the Law as Identity Markers

Jewish history shows the importance of these identity markers. In the 170s and 160s B.C.E., the Seleucid king of the Syrian empire, Antiochus IV Epiphanes, together with allies among elite Jews, banned observance of circumcision, Sabbath observance, and dietary practices. Jews faithful to Torah resisted this attempt at assimilation and continued to practice their covenantal commitments, even when it cost their lives. First Maccabees 2:31-38 describes some Jews who, refusing to fight on the Sabbath, were slaughtered by Antiochus's troops. The same text also recounts:

> According to the decree, they [Antiochus's forces] put to death the women who had their children circumcised, and their families and those who circumcised them; and they hung the infants from their mothers' necks. (1:60-61; cf. 2 Macc 6:10)

Similar deaths followed for those who refused to eat unkosher food (1 Macc 1:62-63; 2 Macc 6:18-31; 7:1-42). For most Jews, dismissing these practices was a betrayal of the covenant, of Jewish identity, and of God.

The question for Galatians is whether Gentiles should observe these identity markers. For most Jews, then and now, there was little expectation that Gentiles had to convert to Judaism to be in right relationship (i.e., justified) with God. Hence, because the majority of Jews did not believe one needed to practice Judaism in order to be in this right relationship, Jews generally did not engage in attempts to convert Gentiles to Jewish practice and belief. Paul agrees with this view. He is consistent with his teaching in 1 Cor 7:20 that church members should "remain in the condition" in which they were called; therefore the Gentiles do not have to practice "works of the law." Indeed, were they to do so, then they would become "Jews." Paul's eschatological point, and one shared by most Jews of the time, was that God is the God of both Jews and Gentiles. Were Gentiles to convert to Judaism, then God would be the God of Jews only. That, Paul and the majority of his fellow Jews, would not accept.

The second major expression, "justification," translates the Greek *dikaiosynē*, a term that can also be translated "righteousness." For Paul, "righteousness" is not primarily a moral quality. Rather, it connotes God's fidelity and faithful action in relationship with humanity. For example, in Rom 3:26, Paul explains that God shows his righteousness/ justification (*dikaiosynē*) at the present time, so as to be just (*dikaion*) and the one who justifies (*dikaiounta*) those who have faith in Jesus.

To speak of being "justified" or "being made righteous" is thus to speak of being placed in right relationship with God. God's righteous action justifies or delivers people from sin. Paul emphasizes God's righteousness in raising Jesus "for our justification" (Rom 4:25) so that those who accept Paul's gospel are "justified . . . in Christ Jesus . . . by his blood" (Rom 3:24-25). Paul's language is forensic: the judge "justifies" a party in a dispute and therefore pronounces that party in right relationship with the court. The decision is that of the judge alone, and in Paul's scenario, that judge is the righteous or faithful God. Justification is thus *by grace*. The "faith" aspect means that one accepts the authority of the judge, and of the judge's gift of Christ.

A further question arises: does this justification come by faith *in* Jesus or by the faith *of* Jesus? The NRSV translates Gal 2:16 as:

A person is justified not by the works of the law but through *faith in Jesus Christ*. And we have come to believe in Christ Jesus, so that we might be justified by *faith in Christ*. (emphasis added)

In the notes, however, the translators suggest an alternative:

A person is justified not by the works of the law but through *the faith of Jesus Christ*. And we have come to believe in Christ Jesus, so that we might be justified by *the faith of Christ*.

The NIV offers the same alternative: "*but through the faithfulness of . . . justified on the basis of the faithfulness of.*"

A similar translation alternative occurs in Gal 3:22. The NRSV reads:

So that what was promised through *faith in Jesus Christ* might be given to those who believe. (emphasis added)

The notes offer an alternative:

So that what was promised *through the faith of Jesus Christ* might be given to those who believe.

Here the NIV offers no alternative.

The disputed phrase in Greek (*pistis Christou*) can be translated by what is called either an *objective genitive* or a *subjective genitive*. For example, the phrase *the love of God* is ambiguous. It can mean "love for God," where love is directed to God. God is the object of our love. This construction is called an objective genitive. But the phrase can also mean God loves us. In this case God does the loving. God is the grammatical subject of the act of loving. This construction in Greek is called a subjective genitive.

Similarly, "the faith of Jesus Christ" can mean "faith in Jesus Christ" where faith is directed to or placed in Jesus Christ. Jesus Christ is the object of faith (objective genitive). The phrase can also mean "the faith or faithfulness that Jesus Christ showed." Jesus is the one who exhibits faith/faithfulness (subjective genitive). This debate about an objective or subjective genitive reading of "faith of/in Jesus Christ" also occurs in relation to Rom 3:25, 26; Gal 3:22; Phil 3:9; and Eph 3:12.

The conventional way of interpreting the phrase in Gal 2:16 has been to read it as an objective genitive: people are set in right relationship by placing *faith in* or directing it to *Jesus Christ.* This approach is consistent with the Reformation view of human weakness and complete reliance on the divine. But some interpreters question that reading for several reasons. First, the second sentence of Gal 2:16 reads, "And we have come to believe in Christ Jesus." Here the verb "believe" (*pisteuo*) indicates that the believer places faith in Christ. Why, then, would Paul both immediately before and after this statement about believing in Christ refer twice more, in the same verse, to *faith in Jesus Christ?* This redundancy commends a subjective genitive reading for the first sentence of the verse.

Second, the subjective genitive understanding that emphasizes the faithfulness that Jesus showed in doing God's will by submitting to crucifixion finds a parallel construction in Rom 4:16. There, Paul refers to "the faith of Abraham." This is clearly a subjective genitive: it refers to the faith that Abraham demonstrated in doing God's purposes (cf. Rom 4:12).

Third, a subjective genitive understanding of *the faithfulness that Jesus Christ exhibited* evokes a larger story of Jesus' obedience to God's purposes, which Jesus' followers are to imitate (i.e., mimesis). In Phil 2:6-11, especially in 2:8, Paul emphasizes Jesus' obedient death on the cross as an example of self-giving love. In Rom 5:12-21 he underlines Jesus' faithful obedience.

However, it is possible that Paul embraces both readings: faith *in* Jesus and faith *of* Jesus. The two are not mutually exclusive.

Galatians 1:10-21—Paul's First Argument: Personal Defense of His Circumcision-Free Gospel

Paul begins the letter with the customary greeting. He identifies himself as sender and the Galatian Jesus-believers as recipients; he then offers a benediction. Paul uses these conventional forms to introduce themes important for the letter. By presenting himself as "an apostle—sent neither by human commission nor from human authorities, but through Jesus Christ and God the Father" (1:1), he asserts his claim of a direct commission from Jesus to go to the Gentiles. It is a power move that declares he acts under God's authority and as God's agent; he is therefore not under the authority of the Jerusalem apostles, and he is no less legitimate than they are, despite their having known Jesus. In 1:2, he affirms his support from "all the members of God's family who are with me" and so asserts that he represents teaching acknowledged by others as correct. The benediction reinforces his message by referring to God's salvific work accomplished in Jesus, "who gave himself for our sins to set us free from the present evil age" (1:4). The point is that commitment to Jesus is all that is required to be set free. There is no "Christ-plus-circumcision" gospel.

After the salutation (1:1-5), a letter usually expresses thanksgiving or a prayer. Instead, Paul breaks with convention to rebuke his readers:

> I am astonished that you are so quickly deserting the one who called you in the grace of Christ and are turning to a different gospel. (1:6)

Resorting to conventional invective, he calls the Galatians confused (1:7) and their new teachers "accursed" (1:9). He then launches his defense of his Christ-only gospel, in which he attacks the teaching he finds contrary to his views.

In 1:11–2:21 Paul unpacks his first major point. He and his fellow apostles are witnesses that "the revelation of Jesus Christ" (1:12) and membership in his church do not require circumcision. He begins with autobiography; his argument here is that his personal experience legitimates his teaching:

> The gospel that was proclaimed by me is not of human origin; for I did not receive it from a human source, nor was I taught it, but I received it through a revelation of Jesus Christ. (1:11b-12)

He repeats the point in 1:16-19 by saying that after his experience on the road to Damascus he did not go to Jerusalem to consult with apostles. Only after three years did he meet, briefly, with Peter (Cephas) and James, Jesus' brother. The implication is that to contradict Paul is to contradict Jesus himself.

Second, he recounts what the Galatians likely already knew: that he had persecuted the followers of Jesus (1:13-14). His change from persecutor to apostle, prompted by divine revelation, further legitimates his gospel.

Third, Paul emphasizes his own credentials:

> I advanced in Judaism beyond many among my people of the same age, for I was far more zealous for the traditions of my ancestors. (1:14)

These traditions included circumcision: according to the Jewish tradition, circumcision is performed on eight-day-old Jewish male babies; Paul had little choice regarding that ritual. However, he also asserts that he is more knowledgeable about Jewish tradition than his peers, and that not only did he learn the tradition; he also practiced it fully. Should the opposing teachers be promoting their "Jewish" credentials, Paul's argument is that his are better.

Finally, he explains his relations with Jesus' followers in Jerusalem. Fourteen years after encountering the risen Christ, he went to Jerusalem not because he was summoned, but "in response to a revelation" (2:2). To these "acknowledged leaders" (2:2; the 1984 NIV's "who seemed to be leaders" better captures the flavor of the Greek and Paul's irony), he explained that Jesus commissioned him to evangelize the Gentiles, and that these Gentiles were not required to follow Judaism's distinctive laws. These leaders, according to Paul, both agreed with his plan and did not require his companion Titus to be circumcised (2:3). Despite a challenge from "false believers" (2:4), Paul prevailed. James, Cephas (Peter), and John (2:9) agreed that Paul would preach to Gentiles, and they would preach to Jews.

Paul and Gentile Mission?

Whether Paul has painted an accurate description of this meeting remains debated. According to Matthew (28:19), Peter, John, and other Galilean apostles are commissioned to "make disciples of all nations" (Gentiles included; indeed, the Greek of Matt 28:19 can be translated "all the Gentiles"). Acts 10 depicts Peter as making the first convert among the Gentiles, the centurion Cornelius, and it shows Paul beginning his missionary activities among Jews in synagogue contexts. Perhaps the division of labor was not as stark as Paul suggests.

That the followers of Jesus agreed that Gentiles could join the church is not in doubt. The conversion of Gentiles to the worship of the God of Israel was a major plank in most Jewish eschatological programs. The practical question for the church concerned how Jews and Gentiles were to relate prior to Jesus' return. Would Gentiles conform to Jewish dietary practices or Sabbath observance? Would Jews give up the practices that proclaimed them to be Israel? With what sort of food was the Lord's Supper to be celebrated? Were there to be two tracks of being Jesus-followers, Jewish and Gentile, or just one? These questions provoked a crisis in Antioch. Paul reports that Peter had been eating with Gentiles, but men sent from James—men whom Paul labels the "circumcision faction" (2:12)—persuaded Peter to withdraw from this table fellowship. Barnabas, Paul's former coworker (see 1 Cor 9:6), followed Peter. Incensed by action he regarded as inconsistent with "the truth of the gospel," Paul condemns Peter for compelling Gentiles "to live like Jews" (2:14).

Why Peter or the men from James shifted their views remains a matter of speculation. Jewish tradition did not generally expect Gentiles to become Jews in the messianic age (cf. Zech 8:23). Perhaps the Jerusalem-based church defaulted to the dietary regulations recorded in Torah. Some sort of compromise was needed, and perhaps one in favor of Jewish practice made sense to James and his associates. Perhaps they thought that kosher food guaranteed that the Gentiles would avoid meat offered to idols (see 1 Cor 8–10). Or perhaps the Jerusalem contingent wanted Peter, engaged in mission to the Jews, to continue to observe the markers of Judaism, and some Gentiles wanted to imitate this Jewish way of life sanctioned by Torah. We do not know.

In Gal 2:15-21, Paul extrapolates the central implication of his commission to proclaim the "truth of the gospel" (2:5, 14). He asserts that Gentiles are justified or set in right relationship with God through "faith in/of Christ" and "not by works of the law" (observing Jewish identity markers) as the teachers were instructing (2:16).

Galatians 3:1–5:15—Paul's Second Argument: Scriptural Defense

Paul begins his second argument by recalling the Galatians' initial experience of the Spirit: "Did you receive the Spirit by doing the works of the law or by believing what you heard?" (3:2). Since they already had the Spirit through believing, he argues, circumcision is unnecessary. Paul's opponents may have argued that agreeing to circumcision would be an appropriate response to this gift.

Then, Paul begins a series of arguments from Scripture. He cites Gen 15:6 to show that Abraham was regarded as righteous, or justified, because he believed God before he was circumcised. Paul then extends the point: it is not Abraham's biological descendants who are his heirs, but "those who believe" (3:7). In the context of Galatians, those who believe are (noncircumcised) Gentiles.

Paul then adduces a second proof-text to anticipate his later claim that the true children of Abraham are Gentile followers of Jesus:

And the scripture, foreseeing that God would justify the Gentiles by faith, declared the gospel beforehand to Abraham, saying, "All the Gentiles shall be blessed in you." (3:8; the citation alludes to Gen 28:14)

Leaving Abraham briefly, Paul picks up the idea of blessing by contrasting the curse that he states comes with the law and the blessing that is obtained apart from it (3:10-14). Here he cites Deut 27:26:

> For all who rely on the works of the law are under a curse; for it is written, "Cursed is everyone who does not observe and obey all the things written in the book of the law." (3:10)

This would have been an excellent verse for Paul's opponents to cite in their promotion of the practice of the markers of Judaism. If they had cited it, then Paul can turn their argument around: for Paul, the verse shows that the Torah "curses" but Jesus blesses. Paul immediately makes another allusion to Deuteronomy (21:21-22):

> Christ redeemed us from the curse of the law by becoming a curse for us—for it is written, "Cursed is everyone who hangs on a tree." (3:13)

Deuteronomy refers to the exposure of the corpse of an executed criminal, but by the first century, some Jewish writers understood the verses to refer to crucifixion (Qumran texts: 11QTemple; 4QpNahum). Paul interprets the reference in terms of Christ accepting this "curse" so that Abraham's blessing comes to Gentiles (3:14). In effect, Jesus takes upon himself the "curse" so that those under that curse can be blessed. In modern terms, the exegesis can be seen to be slippery; in a first-century context, it is quite consistent with the way Scripture could be understood.

Paul then returns to Abraham by way of the prophet Habakkuk. In 3:11 he cites Hab 2:2 to underscore faith: "Now it is evident that no one is justified before God by the law; for 'The one who is righteous will live by faith'" (see also Rom 1:17). Since Abraham is for Paul the epitome of "righteousness" in Israel's Scriptures, the segue is logical. Paul here takes up promises God made to Abraham concerning his "offspring" (literally "seed"). For example, Gen 17:7 records:

> I will establish my covenant between me and you, and your offspring after you throughout their generations, for an everlasting covenant, to be God to you and to your offspring after you.

In Gen 22:18 God tells the obedient Abraham, "By your offspring shall all the nations of the earth gain blessing for themselves." Both Hebrew (*zerah*) and Greek (*sperma*) terms for "offspring" are collective nouns, singular in form but denoting a *plural*. In Genesis, they denote Abraham's physical descendants: Isaac (21:12), Jacob, and their children through the generations. But Paul identifies this singular "seed" or "descendant" as Christ, in whom the Galatians have believed (3:16). By this reading, Paul disenfranchises the Jewish people and replaces them with Jesus-believers both Jewish and Gentile; belief comes to replace ethnicity in determining the heirs of Abraham:

> And if you belong to Christ, then you are Abraham's offspring, heirs according to the promise. (3:29)

Romans 9–11 tells a different story when it comes to the role of the Jewish people.

In Gal 3:17, Paul makes a legal argument to support his claim about proper inheritance. Because these promises to Abraham predate the law of Moses, they take priority.

> My point is this: the law, which came four hundred thirty years later, does not annul a covenant previously ratified by God, so as to nullify the promise.

The "four hundred and thirty years" refers in Exod 12:40 to Israel's time in Egypt. Since Paul's opponents could, and perhaps did, retort that the later revelation, or covenant associated with Moses, supersedes the former given to Abraham, Paul needs to reinforce his point that the Abrahamic covenant supersedes the Mosaic one.

He continues by arguing for the Law's secondary status (3:19-25):

> [It was] added because of transgressions, until the offspring would come to whom the promise had been made; and it was ordained through angels by a mediator. (3:19)

Exodus does not state that the Law was added "because of transgressions." Paul presents the Law as a preventative to keep people from sinning and, perhaps, to teach people what sin is (see Rom 3:20; 7:7). The claim about angels comes again from the Greek version of Deut 33:2. The Hebrew does not mention angels. The "mediator" to whom Paul refers is Moses.

Next, he claims that the law has been superseded: with the coming of Christ, this old Law no longer has a purpose.

> [It was] our disciplinarian until Christ came, so that we might be justified by faith. But now that faith has come, we are no longer subject to a disciplinarian. (3:24-25)

"Disciplinarian" (Greek: *paidagōgos*) referred to the slave who watched over and tutored the master's children. The point is that the law is at best preparatory; those who are mature in Christ do not need it.

Paul concludes this argument by asserting that in Christ, Abraham's offspring, social, racial, and gendered distinctions are irrelevant.

There is no longer Jew or Greek, there is no longer slave or free, there is no longer male and female; for all of you are one in Christ Jesus. (3:28)

The verse may have been used in baptism, as 3:27 suggests. The formula is hinted at elsewhere in Pauline texts (1 Cor 12:13; Col 3:11) as well as in noncanonical traditions (the term "canonical" would be anachronistic for Paul) such as the *Gospel of Thomas* 22; *2 Clement* 12:2-6; and the *Gospel of the Egyptians* (preserved by Clement of Alexandria). It may reflect understandings of Gen 1–2 where God created both "male and female" in the divine image (Gen 1:27). In Gen 2, God creates "the *adam*," the earthling, and then after creating the animals, separates the female and male human beings. In the ancient Mediterranean world, wholeness and unity took preeminence over division. Paul understood Jesus to be a new "Adam" (cf. Rom 5:14). People baptized into Christ conform to the model of this new Adam, the unity of gender, ethnicity, or social status that existed prior to creation.

On the basis of Paul's other letters, this removal of distinctions was not standard social practice in his churches. First Corinthians mandates distinctive gender roles (for example, 11:3; 14:33-36), and Eph 5:22-24 and Col 3:18 as well as the Pastorals (1, 2 Tim, Titus) follow suit. Philemon and the various household codes attest slavery and gender divisions. In Rom 3:1-2, Paul acknowledges much advantage for "the Jew" including circumcision. Thus the point of Gal 3:28 may be that in the eyes of God, no division matters, and, perhaps, that in baptism one becomes a new creation.

An Anti-Jewish Interpretation of Galatians 3:28

A common interpretation of Gal 3:28 suggests that Paul sets an egalitarian gospel over against misogynist Judaism. Similarly, those who propose this comparison typically associate Pauline statements that appear to contradict Gal 3:28 (for example, 1 Cor 14:33b-36 on women's silence in the churches) with Paul's "rabbinic" background. This juxtaposition of "bad Judaism" against "good Christianity" is both historically incorrect and theologically harmful. First, rabbinic texts substantially postdate Paul, and while some passages can be seen as misogynist, they are best compared with the writings of contemporaneous church fathers, who display similar attitudes. Second, the erasure of "male and female" is not necessarily a good thing for women; nor is the erasure of Jewish identity necessarily a good thing for Jews. For the slave, the erasure of the category "free" is another contested point. Third, if the formula does refer to an original "Adam" before the separation into male and female, in antiquity this primal being was generally understood as the ideal male. This is how the *Gospel of Thomas* (114)

weak, Thomas

understood ideal gender roles; in this gospel, Jesus states, "Every woman who will make herself male will enter the kingdom of heaven." Conversely, rarely does one find in Christian apologetics reference to Jewish texts that sound similar to Gal 3:28, for example, *Seder Eliyyahu Rabbah* (and *Seder Eliyyahu Zuta*): "The Prophet Elijah said, 'I call heaven and earth to witness that whether it be Jew or Gentile, man or woman, manservant or maidservant, the Holy Spirit will suffuse each in proportion to the deeds he or she performs.'" Christian texts offer superb "good news"; those who hold these books sacred do not need a false construction of Judaism to promote the gospel.

In chapter 4, Paul continues the argument about inheritance by asserting the Gentiles' identity as heirs and children of God. The Spirit attests this identity; to be circumcised betrays it (4:1-11). In 4:12-20, expressing his concern for the Galatians, Paul observes that their attitude to him has changed because of the teachers (4:15-18). With a surprising cross-gendered metaphor that presents himself as their mother, he reminds them that they are the children to whom he gave birth (4:19-20).

Paul then returns to his scriptural arguments and employs one that, ironically after 3:28, reinscribes gender, social, and ethnic roles. In 4:24, he uses the rhetorical device of allegory to interpret the story of Abraham's two sons: "one [Ishmael] by a slave woman and the other [Isaac] by a free woman" (4:22). Reading this story from Genesis in terms of two covenants, Paul identifies one covenant (Hagar-Ishmael) as sealed at Sinai, of the flesh, located in Jerusalem, and comprising slavery. The other covenant (Sarah-Isaac) consists of freedom that corresponded to the heavenly Jerusalem. Paul thereby reinscribes the institution of slavery. And without considering the negative implications that his allegory might have for those who follow Torah or for slaves, Paul uses a series of antitheses to delineate two lines of descendants: slave and free, flesh and Spirit, flesh and promise.

He connects this Genesis story to the Galatian situation in at least three ways. First, he identifies the Galatian Jesus-followers with Isaac, the son of the "free woman" (Sarah is not named) and the opposing teachers with Ishmael. Paul supplies the element of Ishmael's persecution of Isaac, which is absent from the Hebrew text, though a possible reading of the Septuagint of Gen 21:9 may explain it. Second, in 4:30 he quotes Gen 21:10 to instruct the Galatians to expel the rival teachers: "Drive out the slave and her child." By associating the rival teachers, and followers, with women, slaves, exiles, the wilderness, and disempowerment, Paul makes his case with the rhetoric of shame. Third, he asserts the identity of those who agree with his teachings in 4:31: "We are children, not of the slave but of the free woman."

In 5:2-15, Paul leaves allegory and returns to direct citation. He dismisses the marks of either circumcision or uncircumcision as having no value compared with active faith. There is no Christ-plus gospel. He then exhorts his followers to love by citing Lev 19:18:

> For the whole law is summed up in a single commandment, "You shall love your neighbor as yourself." (Gal 5:14)

For Paul, the summary abolishes all other commandments. For other Jews who saw Lev 19:18 as primary, such as Rabbi Akiva (see the Jerusalem Talmud, *Nedarim.* 9.4), the point was that all the laws should be followed, but under the primacy of this love. After warning the congregation against "devouring one another" (5:15; the warning repeats in 5:26), perhaps indicating how contentious the circumcision issue has become, Paul ends the letter with ethical exhortations concerning a way of life led either by the flesh (opposed to God, 5:19-21) or the Spirit (5:22-26). The exhortation echoes the concerns of the allegory: the way of the Spirit is, for the Galatians, clearly apart from the markers of the Law. The closing exhortation declares circumcision and uncircumcision to be nothing but "a new creation is everything" (6:15).

Contemporary Churches and Identity Markers

Contemporary churches know well a form of the situation that Paul addresses in Galatians. "Christ-plus" gospels seems to abound in our time. Frequently heard are declarations that somebody or some group cannot be Christian if they do, or do not, support abortion; equal rights for gay, lesbian, bisexual and transgendered people; prayer in public schools; women's ordination; inclusive language in worship; evangelism; the flag in the sanctuary; tithing; a particular form of baptism or of celebrating the Sabbath; a particular political party; a particular translation of the Bible; wine at the Eucharist or the rejection of all alcoholic beverages; and so on. "Christ-plus" gospels create litmus tests. They establish boundary markers to determine who is included within the people of God. Thereby they restrict God's grace, which Paul is convinced is available to all people.

This is not to say that people should not celebrate their distinctive identity within the spectrum of groups that constitute the Christian tradition. Nor is it to say that what are considered today to be ethical issues, such as the debates over gender and sexuality issues, are to be eschewed. Paul's argument in Galatians cautions against such boundary markers becoming points of such contention that people are "devouring" each other. Readers of Paul today might take that caution to its logical conclusion and think about the markers—the practices—that people who join the church must adopt, or must give up. Is the church to be a multicultural institution where people can celebrate their distinct practices, or is it a one-size-fits-all model that corresponds to the dominant culture? Just as Jews and Gentiles who followed Jesus in the first century had to negotiate their identities in relation to both their fellow believers and the belief systems of those outside the church, including family, friends, and business associates, today members of the church do well to think carefully about boundary markers that classify people as "in" or "out" of their ecclesial setting.

$\mathscr{E}$phesians

This text traditionally called "The Letter of Paul to the Ephesians" may not be a letter, may not be from Paul, and may not have been addressed to Jesus-believers in Ephesus. Although the opening salutation suggests a letter format, the content is more a treatise or sermon than a letter. While Ephesians identifies Paul as the author, numerous biblical scholars propose that the text was written by a follower who sought to interpret Paul's thinking for a new context. Some aspects of Ephesians differ from Paul's ideas expressed in the uncontested letters, and some aspects seem to promote theologies Paul opposes. While most manuscripts include the words "in Ephesus" in 1:1, almost nothing in the text shows any specific knowledge of anyone or any particular issue in the Ephesian community, or anywhere else.

We begin with a discussion of authorship, which then takes us into Ephesians' vision of God's cosmic, unifying work and the presentation of a household code within that context. We discuss this material using an approach called canonical criticism (supplemented by ideological criticism). The key question here concerns how to interpret diverse—and even potentially harmful—material in the NT.

Authorship: Authenticity and Pseudonymity

The document claims Pauline authorship in the opening verse (1:1) and again at the beginning of a first-person singular "autobiographical" section (3:1-12). Ephesians also mentions Tychicus (6:21), who is elsewhere associated with Paul, though in documents probably not written by Paul (Col 4:7; 2 Tim 4:2; Titus 3:12; cf. Acts 20:4). Nevertheless, Paul's authorship of Ephesians is questioned for at least six reasons.

First, compared to the letters whose Pauline authorship is not in dispute (Rom, 1 and 2 Cor, Gal, Phil, 1 Thess, Phlm), Ephesians manifests a substantially different style. By one count, 9 of its 100 sentences (in Greek) have 50 or more words. In comparison only 3 of 581 sentences in Rom 1–4, 1 of 621 sentences in 1 Cor 1–4; 2 of 334 sentences in 2 Corinthians, and 1 of 102 sentences in Philippians have 50 or more words. These overly long sentences prompted NT scholar Ernst Käsemann to pronounce parts of Eph 1 "the most monstrous conglomeration of sentences in the Greek language." One such example is Eph 4:11-16, which most English translations divide into multiple sentences, but is one sentence in Greek.

Second, Ephesians tends to heap up synonyms, which is not one of Paul's stylistic traits. For example, 1:19 uses four words meaning or connoting "power." Literally it reads, "and what is the exceeding greatness of his *power* for us who believe according to the *action* of the *power* of his *might*." The NRSV translates: "and what is the *immeasurable greatness* of his *power* for us who believe, according to the *working* of his *great power*" (emphasis added).

Lengthy sentences and repeated ideas create a third stylistic difference. Lacking Paul's vitality and spontaneity, Ephesians reads more like a meditation, a carefully crafted presentation of theological views and ethical exhortations.

The fourth argument against authenticity concerns content. Paul's undisputed letters address individual churches (see Gal 1:2b; 1 Cor 1:2) or specific circumstances (Phlm). Ephesians, however, concerns the church universal: "And he has put all things under his feet and has made him the head over all things for the church" (1:22). Paul spent some time in Ephesus (1 Cor 16:8) yet, strangely, there is no personal or obviously contextual address. The comment that the author has "heard of your faith" (1:15) does not suggest close previous interaction.

"In Ephesus" in 1:1?

The words "in Ephesus," which typically appear at 1:1 in Bibles printed today, do not appear in some early manuscripts. The earlier versions of this document may have begun: "Paul, an apostle of Christ Jesus by the will of God, to the saints who are also faithful to Christ Jesus." Later manuscripts added "at Ephesus," as scribes sought to conform this document to other Pauline letters. In Marcion's canon, the same text is called "to the Laodiceans." Some have suggested that Ephesians was originally composed as a cover letter for a collection of Paul's authentic letters.

Fifth, calling into question the authenticity of Ephesians is its dependence on Colossians. Over one-third of the words used in Colossians appear in Ephesians, with some direct quotes. For example, Eph 6:21-22 quotes Col 4:7-8. Some scholars have concluded that 85 percent of Ephesians may have been culled from the undisputed letters and Colossians. Whether Colossians is itself from Paul's hand or is a later text ascribed to the apostle is a question that further complicates using Ephesians in order to understand Pauline thought. Ephesians also has approximately 100 words that do not appear in the undisputed Pauline letters but are more common in late first-century and second-century writings.

Sixth, of relevance for the canonical-critical perspective of this chapter, is that Ephesians shares with the undisputed letters the proclamation of salvation by grace through faith (2:5, 8-9), the salvific effect of Jesus' death on the cross (2:16), and the Spirit's gifts to believers (4:1-12). Yet it differs substantially from these other letters on matters of soteriology, eschatology, Jewish/Gentile relations, and ecclesiology. Concerning soteriology (teachings concerning salvation), Ephesians departs from Paul's future orientation and eschatological urgency (1 Thess 4:13-18; 1 Cor 15:20-28), and instead emphasizes the present. Already Christ and believers have been raised and seated in the heavenly places. Already all things are under Christ's feet or rule (1:20-23; 2:5-6). Although Ephesians refers occasionally to an age to come (1:21; 2:7), these references play little part in modifying the present focus. Ephesians does not refer to Jesus' return.

For Paul, or at least the Paul we can know from the undisputed letters, Jesus' death and resurrection are the beginning of the *future* completion of God's purposes. As the "first fruits of those who have died" (1 Cor 15:20), Jesus points to and guarantees that God's purposes will be completed at the general resurrection of the dead (1 Cor 15:21-28). Paul operates with an "already" and "not yet" tension. The believer-in-Jesus is justified in the present (Rom 3:24), and that believer lives a sanctified life. But only at the end—the eschaton, the final completion of God's purposes (which Paul sees occurring during his lifetime)—does salvation occur. For example, Rom 6:5 states that while believers "*have been* united with him in a death like his," participation in the resurrection is future: "we *will* certainly be united with him in a resurrection like his" (emphasis added). Similarly, in Rom 10:9 Paul states, "If you confess with your lips that Jesus is Lord and believe in your heart that God raised him from the dead, you *will be saved*" (emphasis added).

But in Ephesians, salvation has already occurred: "For by grace *you have been saved* through faith" (2:8, emphasis added). Just as Christ *has been* seated already in the heavenly places (1:20), so his followers, have also *already* been "raised up . . . and seated with him in the heavenly places" (2:6).

Ironically, this view of present salvation seems to correlate with the view of some people in Corinth against whom Paul struggled. In 1 Cor 4:8 he mocks their overemphasis on a present salvation and neglect of its future dimension:

> Already you have all you want! Already you have become rich! Quite apart from us you have become kings! Indeed, I wish that you had become kings, so that we might be kings with you!

The eschatological completion that the opening chapters of Ephesians proclaim becomes tempered at the end of the document. The concluding instructions encourage strength to fight the cosmic battle: "Put on the whole armor of God, so that you may be able to stand against the wiles of the devil" (6:11). Whereas Ephesians (1:20-22; 6:12) borrows from Colossians (2:10, 15), the image of salvation as Christ's victory over all rulers and powers (Eph 6:11-12) gives this participationist soteriology a little more play by recognizing the believers' ongoing struggle against "the rulers . . . authorities . . . and cosmic powers" (6:12). Dualism has become cosmic: one is either of the church, or of the devil. The church's task is not to attack but to defend or "stand firm." Ephesians 6:14-18 delineates the armor: belt of truth, breastplate of righteousness, shoes of proclamation, the shield of faith, the helmet of salvation, and the sword of the Spirit. The church militant has not begun, but the battlements are in place.

Consistent with this reframing of Paul's eschatological views, Ephesians presents the uniting of Jews and Gentiles as already accomplished through Jesus' death (2:11-22). By contrast, as Paul's letter to the Romans makes clear, the process of interaction between Israel and Gentiles, involving mercy and disobedience, continues into the future until "the full number of the Gentiles has come in." Only then "all Israel will be saved" (Rom 11:25-26). Moreover, Ephesians declares that since Christ "has made both groups into one" (2:14), he "has abolished the law with its commandments and ordinances" (2:15). In this "reconciliation" between Jews and Gentiles, as Ephesians describes it, Torah disappears. Paul, conversely, declares emphatically that he does not abolish the law: "Do we then overthrow the law by this faith? By no means! On the contrary, we uphold the law" (Rom 3:31).

None of these topics, individually, confirms non-Pauline authorship. The changes in tone, style, and vocabulary could be the result of Paul's changed circumstances, changed thinking, or the different needs of the audience. Yet whether written by Paul or by a follower in a subsequent generation using his name for authority, Ephesians presents quite different views on salvation (present accomplishment, not future expectation), the law (abolished, not continuing), salvation-history (unity of Jews and Gentiles already accomplished, not a work-in-progress), and ecclesiology (the church universal, not the local church). And, as we are about to see, the differences continue in terms of women's roles. These distinctions are not simply matters of developed thinking; they reverse central convictions in other letters.

These differences also raise the question that canonical criticism engages: What should interpreters make of differences among New Testament texts? Are some texts right and others wrong, some more authoritative and others less so? Do we recognize that all are equally valid even though they say very different things? Or are there some means by which we can evaluate the differing claims? We will return to these questions shortly.

Cosmic and Ecclesial Unity and Supersessionism

At first glance, Ephesians seems to offer a utopian vision of all humanity unified in Christ. But using the lens of ideological criticism (see 1 Thess for more on ideological criticism's focus on exposing dehumanizing claims in texts and their interpretation), we observe some unsavory fallout from this vision.

Ephesians' central proclamation is:

[God] has made known to us the mystery of his will, according to his good pleasure that he set forth in Christ, as a plan for the fullness of time, to gather up all things in him, things in heaven and things on earth. (1:9-10)

The term translated as "gather up" (Greek: *anakephalaiōsasthai*) is a rare composite with connotations ranging from "summing up" (see Rom 13:9) to ending (Ps 72:20 LXX). It can also mean uniting or ruling or concluding. All these connotations fit this document's theology. For Ephesians, God's work "sums up" or "pulls together" or "unites" all things in heaven and on earth, throughout time, for the sake of fulfilling the divine will and establishing divine rule.

For Ephesians, God's work encompasses all time, all space, and all creation. Jesus' followers become part of the divine plan. They are elected by divine grace, chosen "before the foundation of the world to be holy and blameless before him in love" (1:4). They are members of God's family because of their relationship with Christ: "He destined us for adoption as his children through Jesus Christ, according to the good pleasure of his will" (1:5). Exemplifying God's power at work is the resurrection and ascension of Jesus (1:20-22). By chapter 4, everything and everyone is united under this Christian imperium:

There is one body and one Spirit, just as you were called to the one hope of your call-ing, one Lord, one faith, one baptism, one God and Father of all, who is above all and through all and in all. (4:4-6)

With this claim, it is not surprising that one commentator described Ephesians as "the first manifesto of Christian imperialism."

To detail this unity, Ephesians first distinguishes its readers from their past, nega-tive way of life in the Gentile world. They used to be "dead through trespasses and sins" (2:1). They no longer follow "the desires of flesh and senses" and are no longer "by nature children of wrath, like everyone else" (2:3). They do not "follow the course of this world" (2:2) in conformity to dominant values and practices. Because, like Colossians,

Ephesians understands society to be under Satan's control, it sees outsiders as subject to "the ruler of the power of the air, the spirit that is now at work among those who are disobedient" (2:2).

Chapter 4 returns to this emphasis on distinguishing church members from their former societal values: "You must no longer live as the Gentiles live, in the futility of their minds" (4:17). In other words, in the world as Ephesians depicts it, Gentile life consists of futile minds, lack of understanding, alienation from God, ignorance and hard-heartedness, immorality, corruption, and lust (4:17-24). These characteristics of "your former way of life, your old self" (4:22) contrast with a renewed mind, a "new self, created according to the likeness of God in true righteousness and holiness" (4:24). Verses 25-32 list 16 behaviors that are to be "put away" or be characteristics of the "new self." The verses continue the concern with unity and peace with the final three characteristics comprising unity-keeping actions ("be kind . . . tender-hearted, forgiving") that participate in God's activity, "as God in Christ has forgiven you" (4:32). One possible implication of this summary is that, apart from one's relationship with Christ, kindness, tenderheartedness, and the ability to forgive do not exist.

Having emphasized the contrast with the readers' former way of life, Ephesians explains how these new, formerly "Gentile" followers of Jesus, have been brought under the covenant of Israel:

> At one time you Gentiles by birth, called "the uncircumcision" by those who are called "the circumcision"—a physical circumcision made in the flesh by human hands—remember that you were at that time without Christ, being aliens from the commonwealth of Israel, and strangers to the covenants of promise, having no hope and without God in the world. (2:11-12)

God's intervention has "brought [them] near" in Jesus' sacrificial death (2:13) and broken down the "dividing wall . . . the hostility between" Jew and Gentile (2:14). The material here echoes the claim in Gal 3:28 that in Christ Jesus "there is neither Jew nor Greek." By creating "one new humanity in place of the two" and reconciling Jews and Gentiles to God "in one body" (2:14-16), God creates a new humanity in which Gentiles are members of the commonwealth of Israel; they are no longer "strangers." Ephesians does not offer the possibility that peace can exist outside of unity. Like Gal 3:28, it promotes the erasure of difference.

Ephesians 3:1-6 moves the focus to the benefits of Christ for the Gentiles. The writer draws upon the language of "mystery" found in Colossians, but emphasizes not maturity in Christ but Gentile inclusion:

This mystery . . . as it has now been revealed . . . that is, the Gentiles have become *fellow* heirs, members of the *same body*, and *sharers* in the promise in Christ Jesus through the gospel. (3:5-6; italics added)

In describing this mystery of Gentile inclusion, Ephesians utilizes three Greek terms constructed with a prefix (*syn*) that means "with" or "co-." Literally, the Gentiles are co-heirs and co-bodies and co-members/co-partakers of the promise in Christ Jesus (3:6). Ephesians, then, extends the language of mystery beyond salvation encountered in the cosmic Christ as in Colossians to emphasize the unified church in which Gentiles are full participants. Christology leads to and shapes ecclesiology.

However, with the emphasis on unity and Gentile inclusion, there is a casualty. There is no place in this "one body" (2:16) for the practice of Torah, and so of distinct Jewish identity:

He has abolished the law with its commandments and ordinances, that he might create in himself one new humanity in place of the two, thus making peace. (2:15)

Two peoples are made "one" with identity constituted "in Christ Jesus" and built on "apostles and prophets, with Christ Jesus himself as the cornerstone" (2:20). The effect of this vision is not only to write the non-believing Gentiles out of the human story and the divine plan but also to exclude Jews, as Jews. Ephesians takes no thought, as Paul does in Rom 9–11, to God's continuing faithfulness to Israel. What is good news to the Gentiles who have joined the church would not be heard as such to either Jews or Gentiles who find the message of Paul to be scandalous or folly or who are not convinced that they are living in the messianic age.

Wise Living and Household Codes

Ephesians 5:21–6:9 develops the notion of "wise living" in a discussion of how households should operate. At least since Aristotle (d. 322 B.C.E.), management of ideal (elite) households was a topic of ethical discourse. In Greek and Roman philosophical thought, the household was a microcosm of the empire as well as its foundation. Proper household management contributed to the health of the body politic. Both Hellenistic and Jewish authors, including Philo (*De Decalogo* 165–67; *De Hypothetica* 7:1-14) and Josephus (*Contra Apion* 2.199–208), engaged this topic. Ephesians, along with other NT writings (Col 3:18–4:1; 1 Pet 2:11–3:12; 1 Tim 2:8-15; 5:1-2; 6:1-2; Titus 2:1-10; 3:1, Mark 10; Matt 19–20), offers instruction on proper domestic relations. The version in Ephesians is likely based on that in Colossians.

The literary formulation describing respective roles in the household is today called the "household code" (the German *haustafel*, or "house table," is the technical term). The formulation sets out a hierarchical system in which authority resides with the husband/master/father, who "rules over" wife, slaves, and children. Ephesians employs the genre, though with some modifications.

The passage begins by emphasizing mutual submission, which is absent from Colossians: "Be subject to one another out of reverence for Christ" (5:21). This opening tempers somewhat the hierarchical impact of following exhortations. Attention to mutuality also echoes Paul's insistence in 1 Cor 7:4:

> The wife does not have authority over her own body, but the husband does; likewise the husband does not have authority over his own body, but the wife does.

However, while tempering the hierarchy, Ephesians increases the husband's authority beyond the teachings of 1 Corinthians and Colossians. Whereas Col 3:18 simply exhorts, "Wives, be subject to your husbands, as is fitting in the Lord," Ephesians heightens the theological justification: "Wives, be subject to your husbands *as you are to the Lord*" (5:22, emphasis added) because "just as the church is subject to Christ, so also wives ought to be, in everything, to their husbands" (5:24). There is no mutuality in commanding the husband to submit to the wife. He is the head of the wife just as "Christ is the head of the church" (5:23), and, as 1:21-22 notes, Christ is "head over all things" for the church. Some interpreters claim that this image of "head" (Greek: *kephalē*) means that Christ is the *source* of the church, just as the man/husband is the source of the woman's/wife's existence in creating woman from man (Gen 2:21-22). But Eph 5:24 makes it clear that "head" concerns authority over, not source (cf. 1:22). As we have seen, the letter insists: "Just as the church is subject to Christ, so also wives ought to be, in everything, to their husbands" (5:24).

While emphasizing wifely submission and obedience, the passage also urges husbands: "Love your wives, just as Christ loved the church and gave himself up for her" (5:25; also 5:28, 33). This love imitates and reinscribes a cultural value: "Husbands should love their wives as they do their own bodies. He who loves his wife loves himself" (5:28). In antiquity, men were expected to love and care for their bodies; ancient culture did not move into today's psychological diagnoses of self-hate or self-disgust. By concluding that the husband "should love his wife as himself, and a wife should respect her husband" (5:33), the author puts the greater responsibility on the husband to engage in self-sacrificial, self-invested love. In turn, the wife's respect gains the husband social honor. This focus on love mollifies the patriarchal structure somewhat, but does not challenge it.

Ephesians' discussion of marriage is grounded in references to ecclesiology and theology. Both husband and wife are members of the same "body," that of Christ and so of the church (5:30). Ephesians 3:31 appeals to the idea of unity in Gen 2:24 ("Therefore a man leaves his father and his mother and clings to his wife and they become one flesh") not to forbid divorce (see Matt 19:5-6; Mark 10:8) but to bolster marital harmony. It then extends the reference by calling this marital relationship a "great mystery" and relating it "to Christ and the church" (5:32). The language of "mystery" recalls earlier references to the mystery of God's plan to unite the world and time through Christ (see 1:9-10; 3:3, 4, 9). Thus marital relations are not only the microcosm of the empire, but they are also the foundation and sign of God's universal plan. According to Ephesians, while Jew and Gentile are united and difference is erased, when it comes to gender, union, whether in marriage or in the church, preserves difference.

The second relationship in the household codes concerns parents and children. Again, Ephesians addresses the subservient first and grounds the exhortation in Israel's Scriptures:

Children, obey your parents in the Lord, for this is right. "Honor your father and mother"—this is the first commandment with a promise: "so that it may be well with you and you may live long on the earth." (6:1-3; see Exod 20:12; Deut 6:16)

The only instruction for parents is directed to fathers, that they not provoke their children but discipline and instruct them in the ways of the Lord (6:4). The mother receives honor, but she has no responsibility and no authority over her children.

The third relationship likewise focuses on the subordinate.

Slaves, obey your earthly masters with fear and trembling, in singleness of heart, as you obey Christ, not only while being watched, and in order to please them, but as slaves of Christ, doing the will of God from the heart. (6:5-6)

Thus the master, like the husband/father, serves in the place and role of Christ. The verse gives divine sanction to slavery, a fundamental structure of the Roman empire within which perhaps one-third of the population were slaves. As with the exhortation to wives, the theological material adds to the parallel in Colossians. The master is only exhorted not to threaten his slaves (6:9a). Yet the master's absolute control is tempered, for both slave and free "have the same Master in heaven, and with him there is no partiality" (6:9b).

Ephesians changes its Colossians source by emphasizing mutual submission (5:21), love, and the relationship of Christ and the church. These changes could be seen as mitigating the hierarchical system that governed Roman life. However, the command for mutual submission is not carried through into the specific instructions to husbands, fathers, and masters. They are not instructed to submit to wives, children, and slaves.

The emphasis on their submission is reinforced by the analogy of Christ's rule over the church. The sanctioning and indeed sanctification of slavery by making the slave's work a service to the Lord presents submission as a sacred duty. And the comment that it does not matter whether one is a slave or free (6:8) ignores the profoundly dehumanizing realities of slavery. It would seem that Ephesians intensifies the sanctioning of patriarchy and slavery.

Canonical Criticism

The Reverend Jerry Falwell (1933–2007) asserted that the Equal Rights Amendment was "a definite violation of holy Scripture" because it "defies the mandate that 'the husband is the head of the wife, even as Christ is the head of the church.'" The Southern Baptist Convention proclaimed in 1998: "A wife is to submit graciously to the servant leadership of her husband." Opponents of these teachings concluded that by upholding not only male authority but also male supremacy and relegating women to secondary and submissive roles, neither the SBC mandates nor Ephesians can be accepted as gospel.

Our understanding of Ephesians is thus not an arid exercise or even just a historical investigation. Interpretation impacts lives today. How then do readers, seeking to be both faithful to the text and faithful to their own vision of Christian life, negotiate such passages? Ideological criticism helps indicate where the text can be read as promoting dehumanization; canonical criticism provides a few guidelines for negotiating contradictory, and problematic, passages.

Embracing a range of approaches, canonical criticism addresses the form and function of the New Testament writings as sacred Scripture. These approaches explore the formation, final literary shape, and contemporary interpretation of biblical literature as the canon or "rule" of the church. Attention to the canon's formation foregrounds the interplay between emerging traditions and changing social circumstances. Attention to its final literary shape attends to the interplay among biblical writings. Attention to the interpretation of the canon foregrounds not the text's origin or events behind the text but the texts themselves as part of a contemporary theological conversation with other canonical texts and interpretations promoted by communities of faith.

Given that the canon was written by multiple authors addressing multiple communities with multiple issues, it will necessarily express views that appear to be divergent. Canonical criticism highlights the importance of interpreting a passage in relation to the rest of the document of which it is a part, and then in relation to the other documents in the canon. For example, we could conclude that by promulgating a household code that reinscribes patriarchy and slavery, Ephesians violates its major message of the new life in Christ that is manifest apart from prevailing social values. Ephesians celebrates that the followers of Jesus are no longer "following the course of this world, following the ruler of the power of the air, the spirit that is now at work among those who are disobedient" (2:2).

Again readers are instructed, "No longer live as the Gentiles live" (4:17) but live as a "new self" in "the likeness of God" (4:24), who unites or gathers up all things (1:10). By taking over the patriarchal household structure, Ephesians does not live up to its own vision of a new way of life.

This emphasis on "not living as the Gentiles do" but rather on walking as people "created in Christ Jesus for good works" (2:10) provides a means of evaluating interpretations that view the teachings in Ephesians as still relevant rather than as culturally contingent. For example, those today who argue that wives are to submit to their husbands rarely argue that slavery ought to be legalized, or that where it is practiced, it should continue as long as masters do not threaten their slaves. To use a literalist hermeneutic for the relations between wives and husbands, but a liberationist one for the relations between slaves and masters is, at best, inconsistent. Or to absolutize a command—wives, submit to husbands—not only fails to heed Ephesians' emphasis on not conforming to cultural practices, it fails to take into account social realities: Should a wife abused by her husband submit to abuse? Other readers allegorize the instruction to slaves and masters as instructions for employers and employees. But employment status, no matter how bad it might be, is far removed from divinely sanctioned slavery. Still others argue from Eph 6:8—"we will receive the same again from the Lord, whether we are slaves or free"—that slavery and other inequalities today do not matter, because at the eschaton, all will be sorted out. Surely—adding an ideological criticism lens to make visible both the dominant commitments of this text and these interpretations, as well as to identify contrary commitments that are silenced—contemporary practices of compelling human beings into sex slavery or inhuman labor practices require urgent resistance now. Canonical criticism helps here in showing that in Eph 2, living *in this world*, but *not in conformity to it*, is the dominant model.

A second way that canonical criticism offers for assessing a scriptural passage is to compare it with other biblical material. For example, on the question of Jewish/Gentile relations, Paul's vision in Rom 9–11 recognizes Israel's continuing place in God's faithful plans. It is at odds with Ephesians' supersessionist approach as well as with the claims in the Scriptures of Israel. On the question of gender: various NT passages attest to women as equal partners with Paul in ministry as women deacons (Rom 16:1), apostles (Rom 16:7), teachers, and prophets. The two approaches—submission and equality—are not reconcilable, yet both are in Scripture. Thus, along with seeing if a text fits into the concerns of its own literary context, canonical criticism asks how a particular passage fits into the canon as a whole.

A third approach to negotiating divergent teachings and addressing problematic ones is to recognize that all readers set up "a canon within the canon." A "canon within the canon" consists of what the interpreter decides is the Bible's major emphasis or what constitutes the gospel. Martin Luther, for example, formulated a doctrinal "canon within the canon," namely "that which commends Christ." Appealing to central themes that span the New Testament—for example, new life in Christ, unity of the community, love of God and neighbor, mutual submission and service, that which is loving, life-giving, and liberating—some readers will conclude that a passage such as the Ephesian household code contradicts the basic message of the canon. The difficult question concerns what constitutes this "canon within the canon."

As long as there are Christians, there will be diverse ways of understanding the biblical material. What is culturally contingent and what is timeless? What is to be fore-grounded and what is to be set aside? What is applicable to all and what is restricted to an individual or a church in particular circumstances? What is a faithful expression of the good news and what is cultural co-option? The canon speaks with multiple voices. It is the responsibility of its readers to assess the different voices, in the light of what they see to be the primary proclamation of the gospel.

$\mathscr{P}$hilippians

Philippi, "a leading city of the district of Macedonia and a Roman colony" (Acts 16:12), had been by the time of Paul's letter (ca. 50), under Roman control for about a century. In 42 B.C.E., Marc Antony and Octavian defeated Brutus and Cassius at the Battle of Philippi. Settling veterans of the war there, they began the process of romanization. More veterans settled in Philippi after Octavian defeated Antony at the Battle of Actium in 31 B.C.E. Octavian, who would become known as the emperor Augustus, emerged from that battle as the empire's undisputed ruler. In 44 C.E., the emperor Claudius conquered the surrounding (northern) territory of Thrace and made it a Roman province.

By the mid-first century, Philippi's inhabitants were mainly Greeks, Romans, and native Thracians, along with Africans and Gauls. Acts 16:13-16a indicates a Jewish presence in the city, and a third-century inscription confirms a synagogue there. While some were Roman citizens, there were also slaves and freed or former slaves (*liberti*). All were aware of Rome's rule. One entered Philippi through an impressive gate with statues of the city gods. The forum or central square was surrounded by temples including a building devoted to the imperial cult or worship of the emperors Augustus and Claudius and their families, especially Augustus's wife, Livia. The forum displayed statues of the imperial family, of Thracian kings, and of local elites. To the south was the commercial area and agora (the marketplace), along with an impressive 42-seat public latrine (Paul's reference to "human waste" in 3:8 had local resonance!). The city also included a theater and sanctuaries for gods such as Dionysos, Artemis, Apollos, and Isis.

Acts 16, which provides an account of Paul and Silas's missionary work in Philippi, highlights hospitality provided by the textile worker and patron Lydia, the exorcism of a mantic slave girl, the missionaries' imprisonment by the slave's owners for "advocating customs that are not lawful for us as Romans to adopt or observe" (16:21), and a miraculous prison escape. Paul and Silas accuse the local magistrates of having "beaten us in public, uncondemned men who are Roman citizens, and thrown us into prison" (16:37). They receive a public apology, and move on to Thessalonica.

Paul's letter mentions none of these events. Nor is the account in Acts necessarily accurate. For example, the reference to their citizenship—something Paul never mentions in his letters—*after* the imprisonment seems more plot device than factual reporting. Yet the route of Paul's journey as Acts presents it—from Troas in Asia Minor west to Samothace and the port of Neapolis and then further west on the Via Egnatia road to Philippi—is plausible (16:11) as is the general description of the city.

Method: Social-Science Criticism

Our discussion of Philippians is shaped by a social-science approach (see 1 Cor, 1 Pet, and 1–3 John for other examples of this approach). Here we make four observations about the social-science method.

First, New Testament social-science criticism begins with the historical-critical recognition that the biblical texts are shaped by their historical contexts. It then extends this recognition by investigating the cultural practices, values, and social structures that organize those contexts. Social-scientific criticism thus helps to elaborate the social structures and values of the world in which New Testament texts participate. It also helps contemporary readers to avoid projecting anachronistic concepts and values onto first-century texts.

Second, for the NT world, those contexts include a vast array of structures (for example, the empire, household and kinship relations, slavery, provincial and city governance), cultural values (honor and shame; gender constructions), and practices (identity construction, patron-client relationships, euergetism or civic good works). Several may be in play in the same event.

Third, social-science work often draws on cross-cultural analysis to construct models of social structures. Models are then applied to and modified by the specific contexts under investigation. This use of modeling can be helpful in providing a larger framework by which to interpret data; it can also be a liability in that the general model might distort a particular situation.

Finally, the task of identifying social structures and values and interpreting New Testament texts in relation to them is a challenge, and what goes by the name "science" is often substantially an art. A text is not the same as a community, so moving from text to community is difficult. Modeling structures and values in a text is not the same as modeling or mapping a community. Usually there is some connection between the two, but the form that connection takes is not always evident: Does the text report what presently exists, or does it suggest, in a situation of conflict for example, what ought to be? Does it correct current practices? Does it confirm them? Does it envision or introduce new practices?

In interpreting Philippians, we attend particularly to the cultural practice and value of friendship. Because friendship involves different things in different cultures, we need to understand how friendship was practiced in the Roman Empire of the first century.

Following a discussion of the occasion of Philippians, we turn to friendship in Philippians, in Greek culture, and in Stoic thought to see how Paul utilizes common cultural conventions in light of his belief in Christ. In understanding the function of friendship in the letter, we focus on three sets of relationships: Paul and the Philippians, the Philippians with fellow church members, and God with both the Philippians and Paul.

The Occasion of Philippians

Paul writes that he and the congregation have shared "in the gospel from the first day to now" (1:5). He does not specify either the date or circumstances of that "first day" or "now." Presumably his audience understands the details; we do not have access to them. Paul states that he writes from prison (1:7, 13, 17), but he does not say where or why he is imprisoned. Presumably his readers know, but we do not. In addition to reporting Paul's short imprisonment in Philippi (Acts 16:23-40), Acts mentions two places where Paul was imprisoned: Caesarea (23:23–26:32) and Rome (28:16–31), but as we have seen, the historicity of Acts cannot be easily confirmed. Paul's letters also indicate that he faced difficulties in Ephesus, which might mean he was imprisoned there (1 Cor 15:32; 2 Cor 1:8-9; 11:23). Argument can be made in favor of each setting, but none is conclusive.

Further complicating the identification of the letter's occasion is the question of its literary unity. Our letter to the Philippians may be a compilation of at least two, or even three, letters (a suggestion also posited for 2 Corinthians). In this chapter, after indicating the problems with the coherence of the letter as we have it, we choose to analyze the letter as a literary unity.

Philippians: One Letter or Compilation?

Philippians 3:1b, "To write the same things to you is not troublesome to me," suggests that Paul had written a previous letter to the church at Philippi. We know from 1 Cor 5:9 and perhaps 2 Cor 2:3-4 that recipients did not carefully preserve every letter that Paul wrote. The thesis that Paul wrote multiple letters to the Philippian church may also have support from the second-century bishop of Smyrna, Polycarp, who in his own *Letter to the Philippians*, refers to "letters" (3:2)—plural—that Paul had written to them.

It is possible that parts of this initial letter found their way into the text of Philippians as we now have it. The hypothesis of multiple letters spliced together makes sense of several anomalies in the text. For example, in 3:1a Paul writes an

---

apparent conclusion, "Finally, my brothers and sisters, rejoice in the Lord"; such an exhortation typically comes near the end of Paul's letters. The reference in 2:19-30 to travel plans is also oddly placed, for these also typically come at the end, not midway through. However, in Philippians, the text continues for another two chapters. Further, a second exhortation to rejoice in 4:4 suggests that 3:2–4:3 is an interpolation, material inserted into an already completed text.

Also suggesting an interpolation is the shift in content and tone from 1:1–3:1a and then from 3:1b–4:3. Philippians 3:1a speaks of rejoicing and Paul's pastoral care, while 3:2 opens a new subject with a harsh warning: "Beware of the dogs, beware of the evil workers, beware of those who mutilate the flesh." Scholars have even suggested that 4:10-20 derives from a third letter that Paul wrote to the Philippians. According to 4:18, Paul's coworker, Epaphroditus, has just arrived from Philippi with gifts from the congregation, whereas 2:25-30 suggests that he has been with Paul long enough to have become ill, nearly died, and recovered. Such compilation theories—and numerous theories allocate verses in different ways to various postulated letters—attempt to explain anomalies.

However, many interpreters find the hypothesis of compilation unnecessary. They point to various factors to support textual unity. There is no manuscript evidence for separate letters. It is impossible to identify the supposed separate letters on the basis of distinctive vocabulary or themes. Other explanations account for the so-called anomalies relatively easily. To label the material in chapter 2 about Timothy and Epaphroditus as "travel plans" misses Paul's point in 2:1–4:3 of offering examples of the sort of interactions that should mark this community of friends. The discussion of the gift in 4:10-20 also reinforces the theme of friendship and indicates that Paul is the friend of the Philippian congregation, not their client.

The content of Philippians is largely peaceable. Paul thanks the congregation for their support, praises their fidelity, and expresses their common belief in the lordship of Christ. The letter also includes some familiar polemic. Wherever Paul goes, he appears to have opponents who proclaim a variant gospel. Identifying these opponents from his brief, often ambiguous, polemic remains challenging. The possibility exists that four of the five groups he mentions may not be real people at all. They might be stereotypes convenient for Paul's argument.

The first of the possible rival teachers or teachings comprises those who "proclaim Christ from envy and rivalry . . . out of selfish ambition, not sincerely but intending to increase my suffering" (1:15-17). Second, perhaps related to this group, Paul contrasts his coworker Timothy with those who "are seeking their own interests, not those of Jesus

Christ" (2:19-22). Both groups of opponents are found wherever Paul and Timothy are, so they are clearly not restricted to Philippi.

The third group has caused the Philippians "suffering . . . since you are having the same struggle that you saw I had and now hear that I still have" (1:27-30). This group is likely to be comprised of people in Philippi who reject the church's proclamation and are perhaps concerned with the church members' lack of involvement in local civic and imperial observances.

Fourth are "the dogs . . . the evil workers . . . those who mutilate the flesh" (3:2), whom Paul contrasts with "we who are the circumcision" (3:3). Some interpreters propose that 3:2 refers to Jews who follow Jesus and who want Gentile followers to be circumcised and observe other distinct practices of Judaism, such as Sabbath observance and dietary regulations. A comparison of these "dogs" to the Judaizers mentioned in Galatians is sometimes drawn. However, a single reference does not suggest a major threat to the Philippian church. Paul's words may be more of a general warning. Even more likely, the warning bolsters Paul's comment in 2:1 that service for others is the marker of Christian friendship. In 3:2, Paul is resisting status markers, such as circumcision. The verb in 3:2 translated in the NRSV "beware" (Greek: *blepō*; the NIV's "watch out for" comes closer to the Greek but still doesn't quite get the visceral connotation) literally means "see" or "look at," so Paul may be saying, "Observe those who mutilate the flesh" or even the effects of the operation itself, and do not concern yourselves with that marker.

Finally, fifth, Paul refers to "enemies of the cross of Christ . . . their god is the belly . . . their glory is in their shame . . . their minds are set on earthly things" (3:18-21). He contrasts them with himself and the Philippian congregants whose "citizenship is in heaven." The reference to "belly" is unlikely to refer to Jewish dietary observances. Rather, "belly" and "shame" more likely refer to sexual and sensual pleasure. It is by no means clear that Paul here identifies a group active in Philippi.

With such vague targets, whether the congregation is facing any direct threat, either from local Philippians or from others within the Jesus movement, cannot be conclusively determined. The various references do, however, have the literary effect of bonding Paul to the Philippians by suggesting that they are "friends," with shared ideals and common foes. It is to "friendship" we now turn.

A Model of Friendship

In books 8 and 9 of his *Nicomachean Ethics,* the fourth-century B.C.E. philosopher Aristotle detailed his central insights about friendship. Aristotle's observations continued through the writings of the Roman philosopher, orator, and political commentator Cicero (d. 43 B.C.E.); Seneca (d. 65 C.E.), the Stoic moralist and advisor to the emperor Nero;

and other Greek and Roman philosophers and rhetoricians after Paul's time. From their discussions, social-science interpretation can construct a developing model of friendship in Paul's world, at least as far as elite, literate men understood it. Perhaps their views had a trickle-down effect that also influenced lower-status individuals.

According to Aristotle, friendship is based in *koinōnia*, a Greek word denoting the sharing of common activities and aims; the term is often, for the New Testament, translated as "fellowship." Basic to friendship is a unity of mind and purpose that comprises goodwill. "Goodwill" here signals the desire for the other's good. Aristotle identified three types of friendship: one based in a person's usefulness; a second based in pleasure or delight in a person's company; and a third based in shared character or virtue. Aristotle thought the third type was the most enduring and valuable.

All three forms were part of a system of reciprocity in which each person benefited from his (the gender-specific pronoun is deliberate) relationship with the other. Friendships were marked not only by concord, equality, and faithfulness but also by a contract of exchange. In antiquity, then, friendship among elite males was less about "hanging out with someone" and more about forming networks and political alliances to secure long-term, mutual interests. Friends whose relationship was based in shared character or virtue became one soul in sharing hospitality, material possessions, joys, and sorrows.

While repeating Aristotle's emphases, subsequent discussions of friendship also acknowledged various challenges to it. These included the need to distinguish true from false and "flattering" friends, the difficulties of restoring friendships that had been breached, discernment in choosing virtuous friends, and friendship among unequals. Aristotle had emphasized friendship among those of equal power and wealth. He recognized that interactions existed among unequals—father and son, master and slave, benefactor and beneficiary—but he did not think these relationships were "friends." Nevertheless, "friendships" in the sense of mutual support and personal investment among those who were not social equals flourished. These friendships, which usually took the form of patron-client relations, also emphasized common aims, commitment to moral duties, and virtuous character in interactions marked by beneficial reciprocity and obligation. Hellenistic kings and the Roman emperors developed circles of "friends" who offered counsel, performed loyal service, or supplied information.

Speculation about friendships among persons of unequal status intensified the discussion about distinguishing friend from foe, or friend from flatterer. One criterion for discernment concerned "boldness" or "frankness of speech." The flatterer only flattered, whereas a true friend was willing to speak candid criticism.

Another developing emphasis concerned letters of friendship. Letters connected absent friends and maintained the relationship. Seneca stated, "I prefer that my letters should be just what my conversation would be if you and I were sitting in one another's company or taking walks together" (*Moral Epistles to Lucilius* 75.1). Letters engaged both the sender's and the recipient's interests along with those of third parties; thereby they fulfilled the friendship obligation of mutual counsel. All of these characteristics are evident in Paul's letter to the Philippians.

Philippians as a Letter of Friendship

Paul begins by drawing together his intimate friends who are with him and the members of the Philippian congregation:

Paul and Timothy, servants [Greek: *douloi*, literally, "slaves"] of Christ Jesus. To all the saints in Christ Jesus who are in Philippi, with the bishops and deacons. (1:1)

The designation "slaves" could suggest the relationship is between unequals, but Paul's prior relationship with the Philippians, his own reputation, the contents of the letter, and the identity of the "master" immediately belie that impression. Paul and Timothy subordinate themselves as "slaves" compared to the "saints," yet they have honor as slaves of Jesus and not of the Philippian congregation. The term *doulos* (the singular form) will reappear in the Christ Hymn (2:6-11), which depicts Jesus taking the form of a "slave." What in some contexts would denote humiliation becomes, for followers of Jesus, a term of honor. Paul does not identify himself in the salutation as an "apostle" (contrast Rom 1:1; 1 Cor 1:1; 2 Cor 1:1; Gal 1:1, etc.), but he does note the ranks of the "bishops" (Greek: *episkopoi*, literally, "overseers") and "deacons" (Greek: *diakonoi*) among the Philippians. This is the earliest appearance of these church offices, and their duties remain unstated.

Throughout the letter, Paul emphasizes the reciprocal relationship he has with the Philippians, and he exudes the concern for their well-being that attests friendship. He prays for them (1:3-11) and acknowledges that they pray for him (1:19). He recognizes their affection (1:7) and expresses affection for them (1:8). He wants the best for them (1:6, 9-11), which means both their faithful living (1:27-28) and their eschatological salvation (2:1). He declares he speaks with "boldness" or "frankness" (1:20). He notes the suffering (1:20-24, 30) as well as rejoicing that he and the Philippians share: "I am glad and rejoice with all of you—and in the same way you also must be glad and rejoice with me" (2:17-18).

Intimate address defines and solidifies the relationship: the Philippians are his friends, and indeed his "beloved" friends. He calls them "beloved" (Greek: *agapētoi*; 2:12; 4:8) and describes them as those whom he "loves and longs for" (4:1). He uses kinship terms to describe them as "brothers and sisters" (although "sisters" is implied rather than stated; 1:14; 3:1, 17; 4:1; also 2:25), and thereby he constitutes a fictive family comprising himself and the Philippians.

Paul's terminology includes other markers that fit within the construction of "friendship." For example, six times he uses the word *koinōnia*, indicating lives marked by shared activity and common purpose. He rejoices in "your sharing [or "partnership" (NIV)] in the gospel from the first day until now" (1:5; see also 3:15). He appeals to their shared life in the Spirit:

> If then there is any encouragement in Christ, any consolation from love, any sharing [or "common sharing" (NIV) (*koinōnia*)] in the Spirit, any compassion and sympathy . . . (2:1)

In 3:10 he expresses his goal "to know Christ and the power of his resurrection and the sharing of [or "participation in" (NIV) (*koinōnia*)] his sufferings by becoming like him in his death." In 4:14, he acknowledges that "it was kind of you to share [verb form of *koinōnia*] my distress," and the next verse acknowledges their financial gift as an expression of common or shared life: "When I left Macedonia, no church shared [verb form of *koinōnia*] with me in the matter of giving and receiving, except you alone" (4:15).

Another compositional emphasis expresses the shared life and unity of mind that constitute friendship. Thirteen times Paul uses words constructed with the prefix "syn-," indicating "together," "side by side," "beside," "with" or "co-." Two instances (1:7; 4:14) involve the word *koinōnia*. In 1:27, Paul talks about "striving together" or "striving side by side with one mind for the faith of the gospel," and in 4:3 he names those who have "struggled beside me in the work of the gospel." Twice in 2:17-18 he identifies "rejoicing together," and in 4:3 he speaks of "helping together" or "receiving together" two women in dispute. That same verse addresses the Philippians as "my co-companion" or "my fellow-companion" and recognizes that among them are other "co-workers."

Similarly, Paul underlines their unity by utilizing terms of sameness. He and the Philippians share "the same struggle" (1:30). He exhorts them to have "the same mind" (also 2:2, 5; 3:15; 4:2) and "same love." In 2:18, he speaks of the same or mutual rejoicing. These emphases denote classic friendship virtues of shared purpose, harmony, mutual goodwill, and benefit.

Much of this celebration of Paul's friendship with the Philippians centers on their common purpose, which is related to Paul's present circumstances. First, Paul is in prison (1:7, 13-14, 17). He does not say why, although he declares, "I have been put here for the defense of the gospel" (1:16). Comforting the congregation, he explains that his situation has led to the spread of the mission. It has provided opportunity for him to evangelize the imperial guard and has emboldened others to bear witness (1:12-14). He seems to recognize that he might be executed (1:20-24), yet he expresses an expectation of being released soon (1:19) and thereafter visiting the Philippians (1:25-26; 2:24). Whether he is trying to cheer up his recipients or whether he expects to be executed cannot be determined; both attitudes may be operative. Mentioning his expectations to "come to you again" (1:26), Paul uses the term *parousia*. An allusion to Jesus' return is not impossible (but see 2:12). Taking a Stoic view of life in which one determines that which is essential and that which is not (Greek: *adiaphora*, issues to which one might be indifferent), he can celebrate the gospel's progress and his friendship with the Philippians; all the rest is ultimately inconsequential. As Paul summarizes, "For to me, living is Christ and dying is gain" (1:21).

Despite his imprisonment, Paul focuses on "joy" and "rejoicing"; some 14 references make this response a major theme in the letter. He expresses his joy in the congregation's continuing loyalty to him (1:4; 2:17; 4:10), mentions their continuing joy in faith (1:25), instructs them to rejoice with him (2:18; see 2:28-29), and exhorts them to rejoice in the Lord (3:1; 4:4 [2x]). He rejoices in continued preaching of the gospel (1:18 twice) and expresses his own joy (2:2; 4:1).

Yet as the models of friendship indicate, friends share difficulties as well as joys. Paul acknowledges his imprisonment as a time of suffering (1:30; 2:17; 3:10), but "in any case, it was kind of you to share my distress" (4:14; also 1:30). He also assures the Philippians that they need not be concerned about their own suffering, since suffering is a sign of divine honor granted by their divine patron:

> For he has graciously granted you the privilege not only of believing in Christ, but of suffering for him as well. (1:29)

That is, the Philippians provide a service or benefit to Christ by suffering *for* him, as he suffered for them. The model is one of reciprocity. It serves to solidify friendship even as it consoles. Paul states in 2:1, there is encouragement in Christ, "consolation from love," and "sharing in the Spirit" of compassion and sympathy. He can therefore, stoically, conclude, "Do not worry about anything" (4:6).

Friendship and Gifts

In 4:10-20, Paul acknowledges that the Philippians have expressed their friendship for him in sending financial gifts with Epaphroditus (4:18). While he clearly appreciates their gift (4:14), he frames its significance away from any association with patron/client relations.

First, he rejoices that they "revived your concern for me" (4:10). This reviving refers to previous gifts that they had sent him (4:15-16; also 2 Cor 8:1-5; 11:8-9). The imperfect tense of "you were concerned for me" indicates repeated action, but at some point those gifts had stopped (4:10b). Using friendship conventions, Paul accounts for their ceasing to send gifts in terms of the Philippians not having had the "opportunity to show" their appreciation in reciprocating his gift to them of the gospel (4:10b).

Second, exchange among friends of unequal resources typically defined one party as the patron (here, the Philippians) and the other as their client (Paul). A client was subject to the patron's will. Paul had refused financial support from the Corinthians, perhaps precisely to avoid such relationships (1 Cor 9:12-18; 2 Cor 11:9b-12). Therefore, Paul follows his statement of appreciation by asserting his independence. He does not expect them to meet his needs. In fact, he presents himself, stoically, as having no needs at all:

> Not that I am referring to being in need; for I have learned to be content with whatever
> I have. I know what it is to have little, and I know what it is to have plenty. (4:11)

By denying need, he rejects a friendship based in utility. In 4:17 he again asserts his independence and rejects any patron-client relationship. Instead, he insists that he has been "paid in full and have more than enough; I am fully satisfied" (4:18).

But Paul also asserts that his sufficiency does not result from self-sufficiency. Rather, it results from God's care. "I can do all things through him who strengthens me" (4:13). Paul presents himself not only as a "slave" of God, but also as both a friend of God and a client of God his patron. He is independent of the Philippians but dependent on God, who provides the strength he needs for any situation. So too are the Philippians. They are his friends and they are, like Paul, also clients of God's favor, "for all of you share in God's grace with me" (1:7).

He concludes by asserting that the gifts he has received from them were not ultimately for him. The gift Epaphroditus brought was, he says, "a fragrant offering, a sacrifice acceptable and pleasing to God" (4:18). Paul uses language from the Scriptures to reframe their gift to him as an offering or sacrifice to God. A "fragrant offering" was a burnt offering with a "pleasing odor" acceptable to God (cf. Exod 29:18). Paul declares their support for him to be pleasing to God.

Finally, in 4:19, he recalls his claim in 4:13 that God supplies all his needs by declaring that God will do the same for the Philippians. Paul thus presents God as a patron-friend who supplies needs, and he secures his friendship with the Philippians by underscoring their mutual friendship with and dependence on God.

Friendship and Christology

Paul not only secures his friendship with the Philippians and their shared friendship with God. He also addresses issues among the Philippians where friendship has become strained. He mentions two women, Euodia and Syntyche, evangelists and church planters who "struggled beside me [using a *syn*-word] in the work of the gospel" (4:3) but who are not "of the same mind [another *syn*-word] in the Lord" (4:2). To facilitate their reconciliation Paul calls on another friend, his "loyal companion" (4:3). The Greek word underlying "loyal companion" or "true companion" in the NIV, *syn-zygos*, another *syn* formulation, means literally "yoke-fellow." This person's identity is not known.

The appeal to the women and to the rest of the church to be "of the same mind" (i.e., to be friends) is part of a sustained statement about the sort of friendship the "gospel of Christ" creates. This statement begins in 1:27-30 with an exhortation using friendship language: they are to stand "firm in one spirit, striving side by side with one mind for the faith of the gospel."

In 2:1-4 Paul repeats the central qualities of being a community of friends "in Christ . . . in the Spirit" (2:1). As in 1:27, they are to "be of the same mind, having the same love, being in full accord and of one mind" (2:2). Paul rules out "selfish ambition or conceit," urges humility, and instructs them to attend not to their own interests but to "the interests of others."

The rest of chapter 2 provides examples of attending to "the interests of others." In 2:5, Paul instructs them: "Let the same mind be in you that was in Christ Jesus." He then explains the "mind" of Christ in 2:6-11 with what has come to be known as the "Christ Hymn." This was probably a piece of liturgical material Paul is citing rather than something he himself composed; the language is distinct from that in his epistles. The hymn begins by declaring that though Christ "was in the form of God," he "did not regard equality with God as something to be exploited [or grasped]," so he "emptied himself, taking the form of a slave, being born in human likeness" (2:6-7). The slave's sole purpose was to serve his master's will. Jesus "became obedient to the point of death—even death on a cross" (2:8), and this fidelity was rewarded when "God also highly exalted him" (2:9). So too the Philippians can expect that Christ, their friend and patron, will reward them.

Influences on the Christ Hymn

Traditions about Wisdom (see Prov 8:22-31) or the *Logos* (see John 1) may provide the framework for depicting a divine being that lived among humanity. Proverbs describes Wisdom, a female figure (Hebrew: *Chochma*; Greek: *Sophia*) as being with God before creation (8:22-26; this thesis reads Phil 2:6 as indicating preexistence), active with God in creation (8:27-31), and in intimate relationship with God (8:30). Seeking relationship with humanity, Wisdom invites and guides people into faithful relationship with God (Prov 8:32-9:6; Wis 7:22-8:1). The pseudepigraphon *1 Enoch* (41) describes how Wisdom experiences both acceptance and rejection among humans, and eventually returns to God (see discussion of John's Gospel).

Another possible influence on the hymn includes traditions concerning Adam. Originally, Adam bore the form or image of God (Gen 1:26-27), as does Christ at the beginning of the hymn. Like Adam, Jesus had the opportunity to grasp or exploit equality with God, that is, to become godlike (see Gen 3:5), but unlike Adam, he did not do so. While Adam's choice rendered him, according to Paul, a slave of sin and alienated from God, Jesus relinquished (or "emptied"; Greek: *ekenōsen*) his exalted status to identify with Adam's status as a slave [to sin] (Phil 2:7). His crucifixion was the ultimate act of participation in Adam's slavery (2:8). But God's exaltation of Jesus overcomes Adam's wrong and elevates Jesus to the status for which Adam was destined (2:9-11). This approach understands 2:6 not as referring to Jesus' preexistent or heavenly state, but to his earthly existence.

A third influence may be the "servant songs" of Isaiah. The servant "poured out himself to death" (Isa 53:12) and receives universal exaltation (Isa 45:22-23 and, broadly, 52:13–53:12).

Finally, another possible context, if not direct influence, may be the state cult. By depicting Jesus' role in manifesting God's sovereignty over "heaven and on earth and under the earth" (2:10) and in claiming that God's sovereignty is recognized by "every knee . . . and every tongue" (2:10-11), the hymn celebrates a rule and destiny Rome claimed for itself. In 1:27 Paul uses the cognate verb of the noun "citizenship" (Greek: *politeuma*) to emphasize that the way of life of Jesus-believers should be shaped "in a manner worthy of the gospel of Christ."

After the hymn's example of Christ attending to "the interests of others," Paul offers himself as an example of one who manifests the mind and actions of Jesus (2:17-18). He uses ritual terminology to describe himself "being poured out as a libation over the sacrifice and the offering of your faith" (2:17) and so evokes the image of Jesus, who emptied himself (2:7). Non-Jewish recipients of the letter would not need to have worshiped in the Jerusalem Temple to appreciate Paul's imagery; the practice of sacrifice was known among all members of the empire, and sacrifices were common in most large temples. Later, Paul urges his friends in Philippi in mimesis: to "join in imitating me, and observe those who live according to the example you have in us" (3:17). Paul reciprocates Christ's action for them. They as friends should reciprocate his action by "pouring themselves out" for each other. Timothy (2:19-24) and Epaphroditus (2:25-30) serve as further examples of serving others. Epaphroditus followed Jesus' example of being "obedient to the point of death" (2:8; see also 2:30).

Paul's comparison of himself to Jesus continues in chapter 3. He, like Jesus, abandoned his former status of privilege and honor:

If anyone else has reason to be confident in the flesh, I have more: circumcised on the eighth day, a member of the people of Israel, of the tribe of Benjamin, a Hebrew born of Hebrews; as to the law, a Pharisee; as to zeal, a persecutor of the church; as to righteousness under the law, blameless. . . . For his sake I have suffered the loss of all things, and I regard them as rubbish, in order that I may gain Christ. (3:4-8)

He imitates Jesus in regarding all of this tradition and identity "as loss because of the surpassing value of knowing Christ Jesus my Lord" (3:8). He repeats the point for emphasis: "I regard [these identity markers] as rubbish [Greek: *skybala*, literally, excrement], in order that I may gain Christ." Paul's Stoic point is that he has found what is truly important. His Jewish identity markers would have potentially compromised his friendship with the Philippians, since they would be occasions for boasting, so Paul dismisses them.

Throughout, Paul has defined a friendship that is expressed in self-emptying love toward others. The supreme example is Jesus' friendship with God and his actions among humans. And Paul points to the presence of the same self-giving friendship between himself and the Philippians, and in the actions of Timothy and Epaphroditus. While he employs cultural values of friendship, he also resists values and practices of self-promotion, boasting, and concern only for oneself, thereby inviting his readers into a similar way of life.

CHAPTER 12

Colossians

The early Christian movement came into being in a religious marketplace stocked with numerous expressions, groups, and traditions seeking to make meaning, find significance, gain blessing, secure protection, create community, elicit revelation, and effect transformation in an often difficult world. In this chapter we consider Colossians in its polemical relation to those expressions known as "mystery cults" as well as to Roman imperial cult observance. Here the term "cult" should not be given a negative valence, as if "cult" suggests illegitimate, sinister practices. In the technical terminology of history-of-religion, "cult" refers to the formal system of religious practice. The term comes from the Latin for "tend" or "worship"; the English "cultivated" is etymologically related to "cult."

Mystery cults, which existed throughout the Roman empire, provided a context for, and competition with, the early church. Both these cults and the church offered the gift of life after death. Both spoke of possessing an understanding of the secret or mystery of the cosmos (the "mystery"), the knowledge of which would enable people to survive, even transcend, daily struggles. Both offered revelation from and unity with the divine. Both provided membership in a community of like-minded people. Both had rituals suggesting rebirth and salvation from a cruel world and impersonal forces. Many of the mystery cults had founding figures who died and rose again. Many practiced some form of ritual immersion, held special meals, and celebrated holy days.

For example, in the late second-century C.E. novel the *Metamorphoses* (which Augustine called *The Golden Ass*), Apuleius describes the desire to be initiated into the cult of Isis, the Egyptian goddess whose worship was popular throughout the empire, especially in the first two centuries C.E. Isis was understood as a source of knowledge and wisdom; as protector for women, especially in childbirth; as having power over the elements of nature, including the sea and seasons; as effecting rebirth and new life beyond death; and as extending justice and benefits to all. The *Metamorphoses* is a rare exception in describing an initiation into a mystery cult. Initiation rites were closely guarded secrets. Even in this account the narrator says he cannot reveal some details. Nevertheless, attested are practices of fasting, sacrifices, bathing, and visions (including of the gods).

In a dark night, she [Isis] appeared to me in a vision, declaring in words not dark that the day was come that I had wished for so long. [He goes to the priest of the temple of Isis.] Thereupon the old man took me by the hand and led me courteously to the gate of the great temple, where, after that it was religiously opened, he made a solemn celebration and after the morning sacrifice was ended, he brought out of the secret place of the temple certain books written with unknown characters . . . then he interpreted to me such things as were necessary to the use and preparation of mine order . . . Then he brought me when he found that the time was at hand, to the next baths, accompanied with all the religious sort, and demanding pardon of the gods, washed me and purified my body according to the custom . . . commanding me generally before all the rest to fast by the space of ten continual days, without eating of any beast or drinking of any wine, which things I observed with a marvelous contingency. Then behold the day approached . . . [He cannot tell us much of what happens in the temple because he is bound by secrecy, but he can tell us some parts of it]. Listen therefore, and believe it to be true. You shall understand that I approached near unto hell, even to the gates of Proserpine [the underworld], and after that I was ravished throughout all the elements, I returned to my proper place: about midnight I saw the sun brightly shine, I saw likewise the gods celestial and the gods infernal, before whom I presented myself and worshipped them. Behold now that I have told you, which although you have heard, yet it is necessary that you conceal it. (Apuleius, *Metamorphoses*, or *The Golden Ass*, 11.22-23 [Loeb Classical Library; translated by W. Adlington and S. Gaselee; Cambridge, MA: Harvard University Press, 1965])

In understanding how mystery cults, or "religions" function, one approach is to analyze how the foundational stories of the movement and the particular practices it promulgates function together. In this approach, which goes under the rubric of "history of religion," the group's grounding story is known as a "myth." The term does not refer to a "story that is not true." It refers, rather, to the group's defining narrative that explains the world, interprets human experience, and grounds the community in terms of its location in time and place. Myths express meaning. They explain the origins of the world or cosmos (cosmogony) as well as its goals (teleology), usually in supernatural or transcendent terms.

Repeated practices or "rituals" are based in the myths, although it is possible that the practice came first and the story developed later to explain it. Rituals indicate for practitioners their place in the world. They infuse daily life with a sense of the sacred, of meaning. They unite the community in shared practices as well as define the practitioners as distinct from the broader culture. By reenacting the events of the myth, the rituals connect the group members to the defining moments of the movement and so give meaning to time. By looking at the myths and rituals of a particular group within their broader context, we can see how story and practice both draw from and set up worldviews that can either reinforce the prevailing culture or set up alternatives to it.

In this chapter, after initial discussion of the debated question of Colossians' authorship and a summary of its contents, we look at the interaction of its central myth and rituals as well as its polemics against alternative religious or philosophical expressions. Finally we note some reception history in which Colossians is reinterpreted in Ephesians and then serves as a major factor in christological developments.

Author?

Colossians presents itself as a letter written by "Paul" and Timothy to the church in Colossae in the province of Asia (today part of the country of Turkey). Traditionally, the letter has been grouped with Philippians and Philemon as a "captivity letter," from "Paul" in prison in Rome. It constructs a scenario in which "Paul," a prisoner (1:24; 4:3, 10, 18), writes to the Colossians whom he has not visited previously (2:1). Epaphras, the purported founder of the Colossian churches, is currently with "Paul" (4:12). "Paul" sends the letter by Tychicus (4:7-8) and Onesimus (4:9), familiar from other Pauline letters. He instructs that it be read to the churches in Colossae and Laodicea, including the house-church of a woman named Nympha (4:15).

While the letter presents Paul as author, a number of scholars propose that the vocabulary, emphases, and doctrinal content of Colossians indicate it was composed probably after Paul's death, by a disciple. The arguments are plausible, but neither individually nor together will they convince all.

The evidence for non-Pauline authorship is circumstantial rather than definitive. Approximately 87 words used in Colossians do not appear in the seven undisputed letters, and 34 of these do not appear elsewhere in the NT. Colossians lacks important Pauline words like "righteousness/justification," "law," and "salvation." Instead, Colossians uses the language of forgiveness, which is not common in Paul's letters: for example, "in whom we have redemption, the forgiveness of sins" (1:14; cf. 2:13-14; 3:13). However, the sample size is small, and any author can adapt vocabulary to the needs of a new situation.

More significant for the question of authorship is doctrinal content. Colossians employs some familiar Pauline ideas, such as "body" of Christ (1:18), reconciliation (1:22), baptism as burial with Christ (2:12), the old and the new self (3:9-10), and a different societal vision where conventional status markers are not definitive (3:11). But there are substantial differences. For example, in the undisputed letters, the church makes up the body of Christ (see 1 Cor 12:27). For Colossians, Christ is the head of the body, and the body consists not only of all churches but also, ultimately, the cosmos:

He is the head of the body, the church; he is the beginning, the firstborn from the dead, so that he might come to have first place in everything. (1:18)

Next, Colossians does resemble the undisputed letters in promoting a "partici-pationist soteriology" whereby believers are "in Christ" (2:6). Yet the letter changes a crucial orientation found in Paul's formulation. While Paul recognizes the impor-tance of God's work in Christ in the present (Rom 3:24-25a), he is often oriented to the future completion of God's purposes in Christ (Rom 6:4-5; 1 Cor 15:20-28). Colossians, however, moves the focus from the future to the present. It declares that with Christ, they have already died to their old lives and have already risen to a new life; they participate with him in the eschatological, heavenly sphere, freed from any hostile power, whether human or supernatural (1:21-22; 2:12-15; 3:1). The ritual of baptism enacts this central interpretive story by connecting the redemption of the cross with "burial" and resurrection:

When you were buried with him in baptism, you were also raised with him through faith in the power of God, who raised him from the dead. (2:12)

Here we see story and ritual in mutually reinforcing relationship.

Although Colossians includes a few references to the future culmination of God's purposes (3:4, 6, 24-25), the letter's realized eschatology emphasizes the present comple-tion (or realization) of God's purposes. In Colossians, followers of Jesus already have redemption (1:14), and have already "been raised with Christ" (3:1). Further, God's eschatological promises have already been accomplished:

Through him God was pleased to reconcile to himself all things, whether on earth or in heaven, by making peace through the blood of his cross. (1:20)

Already God has "disarmed the rulers and authorities and made a public example of them, triumphing over them in it" (2:15). For "Paul," this victory remains in the future (1 Cor 15:20-28). Further, in the undisputed letters, participation in resurrection remains in the future as well (Rom 6:5; 1 Cor 4). Colossians reformulates these central Pauline emphases.

If Colossians is pseudonymous, this conclusion should not be taken to mean that the letter is what we would call a "forgery" or written deliberately to deceive. Pseudonymity, which was common in antiquity, expressed respect for key figures, spread their influence after their death, evoked their authority to extend teaching within a tradition, and served to secure the relevance of traditions by reinterpreting them for new situations. By using Pauline terminology coupled with Paul's name, Colossians rhetorically suggests a respectful continuity of thought. Close reading of

Colossians, however, in comparison with other letters, suggests not just development but dramatic change.

Even the destination of the letter is not secure. Colossae is in Phrygia in Asia Minor, about 120 miles east of Ephesus, and within 10 to 15 miles of Laodicea and Hierapolis. In the early 60s C.E., a major earthquake struck the area. Laodicea was rebuilt, but there is no report of how Colossae fared until a fourth-century reference indicates it had been destroyed. We have no evidence, aside from this letter, of a late first-century community of Jesus-believers in Colossae. It is possible the city was largely uninhabitable, and the reference to Colossae part of the author's rhetorical fiction along with claims of Pauline authorship. Perhaps Laodicea and Hierapolis were the intended audiences, with the presentation to Colossae blunting the critique so as to enable the Laodiceans and Hierapolitans to hear its address (4:13).

Content and Context: "Philosophy" or "Empty Deceit"

Colossians suggests that among the community of Jesus' followers there is an interest in a competing teaching or "philosophy." The author counters that this alternative teaching is "an empty deceit" (2:8) that offers nothing to the community. They have all they need from divine blessings conveyed through Christ. In history-of-religion terminology, the author promotes the community's "myth" of God's work in Jesus that provides its grounding and ultimate concerns.

We do not know if those advocating this alternative worldview were Jesus-followers or outsiders to the community. Nor do we know how appealing this "philosophy" might have been to church members. There seems to be enough of a concern to warrant a warning against submitting to some regulations or rituals: "Do not handle, Do not taste, Do not touch" (2:21). Yet the author does not berate the readers for adopting this teaching. The tone is not that of Galatians.

The author presents aspects of both the doctrine (myth) and ritual of this "philosophy," though whether its own teachers would agree with the description cannot be known. The myth emphasizes cosmic powers, and the "philosophy" concerns "human tradition, according to the elemental spirits of the universe" (2:8, 20). "Human tradition" expresses a negative verdict, and it rhetorically distinguishes this competing philosophy from what God reveals in Christ (1:9-13, 27). Followers of Jesus possess what is true and permanent; the opponents have what is false and invented. Likely the opponents would make the same claims in reverse.

The phrase "elemental spirits" might refer to the four basic elements of the cosmos (earth, fire, air, water). More likely, given passages like 2:8-15, it refers to cosmic spirits.

These "rulers and authorities" (2:10, 15), sometimes associated with stars and planets, were widely understood to impact human lives with either "blessing" or punishment (we might compare the modern practice of reading one's horoscope). Consequently, various rituals, including prayers and incantations, were performed to appease or find harmony with these powers.

Colossians uses the language of "mystery" (1:26-27; 2:2; 4:3) to explain why Jesus' followers need not be concerned with these spirits. The term itself (the Greek is *mystērion*), as well as how it is used in the letter, suggests that Colossians presents commitment to Christ as a better version of the popular "mystery cults." Colossians uses "mystery" to describe the divine plan, known only to Jesus' followers. According to 1:26, "the mystery that has been hidden throughout the ages and generations . . . has now been revealed to his saints." This mystery is one of incalculable worth, greater than anything any other system can offer:

> To them God chose to make known how great among the Gentiles are the riches of the glory of this mystery, which is Christ in you, the hope of glory. (1:27)

The notion that insiders have access to secrets hidden from others both binds the community together and creates for them a sense of distinctiveness and privilege in relation to the majority culture. Finally, the author details the content:

> It is he whom we proclaim, warning everyone and teaching everyone in all wisdom, so that we may present everyone mature in Christ. (1:28)

Maturity means not listening to the teachers of philosophy and not compromising faith in this cosmic Christ with other rituals and visions.

The two remaining references to this "mystery" in Colossians reinforce the notion that the mystery comprises Christ: "so that they may have . . . the knowledge of God's mystery, that is, Christ himself, in whom are hidden all the treasures of wisdom and knowledge" (2:2-3) and "At the same time pray for us . . . that we may declare the mystery of Christ" (4:3). Using language and imagery familiar to a Gentile audience, Colossians explains both the importance of Christ and why competing cultic claims should have no appeal.

Verses 15-20 of chapter 1 employ motifs familiar from the Wisdom tradition (see Wis 7:22–9:2; our chapter on John's Gospel) to elaborate Christ's cosmic significance and sovereignty:

- "He is the image of the invisible God" (1:15);

- "in him all things in heaven and on earth were created . . . through him and for him" (1:16);

- his power is over "thrones or dominions or rulers or powers" (1:16; see 2:10);

- he is preexistent and the sustainer of all things (1:17);

- "in him all the fullness of God was pleased to dwell" (1:19; see 2:9; 3:11);

- "through him God was pleased to reconcile to himself all things, whether on earth or in heaven, by making peace through the blood of his cross" (1:20).

In addition, it makes other cosmic claims:

- "he is the head of the body, the church" (1:18; see 2:10);

- "he is . . . the firstborn from the dead" (1:18).

Not only do such declarations contest claims of power and revelation made by mystery cults, but they may also contest claims of, and perhaps participation in, the imperial cult. Imperial-critical readings of the NT seek to understand the variety of ways in which early followers of Jesus negotiated the Roman world with its hierarchical social structure, networks of power, provincial alliances, taxes, military power, and assertions—that is, myths—of divine sanction for imperial structures and values. These claims were celebrated in civic rituals, including processions, sacrifices, prayers, hymns, feasts, and displays of images of the emperor and members of the imperial family.

The christological claims of 1:15-20 contest Rome's self-presentation as the agent of the gods in holding supreme earthly and cosmic power, and Rome's propaganda insisting that the *Pax Romana* (Roman peace) to which all nations submit expresses the divine will, reconciles humanity, makes peace, and holds all things together. Colossians sets forth its myth in presenting Christ as a more powerful ruler and more definitive revealer of divine will.

Rituals

With the myth, the grounding story of the cosmic Christ in place, the author turns to the rituals that reinforce and proclaim it. Public sacrifice was the most visible ritual performed for what today we would call both "religious" and social/civic purposes. Individuals also engaged in private rituals that both reflected their beliefs and sought to influence transcendent powers. Colossians mentions a range of practices including "matters of food and drink or of observing festivals, new moons, or Sabbaths" (2:16) as well as "self-abasement and worship of angels" along with "visions" (2:18). Describing these practices in terms of limitations—"Do not handle, Do not taste, Do not touch" (2:21)—the author disqualifies their effectiveness: though they "have indeed an appearance of wisdom in promoting self-imposed piety, humility, and severe treatment of the body, but they are of no value in checking self-indulgence" (2:23).

Ritualized dietary behaviors are common in religions cross-culturally. The same is true of calendars that divide time into sacred and profane. The myth explains the ritual, and the ritual enacts the story: we perform this action or mark this date because the gods did this, or because our savior figure first performed it. For many, the performance of ritual provides a means of making the profane sacred, of connecting to the divine, of securing blessings, transformation and protection, and of reinforcing group membership. A ritualized performance can, of course, turn from a meaningful action into an obsession or a rote behavior, but *pace* Freud, not all rituals are acts of neurosis. Rituals bring meaning to people's lives, and it is possible that for some followers of Jesus, detached from the practices mandated in Torah, rituals associated with mystery cults proved appealing. They connected church members with Jesus' story in a way that engaged the body as well as the mind and spirit.

It is possible that the competing teachers were promoting circumcision (2:11), for the ritual connected the worshiper with Abraham and through him to the broader Jewish community. Moreover, it had biblical support (Gen 17:10-14), and functioned as a marker of self-identity in opposition to the prevailing Gentile culture (for example, 1 Macc 1:60-61; 2 Macc 6:10). Yet Colossians has none of the vituperative commentary found in Galatians, where "Judaizing" tendencies found a receptive audience. Instead, the language of circumcision may be more a recapitulation of language associated with Paul, with the author evoking one of Paul's major concerns. Here in Colossians, the myth of the community—the foundational story—explains that physical circumcision is not necessary, for dying and rising, forgiveness, union with the divine, and even a "true" circumcision are all accomplished apart from it. The author first shifts Paul's focus from a literal to a metaphoric circumcision, and then, second, associates this circumcision, an initiation ritual in Jewish practice, with baptism, the initial ritual for the churches. Third, the author erases the import of physical circumcision, and the other rituals prescribed in Torah, by suggesting that Jesus' death ended them. Finally, the author connects baptism with resurrection:

> In him also you were circumcised with a spiritual circumcision, by putting off the body of the flesh in the circumcision of Christ; when you were buried with him in baptism, you were also raised with him through faith in the power of God, who raised him from the dead. And when you were dead in trespasses and the uncircumcision of your flesh, God made you alive together with him, when he forgave us all our trespasses, erasing the record that stood against us with its legal demands. He set this aside, nailing it to the cross. (2:11-14)

216

The condemnation in Colossians of "worship of angels" in 2:18 can be interpreted in two ways. One view sees the phrase speaking of angels as the object (an objective genitive) of worship; in this reading, the sentence speaks of rejecting the practice of worshiping angels, because only God is worthy of worship. This option is consistent with the letter's suspicion of heavenly powers other than God (1:16; 2:8). Given the fluidity of christological understanding among the first few generations of Jesus' followers, a concern to avoid worshiping angels fits within a broader pattern. Some people regarded Jesus as a mighty angel, similar to Michael (see especially Dan 12:1, "At that time Michael, the great prince, the protector of your people, shall arise"). The concern to distinguish Jesus from angels will reappear in the book of Hebrews.

Another view sees angels as the subject (subjective genitive) of worship. On this less likely reading, Colossians does not approve of angels doing the worshiping. The reference to "visions" in 2:18 might support this latter option along with the reference in Dan 10:2-9 to fasting as a preparation for encountering visions. Why angels should not worship God, though, is not stipulated. A third possibility is that both options are condemned.

The concern for ritual—which includes the form worship takes, the object of worship, practices related to purity, and calendar-based behaviors—and the letter's primary christological claims suggest that the key issue for the letter is how the divine is known. For the author, God is encountered only in Christ, "for in him the whole fullness of deity dwells bodily, and you have come to fullness in him, who is the head of every ruler and authority" (2:9-10). No rituals can effect this encounter: "they are only a shadow of what is to come, but the substance belongs to Christ" (2:15-17). Rituals concerning purity practices and calendrical observances are no substitute for this encounter with the divine, whose reality is known in Christ.

Competing claims about how divine power is encountered always raise the question of authority: How does one know that claims are true? The teachers of "philosophy" or "empty deceit" (2:8) highlight rituals and visions as key to encountering divine powers. If the opponents are followers of Jesus, perhaps they are suggesting that faith in Christ needs supplementing or completing by such practices. This supplementing would not be anomalous: We know from the Pauline letters that some followers of Jesus emphasized spiritual gifts, such as glossolalia and prophecy (see 1 Cor 14), visions (see 2 Cor 12:2), and healings (see Acts, *passim*). If they are not Christ-believers, perhaps they are suggesting that Christ does not reveal the divine. Either way, the author of Colossians assures church members that they are caught up in God's resurrecting power (2:12-13) that is revealed in "Paul's" ministry (1:25-29).

Conflict over the definitive myth and its related rituals may provide insight into the mysterious comment in Col 1:24, wherein "Paul" says:

I am now rejoicing in my sufferings for your sake, and in my flesh I am completing what is lacking in Christ's afflictions for the sake of his body, that is, the church.

At least three meanings have been proposed to explain the verse.

First, "Paul" could be saying that Christ's sufferings were insufficient to redeem humanity, so the apostle completes what is lacking. But this reading is not compelling. The writer's primary point is that Jesus' followers are already raised with Christ (1:14; 2.12) and that "through the blood of his cross" God has reconciled all things (1:20). To claim that Christ's work was lacking would undermine these claims and support the philosophers' possible argument that something more than Christ was needed.

More likely is the second option, which proposes a reference to the exemplary role of "Paul's" sufferings. Here, the apostle's faithfulness to the gospel inspires believers to faithful imitation (mimesis), including suffering. Paul's suffering, in imitation of that of Jesus, was thus "for the sake of his body, that is, the church" (1:24). The idea of the representative as exemplar has cross-cultural resonance, as does recalling the hero's suffering or sacrifice in practices such as fasting and periods of celibacy. To imitate the movement's hero, as well as the representatives of that hero, connected the worshiper in body as well as in spirit to the transcendent.

A third approach, akin to the second, understands these sufferings to belong to the deteriorating period expected before the arrival of the messianic age. This period is often referred to as the "messianic woes." A righteous person's suffering could mean less suffering for others. These latter two interpretations understand "Paul" to be participating in the Christ myth and his sufferings to inspire faithful discipleship. No other practice or belief is necessary.

Ethical and Social Dimensions

In religious systems, myth and ritual usually have a connection to ethics. Likewise, Colossians' story of the Christ leads to an ethical program. The concern for proper behavior is a subtheme throughout the letter, since receiving the gospel means "lives worthy of the Lord, fully pleasing to him, as you bear fruit in every good work and as you grow in the knowledge of God" (1:10). In turn, the ethical vision is set in contrast to the competing philosophy. While the rival teachers focus on ascetic practices and visions, the writer of Colossians offers an alternative "vision:" "Set your minds on things that are above, not on things that are on earth" (3:2). The "things above" have to do with Christ. The "things of earth" refer not to specific physical realities but to anything contrary to God's purposes.

In 3:5-17, the author delineates life in Christ with a list of vices and virtues. Such lists are common in Jewish and Gentile moral literature as well as in Paul's undisputed letters. The language in Colossians intimates concern for ritual action as well as moral performance. For example, by exhorting, "Put to death, therefore, whatever in you is earthly: fornication, impurity, passion, evil desire, and greed (which is idolatry)" (3:5), the author reinforces the concepts of dying and being reborn. By noting that the followers of Christ have "stripped off the old self with its practices" and are now clothed "with the new self" (3:9-10), the author alludes to the ritual of baptism and so reinforces the idea of believers as a new creation. The ethical section concludes by envisioning a new humanity:

In that renewal there is no longer Greek and Jew, circumcised and uncircumcised, barbarian, Scythian, slave and free; but Christ is all and in all!" (3:11)

The wording, which may have originated in a baptismal formula, echoes Gal 3:28:

There is no longer Jew or Greek, there is no longer slave or free, there is no longer male and female; for all of you are one in Christ Jesus." (also 1 Cor 12:13)

In some mystery religions, class and gender roles were set aside, usually on a temporary basis. One well-known example involves the cult of Dionysius, or the Bacchanalia, which had a modest renewal in first-century Rome and whose myths and rituals permeated Roman society. Plutarch, writing in the mid-first century C.E., describes Marc Antony's arrival in Ephesus:

Women arrayed like Bacchanals, and men and boys like Satyrs and Pans, led the way before him, and the city was full of ivy and thyrsus-wands and harps and pipes and flutes, the people hailing him as Dionysus Carnivorous and Savage. (*Vita Antony* 24.3)

His contemporary, Tacitus (*Annals* 11.31), describes how Messalina, the wife of the emperor Claudius, sponsored a Bacchic celebration ("orgy" might be the better term) that featured frenzied dancing from women dressed in skins. The remains of Pompeii, the city destroyed in 79 C.E. when Vesuvius erupted, attest the popularity of this movement. Frescoes preserved in the "Villa of the Mysteries" depict Dionysian initiation rites. A century later, Justin Martyr—a Christian—compares Jesus to Dionysius, noting their divine conceptions, violent deaths, resurrections, and ascensions. Justin also notes that the followers of both use wine in their rituals (*Dialogue with Trypho* 69).

Although Colossians envisions a new humanity in which ethnic ("Greek and Jew") and social ("slave and free") divisions are abolished, it is reluctant to revise gender roles.

They are not included in 3:11. Instead, realized eschatology gives way to traditional hierarchies in the "household code" of 3:18–4:1. (See the ch. on Eph)

In 4:2-4, Colossians returns to the language of mystery and instructions for ritual:

> Devote yourselves to prayer, keeping alert in it with thanksgiving. At the same time pray for us as well that God will open to us a door for the word, that we may declare the mystery of Christ, for which I am in prison, so that I may reveal it clearly, as I should.

Prayers, common throughout ancient religious observance, served as communication between earth and heaven, human and divine. They embraced praise and thanksgiving, entreaty, intercession, and relationship. They took both private and public form. Here, "Paul" calls for communal intercession. The letter closes with final instructions about conduct to outsiders and appropriate speech (4:5-6) and greetings (4:7-18).

Prayer in the New Testament

Prayer permeates the NT. In the Gospels, Jesus instructs his followers on where and how as well as for what and for whom to pray (compare Matt 6:9-13 and Luke 11:1-4). Jesus himself prays (Matt 26:36-46; John 17; these examples would later impinge on christological debate: If Jesus is divine, why does he pray?) as does Paul (Rom 1:8-10; 1 Cor 4–9), the church (Acts 4:3-31), the martyr Stephen (Acts 7:54-60), and others. The writer of the Letter of James provides instruction about praying for healing (5:13-18). Epaphras, the purported founder of the addressed group (1:7), prays for the Colossians (Col 4:12).

Reception History

Reception history, sometimes also called "history-of-effects" or "history of interpretation," concentrates on the afterlife of biblical texts. We noticed, for example, in the chapters on Matthew and Luke, how both gospels reinterpret Mark's narrative, though without displacing Mark from the canon. Whether the authors of the Gospels of Matthew and Luke sought to displace, as opposed to supplement or even correct, remains a debated question. In the chapter on Galatians, we looked at how the Protestant "reformers" understood the letter in the light of their own historical situation, and how that understanding matches up with what we know of first-century practices. In the chapter on James, we will attend to different emphases that emerged at three moments in the 2,000-year reception history. Over time, all biblical texts develop new meanings. As the original context is forgotten or no longer found relevant and new contexts prompt new questions, interpreters formulate new meanings. Indeed, two readers from the same cultural context may adduce two very different interpretations of the same page: individual interests and experiences are not erased by cultural context. Hence there is no singular "Lutheran" interpretation, "Korean" interpretation, or "woman's" interpretation. For Colossians, this process of interpretation is already under way in Ephesians.

Although Ephesians is placed before Colossians in the canon (letters attributed to Paul appear in the order of longest to shortest), historically Ephesians is both later than and dependent on Colossians. Ephesians not only borrows words, phrases, and major themes from Colossians; it also develops them. In the discussion of Ephesians, we commented on this text's expanded household code. Here we focus on christological and ecclesiological developments.

In Col 1:19 the exalted Christ, "in whom all the fullness of God was pleased to dwell," is "the head of the body, the church" (1:18). Colossians adapts an image from 1 Cor 12, where the "body" is the local congregation and the head is part of the body. For 1 Corinthians, this corporeal metaphor functions to unite the fractious members of the congregation. For Colossians, the body and the head are distinct. The body refers not to the local congregation, but to all those who follow Jesus. The image of Christ as "head" and of the church as "body" indicates the vital connection between the two as well as the obedience of the church to Christ. In Colossians, finally, "head" can mean both "source" and "rule," for the church draws its life from the exalted Christ as its source (2:19) and is obedient to his rule as its head (3:15).

Ephesians employs the same head-body metaphor to denote the rule of Christ over all, including the church (1:21-23). But whereas Colossians refers to the "fullness of God" dwelling in Christ (1:19; cf. 2:9), Ephesians redefines the word "fullness." Instead of referring to God's presence in Christ, "fullness" in Ephesians refers to Christ indwelling the church. God has made Christ

the head over all things for the church, which is his body, the fullness of him who fills all in all. (Eph 1:22-23)

The effect of this move—repeated in 3:19 and 4:13—is to portray the church as a cosmic entity sharing in the cosmic rule of Christ. This shift from the local to the cosmic is reflected in how the term "church" (Greek: *ekklēsia*) appears in Colossians. Apart from the more general use in 1:18, the other three uses, two of which come in the final greetings, refer to local congregations (1:24; 4:15, 16). In Ephesians, all the references are to the universal, cosmic church (1:22; 3:10, 21; 5:23, 24, 25, 27, 29, 32).

For a broader insight into the reception of Colossians, we can trace the interpretation of the description of Christ as "first-born of all creation . . . for in him all things in heaven and on earth were created" (1:15-16a). In the late third to early fourth centuries, this description caused much controversy. Some theologians concluded that Jesus was the first creature; others argued that the phrase *presumed* his preexistence. Accordingly, the passage figured prominently in shaping the emerging understanding of a "two-natures" Christology, that is, that Jesus was both fully human and fully divine. Interpreters came to read 1:15-16a and 1:18-19 ("He is the head of the body, the church; he is the beginning, the firstborn from the dead, so that he might come to have first place in everything. For in him all the fullness of God was pleased to dwell") as declaring both natures, beginning with the human and moving to the divine.

That none of this process was self-evident is illustrated by an early church debate over the meaning of 1:19. The claim that "for in him all the fullness of God was pleased to dwell" is repeated in 2:9 but with the addition of one word—"was pleased to dwell *bodily.*" Athanasius argued that this "bodily" reference meant the incarnation. Tertullian and Chrysostom thought it meant the church. The debate was whether, and if so, how, the divine could indwell the physical.

The sixteenth-century reformer John Calvin complained that this early doctrinal debate over "two natures" Christology obscured crucial affirmations in Col 1. Calvin thought attention should focus not on the being of Christ but on his significance for and relation to humanity. For Calvin, the passage was much more about Christ's work rather than his being.

Colossians prompted other doctrinal debates as well. For example, from early on, verses such as 1:20 ("And through him God was pleased to reconcile to himself all things, whether on earth or in heaven, by making peace through the blood of his cross") and 2:15 ("He disarmed the rulers and authorities and made a public example of them, triumphing over them in it") were interpreted as indicating that literally all things, including all humanity, were embraced in God's reconciling work of new creation. Therefore, Colossians was seen as proclaiming a universal salvation. Others read these verses in a more restricted way as referring only to the church, though keeping open the possibility that one day the church might embrace all humanity. Still others found in these verses the problematic question of free will.

Readers will choose what aspects of the text to emphasize (the "canon within a canon"), what method by which to understand the text, and what context should determine meaning. For some, the "original" meaning of the text is paramount; for others, what the text means "today" must take precedence. Debates over both what the text means and how it is to be implemented in terms of belief and practice necessarily continue.

CHAPTER 13

1 and 2 Thessalonians

1 Thessalonians

Likely the earliest extant NT document, 1 Thessalonians dates from the 40s, perhaps as early as 41 C.E. The letter reflects the multiple contexts that shaped Paul's interaction as an evangelist and church founder with the Thessalonian congregation: their urban Hellenistic context, especially its philosophical components; the Roman empire; his Jewish identity; and his understandings of Jesus received from others in the movement, along with his own mystical experience of the risen Lord. By attending to these multiple historical and cultural contexts, we gain some understanding of the social complexities of Paul's apostolic activities.

Along with a combination of historical and literary criticisms, we employ postcolonial criticism/imperial-critical studies in discussing the letter's negotiation of the Roman empire, and ideological criticism in discussing 1 Thess 2:14.

Apostle, Artisan, and Advocate

Both Acts 17:1-9 and 1 Thess 2:2 present Paul and his companions coming to Thessalonica after encountering problems in Philippi. Acts presents numerous details that the letter neither confirms nor denies: Paul's initial preaching in a synagogue, Jewish and upper-status Gentile women converts; the near riot occasioned by claims that Paul was "saying that there is another king named Jesus" (Acts 17:7); the persecution of Paul's host, Jason; imprisonment; and departure for Beroea. Accordingly, we concentrate on 1 Thessalonians as the primary historical source from which to reconstruct Paul's situation.

Unlike the other six undisputed letters (Rom, 1 and 2 Cor, Gal, Phil, Phlm), in 1 Thessalonians Paul does not begin with self-description. Here he simply names himself and his companions Silvanus and Timothy (1:1). Subsequently, he declares he is an apostle. The term "apostle," which is a common term in Greek texts, literally means

not Paul's usual opening in letters

a "sent one" or a person who represents someone else. Paul presents himself as sent by and representing Jesus. While Luke-Acts generally defines an apostle as one who was an eyewitness to Jesus (Acts 1:21-22), Paul has two different criteria: one who has seen the risen Jesus and one who has founded a group of believers (1 Cor 9:1-2).

Instead of opening with his own credentials, Paul begins with a reference to "God the Father and the Lord Jesus Christ" (1:1). Both "father" and "lord" take on contextual nuance. First, in transferring the Thessalonians' allegiance from their pagan gods and in leading them to form a new life "in God the Father," Paul creates a new family with a new parent. He reinforces this alternative familial structure by casting himself as a parent. He cares for the Thessalonians in a "gentle" way, "like a nurse tenderly caring for her own children" (2:7). He shares not only the gospel but also "our own selves because you have become very dear to us" (2:8). He sees himself as their father and the Thessalonian believers are his children (2:11). He declares himself orphaned when he and his coworkers left Thessalonica (2:17). These kinship images reinforce and define their mutual relationships in household terms. As Roman ideology promoted what we today call "family values" and presented the emperor as the "father" of a household made up of the whole empire, so Paul redefines the family in terms of reciprocal love, loyalty, and mutual responsibility: the focus is inward to the members of the church, not outward to the empire as a whole.

In identifying Jesus as "lord," Paul defines the congregation away from their former lives as people who had "turned to God from idols, to serve a living and true God, and to wait for his Son from heaven, whom he raised from the dead—Jesus, who rescues us from the wrath that is coming" (1:9-10).

Idols, which functions as a metonymy for all worship not directed to the God of Israel, had been a normative aspect of their previous, Gentile identity. In Thessalonica, the Greek gods Zeus and Apollo (adapted into the Roman pantheon), Asclepius and Hygeia (gods of healing), Egyptian gods Isis and Serapis, and the Roman imperial cult were honored. Becoming a follower of Jesus impacted the new converts' familial and political worlds.

Despite his parental role and his life-transforming teaching, Paul also mentions that he did not demand financial support from the Thessalonians (2:7; see 1 Cor 9). To the contrary, he recalls the social circumstances in which he preached:

> You remember our labor and toil . . . we worked night and day, so that we might not burden any of you while we proclaimed to you the gospel of God. (2:9)

If Acts 18:3 is reliable, Paul's work or trade involved making tents and other leather products. Our modern image of Paul standing in the agora and gathering a crowd, or speaking in synagogues only to be driven out, comes from Acts, not from Paul's letters. First Thessalonians suggests that he proclaimed his gospel while he worked in an artisan's workshop that was part of an *insula* or tenement building with shops on the street level.

224

By one calculation, a group of perhaps 10 to 20 congregants might typically meet in a shop, where much of the empire's urban population worked. Artisans, such as leather-workers, often belonged to a "voluntary association" or trade association that regularly met in shops, in rented rooms, or at the home of a wealthy patron for meals and network-ing, including paying homage to imperial and local gods.

Roman philosophers and elites express disdain for manual labor. That was not the case among Jews, however, where the idea of teaching one's child a trade was considered admirable. Israel's traditions celebrated the labors of its heroes: Jacob, Moses, David, and Rachel were shepherds; Amos was an agricultural worker. Josephus speaks positively of artisans and their work, especially those constructing the Temple (*Antiquities* 8.69), and rabbinic sources extol physical labor. Mark 6:3 identifies Jesus as a builder or carpenter (*tekton*), and Matt 13:55 makes him the son of a builder. Jesus' Jewish audiences do not cast any aspersion on him for doing manual work. Thus we see a cultural difference between elite non-Jewish and Jewish values.

Paul encourages his Thessalonian converts to engage in manual labor. He exhorts them to "work with your hands . . . so that . . . [you are] dependent on no one" (4:11-12). This instruction suggests that most, if not all, the church members were artisans, not elites. It may also attempt to prevent the members of the congregation from stop-ping their work in order to prepare for the eschaton, and so becoming dependent on others for what we would call religious reasons. The letter does not indicate economic conflict or status distinction (contrast 1 Cor 1:26-29) nor does it indicate that wealthy patrons are part of the group. In 2 Cor 8:2, Paul exaggerates somewhat in mentioning the Macedonians' "great poverty" though they had enough to contribute to his collec-tion. The absence of references to slaves suggests either that Paul knows of no immediate concerns with slaves in the congregation, or that the congregation was comprised pre-dominantly of free (or freed) people.

Hellenistic Cultural Context: Philosophical Practices

The community of Jesus-believers in Thessalonica substantially resembled the struc-tures and practices not only of voluntary associations of artisans and synagogues but also of philosophical schools. Indeed, the second-century Christian writer Justin and the pagan Galen both linked Christianity to philosophical schools, which in their various forms attempted to understand the cosmos and to identify the ways in which humanity could live a good life. Josephus did the same in analogizing the Pharisees to Stoics, the Essenes to Pythagoreans, and the Sadducees to Epicureans. Of the various philosophical groups, the Cynics, Stoics, and Epicureans had the greatest public influence.

Three Greek Philosophies: Cynicism, Stoicism, Epicureanism

Diogenes of Sinope (ca. 300 B.C.E.) is usually identified as the founder of the countercultural movement known as *Cynicism*. Cynics rejected conventional societal values of wealth, status, political power, comfortable housing, social conformity, and familial connections. Free of societal trappings, Cynics sought a lifestyle akin to nature, marked by self-sufficiency and frankness. Diogenes taught that all things belonged to the gods, who were friends of the wise and among whom all property was shared. His male and female followers followed this theological view, spurning materialism, begging for daily resources, and living as itinerants, whether alone or in groups. References indicate that the wealthy and powerful disparaged Cynics for their unkempt appearance, idleness, and public challenges to propriety. Opponents disdainfully called them "cynics" from the Greek word for "dog," a name Cynics seemed to embrace warmly as validating their fundamental outlook.

Stoic philosophy is named after the *Stoa* or colonnade where Zeno gave his teaching in Athens around 300 B.C.E. Largely setting aside the traditional gods, Stoicism affirmed a universe permeated by the divine principle or *Logos*. This nonpersonal God was perceptible through rational thought and nature's harmony and beauty. The Stoic's task was to learn to trust this divine purpose and through rationality to accept all things with equanimity, not being overwhelmed or upset by life's difficulties. Stoics practiced independence from outside influences, mastery of passions, and indifference to sickness or health, poverty or wealth, fame or scandal, abundance or deprivation, life or death. They cultivated virtue expressed in wise choices, courageous endurance, and benefactions for others.

Epicureanism originated with Epicurus, a philosopher from the Greek island of Samos (341–270 B.C.E.), who taught in Athens. Epicureans sought pleasure, the satisfaction of desires, and the absence of pain that resulted from unsatisfied desire. Although their goals are often misunderstood as tantamount to hedonism or personal gratification, the Epicureans taught that only desires that were necessary and natural should be satisfied. Accordingly, they embraced a modest, almost ascetic, standard of living. They sought a state of mind untroubled by pain, the irrational, and false opinions (including misconceptions of the gods). Contemplation of the world and the senses were crucial sources of knowledge for gaining pleasure or inner tranquility. Epicureans taught that the soul did not survive death, that there is no supreme God, and that the cosmos resulted from an accident, not an intentional act of creation. They believed that the gods existed but were unconcerned with human affairs. Epicureans formed communities with a critical stance to society, valued friends, included males and females, and welcomed people of all status.

By comparing the approaches of these philosophical schools with Paul's ideas, we can see how his ethics and cosmology relate to philosophical approaches. We can also see how Paul, by adopting and adapting these culturally familiar structures, makes his proclamation of a Jewish messiah and the God of Israel amenable to Gentiles.

For example, just as some philosophers worked and taught in artisan shops, so did Paul. He and they aimed to convert people to a morally educated life and to encourage nurture beyond conversion through community formation. Because new adherents often experienced discouragement and social alienation created by their shifts in beliefs and practices, Paul like his philosophical counterparts provided encouragement, "pleading that you lead a life worthy of God" (2:12).

Like Paul, philosophers used letters as a means of reeducating and encouraging converts. A series of letters, for example, is ascribed to Diogenes and his various students, including Crates. Both philosophic teachers and Paul also appeal to the practice of imitation (mimesis). Paul attests that the Thessalonians "became imitators of us and of the Lord" (1:6). This imitation is appropriate since Paul assumes that his life embodies the gospel. In turn the Thessalonians "became an example to all the believers in Macedonia and Achaia" (1:7). Subsequently they imitate the churches in Judea by suffering (2:14-16). In particular, Paul and the philosophers present themselves as trustworthy and their work as marked by integrity. Paul declares that his "appeal does not spring from deceit or impure motives or trickery" (2:3); he claims God as a witness to his integrity ("to please God who tests our hearts," 2:4-5a), and he catalogues his renouncing of "words of flattery or with a pretext for greed nor did we seek praise from mortals" (2:5-6). Philosophers cared for new converts by combining frank speech with parental concern, and so by creating communities of mutual affection. Paul also exhorts love for one another (3:12; 4:9-10), urges the Thessalonians to respect their leaders (5:12-13) and to

> encourage one another and build up each other . . . admonish the idlers, encourage the faint hearted, help the weak, be patient with all of them. See that none of you repays evil for evil, but always seek to do good to one another and to all. (5:11, 14-15)

Finally, philosophers debated levels of societal and political involvement, whether "the quiet life," or active participation was more desirable. Paul instructs the Thessalonians:

> Aspire to live quietly, to mind your own affairs. (4:11)

Paul here counters a tendency among some philosophical converts to abandon work, "meddle" in others' affairs, or shun societal involvement. Such activity was often seen as socially irresponsible. In their countercultural stances, self-sufficient attitudes, community loyalty, rejection of (the influence) of Roman gods, and avoidance of markers of status, Paul's Thessalonian congregation and other churches resembled philosophical schools. Just how deliberate is Paul's imitation of philosophical practices is not clear. Nor do these similarities make Paul a philosopher; his self-identification is as an apostle and preacher of the gospel of God. What matters is that these parallels indicate not only Paul's setting within and influence from his Hellenistic cultural context but also his adaptation of his preaching and practice to that Hellenistic discourse.

Roman Imperial Power and the Eschatological Kingdom of God

A further context for Paul's activities in Thessalonica involves the Roman Empire. The city of Thessalonica, founded in the fourth century, had been part of the empire with the rest of the province of Macedonia since 168 B.C.E., and its provincial capital since 149/48. Estimates suggest a population of 40,000 to 50,000. Imperial presence included the governor, his staff and garrison, along with some settlers who moved to the region for trade opportunities.

Roman alliances with provincial elites were an important mechanism for maintaining imperial control, as were inscriptions, coins, and statues. Thessalonica's citizens were able to elect local magistrates (called *politarchs*), and these magistrates—the elite—honored Rome with a temple dedicated to the emperor Augustus and by sponsoring games and other entertainments; funding public works, feasts, and sacrifices; and promoting oaths of loyalty to the emperor. Expressed visually, monetarily, and religiously, Roman power and imperial ideology were well established throughout the province.

Two crucial recognitions are evident in this discussion. First, religion was tightly interwoven with politics, economics, and social interaction; there was no separation of "church and state." The idea that the gods had chosen Rome and its emperor as their agents to do their will, manifest their blessings, and rule their lands permeated the empire. Second, participation in civic religious practices was not mandatory. No law required all residents in the empire to offer sacrifices to an image of the emperor or his gods. Yet many people did so voluntarily in civic festivals, trade associations, and households, to ensure the gods' protection and blessing, or to express political loyalty. Neglect could bring disaster to the city; the refusal to participate in such rites would raise suspicion and hostility from groups of inhabitants. Refusal to participate put the city in danger of disapproval by both the gods and the state.

In thinking about 1 Thessalonians' engagement with Roman power, postcolonial or imperial-critical criticism provides a helpful interpretive lens. Postcolonial criticism emerged in the mid-twentieth century when people who had experienced colonization (in Latin America by the Spanish and Portuguese; in South Asia by the British; in

Central Africa by the French; in Korea by the Japanese, and so on) sought to understand their various and often simultaneous experiences of accommodation, resistance, and reformulating self-identity after independence. Imperial-critical studies especially investigate how the Roman Empire's strategies to pacify its subjects and naturalize its domination are negotiated in NT texts.

Postcolonial work surfaces submerged colonial histories, experiences, and identities, yet the process is never pure. The colonizer always leaves its mark, and the submerged history is necessarily incomplete. In resisting external pressure, the occupied culture may find itself mimicking what it opposes. It may begin to describe its gods as variations of the gods of the empire. It may adopt the colonizer's worship, dress, or language. It may imitate some of the empire's values in violence toward and domination over groups, thereby creating a type of hybridity. The colonized culture becomes a composite of the indigenous and the imperial. This process also works in reverse. The colonizer adapts and adopts aspects of the ethos and culture of the colonized.

Postcolonial criticism and imperial-critical studies pursue such issues in relation to the NT writings and their interpretation through at least four interrelated tasks. The first involves identifying the various ways that texts are embedded in and assume imperial structures. The second concerns the complex and often simultaneous ways in which texts negotiate imperial realities, whether through imitation, accommodation, pragmatic survival, or opposition. Eschatological scenarios, for example, in which God forcibly imposes divine will and destroys those who resist, both oppose and mimic imperial systems. Text, authors, and readers become complicit at times in perpetuating the very structures they find antithetical to the "kingdom" [empire] of God.

A third task concerns the way that ideology shapes biblical interpretation. All interpretation is biased, since the interpreter determines what questions to ask, what data to adduce, how to assess the data, and how to present it. Further, whether conscious of it or not, the conclusions we draw are often influenced by our personal priorities and experiences. For example, interpreters who understand Christianity as about individual salvation, or one's personal relationship with Jesus, may be less likely to foreground the New Testament's statements regarding engagement with the political system and perhaps more likely to foreground texts that advocate quietism. Often interpretation of New Testament texts has been controlled by an ideology that separates the "political" and the "religious" and concludes that anything biblical is "religious" and not political. Imperial-critical and postcolonial work exposes this view to be both an ideology and a false one.

Fourth, this approach may also be instructive for contemporary churches, especially the churches in the (empire of the) United States. It would be both anachronistic and simplistic to map the *Pax Romana* (Roman peace) maintained through army, taxes, alliances, and ideology, onto the *Pax Americana*, the American "peace" promoted in our world through military and economic strategies. The United States is not ancient Rome. It would be equally anachronistic and simplistic to see Christianity as an unequivocal bastion of liberation within either ancient or modern contexts. Nevertheless, a conversation between the analysis of the New Testament and assessment of the policy and social structures of the United States (and other nations) might prove productive. On the one hand, we may see how contemporary political and socioeconomic issues inform the work biblical scholars do. On the other, we may find that biblical writings can speak to both the colonized and colonizer.

Given the pervasive presence of statues of gods and emperors in a city like Thessalonica, Paul's insistence that his followers turned "to God from idols" (1:9) attests a disruption in societal practice. Abandoning idols (probably) meant withdrawal from civic celebrations of the imperial cult and from honoring the city gods. Jesus-followers who participated in trade guilds had to negotiate the expectation that members participate in imperial observance. Followers also had to negotiate their own households where worship was part of the daily routine. Perhaps some accommodated and continued to observe civic celebrations because they thought idols were powerless (cf. 1 Cor 8:4). Perhaps others faced household or social ostracism because of their nonconforming practices. Still others may have imposed their new beliefs upon members of the household, with wives, children, and slaves now forced to conform to the husband/father/master's new interest in Paul's alternative worldview and lifestyle.

For Paul's churches, the central ideology was not the kingdom of Rome, but the kingdom of God. In 2:12 Paul reminds his congregants, "God . . . calls you into his own kingdom and glory." The word translated "kingdom" (*basileia*) could be translated "empire," and it was commonly used for Rome's dominion. Paul simultaneously competes for his congregation's loyalty, imitates imperial language, and accommodates the two by not driving an irreconcilable wedge between them.

Paul's vocabulary has other political nuances. For example, he refers to Jesus' return with the terms *parousia* (2:19; 3:13; 4:15; 5:23) and *apantēsis* (4:17). These terms normally described the approach of an emperor, military leader, or imperial official to a city and his welcome as a conquering hero by the grateful and admiring public. For Paul, Jesus' return mimics but upstages such ceremonies. As an eschatological act, his return will destroy the current Roman order. In 5:3, Paul cites two of the claimed blessings of Roman rule, "peace and security," only to declare that Jesus' coming will suddenly and inevitably shatter this Roman status quo. Those promoting Rome's claims are unaware of God's imminent judgment.

We can see here an instance of colonial hybridity. As Rome sought complete control over its territories, so Paul anticipates God's control over the world. Paul's vision and vocabulary thus simultaneously resist and mimic Roman imperial ideology and practice. As with Paul's philosophic context, we see that he cannot be detached from his social context. How and the extent to which, then, his message can be detangled from that context and applied to new situations remain contested questions.

For some of Paul's congregants, whose negotiation of Roman imperial values and practices resulted in their withdrawal from familial, trade association, and civic celebrations, some sort of local harassment resulted. Paul commends the Thessalonians for receiving the proclamation "in spite of persecution" (1:6; also 3:3-7). The word translated "persecution" (*thlipsis*) could also be translated "oppression, affliction, tribulation." This does not mean empire-wide persecution. It does not indicate public spectacles where believers were tortured to death for public entertainment and instruction. Rather, the most likely scenario is that withdrawal from civic observance — what Paul calls "idolatry"—prompted negative social reactions. Congregants may have been accused of being atheists because they did not honor the gods. Perhaps they were accused of jeopardizing the well-being of the city by offending the gods or being disloyal to the empire or emperor. "Persecution" might involve judicial action, verbal conflict, economic hardship (boycotts; loss of jobs), social alienation, even isolated physical violence.

Polemic and Ideology

Paul does indicate one source of hostility to the Thessalonians receiving the gospel:

> For you, brothers and sisters, became imitators of the churches of God in Christ Jesus that are in Judea, for you suffered the same things from your own compatriots as they did from the Jews, who killed both the Lord Jesus and the prophets, and drove us out; they displease God and oppose everyone by hindering us from speaking to the Gentiles so that they may be saved. Thus they have constantly been filling up the measure of their sins; but God's wrath has overtaken them at last. (2:14-16)

This harsh outburst against fellow Jews for killing Jesus, attacking his followers, and hindering Paul's mission seems to be quite inconsistent with Paul's warm comments about Jews in Romans 9–11. Some have suggested it is so inconsistent it must be an interpolation. Surely, the theory goes, Paul knew better than to accuse "the Jews" of killing Jesus, and surely Paul, a Jew himself, would not so condemn his own people. However, there is no manuscript support for the thesis that the verses were later additions.

What, then, are we to make of Paul's harsh condemnation? The question is urgent. Using this text and the gospel accounts, Christians have repeatedly accused Jews of being "Christ-killers" and as being eschatologically damned. To think about the text and its interpretation, we employ ideological criticism.

Ideological criticism seeks to make explicit social and cultural structures that people take as natural or inevitable or even divinely sanctioned. It similarly attends to how social, economic, and political power structures are inscribed in the biblical texts and in the interpretations readers offer. By attending to the ideological concerns embedded in scholarship itself, we can observe how interpreters across the ages have naturalized and reinscribed cultural constructions, often oppressive ones, in their analyses.

When we interrogate Paul's construction of Jews in this passage, several factors concerning his cultural context, and so how we might understand his statements, emerge. First, what Paul the Jew says here about Jews being under God's judgment is said by other Jews. Israel's own prophets repeatedly condemned the nation for disobeying God. Just slightly later than Paul's time, Josephus interprets Rome's destruction of Jerusalem in 70 C.E. as divine punishment:

> This was the result of God's anger against us for our manifold sins, which we have been guilty of in a most insolent and extravagant manner with regard to our own countrymen; the punishments of which let us not receive from the Romans, but from God himself, as executed by our own hands, for these will be more moderate than the other. (*Jewish War* 7.332-333)

Paul's claims belong to this tradition, although what he has in mind when he declares that "God's wrath has overtaken them at last" (2:16) is not clear. For those who claim that the problematic verses are an interpolation, the reference here is to the destruction of the Temple. Tradition has it that Paul was executed in Rome as part of Nero's persecution in 64; since the Temple was destroyed in 70, the verses must postdate Paul.

One major point, however, distinguishes Paul's views from internal Jewish critique. Prophetic critique and Josephus's political commentary address Jewish communities, although Josephus also has a Roman audience in view. That the prophetic critique is part of the canon of Judaism shows that the communities who considered these texts sacred acknowledged their sins and repented. Further, Josephus contextualizes his condemnation of Jewish sin with accounts of Jewish bravery and loyalty (including his own) and thereby mitigates the strong condemnation. Finally, Josephus is writing in Rome, under the patronage of the Emperor Vespasian; it would not be politically wise for him to condemn Rome. Paul, however, writes 1 Thessalonians not to Jews, but to Gentiles. The form of internal critique, addressed to a new audience, has become external vilification.

Understanding the possible context for this vilification does not excuse the language, but it can help make sense of it. The Roman imperial setting sheds some light on both Jewish opposition to Paul's preaching and Gentile receptivity to it. The claim that a crucified Jewish messiah is the savior of the world not only attracted negative attention from some Gentiles as "foolishness" (1 Cor 1:23), but it also put Diaspora Jewish communities in danger. Already suspect for not participating in imperial cultic activity, including the "worship of idols," Jews were at least tolerated and sometimes respected for adhering to their ancient traditions. But for Gentiles to act in a way similar to Jews, without historical and ethnic connections, created problems. If these Gentiles were synagogue affiliates (God-fearers), or if the broader Gentile community understood converts to be participating in activities associated with Jews, local Jews would be put at risk. Paul's preaching may also have prompted negative reactions from Jews, who rejected the idea that their messiah had come, who found Paul to be misreading their Scriptures, and who found his presentation of Jewish concerns distorted. What was evidently true to Paul was evidently false to many of his fellow Jews.

Another possible clue to Paul's context comes in the reference to "the Jews" as those who "killed the Lord Jesus" (2:15). Ideological criticism highlights Paul's selective omission of Pontius Pilate, the Roman governor. Without Pilate's verdict, Jesus' death could not have happened. Paul selectively targets his own people. Verse 14 may explain why Paul chooses to name only the Jews. He compares the suffering of the Thessalonians with what happened in Judea (the term for "Jews," *Ioudaioi,* could also be translated "Judeans"). The polemic is utilitarian in connecting the suffering of the Thessalonians with those of Jesus and his immediate followers in Judea. It is also rhetorically potent: Paul here places his affiliation not with his fellow Jews, but with his new "family," his Thessalonian Gentile converts.

Another factor influencing Paul's language may involve his expectation of Jesus' imminent return and the final sorting between the saved and the damned. Perhaps Paul has realized that many Jews have not found claims that Jesus is the Messiah convincing. Since they have rejected his claims, he rejects them (2:16; 3:4, 7). Initial eschatological fervor can result in a dualistic view of the world, with the saved few facing opposition from the many damned. A decade or more later, when he writes Romans, not only has his audience likely changed from a predominantly Gentile Thessalonian congregation to a congregation of both Jews and Gentiles, but also his eschatological fervor has tempered somewhat. His plans to preach in Spain suggest he no longer expects Jesus' imminent return. As a result, in Romans 9–11 he has a much more generous understanding of salvation history.

Whatever the circumstances, Paul's language here in 1 Thess 2:14-15 is polemical. By definition polemical language is extravagant and vicious. Interpreters must not misconstrue polemical language as factual report, nor generalize a statement made in a particular context. Moreover, readers must resist misunderstanding any polemical statement as an accurate comment about those of a different ethnicity and religious identity.

Eschatology and Politics

Paul refers several times to a cluster of eschatological events associated with Jesus' return, the final judgment of Rome's world, and the vindication of believers. Jewish eschatological thinking as depicted in apocalyptic literature generally involves several of the following motifs: (1) the division of history into the present evil age and the new age to come; (2) an anticipation of social degeneration before redemption comes; (3) divine intervention (sometimes called "the Day of the Lord") that may or may not involve an agent, for example, an angel, prophet, or messiah; (4) the gathering of the dispersed of Israel from the Diaspora, including the 10 northern tribes exiled by Assyria in 722 B.C.E.; (5) destruction of hostile nations/empires and the conversion of Gentiles not to Judaism but to the worship of Israel's God; (6) a general resurrection and final judgment; (7) a renewal of heaven and earth; and (8) the final triumph of God's will for life, justice, and peace where there is no evil or death.

Drawing upon such traditions, Paul exhorts the Thessalonians to "wait for [God's] Son from heaven, whom he raised from the dead—Jesus, who rescues us from the wrath that is coming" (1:10). He anticipates their vindication when he boasts about them "before our Lord Jesus at his coming" (2:19; see 3:13; 5:23).

Generally dualistic, eschatological worldviews typically divide the world into the elect and the rejected, the saved and the damned. In turn, the division has social consequences. Paul maintains strong boundaries between his congregants as loved and chosen by God (1:4) and outsiders whom he describes negatively as idolaters (1:10), subject to God's wrath (2:16), lustful (4:5), and unconcerned for God's purposes (5:5-7). Such language works as a disincentive for the Thessalonians who might think of returning to their former beliefs and practices. Apocalyptic literature encourages insiders to remain faithful, explains their suffering as indicating the nearness of the end in the divine plan, and provides comfort by describing not only their future participation in God's purposes but also their opponent's destruction.

As Paul assures the Thessalonians that their current suffering will result in future salvation, he also assures them that the eschatological scenario has not gotten off track. Questions seem to have arisen within the congregation about what happens to those among them who have died before Jesus' Parousia (4:13). Perhaps outsiders mocked the group's claims of salvation; perhaps others interpreted the deaths as punishment for abandoning worship of the civic and imperial gods.

Paul offers five forms of consolation. First, he encourages them not to grieve as those "who have no hope" (4:13). Here his dualistic views are in place; that people outside the church had their own views of salvation is not his interest. Second, he affirms those who have died will be raised (4:14). He makes this affirmation because he sees Jesus' resurrection as the beginning of and guarantee of the general resurrection. Thus the truth of Jesus' resurrection assures their own. Third, he affirms, "Through Jesus, God will bring with him those who have died" (4:14b). God's purposes embrace the dead; more, God has the power to raise the dead. Fourth, presenting his eschatological vision (cf. Mark 13), Paul insists that he and the Thessalonians will be alive when Jesus returns:

> We who are alive, who are left until the coming of the Lord will by no means precede those who have died. For the Lord himself, with a cry of command, with the archangel's call and with the sound of God's trumpet, will descend from heaven and the dead in Christ will rise first. Then we who are alive, who are left, will be caught up in the clouds

together with them to meet the Lord in the air; and so we will be with the Lord forever. (4:15-17)

This reconfiguration of the imperial *parousia* into the return of Jesus co-opts, or reframes, Roman propaganda.

Fifth, Paul assures the congregation concerning the "times and the seasons" (5:1). He has already instructed them that the "day of the Lord" (5:1-2) will come "like a thief in the night," a notion familiar from the Synoptic tradition and perhaps reflecting Jesus' own words (see Matt 24:43//Luke 12:39). This emphasis on suddenness and surprise differs from traditional *parousia* scenarios but is consistent with Jewish apocalyptic writings. Cities usually know when to expect the conquering hero. Paul also adapts the *parousia* idea by connecting it with the "day of the LORD," a term from Israel's Scriptures that can refer to God's imminent intervention to defeat the enemies of the covenant community (Amos 5:18-20; Isa 13:6, 9, 13; Zech 12:3-6; 14:1-5, 6-9), or God's judgment on Israel and Judah (Amos 5:18-20; Zeph 1:7-10, 14-18; 2:2-3; 3:8; Zech 13:1-2). For Paul, the image assures the Thessalonians of their own salvation and of their enemies' destruction. Dualistic imagery reinforces their new identity, provides them an incentive to ethical behavior, and gives them assurance that their hopes will be fulfilled:

> But you, beloved, are not in darkness, for that day to surprise you like a thief; for you are all children of light and children of the day; we are not of the night or of darkness. (5:4-5)

2 Thessalonians

There has been considerable debate about this short letter's author. It is written in Paul's name, and Pauline authorship was widely assumed in the early church. From the late eighteenth century, however, opinion has gradually changed. Today many scholars think 2 Thessalonians was written a generation or so after Paul's death, in imitation of 1 Thessalonians but displaying changes in vocabulary, tone, and content. The imitation includes an almost identical salutation (1:1-2), the goal of God's kingdom (1:5), Jesus' Parousia (1:7-12; 2:1-17), imitation, (3:7-9), self-support (3:8-9), and instruction to work (3:6-13). Yet significant differences suggest a new author.

Some typical Pauline terms (sin, apostle, proclaim, nation, dead, body, etc.) do not appear in the letter. Conversely, 10 terms appear only in 2 Thessalonians. Another 11 do not appear elsewhere in Paul's letters but do appear in later NT texts. Typically, familiar terms appear with different nuances. In 2 Thess 1:5, the "kingdom/empire of God" is only the future, whereas in Paul's letters it is also a present reality (Rom 14:17). Second

Thessalonians links "affliction" (*thlipsis*) and divine retribution (1:4-6), which Paul does not do. Likewise, only 2 Thessalonians uses the noun "revelation" (*apocalypsis*) for Jesus' Parousia (translated as the verb "is revealed" in 1:7). The letter lacks references to Jesus' death and resurrection and does not cite Israel's Scriptures. Twice it appeals to the importance of traditions passed on by the writer (2:15; 3:6). To be sure, changes in Paul's circumstances as well as those of the Thessalonian community can prompt such changes. Thus the authorship question cannot be resolved.

Whether written by Paul or in his name, the letter's eschatological concerns differ from the imminent sense of Jesus' return in 1 Thess 4. Jesus had not returned to raise the dead and unite with the living. Eschatology required rethinking. So far, in the various claims over the centuries concerning the dating of the return of Jesus, it always has.

This letter reconfigures eschatological expectations in three ways. The first concerns whether Jesus has already returned. First Thessalonians 5:1-2 emphasizes the suddenness of Jesus' future return. Second Thessalonians deals with a claim that Jesus had already come and the community had failed to note it:

> As to the coming of our Lord Jesus Christ and our being gathered together to him, we beg you, brothers and sisters, not to be quickly shaken in mind or alarmed, either by spirit or by word or by letter, as though from us, to the effect that the day of the Lord is already here. (2:1-2)

The author rejects this view.

Second, rather than highlight the imminence and surprise of Jesus' return, 2 Thessalonians outlines a sequence of events leading up to Jesus' Parousia. A time of rebellion (2:3a) leads to a revelation of "the lawless one" (2:3b, 6), an eschatological figure who will usurp God's role (2:4), perform Satanic signs (2:9), and deceive those who refuse to know God's truth and salvation (2:10-12). From this description, coupled with references in 1 and 2 John and a few additional texts from the Scriptures of Israel, especially Daniel and Ezekiel, we will develop the notion of the "antichrist," the demonic opposite to Jesus (see the chapter on the Johannine letters). Then "the Lord Jesus will destroy [him] with the breath of his mouth, annihilating him by the manifestation of his coming" (2:8). Those aligned with the man of lawlessness and with "unrighteousness" (2:12) will be condemned, and those faithful to the gospel will be saved (1:5, 10; 2:14, 16). Compared to 1 Thessalonians, this letter emphasizes divine vengeance: "It is indeed just of God to repay with affliction those who afflict you" (1:6). When "the Lord Jesus is revealed from heaven with his mighty angels in flaming fire," he inflicts "vengeance on those who do not know God . . . These will suffer the punishment of eternal destruction, separated from the presence of the Lord and from the glory of his might" (1:7-9). The conception and expression of this scenario imitates crushing assertions of Roman imperial control over hostile peoples, even while the scene contests the ultimacy and supremacy of Roman rule over the world by asserting God's sovereignty. The effect of this timetable is to maintain the certainty of Jesus' return while recognizing the passing of a significant period of time before his coming.

Third, with diminished expectations of Jesus' imminent Parousia, the present gains increased significance. Marked by affliction, it is a time for congregants to prove themselves worthy of God's empire: to "stand firm and hold fast to the traditions that you were taught by us" (2:15). It is the time of experiencing God's power to "strengthen them in every good work and word" (2:17), of being protected from the evil one (3:3), and obeying the writer's teaching (3:4).

Finally, repeated is the theme of 1 Thess 4:11-12 and 5:14 that congregants follow Paul's example and not be idle or disruptive:

> Anyone unwilling to work should not eat. For we hear that some of you are living in idleness, mere busybodies, not doing any work. Now such persons we command and exhort in the Lord Jesus Christ to do their work quietly and to earn their own living. (3:10-12)

Eschatological prediction can give rise to disappointed expectations. Convinced by Paul's apocalyptic urgency, congregants may have prepared for the end—why work when Jesus was about to return? Perhaps new members were attracted to the care the congregants showed toward each other. Mutual love can entice those less motivated to receive care without reciprocation. Others, perhaps, were unable to find work, and yet the author condemns them for laziness. This too reflects ideological thinking. It presumes that lack of work is the individual's fault and not part of a larger economic system.

But since Jesus had not returned, the church needs to adapt both its timetable and its emphases. And as ideological critique continues to reveal how readers regard as natural what is culturally constructed, or impose their own worldviews on another culture's system, interpreters need to adjust their understandings of the texts and their own perspectives.

$\mathcal{T}$he Pastorals:
1 and 2 Timothy, Titus

In the thirteenth century, Thomas Aquinas identified 1 Timothy as "virtually a pastoral rule." Along with 2 Timothy and Titus, it instructs leaders—or "pastors"—of ecclesial communities. Consequently, the three letters came to be known collectively as the "Pastoral Epistles."

These letters are conventionally regarded as dating to the late first or early second century and thus classified as pseudonymous in that they are written in Paul's name but not written by him. The use of Paul's name is not intended to deceive but to reinterpret the Pauline tradition to address new situations. Whether the three were composed by the same author or school remains debated, but the consensus is that they represent a related view of church, society, and Christology.

This chapter begins by reviewing the historical-critical question of Pauline authorship and briefly summarizing some major themes. We then consider parts of the Pastorals through a feminist-critical and more broadly liberationist lens. We locate the letters in the struggle for Paul's legacy, especially as it impacts debates over slavery and gender roles in both early and contemporary church communities.

Authorship

Doubts about Paul's authorship of the Pastorals surfaced early. In the 140s, Marcion, the great advocate of Paul, excluded them from his canon. Tatian (d. ca. 170) rejected 1 and 2 Timothy but not Titus. The Muratorian Canon from Rome, which may date from circa 180 or may be from as late as the fourth century (this Latin list of the books of the New Testament appears in a very poorly preserved seventh century codex), included them, but they are missing from the collection of Pauline letters known as P46 (part of the Chester Beatty Papyri) and dating circa 200.

Modern biblical scholarship presents six arguments in favor of the Pastorals' pseudonymity. As with the question of pseudonymity applied to Ephesians, Colossians, and 2 Thessalonians, the evidence is circumstantial rather than definitive.

The first argument concerns vocabulary and style. By one count, the Pastorals have 175 *hapax legomena* (words used once only in the NT), about half of which are typical of second-century writers. The Pastorals also lack typical Pauline vocabulary such as "in Christ" and numerous particles (for example, "then," "therefore") common in Paul's letters.

The second argument notes that although the Pastorals employ some familiar Pauline ideas, they neglect or reinterpret others. They include, for example, discussion of salvation through Christ and not through works (1 Tim 1:15; 2:4-6; Titus 3:5), yet the cross receives little or no attention. The Pastorals say much about the church, but nothing about "the body of Christ." They mention the return of Jesus, but eschatology has no urgency or weight. Rather, they present a church that is here for the long haul. Nor do they share Paul's attention to Israel's salvation-history. Finally, the Pastorals use some Pauline words but with significantly different meanings: "righteousness" becomes an ethical concept rather than referring to God's saving power; "faith" becomes "the faith," a body of doctrine.

Third, it is difficult to fit these letters into a reconstruction of Paul's life based on the uncontested letters and even Acts. For example, according to Titus 1:5, Titus is "left behind in Crete," but there is no external evidence that Paul traveled to Crete. On the other hand, Acts is not necessarily reliable as a full account of Paul's travels, and the uncontested letters do not contain complete information.

Fourth, the Pastorals deal with opponents in a way that differs from the seven uncontested letters. There, Paul argues with those who teach something he opposes. The Pastorals make no argument. The writer simply orders Timothy:

> Have nothing to do with stupid and senseless controversies; you know that they breed quarrels. And the Lord's servant must not be quarrelsome. (2 Tim 2:23-24)

Fifth, the Pastorals recognize a developed church order composed of elders (Greek: *presbyteroi*) and deacons (Greek: *diakonoi*; 1 Tim 3:1-13). This institutional structure differs from Paul's charismatic structure of Rom 12 and 1 Cor 12–14. A charismatic structure is based not on set offices and positions but on gifts given by God's grace or by the Spirit to individuals in the church. The word "charismatic" has as its root the Greek word for grace—*charis*—referring to God's gracious provisions of gifts that equip individuals to serve the church's common good. The closest the Pastorals get to a charismatic structure is the recognition that male leaders have been given a gift (Greek: *charis*; 1 Tim 4:14; 2 Tim 1:6). The closest Paul seems to get to an institutional structure occurs in Phil 1:1, where he names "bishops" (Greek: *episkopoi*) and "deacons," but Paul gives no job descriptions for the roles. Then again, the pastorals could be Paul's own development of these roles, or Philippians could be indicative of a broader use of leadership roles in the churches that Paul has chosen to ignore in order to address the entire congregations of Corinth, Galatia, and so on.

Sixth, the Pastorals' presentation of social and gender roles differs significantly from Paul's. In Gal 3:28, Paul says:

> There is no longer Jew or Greek, there is no longer slave or free, there is no longer male and female; for all of you are one in Christ Jesus.

In the undisputed letters, Paul also speaks of women's subordination to men (for example, 1 Cor 14:33b-36), and he assumes slavery in Philemon. Yet Paul approves of women deacons (Phoebe in Rom 16:1), prophets (1 Cor 11), and coworkers (Priscilla in Rom 16:3). The Pastorals are in accord with 1 Cor 14 and with Philemon; they do not reflect the greater openness to women's roles expressed in the Corinthian letters or Romans.

These arguments, whether taken alone or cumulatively, do not prove pseudepigraphy. It is possible that Paul wrote the letters after he was released from prison in Rome. It is possible that the letters' theology and church structure represent reasonable developments. It is even possible that their lack of argument fits with their address to Paul's coworkers: Timothy in Ephesus (1 Tim 1:3) and Titus in Crete (Titus 1:5); addressing his friends, Paul takes a different tone than he adopts when writing to congregations whose members might have some doubts about his credibility. Other interpreters, who reject the notion of pseudonomony but recognize the problems, propose one of Paul's associates or a scribe (an amanuensis) wrote the Pastorals. But it is the substantial differences in theology and ecclesial structures that suggest to us that the Pastorals were composed in the late first or early second century and were designed to reinterpret the Pauline tradition for new circumstances.

Concluding that these three letters were probably not written by Paul does not mean that they can be dismissed or relegated to secondary canonical status. Whether written by Paul, a disciple, or a faithful follower years after Paul's death, the Pastorals are part of the Christian canon and need to be interpreted as such.

Major Themes

Four themes in the Pastorals—doctrinal faithfulness, church structure, social compliance, and personal piety—serve to order the community of faith, maintain its confession, and enhance its social acceptability. The themes suggest the recipients' new situation: no longer facing eschatological concerns, the followers of Jesus needed to determine how to live in the world; would they accept the status quo, fight against it, withdraw from it, or adapt carefully depending on the circumstances? How would they determine orthodoxy (correct belief) and orthopraxy (correct living in the world and practicing through ritual and piety their confessional commitments)?

1. Doctrinal Faithfulness and Unfaithful Opponents

For Paul, "faith" (Greek: *pistis*) is a transformative experience that cannot be reduced to a creed. "Faith" for Paul can refer to Jesus' faith or faithfulness in offering his life on behalf of humankind. It can also refer to the trust or lived commitment that individuals place in the gracious God who offers them salvation and shapes their way of life. Paul argued for this broad and active connotation of the term based on his understanding of Israel's Scriptures, his personal revelations, and the logic of his arguments. For Paul, "the righteousness of God is revealed through faith for faith; as it is written, 'The one who is righteous will live by faith'" (Rom 1:17).

In the Pastorals, the term "faith" undergoes a significant narrowing in meaning. Instead of a transformative experience, a reference to Jesus' fidelity, or a relationship established with the divine, it now means "*the* faith," a body of doctrine, a set of beliefs that determined who was in the church and who was outside. For example, 1 Timothy is addressed to "my loyal child in *the* faith" (1:2; see Titus 1:4; emphasis added). It predicts that "in later times some will renounce *the* faith" (4:1; emphasis added). Second Timothy declares, "I have fought the good fight, I have finished the race, I have kept *the* faith" (2:7; emphasis added).

The Pastorals elaborate this sound teaching or "the faith" in short passages that may well be citations from early creedal statements or, possibly, hymns. For example, 1 Tim 2:5-6 proclaims:

> There is one God;
>> there is also one mediator between God and humankind,
> Christ Jesus, himself human,
>> who gave himself a ransom for all
> —this was attested at the right time.

Similarly, 1 Tim 3:16 offers a creedal statement:

> Without any doubt, the mystery of our religion is great:
>> He was revealed in flesh,
>>> vindicated in spirit,
>>>> seen by angels,
>> proclaimed among Gentiles,
>>> believed in throughout the world,
>>>> taken up in glory.

For the Pastorals, the center of "the faith" concerns Christ's salvific action. Three examples demonstrate this concern:

Christ Jesus came into the world to save sinners. (1 Tim 1:15)

God our savior . . . desires everybody to be saved . . . for there is one God; there is also one mediator between God and humankind, Christ Jesus, himself human, who gave himself a ransom for all. (1 Tim 2:4-6)

The saying is sure: If we have died with him, we will also live with him; if we endure, we will also reign with him; if we deny him, he will also deny us; if we are faithless, he remains faithful—for he cannot deny himself. (2 Tim 2:11-13; see also Titus 3:4-7)

What Is a Ransom?

The image of "ransom," used in the confession of 1 Tim 2:6, denotes a setting free or release from a captivating power. It can refer to the release of prisoners of war and slaves. It appears in the Hebrew Scriptures to denote God setting Israel free from slavery in Egypt (Exod 6:6; Deut 7:8). Often, but not always, it refers to a price paid to purchase the release. For 1 Timothy, humans are captive to sin, for which the writer blames the deception of Eve, but not Adam, as Paul does in Rom 5:12-21. The writer also says that "deceitful spirits and . . . demons" are at work (4:1), and some, notably "younger widows," "have already turned away to follow Satan" (5:14-15). The claim that Christ "gave himself a ransom for all" (1 Tim 2:6) means that Christ gave his life as the payment to free humans from sin and Satan's control. The verse raises, but does not answer, the question as to whom the price of his life was paid. Are we to understand it was paid to Satan, who deceived Eve (but not Adam)? Or does the term "ransom" denote the act of setting free or release from sin and Satan without inferring anything about the transaction of a payment?

Comments about Jesus' death as a "ransom" echo Matt 20:28 and Mark 10:45. They are not, however, found in Paul's uncontested letters. Nor do the undisputed letters use the language of mediator for Jesus; in those earlier texts, Paul reserves the term "mediator" for Moses (Gal 3:19-20). Indeed, Gal 3:20 precludes the idea that Jesus is a mediator: "Now a mediator involves more than one party; but God is one." However, the book of Hebrews, which may postdate Paul, does use "mediator" to describe Christ's work: he is the "mediator of a new covenant" (9:15; see also Heb 8:6; 12:24).

A faith detailed in creeds does not require argument. Further, since for the Pastorals the creeds are correct, then anything that runs contrary to them must be false. Thus 1 Tim 6:3 (also 1:3) condemns

> whoever teaches otherwise and does not agree with the sound words of our Lord Jesus Christ and the teaching that is in accordance with godliness.

Second Timothy 4:3 is even more direct:

> For the time is coming when people will not put up with sound doctrine, but having itching ears, they will accumulate for themselves teachers to suit their own desires.

The response to false teaching is not engagement but attack. Titus 1:13 urges, "Rebuke them sharply, so that they may become sound in the faith." The Pastorals simply declares the opponents "conceited, understanding nothing" (1 Tim 6:4) and inspired by "deceitful spirits and teachings of demons" (1 Tim 4:1). Whoever these people are, the response is clear: "They must be silenced" (Titus 1:11).

For the Pastorals, the major problem does not come from Roman imperial structures or social pressures; it comes from internal struggles among those who share commitment to Jesus. What exactly the author's opponents were teaching is difficult to determine. We do not know if the Pastorals are speaking of former community members or present ones.

Although reconstructing the position of one group on the basis of the opposing group's polemic is speculative at best, a few suggestions can be made about the teaching the Pastorals condemn.

Titus speaks of "many rebellious people, idle talkers and deceivers, especially those of the circumcision" (1:10). The reference to "circumcision" could indicate followers of Jesus who either have Jewish identity or who insist that men be circumcised to belong to the family of Abraham. However, the Pastorals do not display a concern for Torah. Moreover, when Paul speaks of people of "the circumcision," he is typically complimentary; for example, Phil 3:3, "It is we who are the circumcision, who worship in the Spirit of God and boast in Christ Jesus." The potentially negative uses come in the later and probably pseudonymous texts, such as Col 4:11.

The Pastorals condemn "myths" and "genealogies" (1 Tim 1:4, 14; 4:7; 2 Tim 4:4; Titus 1:4; 3:9), but provide no content. Titus's description of "Jewish myths" (1:14) suggests that the myths may comprise interpretations of Israel's Scriptures. There was disagreement over how to understand these texts that are open to multiple understandings. Unlike Marcion, who sought to jettison these Scriptures from any authoritative place in the church, 2 Tim 3:16-17 insists that these texts are of direct relevance to the followers of Jesus:

243

All Scripture is inspired by God and is useful for teaching, for reproof, for correction, and for training in righteousness, so that everyone who belongs to God may be proficient, equipped for every good work.

By "Scripture," the Pastorals mean the Scriptures of Israel (at least Torah and Prophets as well as a number of the Writings and the Psalms), what the churches will later call the "Old Testament." The Pastorals thus may be participating in the early church debates over the role of these texts: attribute them no authority; accept but reinterpret; accept parts but not others. The point here is that the texts have authoritative status. Subsequently, the two verses were used to support the claim that the texts of the Bible, as divinely inspired, were also scientifically and historically inerrant.

Questions of the role of the Scriptures of Israel in the life of the church surface elsewhere in the canon. According to Matt 5:17-18, Jesus states:

Do not think that I have come to abolish the law or the prophets; I have come not to abolish but to fulfill. For truly I tell you, until heaven and earth pass away, not one letter, not one stroke of a letter, will pass from the law until all is accomplished.

It is possible Matthew is responding to other followers of Jesus, perhaps influenced by Paul's Letter to the Galatians, who sought to jettison the Scriptures of Israel from the church or at least thought to eliminate Israel's distinct practices. Conversely, Heb 8:13 asserts:

In speaking of "a new covenant" [the term can also be translated "new testament"] he has made the first one obsolete. And what is obsolete and growing old will soon disappear.

Gnostic Teachings?

We know that some second-century followers of Jesus, typically called "Gnostics," appealed to the Genesis narratives of creation to support their own theologies and views on gender. Some saw Eve as a figure of Wisdom rather than of sin, and perhaps the Pastorals, given their concern for constraining women's roles and their appeal to Genesis in making the argument for restraint, sought to counter this teaching. Some offered new cosmologies (genealogies?) about how the world was created. However, any connection between the opponents' views and alternative readings of Genesis or later "Gnostic" texts remains speculative. The same problem in determining the content of the opposing "myths" confronts us in another comparably late text, 2 Pet 1:16, which reads, "For we did not follow cleverly devised myths when we made known to you the power and coming of our Lord Jesus Christ."

244

Another condemned "myth" may appear in 2 Tim 2:18. Here the author records the claim by two otherwise unknown figures, Hymenaeus and Philetus, that the resurrection has already taken place. The claim, which resembles that which Paul rejects in 1 Corinthians, created more than a creedal challenge. Some proponents of realized eschatology asserted both the completion of the final judgment (one was already saved in the eschatological sense) and the end of any possibility of sin by or in the flesh. The danger of such thinking was then to live without accountability either to God or to other people. In cases where realized eschatology is stressed alongside a soteriology of grace versus works, "antinomianism"—living a lawless life—is a possible result. First Timothy 1:20 claims that Hymenaeus and Alexander blasphemed and were "turned over to Satan." This latter phrase echoes Paul's exhortation in 1 Cor 5:5 to "hand over to Satan" a man who is living with his stepmother.

Finally, 1 Tim 4:3 condemns as hypocritical liars the opponents who "forbid marriage and demand abstinence from foods, which God created to be received with thanksgiving by those who believe and know the truth." Pauline connections again reappear: Paul mentions the slogan "It is well for a man not to touch a woman" (1 Cor 7:1), which probably refers to abstinence from sex, and dietary restrictions are a concern in Rom 14. The "opponent's" demand for dietary abstinence could be related to eating "meat offered to idols" (see, for example, 1 Cor 8–10; Acts 15:20; Rev 2:14, 20) and so participation in Rome's civic as well as familial life. The Pastorals could also be responding to ascetical practices such as fasting and celibacy, as are suggested in Col 2:21.

For these three Pastoral Epistles, doctrinal issues are not only matters of orthodoxy but also orthopraxy. The body, because it manifests these practices, is the site of Christian identity. A suffering body identifies with the suffering Christ. A body that disciplines itself shows its fidelity to Christ. The body that maintains its purity shows its Christian identity to the world. And the body that refuses certain foods and refuses sexual relations is a body that, according to the Pastorals, does not manifest the faith.

2. Church Order

A second means of stabilizing the community, maintaining its confession, and enhancing its social acceptability is church organization. Both 1 Timothy and Titus, which devote considerable attention to this issue, secure church order not through Paul's charismatic authority (1 Cor 12–14) but through a male hierarchy. This structural change attests a change in ecclesial image. Paul imaged the church as "the body" of Christ, in which all the limbs work together (1 Cor 12:27). For the Pastorals, the church is the "household of God . . . the pillar and bulwark of the truth" (1 Tim 3:15). The household metaphor introduces and imitates standard cultural notions of hierarchy and patriarchy. Church leaders must be competent household leaders in controlling subordinate wives, children, slaves (1 Tim 3:4-5, 12; Titus 1:6).

First Timothy provides job descriptions for bishops (3:1-7) and deacons (3:8-10). These officeholders must be males, well-established in "the faith," and competent in running their own households, "for if someone does not know how to manage his own household, how can he take care of God's church?" (3:5). The bishop "must be above reproach, married only once, temperate, sensible, respectable, hospitable, an apt teacher" (3:2). The Letter of Titus, whose recipient has been "left behind" in Crete to "appoint elders in every town" (Titus 1:5), repeats similar instructions about bishops (1:5-9). The requirement to be "married only once" (1:6) can also be translated "the husband of one wife." While the meaning is debated, most likely it disqualifies a divorced and remarried man, or even a remarried widower. The idea of fidelity to the one spouse is already grounded in Jesus' injunctions against divorce (for example, Matt 5:32; 19:9; Mark 10:9-12; 1 Cor 7:10).

"Deacons likewise must be serious, not double-tongued, not indulging in much wine, not greedy for money" (1 Tim 3:8). Titus 1:7 forbids bishops being "addicted to wine." For both texts, the issue is not abstinence but overindulgence. The concern for drinking also appears in 1 Tim 5:23, which endorses lenience rather than abstinence: "No longer drink only water, but take a little wine for the sake of your stomach and your frequent ailments." The verse may reject some previously sanctioned ascetic practices. If so, it is consistent with passages endorsing sexual union rather than celibacy and eating rather than fasting or following dietary restrictions.

Fundamental to the Pastorals' concern with church order are the roles of "Timothy" and "Titus." The letters present "Paul" as commissioning them to convey his teachings (2 Tim 2:14; 4:2) and to imitate him (2 Tim 1:13). They are to model for the congregations the decorum worthy of the "household of God." For example, Timothy is told "let no one despise your youth, but set the believers an example in speech and conduct, in love, in faith, in purity" (1 Tim 4:12). Thus the Pastorals not only interpret Paul's legacy for the needs of the second- and third-generation churches; they also claim Paul's authority.

The Struggle for Paul's Legacy

Other churches will take Paul in different directions. The *Pseudo-Clementine Epistles*, also second-century, regard Paul as the destroyer of the traditions associated with Jesus and promote Peter as the appropriate leader. Those who authored and celebrated the second-century *Acts of Paul and Thecla* promoted Paul as a teacher of asceticism and as an apostle who, albeit reluctantly, endorses Thecla's role as evangelist. In this apocryphal Act, a young woman, Thecla, is so taken with Paul's preaching of "the gospel of the virgin life" that she breaks her betrothal, scandalizes friends and family, and through a series of persecutions because she is seen as destroying families and threatening civilization, proves herself faithful. How historical this story might be in all, or any, of its details is debatable. What it does attest is the association of Paul with a tradition that endorsed celibacy (cf. 1 Cor 7). The Pastorals' emphasis on marriage and producing children may be a socially accommodationist response to such developments.

3. Social Compliance

The Pastorals distinguish between the followers of Jesus and others not only in terms of doctrinal views and ecclesial allegiance but also by moral actions via "vice lists" (for example, 1 Tim 1:9). Their morality includes submission to those with political authority:

> First of all, then, I urge that supplications, prayers, intercessions, and thanksgivings be made for everyone, for kings and all who are in high positions, so that we may lead a quiet and peaceable life in all godliness and dignity. (1 Tim 2:1-2)

Titus 3:1 similarly insists that Jesus' followers be "subject to rulers and authorities" (cf. Rom 13:1; 1 Pet 2:13-17; Rev 13).

The church is not encouraged to engage in overt evangelization, as Matthew's Great Commission (28:16-20) commands, nor is it withdrawn from the evil "world," as John's Gospel intimates. Instead, members are to "speak evil of no one . . . and show every courtesy to everyone" (Titus 3:2). A bishop "must be well thought of by outsiders, so that he may not fall into disgrace and the snare of the devil" (1 Tim 3:7).

By manifesting such behavior, the church communities as "the household of God" (1 Tim 3:15) create the ideal household. They are socially compliant and imitative, resisting any move toward less hierarchical structures.

4. Personal Peity

Lives are to be marked by "godliness" or piety (Greek, *eusebeia*). So 1 Tim 6:3 speaks of "teaching that is in accordance with godliness [*eusebeia*]." And "Timothy" is exhorted:

> Train yourself in godliness, for, while physical training is of some value, godliness is valuable in every way, holding promise for both the present life and the life to come. (1 Tim 4:7-8)

This *eusebeia* embraces socially conformist living (1 Tim 2:2); the duty of children to their families (1 Tim 5:4); contentment, not "gain" (1 Tim 6:5-6); personal qualities such as "righteousness, godliness, faith, love, endurance, gentleness" (1 Tim 6:11); and lives that, having renounced "impiety and worldly passions" are "self-controlled, upright, and godly" (Titus 2:12). Titus 1:1 relates *eusebeia* to "the knowledge of the truth." And 1 Tim 3:16 uses the term to sum up "our religion," whose mystery is "without any doubt . . . great."

Godliness also means "contentment" with "food and clothing" (1 Tim 6:6-8). Wealthy believers are warned against not money itself but "the love of money" because "the love of money is a root of all kinds of evil, and in their eagerness to be rich some have wandered away from the faith and pierced themselves with many pains" (6:10). These verses follow instructions against the opponents' teaching that "godliness is a means of gain" (6:4b-6). Perhaps the author was combatting a form of what today is known as the "prosperity gospel." The rich are instructed not to be haughty, "or to set their hopes on the uncertainty of riches," but to depend on God: "Be rich in good works" and generosity, thus "storing up for themselves the treasure of a good foundation for the future" (1 Tim 6:17-19). Similarly, wealthy women are not to adorn themselves ostentatiously, but are to do good works (see 1 Tim 2). Such teaching about wealth management suggests some wealthier people among the communities that the Pastorals address. Their presence may account, in part, for the letters' emphasis on societal accommodation and cultural imitation.

The Pastorals attest to a process of institutionalization. The church is establishing itself as a permanent member of society. Its doctrinal affirmations are secured, its leadership structure is regularized, the transition to the next generation is accomplished, its place in the world is defined, its expectation of a moral quality of life is clear, and its traditions—notably Paul's legacy—are controlled.

Liberationist Critiques

The Pastorals' vision of the church as societally accommodated and culturally imitative raises significant questions for contemporary interpretation. Do its teachings on slavery and on sexuality/gender have continuing, regulating authority for churches, or should they be confined to their own time? We have seen the significance of these issues in our discussions of Colossians and Ephesians.

Here we employ a generally liberationist, and more specifically feminist, approach to consider these questions. Both approaches are concerned with the impact of the interpretation of biblical texts on individuals and societal practices. Both approaches evaluate interpretations in terms of whether they promote well-being—whether they are liberating, life-giving, and loving (as the interpreter defines these results)—or whether they oppress and confine. According to this approach, an interpretation is not authoritative simply because it can find support in some biblical verses. The

248

interpretation may faithfully replicate the claims of a passage, but if those claims are damaging, the interpretation is contrary to a liberative direction in the Scriptures as a whole and so cannot be binding for contemporary readers. The authority of an interpretation is to be assessed in terms of its impact on people's lives. At the same time, a feminist hermeneutic must recognize that different readers will have different views of what constitutes "liberation."

Slavery

The Pastorals sanction slavery, not only as a Roman institution, but as a system that attests orthodoxy, correct doctrine:

> Let all who are under the yoke of slavery regard their masters as worthy of all honor, so that the name of God and the teaching may not be blasphemed. Those who have believing masters must not be disrespectful to them on the ground that they are members of the church; rather they must serve them all the more, since those who benefit by their service are believers and beloved. Teach and urge these duties. (1 Tim 6:1-2)

Titus 2:9-10 similarly commands:

> Tell slaves to be submissive to their masters and to give satisfaction in every respect; they are not to talk back, not to pilfer, but to show complete and perfect fidelity, so that in everything they may be an ornament to the doctrine of God our Savior.

Neither passage provides instruction to masters, which may suggest that the author speaks from the perspective of some wealth, property (including slaves), and position. Not surprisingly, the Pastorals have been used across the ages to support slavery in various contexts, including the United States.

Yet the Pastorals may convey a mixed message. In a standard vice list, 1 Tim 1:10-11 condemns as being "contrary to the sound teaching that conforms to the glorious gospel of the blessed God" several behaviors. We leave three contested terms in the original: "the law is laid down not for the innocent but for the lawless and disobedient, for the godless and sinful, for the unholy and profane, for those who kill their father or mother, for murderers, [*pornois, arsenokoitais, andrapodistais*], liars, perjurers . . ." (1:9-10).

The third Greek term is often translated "slave traders" (NRSV, NIV) though it can also mean "kidnappers." Slave trading, the procuring and selling of slaves, often after military defeat, was one way of maintaining the slave supply. The supply was also maintained by reproduction: children of slaves, including children of a slave and a master, were slaves. People could also sell themselves and household members into slavery in order to pay off debt or gain food and housing. If the verse is condemning all slave trading, then it could be understood as condemning the whole slave system. That, however, would contradict 1 Tim 6:1-2 and Titus 2:9-10. The likely reference is to selling kidnapped people into slavery.

The condemnation may refer to a more specific form of kidnapping. The second Greek term, *arsenokoitai*, concerns being "in bed with or sleeping with a man" (NRSV: "sodomites"; NIV: "those practicing homosexuality"). The first untranslated term, *pornoi*, can have a general meaning of "the immoral" or more specifically, a male prostitute (NRSV: "fornicators"; NIV: "the sexually immoral"). Taken together, the three terms can describe a scenario of male prostitutes, men who sleep with them (in pederastic relationships or, more likely given the third term, in brothels or in the context of a master using the body of the slave for sexual purposes), and kidnappers who procure slaves for such abusive relationships. This condemnation leaves slave trading in general unthreatened. It also has significant implications for those who claim 1 Tim 1:9-10 condemns all forms of male same-sex sexual relations.

The Pastorals' concern is with societal compliance and reputation. They reject any notion that being "in Christ" where there is neither "slave nor free" (Gal 3:28) might mean Christian masters should free slaves. A liberationist reading of this material rejects its sanctioning of slavery.

Women

The Pastorals exhort women to be silent and obedient, not to teach or preach, to be modest, to conform to the Roman status quo. What prompts each instruction must remain speculative. We can, however, construct a plausible context. That context, in turn, may help readers decide the extent to which, if any, the injunctions should have authority for churches today.

Our starting point is 1 Tim 2:9-15 and its idealistic prescription for limited and domesticated roles for women in church communities. The instructions concern both gender and class. Mandates to dress modestly and forgo elaborate hairstyles, gold, pearls, and expensive clothes indicate that (relatively) wealthy women are in view (2:9-10). Perhaps these women functioned as patrons in hosting meetings in their houses, dispensing benefits, and providing relief for poor members. They are told to contribute not through influence and displays of "wealth" but with "good works" (2:10).

Next, women are to learn in silence (2:11). Perhaps the wealthier women had or sought prominent roles in the church. In exhorting silence, the author uses language similar to 1 Cor 14:33b-36. The prohibition in 1 Cor 14 has often been seen as an interpolation, perhaps added by the same school responsible for the Pastorals. In 1 Corinthians, the instruction contradicts the obvious public role of women in worship (1 Cor 11:5). If the passage in 1 Cor 14 is original to Paul, then he may well have been addressing a specific problem, whether prophecy by wives that dishonored their husbands, or unintelligible glossolalia that disrupted the communal gathering.

First Timothy 2:12 then takes a step beyond 1 Corinthians. First it generalizes the gender relations: "I permit no woman to teach or to have authority over a man; she is to keep silent." Second it provides a scriptural basis for the command: "For Adam was formed first, then Eve; and Adam was not deceived, but the woman was deceived and became a transgressor" (2:13-14). Both moves ensure the injunctions transcend a specific occasion and present the teaching as timeless and universal. Such a prohibition may indicate, ironically, that women were teaching or at the very least sought to do so.

Confirmation of women teaching is provided not only by the several references elsewhere in the Pauline corpus to women's public roles in the church (see especially Rom 16; 1 Cor 7), by the Gospels (for example, the Samaritan woman of John 4), Acts, and other texts both canonical and noncanonical, but also from 1 Tim 4:7. The NRSV reads, "Have nothing to do with profane myths and old wives' tales." The Greek is less clear. The term "old wives" does not literally appear, and the phrase could be translated "Refuse vile [or "godless" NIV] and even foolish myths." Determining the content of these "myths" is, as we have seen, difficult. Four verses earlier, the author attacks those who "forbid marriage and demand abstinence from food" (4:3). Perhaps some women (as well as men) were rejecting the social roles for women as wife and mother. For women in particular, marriage was not always a choice. Marital arrangements were usually made for economic or political alliance rather than love. Death in childbirth was an inevitable risk. Despite the first-century Roman philosophical development of the ideal of husbands and wives as partners, and despite the call in Ephesians that husbands love their wives as Christ loved the church, not all women (or men for that matter) were happy in their legal relationships. Perhaps the gospel message, as they understood it, was an opportunity for experiencing freedom from an unwanted marriage, unwanted sexual relations, and potentially deadly pregnancies and childbirth.

To ground their teachings against women's leadership roles, the Pastorals appeal to Scripture. They do not choose Gen 1:26-27, with its creation and commission of men and women equally in the image and likeness of God. Rather, 1 Tim 2:13-14 takes two arguments from Gen 2:14–3:18, the account of Adam and Eve. Explaining why women cannot teach or have authority over a man, and why women are to keep silent, the letter avers first that "Adam was formed first, then Eve." In this argument, the order of creation imparts status: the woman, formed after the man, is derivative and subordinate. The author could have understood the woman as superior since she is constructed from human bone rather than dirt, or as the culmination of creation since she follows the creation of both the man *and the animals,* or as equal to the man, as Gen 1 suggests.

Then, the author insists that "Adam was not deceived." The comment runs contrary to Rom 5:12-21. There, Paul holds Adam responsible for allowing sin and death to enter the world. Likely the author is suggesting that while woman is responsible for sin, death, and false teaching, the man deliberately transgressed God's commandment and so gave up life in Eden in order to be with her. He was not "deceived" when he took the fruit; rather, he chose to sacrifice himself for her. However, in 2 Cor 11:3, Paul does acknowledge that "the serpent deceived Eve by its cunning."

Other readers might have concluded that the man was equally at fault, or even more so, since the commandment not to eat the forbidden fruit came to him, prior to the woman's creation.

Finally, 1 Tim 2:15 explains the remedy for women's transgression:

> She will be saved through childbearing, provided they continue in faith and love and holiness, with modesty.

Nowhere else does the New Testament suggest that women and men have different paths to salvation.

Some interpret this verse as meaning that women will be saved by means of the *birth of one child*, that is, Jesus. But verse 15 does not point in any clear way to Jesus. Moreover, grammatical construction rules against this reading. The preposition "through" (Greek: *dia*) can mean "because of," but usually it takes this meaning when the following noun is in the accusative case. Here, "childbirth" is in the genitive case. The construction *dia* + a genitive noun means "through" or "by means of" childbearing. Others claim that women will be saved from *dying in childbirth*, but the emphasis on continuous fidelity in verse 15b suggests a time beyond childbirth.

Thus for 1 Timothy, women are saved by conceiving and bearing children. Why is this declaration made? First Timothy 4:3 mentions those who forbid marriage. Some have seen the vile and even foolish myths of 4:7 as (in part) also forbidding or discouraging marriage (see 1 Cor 7:8; Matt 19:12) and celebrating women's celibacy as in the apocryphal *Acts of Paul and Thecla*. Against these views, 1 Timothy upholds the cultural norm: women are to marry, engage in sexual intercourse with their husbands, and bear children. To refuse is to risk damnation.

Second Timothy 1:5 reaffirms the same household model by appealing to "Timothy's" grandmother and mother:

> I am reminded of your sincere faith, a faith that lived first in your grandmother Lois and your mother Eunice and now, I am sure, lives in you.

There may be a connection here between the Pastorals and Acts, since Acts 16:1 describes Timothy as "the son of a Jewish woman who was a believer; but his father was a Greek." Acts and the letter both indicate, by the example of Timothy, the role mothers might play in the religious training of their children (even to the point where the child would follow the religion of the mother rather than that of the father).

Securing this domesticated role for women are the prescriptions concerning church officers in which bishops and deacons are to be men, with each leader assuming the authoritative role in his own household. The bishop "must manage his own household well, keeping his children submissive and respectful in every way" (1 Tim 3:4-5); "Let deacons be married only once, and let them manage their children and their households well" (3:12; contrast the reference to "Phoebe the deacon" in Rom 16:1). Thus, when in 2 Tim 4:19-21, the author greets Prisca and Aquila as well as Claudia, the injunctions bring these women under the prohibitions, suggest that they had no official teaching or preaching function, obeyed their husbands, and stayed silent.

The Pastorals' interest in the domestication of women concerns not only wives but also widows, women not under a husband's control. According to 1 Tim 5:16, a "real widow" gives herself to "supplications and prayers night and day" rather than to "pleasure" (5:5-6). Other wealthy widows, not the church, will support her financially (5:16). Widows with children or grandchildren are to receive support from them. Offspring who fail to provide for widowed mothers and grandmothers are "worse than an unbeliever" (5:8).

To be "put on the list" for receiving church support (5:9), widows must be at least 60 years old (given life expectancy of the time, the list would not have been extensive), have married only once, have served the church community, have raised children, and have "washed the saints' feet" (5:10). This final concern puts the widow in the model of Jesus (see John 13), or, perhaps the unnamed woman of the city who anointed Jesus (Luke 7) and her counterpart, Mary of Bethany (John 12). Whether the "saints" include other women is not made explicit, but given the tenor of the letter, this seems doubtful. While such widows show humility and manifest service, they cannot exercise official leadership or teach. This concern with financial provision is a means to a larger end, namely, control over widows by the ecclesial leadership.

The Pastorals give the impression that younger widows have considerable power and therefore pose particular threats to the ecclesial order. Finding their sexual passion and social freedom dangerous, the author constructs them as vulnerable to "sensual desire" and alienation from Christ. The "first pledge" (5:12) that they violate may be a vow to live celibately following the husband's death. The author acknowledges the women's desires and relative freedom to obtain them (cf. 5:5-6), though the acknowledgment is not positive.

One means of controlling these women is to deny them financial support: "Refuse to put younger widows on the list" (5:11). Another is to stereotype widows who are not under a husband's control as "idle, gadding about from house to house . . . gossips and busybodies" (5:13). The solution? "I would have younger widows marry, bear children, and manage their households" to prevent them turning to follow Satan (5:14-15). Domesticated younger widows, safely remarried and relocated in their own homes with children, no longer threaten the writer's view of ideal society.

The second chapter of Titus provides additional instruction designed to regulate women's behavior. Older men are to be "temperate, serious, prudent, and sound in the faith, in love, and in endurance" (2:2). Young men are to be self-controlled. But women are to police each other's behavior:

> Older women [are to be] reverent in behavior, not to be slanderers or slaves to drink; they are to teach what is good, so that they may encourage the young women to love their husbands, to love their children, to be self-controlled, chaste, good managers of the household, kind, being submissive to their husbands. (2:3-5)

The women first are stereotyped as liable to slander and drunkenness. Then they are given the role of controlling other women. Women here are allowed to teach, but only other women, and the content of their teaching is wifely subordination.

For the author, such social maintenance is necessary, for even inside their homes the writer thinks women are vulnerable. In the (eschatological) last days,

> people [teachers] will . . . make their way into households and captivate silly women, overwhelmed by their sins and swayed by all kinds of desires, who are always being instructed and can never arrive at a knowledge of the truth. (2 Tim 3:2-7)

The idea of men teaching women, in the homes of the women, is not anomalous; we saw the same scenario in Luke 10:38-42, when Jesus entered Martha's home and taught. The problem is not the setting, but the teacher. There is condemnation aplenty in 1 Timothy for both the teachers (male and female?) and for their women hosts, and perhaps patrons. The teachers might include those who "forbid marriage and demand abstinence from foods" (1 Tim 4:3). The language and scenario of 2 Tim 3:1-5 echoes the condemnation of the young widows in 1 Tim 5:13.

Our discussion of these passages from a liberationist-feminist perspective requires us to think carefully about the values the texts promote. Women's silencing becomes a sacred duty, not just a cultural accommodation. Submission, not partnership, is the required order. Yet the continual insistence on women's submission and silence suggests that the actual situations among the Pastorals' readers were by no means so ordered. Further, we know that there were competing narratives, such as the *Acts of Paul and Thecla*, that promoted women's independence, gained by eschewing marriage or by taking vows of celibacy. The Pastorals could be responding to such teachings by insisting on marriage and the production of children.

The Pastorals do not speak the only word on the roles of women. Contemporary readers have to determine how consonant its submissive vision is with other biblical visions and with their understanding of the "good news."

CHAPTER 15

$\mathscr{P}$hilemon

The brief letter of Philemon comprises 25 verses, a tragic legacy, and numerous questions. The letter has been used at various times in the last 2,000 years to justify slavery and to provide biblical sanction for the submission of slaves and especially the return of runaway slaves to their masters.

In this chapter, we suggest that Philemon does not offer a carefully thought-out and sustained argument about these issues. Nor can a universal ethic be drawn from the text. Paul does not address the topic of slavery in general; rather, he engages the very specific situation.

Further, the details of that situation and of Paul's response remain vague. How did Onesimus find himself with Paul? Did he run away and, if so, why? What "duty" and "good deed" does Paul expect Philemon to perform upon Onesimus's return? Is Onesimus even a slave, or is he Philemon's estranged brother?

In this chapter, we use five interconnected methods to discuss the letter. We employ historical-criticism to ask questions about the letter's complex circumstances of origin and address. We employ reader-response approaches to highlight various interpretations formulated by readers. We employ the related approach of reception history (see the discussion of Galatians and James) to observe how Philemon has been read at crucial times in the church's history. We employ a literary approach that focuses on the characters (Paul, Philemon, Onesimus) and that entails a careful scrutiny or "close reading" of the letter. And fifth, in rejecting any reading that interprets the text as supporting contemporary human slavery, we employ ideological criticism to declare such a reading unacceptable.

Throughout, we engage four different and contested interpretations of the letter. These include the following:

- Paul is returning the newly converted but runaway slave, Onesimus, to his owner, Philemon, and will make restitution for whatever damage Onesimus has caused, be it stealing from his master or loss of labor in his absence.

- Paul is encouraging Philemon, in light of the gospel, to manumit (free) the newly converted Onesimus and treat him as a brother rather than as a slave.

- Paul wants Onesimus as his own slave and exhorts Philemon to transfer ownership to Paul.

- Onesimus is not a slave, but Philemon's newly converted yet estranged, biological brother. Paul seeks to heal the fractured familial relationship.

We do not attempt to decide the "best" reading. Rather, we highlight factors involved in the interpretive decisions that create these readings and the consequences of them. This approach reminds us of how much we do not know, of how conventional wisdom comes to be accepted by generations of readers, of the key role interpreters play in making meaning of texts, of why attention to each word matters, and of the far-reaching consequences of interpreting NT texts.

Paul's Address to Philemon

Paul introduces himself as "a prisoner of Christ Jesus" though we do not know where he was imprisoned. The reference to this imprisonment is what helps to classify the Letter to Philemon together with Colossians and Philippians as "Captivity Epistles." Already we recognize that if we read Philemon together with Colossians, we will obtain an interpretation that supports the view that Paul supports the institution of slavery (see Col 3:22-25). If we determine that Colossians is a deutero-Pauline letter, our interpretation of Philemon might differ.

In the salutation, Paul identifies Timothy as a co-sender and "our brother" (1). Timothy is not Paul's "brother" in the physical or legal sense; they are related through belonging to the household of Christ. The important term "brother" will echo in verse 7, where Paul refers to Philemon as a "brother" in Christ and again in verse 16, when Paul speaks of Philemon treating Onesimus as a "brother."

The letter is addressed first to Philemon (1b). By describing Philemon as a "beloved friend" (the literal translation; see also Rom 1:7; Phil 2:12; on "friendship" language, see the chapter on Philippians), Paul expresses an intimate relationship. Paul then reinforces this intimacy by addressing Philemon as a "coworker." This term probably evokes their previous shared work in church planting and teaching. Paul elsewhere applies this term to Aquila and Prisca, Urbanus, Timothy, and numerous others (Rom 16; Phil 4:3). Verse 19 suggests that this coworker relationship resulted from Paul's conversion of Philemon.

Paul addresses others along with Philemon: "Apphia our sister . . . Archippus our fellow soldier . . . and the church in your house" (2). Apphia and Archippus are likely leaders of a local community or house-church of Jesus-followers. However, the singular "your" in "in your house" keeps the focus on Philemon, as does the singular pronoun "you" throughout 4-21.

Addressing Philemon as a beloved coworker is a key part of Paul's approach. Especially in the first half of the letter, Paul presents himself deferentially. In the thanksgiving section (4-7), he praises Philemon's faith in Christ, his love, the good he does, and the ways he has "refreshed" the saints (7). This latter reference probably indicates the hospitality, financial resources, and benefactions Philemon as a patron has provided community members. Paul also underlines the honor Philemon has gained among "all the saints." The approach is diplomatic, and it is hardly the countercultural view of honor that surfaces in other epistles, such as 1 Corinthians. Paul does not invoke his authority as an apostle or as the one who converted Philemon (19). His approach is more indirect: after honoring Philemon, he appeals to compassion three times (7, 12, 20). Unfortunately, English translations often mask the emotional force of his address. The NRSV (cf. the NIV) translates 7b as "the hearts of the saints have been refreshed through you, my brother." The term for "heart" is *splanchna*. It literally means "bowels" or "guts" (considered the seat of the emotions). It is from the same root as the term for "compassion." Verse 12 in the NRSV (again cf. the NIV) reads, "I am sending him, that is, my own heart, back to you." "Heart," again *splanchna*, expresses Paul's compassion. Finally, in verse 20, Paul writes, "Refresh my heart in Christ." In showing compassion to Onesimus, Philemon will be acting in a Christlike and compassionate manner to both Onesimus and Paul.

Paul exhibits not only compassion but also love. He refers to Philemon as "beloved," (1b, translated in NRSV as "dear friend") and gives thanks for Philemon's love for other Jesus-followers (5, 7). Paul makes his "appeal on the basis of love" (9) rather than of apostolic authority (8). In verse 8, Paul explicitly forgoes the use of his authority when he says, "though I am bold enough in Christ to command you to do your duty." The term "bold" (Greek: *parrēsia*) is related to the interactions of friendship (see the chapter on Phil).

Along with expressions of compassion and love, Paul exerts communal pressure on Philemon. By addressing the letter not just to Philemon but "to the church in your house" (2), Paul creates the potential for public shame. Had the letter been read aloud to the congregation, the members would have expected Philemon to respond positively. The apostle's recognition of the honor Philemon gained from beneficent actions to other Jesus-followers (4-7) pressures him to protect that honor. Paul's self-description as "an old man" (Greek: *presbytēs*) and "prisoner" (9) further intensifies this not-so-subtle pressure. For Philemon to deny an apostle would be disobedient. To deny an old man and a prisoner who was also the one who brought him the gospel would be disgraceful.

In setting up his rhetorical strategy, Paul does not mention Onesimus until verse

10. This means he has spent nearly half the letter building connections. He has avoided anything controversial concerning Onesimus, and he has not given Philemon any directive about what he should do. Rather, Paul establishes several obligations between himself and Philemon. For example, the reference to Philemon's house as the meeting place for Jesus' followers (1) as well as his generosity to them (4-7) suggests that Philemon has greater wealth and resources than Paul. That Paul expects Philemon to show him hospitality suggests that Paul is materially indebted to him (22).

Paul also asserts Philemon's indebtedness to him: "I say nothing about your owing me even your own self" (19). By "saying nothing," the apostle reminds Philemon that he owes that which is precious to him. Most interpreters understand this verse to mean that Paul had been responsible for Philemon's conversion and so that Philemon is in Paul's debt. By reminding Philemon of this identity, Paul leaves him with no choice but to comply. Paul can easily be "confident of [his] obedience" (21).

Onesimus

Paul first mentions Onesimus in verse 10: "I am appealing to you for my child [Greek: *teknon*], Onesimus, whose father I have become during my imprisonment." For what he is appealing remains uncertain. So does the "duty" Paul wants Philemon to perform concerning Onesimus (8). What "good deed" (14) Paul wants Philemon to do but will not command him to do must also remain a matter of speculation.

The most common interpretation understands Paul's use of "child" and "father" terms to mean that Paul has converted Onesimus. Paul elsewhere uses paternal imagery (sometimes maternal imagery; so Galatians) to describe his relationship to those he converted (see 1 Cor 4:15). In this understanding of the occasion of the letter, Paul writes on behalf of this repentant, converted, runaway slave, Onesimus, to ask Philemon to receive him without punishment.

Slavery in the Roman Empire

For first-century Romans, slavery was "natural"; it was part of the way the world worked. The empire was a slave economy, and it depended on the labor and skills of an extensive slave population. As products of their time, Philemon and other followers of Jesus owned slaves, or were themselves slaves. Ephesians, Colossians, the Pastorals, and 1 Peter offer instructions for slaves and slave owners. New Testament writings also use the language of slavery, especially slavery to God (Matt 6:24) and to Christ (Rom 1:1), without critique of the institution.

The writings also use it to image Jesus and disciples (Phil 2:6-11; Matt 24:45-51), and Jesus speaks of slaves in parables again without critiquing the institution.

Slaves were regarded as property, could not choose how to support themselves, and lacked freedom of movement, association, and dwelling. As property, slaves could be sold, mortgaged, taxed, leased, bequeathed, and insured. The owner named children born in slavery and renamed those acquired later in life. A slave's body usually bore some mark of ownership, whether a branding, collar, or plaque. Chains were commonplace. Kinship relationships were shattered. Deference in compliance was normative.

Rural slaves (*rustici*) worked often on large landed estates. Urban slaves (*urbani*) were concerned with household matters. Some slaves were well educated and provided land-management, financial, literary or scribal, educational, legal, medical, and entertainment skills. Indeed, some slaves owned other slaves. These roles increasingly blurred the distinction between slave and free. Further blurring the distinction was the fact that slaves could acquire power and honor by association with and service to a high-ranking person. Being a slave in the imperial household, for instance, or in the service of a powerful senator meant greater power and honor than many free persons had.

Greek and Roman literary sources indicate that slaves were expected to obey, submit, and be loyal to their masters. Slave owners, according to these sources, express contempt for and suspicion of slaves, especially in terms of stealing property. They also fear rebellions.

There is substantial evidence for the cruelty with which slaves were treated. Sexual abuse of both male and female slaves was commonplace, except that the culture did not see such usage as "abusive"; it was "natural," the way the world worked. So too were poor housing, clothing, and nourishment. Also common were beatings, floggings, and torture. But there is also evidence for humane treatment of slaves. Some slaves were allowed to live in marriage-type relationships. Slave women who bore numbers of children could be exempted from work. In their agricultural treatises, the Roman writers Marcus Terentius Varro (116–27 B.C.E.) and Lucius Junius Moderatus Columella (ca. 4–ca. 70 C.E.) urged that slaves receive food, clothing, and even rest so that they would be more productive. Some elite writers formed close relationships with educated and skilled slaves (for example, Cicero's relationship with Tiro). In such treatment, slaves were always dependent on their masters' disposition.

Manumission was practiced, often as a reward for faithful service. It could be effected in various ways, such as in an owner's will or before a magistrate. Technically, the practice of manumission released slaves from their compulsory servitude and conferred on the former slaves the status of "freed" persons. In reality, manumission came at a price. Sometimes the slave had to pay the fee for the manumission. Ongoing obligations were normal as freedpersons became clients of their former masters, now their patrons. "Freedpersons" were often identified in relation to their "former" masters. Manumission could be revoked if freedpersons failed to perform these obligations.

The problem with this scenario of Onesimus the returning, runaway slave, centers on whether it fits both the few details of the letter and the social structure of Roman slavery. For example, if Onesimus were a fugitive slave, how did he encounter Paul in prison (10)? If he were seeking sanctuary, fleeing to a prison makes little sense. Fugitive slaves usually found asylum at the statue of an emperor or in a temple, blended into an urban population, or joined the army.

Moreover, Paul does not rebuke Onesimus for running away or even for doing something contrary to Philemon's wishes. Nor does Paul mention Onesimus's repentance for such actions. Paul neither mentions Onesimus's seeking his freedom nor does he plead with Philemon not to punish Onesimus, a surprising omission given that punishment would have been expected in the case of a fugitive slave.

A second scenario suggests that since Paul has converted Onesimus (10), he wants Philemon to manumit him. The problem here is that the instructions to slave masters in Col 4:1 and Eph 6:9, and to slaves in 1 Tim 6:2 show no expectation that conversion of a slave meant manumission. On the other hand, all three of these texts are suspect in terms of their authorship; had Paul intended, in his Letter to Philemon, the manumission of Onesimus, Paul's followers could have controlled the apostle's legacy by insuring that obedience rather than freedom was Paul's focus for slaves.

A third theory proposes that Onesimus, Philemon's slave, did not run away at all. Perhaps Philemon sent him on behalf of the local congregation to assist Paul in prison. While this option explains some parts of the letter, it does not explain others. Had Paul received such aid, why does he not express appreciation as he does in Phil 4:15-20? Moreover, in such circumstances, what "duty" does Paul ask Philemon to perform (8)? What "good deed" does Paul want Philemon to carry out?

All three of these views begin with the presupposition that Onesimus is Philemon's slave, a presupposition that has been in place for millennia. Concerned that some churches were developing the reputation for freeing slaves, the church father from Antioch and later bishop of Constantinople, John Chrysostom (347–407), actively promoted the interpretation that the Letter to Philemon was about reconciling a fugitive slave with his master. Chrysostom sought to protect his churches: slavery was a basic institution of the Roman empire, and promotion of manumission suggested that Christians were subversive. Thus, in his reading of Philemon, Chrysostom concluded that the master should receive Onesimus and treat him humanely. Similar interpretations appear in the relatively contemporary writings of other Christians, including Athanasius, Basil of Caesarea, Ambrosiaster, Theodore of Mopsuestia, Gregory of Nyssa, and Jerome.

This Christian reading remained the letter's dominant interpretation until the present. For obvious reasons, it was popular among advocates of slavery in the American colonies. The Puritan Cotton Mather (1663–1728)—followed by many others into the nineteenth century—argued that Philemon showed masters that christianizing African slaves made them more obedient and more economically productive. Supporters of slavery found in this letter divine sanction for returning fugitive slaves.

But some hearers resisted this reading. A white Presbyterian missionary preaching to slaves in Georgia, the Reverend Charles Colcock Jones, provides this account of responses to his preaching:

> I was preaching to a large congregation on the *Epistle of Philemon:* and when I insisted upon fidelity and obedience as Christian virtues in servants [= slaves] and upon the authority of Paul, condemned the practice of *running away,* one half of my audience deliberately rose up and walked off with themselves, and those that remained looked anything but satisfied, either with the preacher or his doctrine. After dismission, there was no small stir among them; some solemnly declared "that there was no such an Epistle in the Bible"; others "that they did not care if they ever heard me preach again!" (Quoted in Brian Blount, *Then the Whisper Put On Flesh: New Testament Ethics in an African American Context* [Nashville: Abingdon, 2001], 121)

Today, a different form of resisting reading is in place, but it springs not from, or only from, an understanding of the gospel as promoting liberation (for example, Col 3:11, "In that renewal there is no longer . . . slave and free, but Christ is all and in all"). It also follows from a close reading of the letter. When we read Philemon carefully, we find that we may be importing into its interpretation the fugitive slave scenario because that is how the text has traditionally been interpreted. The letter does not unambiguously identify Onesimus as a slave. It does not present Philemon as his master. It makes no direct statement indicating that Onesimus belongs to Philemon. It makes no reference to the flight of a slave or his fugitive status. In fact, its only explicit reference to slavery comes in verse 16, where Paul exhorts Philemon to accept Onesimus "no longer as a slave [Greek: *doulos*] but more than a slave, a beloved brother—especially to me but how much more to you, both in the flesh and in the Lord."

The little word "as" is crucial in introducing a comparison or analogy. Accepting Onesimus "no longer as a slave" could suggest that he was never actually a slave, even while it evokes slavery to suggest Philemon's previous dishonorable treatment of Onesimus.

These observations lead some interpreters to conclude that the slave scenarios do not fit the occasion of the letter because Onesimus is not a slave at all. Instead, a fourth interpretation proposes that the letter is about a fractured relationship between two biological brothers—Onesimus and Philemon. On this reading, Paul's exhortation to Philemon to receive Onesimus "no longer as a slave but more than a slave, a beloved brother—especially to me but how much more to you, both in the flesh and in the Lord" (16) does not involve a literal slave. Instead, it forms the first part of a rhetorical couplet that continues in the next verse, where the thought is completed: "So if you consider me your partner, welcome him as you would welcome me" (17).

The verses draw a comparison. Philemon is not to regard his brother Onesimus as a slave, a lowly person without honor, but as a "brother." The reference to "in the flesh" (16) means the actual sibling relationship shared by Philemon and Onesimus. The reference to "in the Lord" means the kinship established through their common belief in Jesus. Now that Onesimus has become a follower of Jesus (10), the fractured sibling relationship can be repaired.

The repair, though, involves an act of justice. Verse 18 might suggest Onesimus has done some wrong against Philemon concerning money. If so (and it is not clear), Paul offers to take care of that matter to secure the reconciliation.

Philemon's Response

Verses 11–14 elaborate the situation. Paul is sending Onesimus, now a follower of Jesus, back to Philemon, also a Jesus-follower. Verse 11 describes the new situation with a nice double pun. Previously, says Paul, Onesimus was "useless" (*achrēstos*) to Philemon, but he is now "useful" (*euchrēstos*). The two Greek terms commonly designated moral character. Moreover, *chrēstos*, "useful," sounds like the noun "*Christos*," Christ. The prefix *a* negates the word, and *eu* means "good" (as in *eu-angelion*, "good news" or "gospel"). Thus Paul highlights the impact of Onesimus's conversion: "formerly" Onesimus was "Christ-less" or "without Christ" but now he is "well-Christed" or a "good Christian." Enhancing the pun and the point, "Onesimus" means "beneficial" or "useful." Paul uses a cognate term in verse 20: "Yes, brother, let me have this benefit [Greek: *onaimēn*] from you in the Lord." The verse could suggest Paul's desire to keep Onesimus with him, but it can more generally mean that the "benefit" is that Philemon will do the right thing (whatever that may be).

Paul tells Philemon that Onesimus has become "useful both to you and to me" (11). That is, Onesimus is now in a useful relationship to both Paul and Philemon. How Onesimus will be "useful" to Philemon remains unstated: As a slave? A fellow follower of Jesus? A reconciled brother? As the connection between Paul and Philemon?

Paul expresses his affection for Onesimus in verse 12: "I am sending him, that is, my own heart, back to you." In verse 13 he states that he wanted to keep Onesimus "so that he might be of service to me in your place during my imprisonment for the gospel." The term "service" (Greek: *diakoneō*) could refer to ministerial activity, or to activities performed by servants or slaves. The emphasis is that Onesimus serves Paul in the place of Philemon.

Finally, Paul states that he is sending Onesimus back to Philemon "in order that your good deed might be voluntary and not something forced" (14). Just as the "duty" that Paul wants Philemon to perform (8) is not clear, it is not clear here what "good deed" Paul expects Philemon to perform (14).

The dominant interpretation is that Paul wants Philemon to receive Onesimus back as a slave, though without punishing him for running away. On this reading Paul the "prisoner" (1), joins with another criminal, the fugitive thief Onesimus, to intercede with an aggrieved master. Supporting this view is a possible intertextual echo in verse 15: when Paul speaks of Philemon's having Onesimus back "forever" (Greek: *aiōnion*), he could be alluding to Exod 21:6, which states that a slave who refuses manumission will remain with the master "for eternity" (LXX: *ton aiōna*).

If this understanding is accurate, it is difficult to explain why Paul does not appeal repeatedly to Philemon's mercy and grace. Further, nowhere does Paul speak of Onesimus as a fugitive. The closest he gets is in verse 15: "Perhaps this is the reason he was *separated* from you for a while" (emphasis added). The term for "separated" could mean "run away," but its basic meaning is simply "depart" or "left" (for example, Acts 18:1). Moreover, the use of the passive "was separated" challenges the claim that Onesimus is a fugitive. The verb could mean that Onesimus had been separated from Philemon in terms of faithfulness to Christ. Now, with his conversion, Onesimus is no longer separated spiritually. Finally, the appeal to Exod 21:6 seems extremely subtle.

A second option is that the "good deed" Paul wants is that Philemon manumit Onesimus. By setting Onesimus free, Philemon "might have him back forever, no longer as a slave but more than a slave, a beloved brother" (15-16). Paul's appeal here is based on Onesimus's new identity as a brother in Christ (10). Onesimus cannot, so the argument goes, return as a slave. His relationship to Philemon "in Christ" transcends the social stratification of slavery.

This interpretation is not arguing that slavery itself is a social evil but that followers of Christ should not enslave another follower of Christ. The view is prompted by religious confession, not social analysis. In this construction, Philemon's granting of manumission will confirm the change in Onesimus's identity from "slave" to 'brother." Paul underlines this suggestion of manumission by comparing himself to Onesimus as a free partner: "So if you consider me your partner, welcome him as you would welcome me" (17). The term "partner" (Greek: *koinōnos*) suggests much more than the English idiom "business partner" and even more than a spousal connection. The noun *koinōnia*, often translated "fellowship" or "friendship" (see discussion of Philippians), is Paul's common way of describing the church community. Paul uses it in verse 6 to describe Philemon's own fidelity: "I pray that the sharing [Greek: *koinōnia*] of your faith may become effective when you perceive all the good that we may do for Christ."

A third view interprets the "good deed" in relation to transfer of ownership. In verses 11-14, Paul emphasizes that while he was in prison, Onesimus has become "useful" to him. In verses 13-14, Paul expresses a claim on Onesimus and a preference for his ongoing service; the Greek for service is from the verb *diakonein*, the same term that provides the word "deacon"; thus the "service" could have a ministerial function:

> I wanted to keep him with me, so that he might be of service to me . . . but I preferred to do nothing without your consent.

That is, Paul did not keep Onesimus without Philemon's consent; rather he is sending him back to Philemon "in order that your good deed might be voluntary and not something forced" (14).

On this reading, the "good deed" is not Onesimus's manumission, but Philemon's gift of Onesimus to Paul. In verse 20 Paul again seems to appeal for this gift: "Yes, brother, let me have this benefit from you in the Lord." The "benefit" is Philemon's donation. In verse 21, Paul describes Philemon's act of donating Onesimus to him as "obedience," an act that Paul requires of Philemon because he owes his life in Christ to Paul (19).

This third possibility of transfer-of-ownership has a further dimension. In verses 18-19, Paul promises that "if he [Onesimus] has wronged you in any way, or owes you anything, charge that to my account." This "debt" is typically interpreted to be something Onesimus stole from Philemon. The letter, however, says nothing about theft. Perhaps Paul is offering to compensate Philemon for loss of income while Onesimus was with Paul. Or, if the "good deed' involves Philemon giving Onesimus to Paul, it could involve compensating Philemon for his loss. Or, we might emphasize the word "if": Paul does not actually say that Onesimus has created any wrong. He raises a possibility and leaves it to Philemon to make the determination.

A fourth possibility for "the good deed" begins with the presupposition that Onesimus is not a slave. On this reading, the "good deed" involves Philemon being reconciled with his brother Onesimus in an honorable way. How we understand the "good deed" is thus necessarily related to how we understand Onesimus's status.

Paul ends the letter by affirming in verse 22 his expectation of Philemon's hospitality: "One thing more—prepare a guest room for me, for I am hoping through your prayers to be restored to you." This seemingly offhand comment contains an implicit threat. Paul holds Philemon accountable. The apostle will personally determine if Philemon has acted in the contexts of love, compassion, and brotherhood to do "his duty" (8) and "good deed" (14). The term translated "restored" in verse 22 comes from the same root as the word usually translated "grace" (Greek: *charis*) and has the literal meaning of "to give as a gift, to favor" and even "to forgive." Paul's restoration is not simply his release from prison (his own "manumission") but the affirmation of his relationship to Philemon. That relationship will be damaged if Philemon does not do his "duty" (8) or the "good deed" (14), whichever of the four options that might be.

Conclusion

The greetings (23-24) and final benediction (25) are conventional, but conventions have rhetorical force. Paul mentions Epaphras, a "fellow prisoner." The reference might suggest that Onesimus was helpful not only to Paul in prison but also to others sharing the apostle's difficulties. References to the coworkers "Mark, Aristarchus, Demas, and Luke" locate Philemon and his congregation within a broader community. They also stand as witnesses to Paul's letter, and so as witnesses to Philemon's response.

The final verse, "The grace of the Lord Jesus Christ be with your spirit" (25), sounds once more the concern for Philemon's appropriate action. The term for "grace" (Greek: *charis*) connects to Paul's promise of restoration (22), while adding a final suggestion. Paul prays that Philemon show that same grace.

The Letter to Philemon leaves us with numerous questions: Was Onesimus a slave or a brother? What good deed does Paul want Philemon to do? Did Philemon do it? Did Paul or one of his associates witness the result of the letter? For people in the church today, the questions continue. Few would argue for the legitimacy of slavery, but many might still find lessons, or at least good questions, in this letter: Should Christians treat Christian workers differently, more generously or beneficently, than non-Christian workers? Should public shaming be used to prompt moral behavior? To what extent should Christians be involved in patronage systems? How should Christians in the "free world" treat those who are in prison? Should Christians be active in stopping human trafficking today? One of Philemon's legacies is that, like much biblical material, it often prompts people to ask important questions.

$\mathscr{H}$ebrews

W hat is sometimes called "Paul's Letter to the Hebrews," is not a letter, probably not written by Paul, and was not sent to "Hebrews," if that term means Jews who were not followers of Jesus. The document, more a treatise or sermon, reinterprets the Scriptures of Israel as pointing to Jesus. By one count, Hebrews explicitly cites the Psalms 18 times, the Pentateuch 14 times, and the Prophets 7 times. There are also numerous allusions to biblical verses, figures, and events, all of which the author sees as a rough draft that is completed or perfected by Jesus and his church. This contrast between the draft and the completed or perfect version, the shadow and the real, the earthly and the otherworldly, complements philosophical views popularized by Plato (d. 348/347 B.C.E.) and still influential in the first century, for example, in the writings of Jesus' contemporary the Jewish philosopher Philo of Alexandria (d. ca. 50 C.E.). This reading strategy of understanding an original text to anticipate and then be replaced by a second text is known as "typology."

In this chapter, after discussing authorship, date, and setting, we elaborate Hebrews' use of typology. We conclude with some reflections on how Christians in a multireligious world might understand what the church traditionally calls the "Old Testament."

Authorship, Date, and Circumstances

Attempts to ascribe Hebrews to Paul falter on several counts. First, the document does not claim Pauline authorship. Second, whereas sometimes Paul appeals to his own life story in his letters, Hebrews makes no such claims other than to say that the author received the gospel not from Jesus but from "those who heard him" (2:3b). Third, Hebrews is very different in style and content from Paul's undisputed letters, and its Christology is distinct not only from that in Paul's letters but also from the rest of the New Testament canon. Whereas Paul states that Jesus "descended from David according to the flesh" (Rom 1:3), for Hebrews, Jesus is a high priest after the order of Melchizedek.

Numerous suggestions have been made about the authorship of Hebrews. Tertullian, the second-century North African theologian, proposed Paul's associate Barnabas. Eusebius of Caesarea, the fourth-century historian, nominated Paul. His slightly later contemporary Jerome observes that the church in the (Roman) west did not deem Hebrews canonical. Martin Luther, noting the text's philosophical interests, proposed Apollos, the Alexandrian teacher known from Acts and 1 Corinthians. Adolf von Harnack, the German Protestant historian and theologian, proposed Priscilla, Paul's coworker. Origen, the third-century Alexandrian Christian scholar, may have the last word: "God knows."

Proposing a date for Hebrews, like determining its authorship, is a similarly uncertain enterprise. Hebrews, which shows extensive interest in Israel's sacrificial system, is the only New Testament text to develop a Christology that understands Jesus both as ultimate sacrifice and ultimate high priest. Some scholars have suggested it provides a theological explanation and possibly justification for Rome's destruction of the Jerusalem Temple in 70 C.E. as well as responds to the victory celebrations in 71 that supported the reigns of the Flavian emperors, Vespasian (69–79) and his son Titus (79–81). The Flavians displayed Roman military power with a parade of troops, captured Judeans, and plunder taken from Jerusalem. Coins named "Judea Capta" depicted Judea as a mourning, bound woman. The Arch of Titus, still standing in Rome, represented scenes from the triumph. The Arch even depicts Titus's ascension into the heavens at his death. Hebrews offers an alternative narrative: that the true sacrifices at the true altar continue in heaven; that Jesus, not Titus, is the true exalted beloved son (1:13); that the triumph belongs to God, not Rome. This approach dates Hebrews to the last decades of the first century.

However, these arguments are not without problems. For example, Hebrews is not explicitly interested in the Jerusalem Temple. Its descriptions of Israel's sacrificial system and high priesthood come not from first-century Jerusalem but from the Exodus narrative. The altar and priesthood that Jesus replaces are not those of the Temple but of the wilderness sanctuary. Such details can suggest that Hebrews was written before 70 C.E. as much as it might point to a post-70 date. Most scholars settle for Hebrews being written perhaps late first century or early second century.

Hebrews and *1 Clement*?

Some scholars have attempted to date Hebrews by noting that *1 Clement* seems dependent on Hebrews for part of its Christology. Describing Jesus as "the High Priest of all our offerings," "greater than the angels," and "inheriting a more excellent name," *1 Clement* 36 both echoes and directly quotes Heb 1:1-7. Clement also cites passages from the Septuagint that Hebrews also employs, including "You are my Son, today I have begotten you" (*1 Clement* 36:4//Heb 1:5, citing Ps 2:7) and "Sit at my right hand until I make your enemies a footstool of your feet" (*1 Clement* 36:5//Heb 1:13, citing Ps 110:1).

Some interpreters see descriptions in Heb 11:37 and *1 Clement* 17:1—of those who were faithful to God's purposes as going "about in the skins of sheep and goats"—as referring to Nero's persecution of Jesus' followers in Rome in 64–65. The Roman historian Tacitus refers to Nero having "Chrestians" (his spelling) "covered with the skins of beasts, they were torn by dogs and perished" (*Annals* 15.44).

However, the connection between the two verses and Nero's persecution is not certain. First, Heb 11:37 employs language for torture and death familiar from early Jewish texts about martyrs, such as a writing known as the *Lives of the Prophets* ("stoned . . . sawn in two . . . killed by the sword"). The historical value of this text is not clear in terms of its claims regarding the prophets of Israel, but its description of martydoms is conventional. Second, a reference to "destitution" follows the phrase concerning sheep and goat skins, which suggests poverty, not torture. And third, the reference in Heb 10:32 to a previous "hard struggle with sufferings" is too vague to use for dating, given sporadic local harassment.

Further complicating this matter is the uncertain date of *1 Clement*. A reference in *1 Clement* 5 might suggest it was written sometime after the deaths of Peter and Paul (perhaps in the 60s). Mid-second-century writings, those of Hegesippus (died c.180) and Dionysius of Corinth, refer to *1 Clement*. Consequently, *1 Clement* could be written circa 90–140. Hebrews would be earlier, but how much earlier is not clear.

On the question of Hebrew's genre, again, problems arise. Hebrews is not a letter, although it has some standard letter features in its final section: a reference to Timothy, who will travel with the author (13:23); greetings from Italy to leaders (13:24); a closing benediction (13:25). The document's opening, though, lacks letter features such as the identification of sender and recipients and a thanksgiving. Nor does it place exhortations (paraenesis) at the end as letters do. Rather, the document alternates exhortation sections with exposition (2:1-4; 3:7–4:11; 5:11–6:12; 10:19-39; 12:1–13:17). When Hebrews does describe itself, it is as "my word of exhortation" (13:22).

Finally, Hebrews is not written to "Hebrews." It does not seek to evangelize Jews. Even the extensive citations from and allusions to the Septuagint do not determine a Jewish readership, even with the communities that claimed Jesus as Lord, since these texts comprised the Scriptures of Gentile churches. As with authorship, so with the intended audience, numerous suggestions have been made: Jewish followers of Jesus tempted to return to traditional observances after having been inspired by Paul's letters to give them up? Gentile followers tempted by the Septuagint to follow the commandments in Torah? Any followers of Jesus concerned about their relationship to and the meaning of the sacrificial system described in the Pentateuch and so regarded as inaugurated by God?

What can be determined is that Hebrews addresses readers (whether real or hypothetical) who had lapsed in their commitment to Christ (6:4-6), who had not made sufficient progress toward a mature faith (5:11-12), who grow "weary or lose heart" (12:3), and who were facing opposition of various sorts (10:32-36). For all these readers, the document encourages steadfastness in surety of the Parousia, "all the more as you see the Day approaching" (10:25) and confidence by demonstrating how Christ fulfills what the Scriptures of Israel anticipate. In this encouragement, the author develops both a distinctive Christology and a distinctive understanding of the role of Israel's history, practices, and beliefs.

Plato's Worldview

For Plato, earthly reality, which we perceive with our senses, is partial rather than complete, changing rather than permanent, and marked by imperfection, loss, and disease. But another world, known through the mind, consists of pure ideas or forms. It is spiritual, uncorrupted, and perfect. Plato's best-known articulation of this idea is his allegory of the Cave (*Republic*, Book VII, 514a–520a). In this story, told by Socrates, prisoners are chained to a cave wall. Behind them is a large fire, and in front of the fire, people and animals move about. The prisoners can only see, reflected on the opposite wall, the shadows of these figures. For the prisoners, who have seen nothing else, the shadows are reality. The philosopher, according to Plato, is the prisoner made free, the one who can see true reality.

Understandings of what can be perceived through the senses and what can be known by the mind permeate Hellenistic texts. For Philo of Alexandria, the heavens, where God dwells, present the ideal forms, but God graciously provides humanity access to knowledge of this perfected realm. The Torah (the Law of Moses) is a type of the Law of Nature (the Law of God). To live in accordance with Torah is to live according to the divinely established cosmic order. The Wisdom of Solomon (in the OT Apocrypha/deuterocanonical literature) describes Wisdom, who reveals God to human beings, as "a reflection of eternal light, a spotless mirror of the working of God, and an image of his goodness" (7:26). Hebrews 1:3 similarly describes Jesus as "the reflection of God's glory and the exact imprint of God's very being."

When Jewish texts use typology, both the material and the real are valued. Wisdom is a "reflection" of the divine, and *therefore* important. Torah is the sensory image of the mind of God, and *therefore* important. However, when typology moves into Christian texts, it often takes a more dualistic model. This form of typology is known as *supersessionism* because it understands the NT to supersede and so make obsolete the earlier Scriptures. It is also known as *replacement theology* since it replaces Israel's role in salvation history, along with Israel's images, covenant, and Scriptures, with its own.

In most cases in Hebrews and elsewhere in the NT, the prototype or shadow is rejected. For example, Col 2:16-17 sees Torah as the shadow, pointing to and made obsolete by Christ. Colossians presents "matters of food and drink or of observing festivals, new moons, or Sabbaths" as "only a shadow of what is to come, but the substance belongs to Christ." For Hebrews' typological reading strategy, Israel's Scriptures present a "sketch and shadow," a "mere copy" of what is "real," "heavenly," and "true." Once Jesus has accomplished his work, Moses and the Torah are no longer necessary. The wilderness tent where the children of Israel worshiped in between the Exodus from Egypt and their arrival in the land promised to their ancestors anticipates the heavenly altar:

> They offer worship in a sanctuary that is a sketch and shadow of the heavenly one; for Moses, when he was about to erect the tent, was warned, "See that you make everything according to the pattern that was shown you on the mountain." (8:5; see also 9:23, which describes the tent and its vessels as "sketches of heavenly things")

Jesus however, is located "in the sanctuary and the true tent that the Lord, and not any mortal, has set up" (8:2); he is not in "a sanctuary made by human hands, a mere copy of the true one" (9:24; see similar wording in Stephen's speech, Acts 7:48).

This typological reading strategy also provides the basis for Hebrews' insistence that Jesus' sacrifice is qualitatively better than anything Levitical priests, who served in the wilderness sanctuary as well as in the Jerusalem Temple, could offer:

> Since the law has only a shadow of the good things to come and not the true form of these realities, it can never, by the same sacrifices that are continually offered year after year, make perfect those who approach. (10:1)

Such contrasts of earthly and heavenly, temporal and eternal, concern not only institutions, but the very nature of revelation. In its opening verses, Hebrews sets Christ as the culmination of the divine plan:

> Long ago God spoke to our ancestors in many and various ways by the prophets, but in these last days he has spoken to us by a Son. (1:1-2a)

God's speaking to "our ancestors," a point reiterated in the list of ancient worthies in chapter 11 (see also 3:7; 4:3, 12-13; 5:5-6; 7:21), serves in this text to show that all of history has consistently pointed to Christ.

Superiority of Jesus to Angels

The ancient Mediterranean world was full of speculations about supernatural beings—angels and demons, ghosts and spirits, gods and goddesses. Some followers of Jesus, believing that their "Lord" (Greek: *kyrios*) was more than human but also holding to the Jewish view that there is but one Deity, found articulating understandings of Jesus (Christology) difficult. In the first century, the defining affirmations of the Councils of Nicea (325) and Chalcedon (451), that Jesus was "very God of very God . . . being of one substance with the Father," and "truly God and truly human," had not yet been formulated.

Hebrews begins by affirming, on the basis of scriptural citation, that Jesus is more than human but he is not an angel. The writer compares Jesus the Son to the angels with a "chain" or *catena* of citations or what we might call today "proof-texts" (i.e., texts taken out of context in order to make a particular theological argument). In 1:5, Hebrews cites Ps 2:7 (see also 2 Sam 7:14) to affirm that God is the Father of the Son. Then, in 1:6, Deut 32:43 (LXX)— "Praise, O heavens . . . worship him, all you sons of gods"—is adduced to show that angels worship the Son. Third, 1:7 appeals to Ps 104:4 (LXX)—"You make the winds your messengers [Greek: *angeloi*, or "angels"], fire and flame your ministers"—to demonstrate that angels are ephemeral while the Son is permanent. The next argument, found in 1:8-9, asserts that the Son possesses both a (greater) kingdom and a superior identity to the angels, because he is God's anointed. The proof-text is Ps 45:6-7, "Your throne, O God, endures forever and ever . . . Therefore God, your God, has anointed you."

To explain that the Son was active in creation (cf. 1:2) and is unchanging, 1:10-12 appeals to Ps 102:25-27, "Long ago you laid the foundation of the earth . . . They will perish, but you endure . . . you are the same, and your years have no end." Finally, the frequently cited Ps 110:1 (see Matt 5:35//Luke 20:43; Acts 2:35), "The LORD says to my lord, 'Sit at my right hand until I make your enemies your footstool,'" supplies the argument in 1:13 that God has exalted the Son and guarantees his triumphs. Verse 14 concludes the contrast by declaring that while the Son is exalted with God, the angels are sent out on divine service.

Four of the texts cited originally referred to Israel's kings. Psalm 2, probably recited at a coronation, celebrates the king as God's anointed agent or son. Second Samuel 7 narrates God's promise to establish from David's lineage an eternal kingship. Psalm 45 celebrates a king's wedding and praises his righteous rule. Psalm 110, which Hebrews also cites in 4:14; 7:26; 8:1; 10:12-13; and 12:2, also celebrates a coronation. But regardless of these circumstances of origin, the writer of Hebrews now interprets the verses as declarations about the exalted Christ.

Other *Catenae* in the New Testament

This is not the New Testament's only *catena* or "chain" of Scriptures. In Rom 3:10-18, Paul links citations to repeat the point that "there is no one who is righteous, not even one" (Rom 3:10). The chain comprises Scriptures that name sin against God (3:10-12, 18), sinful speech (3:13-14), and sin against others (3:15-17). The citations are also linked by references to parts of the body that engage in sinful activity, "throats" (3:13a), "tongues" (3:13b), "mouths" (3:14), "feet" (3:15), and "eyes" (3:18). This form of citing biblical verses also appears in 1 Pet 2:6-10 as well as among the Dead Sea Scrolls. Similar to Hebrews' presentation of Jesus the Son, the scroll called 4Q *Florilegium* ("4" indicates cave 4, the cave where the scroll was discovered; Q stands for "Qumran"; Florilegium means an anthology) draws together texts from 2 Sam 7:10-14; Ps 2:1; Exod 15:17-18; Deut 23:3-4; and Amos 9:11 (along with brief interpretative comments) to present a portrait of an eschatological Davidic Messiah.

Superiority of Jesus to Moses

Moses does not have the same role in Judaism that Jesus plays in Christianity. Moses is not worshiped, yet he is a revealer, the giver of the Torah, with whom God spoke "face to face" (Exod 33:11; Num 12:8). For Matthew's Gospel, parallels between Jesus and Moses enhance the status of both. For Hebrews, Moses, despite his fidelity, is far inferior to Jesus.

According to 3:1-6, Jesus' faithfulness initially links him to Moses, for Jesus "was faithful to the one who appointed him, just as Moses also 'was faithful in all God's house'" (3:2). This phrase echoes Num 12:7, in which God states that "my servant Moses" is "entrusted with all my house"; here, *house* probably refers to God's people. Yet having recognized Moses's fidelity in leading the people, verse 3 asserts that "Jesus is worthy of more glory than Moses."

Verses 5 and 6 offer three proofs for the claim of Jesus' superiority. First, Moses was a "servant." In the biblical tradition, to be a "servant of God" is a positive, even exalted role. But Hebrews takes the image out of that context and places it in terms of household arrangements. Jesus has greater status than a "servant" because he was "faithful over God's house *as a son*" (3:6, emphasis added). Second, Hebrews claims that while Moses spoke of future things, Jesus enacts this future, the time of salvation (1:2). Third, while Moses served faithfully "*in* all God's house," the exalted Christ has far greater dominion in being "faithful *over* God's house" or people (emphasis added).

In 3:7–4:13 Hebrews develops this contrast between Moses and Jesus in two more ways. The first example is in the context of an exhortation of readers also to fidelity. As is typical of Hebrews' structure, this ethical exhortation or *paraenesis* follows doctrinal instruction (2:5–3:6). Second, it draws from the account of Moses a reference to the Israelites who resisted his leadership. Hebrews 3:7-11 begins by quoting Ps 95:7-11, which speaks of Israel's rebellion and subsequent 40-year punishment in the wilderness:

> "Today, if you hear his voice, do not harden your hearts as in the rebellion, as on the day of testing in the wilderness, where your ancestors put me to the test, though they had seen my works for forty years. Therefore I was angry with that generation, and I said, 'They always go astray in their hearts, and they have not known my ways.' As in my anger I swore, 'They will not enter my rest.'"

By quoting the psalm, Hebrews creates an analogy between readers and the wilderness generation. At Kadesh (Num 14), Israel sought to return to Egypt and to slavery. The allusion locates readers in a similar crisis marked by inconsistent commitment to God and uncertainty about their future. Reflection on the wilderness generation should both warn them of the consequences of infidelity and strengthen their faith. Heb 3:8a cautions against hardened hearts (see Ps 95:8a) or lives that resist God's purposes. To prevent this sclerosis, the author instructs readers to exhort one another not to be deceived by sin and to hold firm their confidence in God (3:13-14). Verse 19 summarizes the consequences of hardheartedness and disobedience: "So we see that they were unable to enter [the promised land] because of unbelief."

The link between the wilderness generation and the readers continues in 4:1-2. Both received good news—"For indeed the good news came to us just as to them"—but "the message they heard did not benefit" that earlier generation, because they did not believe. While they were disqualified from their "rest," "we who have believed enter that rest." *Their* disqualification is emphasized in verse 3 with another citation of Ps 95:11, first cited in 3:11.

Hebrews 4:4-6 then redefines this "rest" not as the literal promised land (the material) but as a heavenly reality (the ideal). This "rest" "remains open" (4:6), and its entry date is "today" for those who hear God speaking (4:7). It is a "sabbath rest" (4:9), an image from the creation story here given soteriological and eschatological dimensions. Readers who do not respond to God's voice heard in the Son (1:2) will not enter this "rest" just as the wilderness generation failed to enter the promised land.

This interpretation of Ps 95:7-11 concludes in 4:11 with an urgent exhortation that associates the redefinition of "rest" with the example of those who failed to obtain it: "Let us therefore make every effort to enter that rest, so that no one may fall through such disobedience as theirs."

Modern Middle East Politics

The redefinition of "rest" away from the land of Israel to a heavenly realm creates a difference in understanding regarding the land of Israel between many Christians and many Jews today. For religious Jews in general, then and now, the land was the "promised land," and the Torah reiterates that unconditional promise throughout Genesis. Even when the Sinaitic covenant, explained in Deuteronomy, states that infidelity to God and morally reprehensible behavior will cause a loss of the land, Israel's Scriptures do not see this loss as permanent. Indeed, Ezekiel (36:22-29) and Zechariah (13:1) both suggest that only in the land, following exile, will Israel fully be in accord with God's ways. God's promises of land to the descendants of Abraham remain a major theme in the Scriptures and subsequent Jewish liturgy.

Other Jews who do not accept supernatural claims to the land, and who perhaps do not even believe in God, still recognize Israel as the homeland of the Jewish people. That some Jews do not believe in God, or do not believe in a God who deals in real estate, may seem contrary to the idea that Jews are part of a religious system, and a religious system has something to do with the category of "theology" or "belief." However, the Jewish people never settled down to be a "religion," if by that term we mean a system that one enters by belief. Although one can, and many through the centuries did, convert to Judaism, the Jewish people never abandoned their sense of being a "people," that is, an ethnic group. One is thus born a Jew, whereas, to use the popular terminology (but see the discussion of John 3), one is "born again" a Christian.

Today, Christians have various theological understandings of this promise of the land. A reading of Galatians indicates to some Christians that all the promises Torah connects to Abraham are delivered to Abraham's "offspring," Jesus, and through him to his followers. Thus the Jews are disinherited. Hebrews redefines the promise of land to a promise of eschatological, heavenly rest and then dismisses the Torah as obsolete. The Jews are again disinherited. For a late first-century audience, such disinterest in the land among the followers of Jesus makes good sense: most were Gentile; most had no connection to the land; many anticipated the Parousia and so regarded the land as ultimately irrelevant. Only with the rise of Constantine did the special Christian focus on the "holy land" begin.

Other Christians today see the children of Abraham, Isaac, and Jacob—that is, the Jewish people—as still in possession of the promises of the faithful God (see

Rom 9:4; 15:8) and therefore as maintaining a theological claim to the land of Israel. And others, also informed by their theologies, opt for different futures for the Middle East. Some insist that the land be divided, as the original United Nations plan had it, into the (Jewish) state of Israel and the state of Palestine, others suggest that there be a single state with a Palestinian (Muslim) majority and so the Jewish state of Israel be eliminated, and still others prefer that the Palestinian population be absorbed into greater Israel. The biblical text, and its role in setting public policy, continues to be of major import.

Jesus as High Priest

The image of Jesus as high priest begins in 2:17 and develops after the author establishes Jesus' superiority to Moses. This image of "great high priest who has passed through the heavens" (4:14) derives neither from the Gospels nor Paul. These texts see Jesus as descended from the house of David, which is not a priestly line, a point Hebrews acknowledges:

> For it is evident that our Lord was descended from Judah, and in connection with that tribe Moses said nothing about priests. (7:14)

Priesthood, established in Israel's Scriptures and continuing in Judaism today, is an inherited position and not a vocation; priestly status carries on the paternal line. Priests are descendants of Moses's brother Aaron. Levites are descendants of Aaron's ancestor and Jacob's son, Levi. Thus in Judaism, one is a priest if one's father is a priest, and the same point holds for Levites. Although today the roles of both priests and Levites are limited because there is no longer a Temple in which they would engage in their duties, Jewish tradition still recognizes certain liturgical roles for both in the context of synagogue worship.

Hebrews needs to delineate Jesus' qualifications to serve as a priest, since clearly his father was not of the priestly line. The first argument emphasizes that as high priest, Jesus can identify with human frailty:

> We do not have a high priest who is unable to sympathize with our weaknesses, but we have one who in every respect has been tested as we are, yet without sin. (4:15)

Second, Hebrews deflects the question of paternal descent by arguing that one can become a high priest "only when called by God, just as Aaron was" (5:4; referring to Exod 28:1-5). Divine call trumps lineage. Heb 5:5 elaborates:

> Christ did not glorify himself in becoming a high priest, but was appointed by the one who said to him, "You are my Son, today I have begotten you."

The writer uses the key text, Ps 2:7, that began the *catena* in 1:5.

Third, 5:6 quotes Ps 110:4 to establish Jesus' role: "You are a priest forever, according to the order of Melchizedek." The opening verse of this psalm appears in 1:13 to celebrate Jesus' exaltation to God's right hand. Regarding this connection to Melchizedek, the writer anticipates: "We have much to say that is hard to explain" (5:11). But before the explanation, *paraenesis* again interrupts. Readers are urged to "go on toward perfection" in mature understanding and with faithful living (6:1-20). The *paraenesis* concludes by returning to Jesus' identity as "a high priest forever according to the order of Melchizedek" (6:20).

The explanation begins by evoking the two scriptural references to this mysterious figure. First, Ps 110:4 (cited in 5:6 and alluded to in 7:3) again provides the proof-text: "You are a priest forever according to the order of Melchizedek." Hebrews 7:3 then applies the reference to Jesus:

> Without father, without mother, without genealogy, having neither beginning of days nor end of life, but resembling the Son of God, he remains a priest forever.

Jesus' association with Melchizedek replaces the criterion of lineage. Jesus "has become a priest, not through a legal requirement concerning physical descent, but through the power of an indestructible life" (7:16).

This aligning of Melchizedek and Jesus is the basis for a contrast between Melchizedek's eternal priesthood, to which Jesus belongs, and priests descended from Abraham.

To make this case, the author draws a second proof-text from Gen 14:18-20. According to Genesis, Melchizedek of Salem, both a king and a "priest of God Most High," blesses Abraham. In response, Abraham gives him "one tenth of everything." The author concludes from this description that Melchizedek, a "priest forever" (7:3), is greater than Abraham both because Melchizedek blesses Abraham and because he receives tithes from Abraham. It follows that if Melchizedek is greater than Abraham, he is greater than any of Abraham's priestly descendants. Melchizedek has an ancestry "without beginning" and is a "priest forever" (7:3, 10). Abraham's descendants, like Abraham, are linked to time, having both a beginning and an end.

The contrast between the Levitical priesthood and the superior "order of Melchizedek," to which Jesus belongs, continues in 7:11-28 and into chapters 8 and 9. The author explains that the Levitical priesthood cannot provide perfection. Priests sin, but Jesus does not. Priests function under a Law that was "weak and ineffectual" (7:18), but Jesus offers a "better hope through which we approach God" (7:19). God guarantees Jesus' "forever priesthood" with an oath, but does not do so for the Levitical priests, and thus the author can conclude that Jesus guarantees a "better covenant" (7:20-22, citing Ps 110:4 again). Jesus is always able to save "since he always lives" (7:23-25), something Levitical priests cannot do. As exalted high priest, Jesus ministers in a heavenly sanctuary of which the earthly sanctuary is but "a sketch and shadow" (8:1-5; 9:1-10). Jesus is superior to the Levitical priests in not having to offer sacrifice for his own sins (7:27). Finally, as the eternal high priest, Jesus does not offer continual sacrifices comprising the blood of "goats and calves." He offers his own blood as the singular sacrifice that removes sin permanently.

A Better Covenant

Developing the reference in 7:22 to a new or better covenant, Hebrews 8 (and 9:15) foregrounds Jeremiah's promise (31:31-34) of a new covenant and presents Jesus as the fulfillment of that promise:

> Jesus has now obtained a more excellent ministry, and to that degree he is the mediator of a better covenant, which has been enacted through better promises. For if that first covenant had been faultless, there would have been no need to look for a second one. (8:6-7)

In its original context, Jeremiah's oracle addressed the destruction of Jerusalem, including the Temple, and the deportation of much of its population to Babylon in the sixth century B.C.E. Jeremiah (31:32) interpreted the catastrophe as God's punishment for the people's infidelity to the covenant made through Moses. But Jeremiah announces good news. God will initiate a new covenant in which the people will know God, and their sins will be forgiven (31:33-34). This new covenant will not be written on stone, but inscribed on the heart. People will no longer require instruction, for they will all recognize God.

Hebrews interprets Jeremiah's declaration in relation to Jesus. It presents Jesus establishing this "new covenant" (8:8; the Greek—*diathēkēn kainēn*—can be translated "new testament") to replace the earlier, broken one. The author concludes by reinterpreting Jeremiah:

In speaking of "a new covenant" he has made the first one obsolete. And what is obsolete and growing old will soon disappear. (8:13)

Typological Supersessionist Reading in 2 Corinthians

This contrast between the original covenant and the one Jesus establishes appears in other New Testament texts. For example, 2 Cor 3:7-11 juxtaposes the "ministry of death, chiseled in letters on stone tablets" with the "ministry of the Spirit come in glory." It similarly contrasts the "ministry of condemnation" with the "ministry of justification." Taking the same typological approach as Hebrews, it presents a supersessionist argument: "What once had glory has lost its glory because of the greater glory; for if what was set aside came through glory, much more has the permanent come in glory."

It is this type of presentation that leads to the stereotype of the "Old Testament God of Wrath" versus the "New Testament God of Love," and the related dichotomy of the "Old Testament" focus on "works" or "law" versus the "New Testament" focus on "grace." The stereotypes, which are based on selective readings of both texts, create a misunderstanding of the Christian Bible (both Old Testament and New), a misunderstanding of the nature of God, and a misunderstanding of the Jewish tradition based in the Scriptures of Israel.

Justifying this claim, the author returns to the theme of Jesus' high priesthood and ultimate sacrifice. The writer describes the "imperfect" wilderness tabernacle and concludes that its worship "cannot perfect the conscience of the worshiper" (9:9). Only the exalted Jesus, heavenly high priest, and his perfect sacrifice, can do this.

The presentation is marked throughout by contrasts as well as correspondences between old and new, temporal and eternal, repeated and unique, earthly and heavenly, shadow and reality. Jesus enters not an earthly tabernacle but the "the greater and perfect tent" (9:11). He offers not continual sacrifices but a "once for all" sacrifice consisting not of "the blood of goats and calves" but "his own blood, thus obtaining eternal redemption" (9:12). Hebrews 9:13-14 argue from the lesser to the greater to contrast the external purification accomplished by animal sacrifices with the greater purifying of "our conscience from dead works" through "the blood of Christ."

In 9:15-28 Hebrews turns to the efficacy of blood offerings. Moses sprinkled "the blood of the covenant" (quoting Exod 24:8) on the scroll of the law, on the people (9:19), the tabernacle, and the liturgical vessels (9:21) to purify these "sketches of the heavenly things" (9:23). But "the heavenly things themselves need better sacrifices than these" (9:23). Christ entered not a sanctuary that was an inferior copy but "heaven itself" (9:24). He did not make continual sacrifices of animal blood but sacrificed himself "once for all . . . to remove sin" (9:25-26).

This attention to blood follows from the claim, in 9:22, that "under the law almost everything is purified with blood, and without the shedding of blood there is no forgiveness of sins." This too is a selective reading of both Israel's Scriptures and the Jewish tradition. The biblical tradition suggests rather that God graciously forgives sins without the need for sacrifice. For example, Gen 18:26 records God saying, "If I find at Sodom fifty righteous in the city, I will forgive the whole place for their sake." No sacrifice was required. Psalm 130:4 affirms of God, "But there is forgiveness with you, so that you may be revered." In Num 14:19, Moses prays, "Forgive the iniquity of this people according to the greatness of your steadfast love, just as you have pardoned this people, from Egypt even until now." The next verse states, "Then the LORD said, 'I do forgive, just as you have asked' "—no reference to sacrifice appears. The Prayer of Manasseh (7) in the Apocrypha (deuterocanonical texts) reads, "You have promised repentance and forgiveness to those who have sinned against you, and in the multitude of your mercies you have appointed repentance for sinners, so that they may be saved." God is not, in the general Jewish view, hampered by the lack of animal sacrifice. God is merciful and forgives sin wherever and whenever a contrite heart atones. Hebrews, together with Christians today who insist on blood sacrifice as necessary to atone for sin, differs from the general Jewish community in the first century and through the centuries today, in what is required for atonement and reconciliation.

By Faithfulness

The discussion of Jesus the high priest ends in 10:18. Another exhortation follows to "hold fast to the confession of our hope," to "provoke one another to love and good deeds," to meet together regularly, and not to "persist in sin" (10:23-26). This section concludes by citing Habakkuk's insistence (2:4) that the "righteous ones will live by faith" (10:38; also Rom 1:17; Gal 3:11), and by defining the addressees as being "not among those who shrink back and so are lost, but among those who have faith and so are saved" (10:39). These references to faith establish the context for the catalogue in chapter 11 of biblical figures who exemplify fidelity.

Hebrews 11:1 defines faith as "the assurance of things hoped for, the conviction of things not seen." We see here the distinction from Paul, who understands "faith" as a transformative experience, and the Pastorals, who present "the faith" as a series of doctrinal affirmations. The first clause in Heb 11 emphasizes faith's eschatological orientation: it hopes for, and is certain about, the completion of God's purposes at Christ's return (10:25, 37). The second clause recollects the typological model. There is more to be seen—ideal forms and heavenly rest—than are available to present existence. Hebrews 5–10 has already detailed some of what exists but is "not seen": the heavenly sanctuary in which Jesus the high priest has offered his perfect sacrifice to effect forgiveness of sin.

The phrase "by faith" appears some 18 times in Heb 11, where it is associated with a multitude of biblical figures. From the primeval history, Hebrews commends Abel, who offered an appropriate sacrifice (11:4; cf. Gen 4:2-16); Enoch, who pleased God (11:5-6; cf. Gen 5:22-24); and Noah, who obeyed God (11:7; cf. Gen 6:9-22). From the time of the patriarchs and matriarchs, 11:8-19 offers a lengthy example involving Abraham and Sarah (Gen 12–23), including Abraham's willingness to sacrifice his son Isaac. For Hebrews, this near sacrifice depicted in Gen 22 anticipates the sacrifice of the Christ as well as his resurrection, since Abraham knew that God can "raise some-one from the dead" (11:17-19). Then follow brief references to Isaac (Gen 27:27-30), Jacob (Gen 48:15-20), and Joseph (Gen 50:24-25). The list gives the impression that everything in Genesis is pointing to Jesus.

Another longer section focuses on Moses, the Exodus, and entry into the land (11:23-31; cf. Exod 2–14). Moses, who models faithful endurance in the midst of ill-treatment (11:23-28), contrasts the faithless wilderness generation that failed to achieve "rest" (see 3:7–4:13). Rahab, the prostitute from Jericho (Josh 2; 6:12-21; see also Matt 1:5; Jas 2:25), exhibits faithfulness in receiving "the spies in peace" (11:31).

In 11:32, the style changes. The names span the narratives in Judges, 1 and 2 Samuel, and the Prophets, but without elaborating their deeds:

And what more should I say? For time would fail me to tell of Gideon, Barak, Samson, Jephthah, of David and Samuel and the prophets . . .

The author presumes that readers are familiar with the accounts. In 11:32-39, the style again changes as lists of names give way to cataloguing the hardships

[of those] who through faith conquered kingdoms, administered justice, obtained prom-ises, shut the mouths of lions, quenched raging fire, escaped the edge of the sword, won strength out of weakness, became mighty in war, put foreign armies to flight. (11:33-34)

Some of these events evoke biblical figures. Conquering kingdoms could refer to the judges. Administering justice suggests David. Lions suggest Samson (Judg 14:6) and Daniel (Dan 6), as does fire (Dan 3). Verses 35-39 emphasize death, persecution, and resurrection, evoking the prophets as well as the Maccabean struggle against Antiochus Epiphanes.

These verses highlight threats to those who show active faith, and thereby they both warn and challenge the addressees. They also subsume the major figures and events of Israel's Scriptures into a new narrative with a new construction of faith. The history of Israel is now the history (only) of Jesus' followers. Locating themselves in this narrative, the readers of Hebrews can persevere in faith, assured of the permanent, the real, and the salvific.

The last two chapters of the text turn from instruction to exhortation. Readers are to "run with perseverance . . . looking to Jesus the pioneer and perfecter of our faith" (12:1-2). Faithful living requires that they "endure trials" (12:7), "pursue peace" (12:14), not refuse God who is speaking (12:25), practice love and hospitality (13:1), and remember and obey their leaders (13:7, 17). The writer concludes with a benediction that God will "make you complete in everything good so that you may do his will" (13:20-21).

Hebrews and Contemporary Readers

For Christian readers today, living in an interreligious context and aware of how in the name of Christ, people have been oppressed, exiled, enslaved, and slaughtered, Hebrews raises stark challenges.

Supersessionism, practiced by any religion, can be dangerous. It often creates an attitude of superiority that leaves people complacent ("I'm saved and you're not") rather than challenges adherents to live a life of service and love. It can promote a lack of interest in and devaluation of other people's traditions. It can undermine expressions of "love of neighbor." It can also lead to misunderstandings, since it reads another religious tradition through its own lens rather than allowing a tradition to define its own practices and theologies.

For example, Hebrews is frequently read as presenting Christianity as the "ideal" religion and Judaism as an imperfect and inadequate forerunner, a tradition whose covenant never worked and is now obsolete. Some Christians would say that this is how it is. Christianity *is* superior to Judaism and to any other religion. Their truth is that Jesus' perfect sacrifice cleanses people "once for all" of sin (Heb 10:10). Without that sacrifice, there is no relation with God. In this view, the promises God makes to Abraham, Isaac, Jacob, Moses, and so on, are transferred from Israel (that is, Jews) to the followers of Jesus (cf. Gal 3:16).

Those who hold these views should not automatically be viewed as anti-Semitic or anti-Jewish; they are reading the text "faithfully" as they define faithful reading.

Other Christians would insist on a very different understanding. While they might claim truth for their own tradition, they refrain from pronouncing judgments on other religious traditions, and they refuse to disparage them. Some use canonical criticism to insist that since divine grace saves, it is not the role of Christians to pronounce who will be saved and who will be damned. Others maintain that God is faithful to Israel "according to the flesh" (Rom 9:4-5) and regard the covenant with the Jews as valid (Rom 11:25-32).

It may be inevitable that people think that their tradition is "better"; indeed, supersessionism may be built into religious discourse. New movements see themselves as completing, or fulfilling—and thus as superior to—what is already in place. The followers of Jesus saw themselves as heirs to Israel's traditions, as did the people who wrote the Dead Sea Scrolls and the rabbinic tradition. They did not consider that they could all be right. Martin Luther and the Protestant churches saw themselves as more faithful to the biblical vision than the Roman Catholic Church. The Catholic church, in its own Reformation, saw itself as the faithful congregation. John Wesley, the founder of Methodism, offered a new view of the Anglican tradition. The Mormon Church reinterprets biblical tradition in light of its own new revelation, and so on.

In making proclamations about the superiority of one tradition over another, all people would do well to become more aware of how theological teaching can impact interpersonal behavior and even international politics. One strategy is to listen to how those of another religious tradition define themselves, rather than impose definitions on them from the outside. And in claiming to perfect an earlier tradition, worshipers might recognize that what they see as a perfection, others might see as an aberration. On the specific question of the new covenant as Hebrews presents it, readers finally would do well to note that the promises and perfection Hebrews offers have yet to become a present reality, either personally or for the church as a whole. Jeremiah 31:33-34, cited in 8:10-12, says:

This is the covenant that I will make with the house of Israel after those days, says the LORD: I will put my law within them, and I will write it on their hearts; and I will be their God, and they shall be my people. No longer shall they teach one another, or say to each other, "Know the LORD," for they shall all know me, from the least of them to the greatest, says the LORD; for I will forgive their iniquity, and remember their sin no more.

Teaching still continues. As does sin.

$\mathscr{J}$ames

Historical criticism focuses on the origins of biblical writings: who wrote what to whom, when, where, why, and how. Another approach, called *the history of the interpretation* or *reception history*, focuses on the ways interpreters across two millennia have made meaning of Scripture in different circumstances. Interpretation is shaped not only by the texts themselves but also by the context in which interpretation takes place and by the agenda of interpreters. Reading is never a decontextualized act—the questions we ask of the text and the meaning we derive from it are inevitably influenced by our own concerns and context.

In this chapter, we first employ historical criticism to address the questions of author and audience; this historical perspective also aids us in addressing the relationship of this letter to the Pauline texts, the Scriptures of Israel, and the traditions surrounding Jesus. Then, employing reception history, we turn to three "moments" in the interpretation of James. The first, which focuses on the letter's reception in the first few centuries of the church, provides the occasion to discuss canonical development. The second concerns Martin Luther's dismissal of James as an "epistle of straw." The third centers on a contemporary liberationist reading. By looking at these three moments, we can track different emphases that emerge in different circumstances.

James in Historical Context

We do not know when the Letter of James was written, by whom, or where. The writer self-identifies as a "servant of God and of the Lord Jesus Christ" (1:1). In the first few centuries, readers associated the document with both James the brother of Jesus (Mark 6:3; Gal 1:19; Acts 12:17; 15:13) and James the son of Zebedee (Mark 1:19). The three other NT figures named James—the son of Alphaeus (Mark 3:18), James the younger (Mark 15:40), and the father of Jude (Acts 1:13)—were not considered viable candidates. The name "James" is an Anglicized version of the Greek *Iakōbos*, which could also be translated "Jacob." The name suggested to early interpreters that "James" was written by a person of Jewish descent. Most English translations of the Bible render the Greek term "Jacob" when the subject is a figure from the "Old Testament," but "James" when the figure is a follower of Jesus. The different translations of the same name necessarily express the translators' own ideological views.

Today, scholars question both ancient attributions, whether to the brother of Jesus or to the son of Zebedee. Many observe that the Greek is too high quality for a Galilean fisherman like James the apostle or an artisan, as Jesus' brother would have been. Since James the apostle was killed in 44 C.E. (Acts 11), his death would indicate a very early date of composition, which many scholars find unlikely given the letter's apparent engagement with Paul's thought. Several other factors call into question the authorship of James of Jerusalem: his commitment to the Law (see Acts 15:14-21) is contrary to "the law of freedom" mentioned in 1:25; it seems unlikely that Jesus' brother would mention Jesus only twice (1:1; 2:1); and claims about his authorship emerged slowly in the first centuries. Ultimately we cannot identify the author.

Nor is the writing's audience clear. The greeting, "to the twelve tribes of the Dispersion" (1:1), could indicate that it was written to Jews in the Diaspora. Yet this greeting could have a symbolic rather than geographical meaning: the readers are "dispersed" from their homeland, which is the (heavenly) kingdom of God.

Concerning a date, if James, brother of Jesus, is the author, the document must have been written in Jerusalem by 62, when James was killed (Josephus, *Antiquities* 20.200). However, the arguments used to support an early date are based on silence—the text's lack of christological development and sophisticated ecclesial structures. That the letter lacks an expectation of imminent judgment does not necessarily indicate a relatively late date, any more than heightened eschatology indicates an early one. The followers of Jesus did not have one form of eschatological speculation. Moreover, the author as well as the intended audience may well have had other texts and teachings that spoke to matters of eschatology, Christology, and ecclesial structures. That a text does not mention a specific issue does not indicate the issue held no interest for either author or audience.

More convincing for us is that this document is a relatively late text. We do not regard it as written by James the apostle or James the brother of Jesus but by someone from within the Jewish community who sought to actualize the teachings of Jesus for Diaspora churches and to correct misunderstandings of Paul's thought.

James Reading Paul

James 2:21-24 reads:

Was not our ancestor Abraham justified by works when he offered his son Isaac on the altar? You see that faith was active along with his works, and faith was brought to completion by the works. Thus the Scripture was fulfilled that says, "Abraham believed God, and it was reckoned to him as righteousness," and he was called the friend of God. You see that a person is justified by works and not by faith alone.

According to Paul, Abraham was justified, was put in right relationship with God, by faith. Paul is adamant that Abraham did not perform any "work"; Rom 4:2-3 (citing Gen 15:6) explains, "If Abraham was justified by works, he has something to boast about, but not before God." Rather, "For what does the scripture say? 'Abraham believed God, and it was reckoned to him as righteousness.'" For Paul, "works" refers to the performance of those laws that marked Jews as distinct from Gentiles: circumcision, dietary regulations, and so on. "Faith" meant both the faithfulness Jesus himself displayed and the trust that his followers put in God's righteous act of raising him from the dead.

However, Paul did not expect Jesus' followers simply to "have faith." Paul's letters typically end with ethical exhortation (*paraenesis*). For Paul, justified people, who have died to the power of sin and who have Christ dwelling in them, perform good works, not those of circumcision or dietary practices, but those of loving their neighbors (another "law"—Lev 19:18—but not one that was distinctive to Jews). As Paul exhorts his Roman readers:

Owe no one anything, except to love one another; for the one who loves another has fulfilled the law. (13:8)

By the time James writes, if our dating of this letter to the period after Paul is correct, the meanings of both "faith" and "works" have changed. For James, "works" no longer refers to ritual law that sanctified the body, reflected Israel's covenant, and kept Jews from assimilating. "Works" now refers to any moral action. Faith is no longer the marker of a new person; "faith" has come to mean a set of beliefs. This same shift occurs in the Pastorals, which speak not of "faith" but "*the* faith" as doctrine. James 2:18-19 shows the shift:

But someone will say, "You have faith and I have works. Show me your faith apart from your works, and I by my works will show you my faith. You believe that God is one; you do well. Even the demons believe—and shudder.

With the change in meaning of both "faith" and "works," Paul's teaching became distorted. If "faith" means not a transformed life but a set of beliefs, one could easily ignore moral actions. Belief alone becomes the litmus test for salvation. So James has to insist that for Abraham,

faith was active along with his works, and faith was brought to completion by the works. Thus the scripture was fulfilled that says, "Abraham believed God, and it was reckoned to him as righteousness," and he was called the friend of God. You see that a person is justified by works and not by faith alone. (2:22-24)

For James, "just as the body without the spirit is dead, so faith without works is also dead" (2:26).

James Reading Israel's Scriptures

James's appeal to Abraham is one of the letter's numerous allusions to the Scriptures of Israel. There are striking connections between James and Wisdom literature, particularly Proverbs, and with Lev 19. For example, echoing Prov 2:6-7, James states that wisdom comes from God (1:5). James consistently condemns oppressing the poor and showing partiality to the rich, as do Prov 14:31 and 18:5. Both Proverbs (10:12) and James (5:20) assert that love covers offenses. Proverbs (3:34 LXX) and James (4:6) state that God favors the poor (Greek: *tapeinos*) and that riches are fleeting (Prov 11:28; Jas 1:10-11). The sometimes-heard canard that Judaism regards the poor as sinful and the rich as righteous is precisely that, a groundless claim.

James is rightly seen as a type of Wisdom literature: it does not focus on the nature of Christ, the role of the cross or resurrection, or on life after death; instead, it provides instruction on how to live a moral life. In antiquity, there was an extensive tradition of instructive or hortatory literature that guided people in right living. Jewish writings such as Proverbs as well as the Wisdom of Jesus ben Sirach (Ecclesiasticus, in the deuterocanonical corpus/Old Testament Apocrypha), the *Letter of Aristeas*, the *Sentences of Pseudo-Phocylides*, and the *Sentences of Syriac Menander* (in the Pseudepigrapha) are among the numerous documents that belong to this tradition. Accordingly a number of common terms and topics appear. For example, in 3:13–4:10, James shows considerable affinity with the extensive traditions (called *topoi*) about envy and friendship (see the chapter on Philippians). The emphasis 1:2 places on the joy of the virtuous life tested in adverse circumstances is found in the Latin writer Seneca and Greek writer Epictetus.

James draws a number of exhortations from Lev 19. These include commands such as "love your neighbor" (Lev 19:18, Jas 2:8), do not swear falsely (Lev 19:12; Jas 5:12), do not withhold wages (Lev 19:13; Jas 5:4), be impartial (Lev 19:15; Jas 2:1, 9), do not speak evil (Lev 19:16; Jas 4:11), and rebuke your erring neighbors so that they do not sin (Lev 19:17b; Jas 5:20). The laws promote and preserve community.

Finally, James incorporates prophetic material. The rejection of "friendship with the world" in favor of loyalty to God (4:4) reflects an extensive prophetic focus on covenant loyalty. Covenant loyalty urged Israel to be faithful to the one God and to a way of life committed "to do justice, and to love kindness, and to walk humbly with your God" (Mic 6:8). The emphasis on fading earthly wealth (1:9, 11) echoes Isa 40:6-7.

Condemnation of the oppressive rich (5:1-6) recollects Amos 2:6-7; 8:4-6; and Isa 3:14-15; 5:8-9. Finally, the emphasis on caring for orphans and widows (1:27) draws on Isa 1:17, 23, as well as on Deuteronomy.

James Reading Jesus

James also draws extensively from Jesus traditions, with striking connections to the Sermon on the Mount in Matt 5–7. Included are exhortations to joy in the midst of trials (Jas 1:2//Matt 5:11-12); the goal of perfection (Jas 1:4//Matt 5:48); warnings against anger (Jas 1:20//Matt 5:22); blessing for the poor (Jas 2:5//Matt 5:3); keeping the law (Jas 2:10//Matt 5:19); blessing the merciful (Jas 2:13//Matt 5:7); doing God's will (Jas 2:14-16//Matt 7:21-23); blessing peacemakers (Jas 3:18//Matt 5:9); and warnings against swearing oaths (Jas 5:12//Matt 5:34-37). While some documents of the early church focus on Christology, James keeps the teachings of Jesus paramount. Whether James had access to Matthew's text, or possessed a series of quotes like the proposed Q source, remains debated.

The Early Church Reading James

From the second to the fourth centuries, the Letter of James gradually attained recognition as an authoritative document, or, as Jerome put it in the late fourth century, "little by little" (*De Viris Illustribus* 2). Two texts, *1 Clement* (written from the church in Rome to the church in Corinth ca. 95) and the *Shepherd of Hermas* (ca. 150), perhaps reflect some influence from James.

---

1 Clement and *Shepherd of Hermas* Reading James, Perhaps

Like James, *1 Clement* (10:1) presents Abraham as a moral exemplar: "Abraham, who was called the 'friend,' was found faithful in that he rendered obedience unto the words of God." *First Clement* (12:1), like James, appeals to Rahab (see Josh 2; 6) as a model of hospitality: "For her faith and hospitality Rahab the prostitute was saved"; Jas 2:25 states, "Likewise, was not Rahab the prostitute also justified by works when she welcomed the messengers and sent them out by another road?" Hebrews also mentions Abraham and Rahab as examples of faith. However, how much influence James has on *1 Clement* is not secure.

James's possible influence on the *Shepherd of Hermas* includes opposition to being double-minded (1:8; 4:8); the struggle against the devil (3:15; 4:7); wealth as an obstacle to relationship with God (1:9-12; 2:5-7; 4:13-17); the oppression of the poor by the rich, who will be judged by God (1:27; 2:6; 5:1-6); warnings against destructive speech (3:6-10; 4:11); the importance of long-suffering (1:4; 5:7-10); the connection of faith and prayer (1:5-8; 4:3; 5:17-18); the power of giving and destroying life (1:21; 4:12); sins of omission (4:17); and the importance of mutual correction (5:19-20). Yet these themes permeate ancient literature, so direct influence is not certain.

The *Muratorian Canon* (its name comes from the scholar who discovered the manuscript in 1740) lists texts that its compiler deems valuable for reading in churches, texts that should not be read in a worship context (for example, letters in Paul's name to Laodicea and Alexandria and other writings associated with Gnostic and Montanist groups), and texts that might be useful for private reading but not ecclesiastical proclamation (for example, the *Shepherd of Hermas*). This canon identifies 22 of the 27 writings that will later comprise the New Testament as acceptable for public worship. James is missing along with 3 John, Hebrews, and 1 and 2 Peter. This absence suggests that the compiler did not know the letter: had it been regarded as dangerous or worthy of private study, it would have warranted mention. However, included among the approved texts are the Wisdom of Solomon (now listed in the deuterocanonical literature, or the Old Testament Apocrypha) and the *Apocalypse of Peter*. Two contemporaneous North African writers, Tertullian (d. 215) and Cyprian of Carthage (d. 258), also do not cite James.

Origen, writing circa 250 in Alexandria, includes James in his list of authoritative texts; he quotes it 36 times and engages 24 verses. Although Origen regards its author as "the brother of the Lord" and "James the Apostle," thereby conflating the two figures, he notes that not all the churches regard it as having value.

The church historian Eusebius (ca. 324–25) supports the view that James was written by the Lord's brother, although he acknowledges the attribution is disputed. He regards the letter as having apostolic authority and attests its use by many churches in worship (*Ecclesiastical History* 2.23.25). However, like Origen, his endorsement is tempered. Eusebius classified Christian writings into four categories based on their recognition by earlier church fathers, the use of what he calls "apostolic style" and language, and content he deems orthodox. He identifies documents recognized by all the churches (for example, four gospels; Paul's letters), inauthentic documents (for example, *Shepherd of Hermas*), heretical works, and those of "disputed value." Eusebius places James in this last category (*Ecclesiastical History* 3.25.3).

Citations of James in the fourth century indicate increasing influence and acceptance. In a letter of 308–9 to church leaders in Antioch, the bishop Marcellus of Rome quotes 3:1-8 on the use of the tongue. A century later, also in Rome, Rufinus includes James on his canonical list. In Alexandria, Athanasius (d. 373) includes James in his important Easter Letter of 367. Like Eusebius, Athanasius categorizes texts: those useful for worship contexts, texts for personal edification, and texts rejected as heretical. James now appears in the first category. Cyril of Jerusalem (d. 386) recognizes James as canonical.

Yet even by the mid-fourth century in some locations, James's value remains questionable. In Cappadocia, Gregory of Nyssa (ca. 335–395) and Basil the Great (ca. 329–379) largely ignore it. Gregory of Nazianzus (ca. 329–390) lists it in his canon but rarely cites it. In Antioch, the moralist monk John Chrysostom (d. 407) cites James some 48 times. The Council of Carthage in 397 includes it in its canon. Augustine of Hippo (d. 430) is said to have written a commentary on it but it has not survived.

It is possible that the Epistle's varied reception is based not only on questions of its authorship but also on its contents. The church fathers were much more interested in doctrine (especially Christology) and liturgical practices than ethical exhortation. James mentions Jesus only in 1:1 and 2:1 and has nothing to contribute on the questions of Jesus' nature, the configuration of the Trinity, or liturgy and sacraments.

Yet on the basis of its ethical teaching, by the end of the fourth century, the text is securely located in the canon. The sense remains, though, that it had tertiary status in churches, a poor relation to the Gospels and Paul's letters.

The Formation of the Canon

The letter's reception history demonstrates that the process of the formation of the New Testament canon took approximately four centuries. The decisive factor for a book's admission to the canon was not committee vote, but how useful it was for early Christian communities.

All of the writings present in the NT canon were *written* between circa 40s and 130 C.E. The earliest text is likely to have been 1 Thessalonians; the latest, 2 Peter and Acts. It is impossible to speak of an "original" text per se; what we have are copies of copies. These documents were read in worship, studied by catechumens and church leaders, and copied by the faithful.

Beginning in the second century, documents began to be *collected.* The late text, 2 Pet 3:15-16 (ca. 120), refers to a collection of Paul's letters. Around 140, Marcion in Rome attests a two-part collection that included Paul's letters (without the Pastorals) along with Luke's Gospel. By the 150s–60s, Tatian, from Syria, assembled a document known as the *Diatessaron* (Greek for "through the four"), a continuous narrative about Jesus compiled from the four gospels. Tatian's harmonization, which circulated widely, was not only very popular; it was also the standard gospel text in Syria into the fifth century.

These collections as well as the Muratorian canon indicate a *selection* process. By this point in the canonical process, two criteria had emerged to help with the selection. First, the document was to have some connection to Jesus, ideally based on eyewitness testimony. Second, despite the addresses of Paul's letters, the text had to be useful for the whole church, and as having widespread acceptance (the criterion of "catholicity"). Origen (d. 253–54) emphasizes widespread acceptance from his familiarity with churches in Rome, Athens, Antioch, Arabia, Cappadocia, and Israel. By the mid-third century, he observes acceptance for the four gospels, the 13 letters in Paul's name, 1 Peter, 1 John, Acts, and Revelation. He also observes sporadic use of 2 Peter, 2–3 John, James, Hebrews, and Jude. He rejects the *Gospels of the Egyptians, Thomas, Basilides,* and *Matthias.*

In the Easter Letter of 367, Athanasius proposed a collection of 27 authoritative writings, which he called "canon," the Greek word for a rule or measure. He also identified writings that were to have no place in the church and writings that could have a limited instructional role. Those texts of limited value included the deuterocanonical Wisdom of Solomon, Sirach, [Greek] Esther, Judith, and Tobit, along with the *Didache* and the *Shepherd of Hermas.* Many, but not all, churches agreed with his proposal, though the canonical status of some writings, such as the book of Revelation, continued to be contested. Various councils subsequently *ratified* Athanasius's proposal, including the Council of Carthage in 397.

Luther Reading James: Faith and/or Works

The Protestant reformer Martin Luther did not think that the Letter of James held the same doctrinal import as most of the other New Testament writings. Although not rejecting it entirely, in his printed New Testament of 1522, he moved James along with Jude, Hebrews, and Revelation to the end of the book, and he did not give these texts page numbers in the table of contents.

Luther did not forbid people from reading James, and he acknowledged that it contained "good sayings." His objections, nevertheless, were substantial. The first concern was authorship. A few years earlier, in 1516, Erasmus had expressed doubts over its apostolic authorship and authority. Luther, agreeing with these doubts, suggested that James was written not by the brother of Jesus but by the son of Zebedee.

Second, for Luther, canonical writings were supposed to "show you Christ," particularly the cross and the resurrection; James does not do so. Third, Luther agreed with Erasmus's objection to the prevailing interpretation of 5:14-16:

> Are any among you sick? They should call for the elders of the church and have them pray over them, anointing them with oil in the name of the Lord. The prayer of faith will save the sick, and the Lord will raise them up; and anyone who has committed sins will be forgiven. Therefore confess your sins to one another, and pray for one another, so that you may be healed. The prayer of the righteous is powerful and effective.

This passage was widely interpreted to support two sacraments, rituals understood to convey Christ's grace, that were observed by the Roman Catholic Church: confession and extreme unction (administering last rites to assure a dying person of God's gracious favor). For Luther, neither confession nor extreme unction was a sacrament. For him, there were only two sacraments instituted by Christ: baptism and Eucharist.

Fourth, beyond authorship, Christology, and sacraments, Luther's major objection was that James did not proclaim the gospel as he understood it. In his 1522 "Preface to the New Testament," and his "Preface to the Epistles of St. James and St. Jude," Luther writes:

> In sum, Saint John's Gospel, and his first letter, Saint Paul's letters, especially Romans, Galatians, and Ephesians, and Saint Peter's first letter are the books that show you Christ and teach you everything that is necessary and beneficial for you to know even though you were never to see or hear any other book or doctrine. Thus Saint James's letter is really a letter of straw when compared to these ones, for it has nothing of the nature of the gospel about it.

As we saw in our discussion of Galatians, for Luther, the "gospel" or "good news" is justification by faith. Luther's slogan therefore was "by faith alone"—*sola fide*—in the crucified and risen Christ. From this, as Paul also taught, would come good works. In Luther's words, "Good works don't make a good man [sic], but a good man bears good fruit."

In Luther's view, Jas 2:14-26 was especially egregious, because the passage cites Abraham as an example not of *sola fide*, as Luther understood Rom 4, but as an example of one who expressed his faith in works: "You see that a person is justified by works and not by faith alone" (2:24). The idea of justification by "faith *plus works*" was everything Luther and his reading of Paul resisted.

There is much dispute about whether Luther understood either Paul or James accurately and whether he was right to set the two against each other. We have already seen that the terms "works" and "faith" have different connotations, even in the New

Testament. Like all readers, Luther read the Bible through his own subject position, in terms of his own issues and the issues of his age.

Today, interpretation is often seen to be a dialogue between interpreters and text and not just a monologue whereby interpreters use the text for their own purposes. This dialogue is more likely where the church is informed by history and when the concerns of the original authors and their circumstances are considered relevant to the interpretive task. Dialogue between reader and text requires understanding something of how the text might have addressed its circumstances of origin (as best as they can be determined), what it has meant over time, and how individual readers and ecclesial communities understand it today. The strength of this dialogue is that it takes human history and community seriously, and it allows thoughtful assessment of the meaning that interpreters make of a text.

Luther's soteriological and christological foci indicate another potential problem with interpretation. The Reformer's predetermined theological agenda stops him from appreciating James's formulation of Christianity based not on doctrine but on lived faithfulness. Luther concentrates only on James's treatment of faith and works, and he sets aside the rest of the letter's often demanding instruction about how this life of faith is to be lived. Moreover, although Luther recognizes diverse voices within the canon, the effect of elevating his reading of Paul over James is to marginalize the latter, rather than to listen to the textual conversation. All readers set up a "canon within a canon" whereby certain voices or verses prevail over others. However, when only one voice prevails, other profound meanings are often ignored.

Historical Approaches and Questions of Faith

During the Renaissance, emphasis on the Bible's original languages—Hebrew and Greek—enabled evaluation of the various manuscripts, and so the discipline of textual- or text-criticism developed. This approach shaped Erasmus's influential Greek New Testament of 1516. Its historical sensitivity impacted Martin Luther and his fellow Reformers in the first half of the sixteenth century.

With the eighteenth-century Enlightenment came a renewed emphasis on reason, and this too influenced biblical interpretation. The quest to find scientific cause-and-effect explanations for natural events extended to religious texts. The Bible was increasingly seen as a document like any other, open to historical investigation. The struggle for how to read the Bible—as divine word that cannot be questioned, as historical text open to any and all questions—continues to impact its interpretation to this day. In our view, historical study, even when it considers questions of authorship or points to possible contradictions, should not undermine one's religious confession. Faith and reason need not be in conflict.

A Liberation Scholar Reads James

Elsa Tamez, a Latin American feminist liberation theologian and professor of biblical studies at the Latin American Biblical University (UBL) in San José, Costa Rica, engages James in her social circumstances. We note several of her reading strategies on the following pages, and we add to them our own observations. (Elsa Tamez, *The Scandalous Message of James: Faith without Works Is Dead* [New York: Crossroads, 1990].)

Tamez begins by suggesting that if the letter had been written to Latin American Christian communities in the 1990s, it would have been "intercepted" by national security forces. They would have found its denunciation of arrogant merchants (4:13-17) and exploitative landowners subversive. James issues a cry for economic justice and a manifesto for changing the old ways:

> Come now, you rich people, weep and wail for the miseries that are coming to you.
> . . . Listen! The wages of the laborers who mowed your fields, which you kept back
> by fraud, cry out, and the cries of the harvesters have reached the ears of the Lord of
> hosts. (5:1-4)

Tamez also wonders whether the hesitations of the church fathers to recognize James's authority and Luther's dismissal of its instruction by elevating faith also "intercept" the epistle by not taking its contents seriously.

A liberation-theological approach to Scripture understands salvation not primarily in terms of redemption from personal sins but in terms of reforming social structures and creating physical transformation. Not only does it read Scripture to find a message of justice for the poor and oppressed; it also understands Scripture to express a preferential option for the poor. That is, the poor occupy a privileged place in God's purposes. Consequently, liberative readings emphasize both the reader's context and the impact of the interpretation. They cannot be isolated from action or praxis, a way of life that works for the benefit of the poor.

This approach has been appreciated for its emphasis on the biblical theme of justice for the poor that begins with the Torah, continues in the Prophets of Israel, and finds renewed emphasis in the words of Jesus and his followers. Liberative readings have also been appreciated for their emphasis on human partnership with God in bringing about societal transformation in accord with God's purposes. They have also been criticized for elevating the social and political, while diminishing the spiritual; for redefining the concept of salvation; and for a tendency to a somewhat dualistic view of good (the poor) versus evil (the rich and usually the West). Occasionally they have employed negative stereotyping of the Bible's Jewish content and context, with those against whom Jesus and Paul struggled seen as "Jews" and this reified Jewish culture mapped onto whatever social evils impact the present reader. More recently, "Rome," for some, is a negative stereotype, with Jesus and Paul and the rest of the New Testament sometimes seen as only opposed to the forces of empire rather than also complicit through the inevitable process of hybridity (see the discussion in chapter 13 on the Thessalonian correspondence). On other occasions, liberation-theological readings replace Jewish history—for example, the Exodus is about any subjugated people—with new situations. The goal of reading for liberation does not justify the means, if the means include negative stereotyping or the erasure of anyone's history.

With her liberationist goals foregrounded, Tamez proposes reading James from three interrelated angles, that of oppression and suffering, of hope, and of praxis. We consider each in turn, starting with oppression and suffering.

First, Tamez proposes that James writes within the context of socioeconomic oppression. James is addressed to "the twelve tribes in the Dispersion" (1:1). The term "Dispersion" (the Greek is *Diaspora*) historically refers to people of Israel scattered to areas outside the land of Israel. In Tamez's view, it also functions as a sociological term to indicate those on the margins of society who have been displaced because of religious commitments or socioeconomic conditions. She understands the reference to "twelve tribes" to indicate those among Jesus' followers who have been socially displaced, are homeless, and live in tension with the local society's more powerful members.

This interpretation exemplifies classic features of a liberation approach. It enacts the thesis that God has a preferential option for the poor. It sees the Bible's message as one of liberation for all suffering political and economic oppression. In this approach, Moses at the Exodus or Jesus at the cross or Paul in prison represents just practice as resistance to political, colonial, or economic oppression. The community suffering today finds strength and inspiration from these biblical antecedents.

Tamez also supports her thesis of a congregation on society's margins by appealing to James's warnings concerning social status. James 1:9 (see also 4:6) proclaims, "Let the believer who is lowly boast in being raised up." The term "lowly" (Greek: *tapeinos*) indicates for Tamez a low social status (cf. Luke 1:52, Mary's Magnificat). In 1:27, James mandates care for widows and orphans. The exhortation draws on numerous references in Israel's Scriptures to widows, orphans, and resident aliens as being society's most vulnerable and requiring support (for example, Deut 24:17; Ps 68:5; Jer 49:11). For these antecedent Scriptures, care for the poor is *law*; it is required. For the church, especially those churches that highlight faith over works, a new reasoning is needed to maintain social programs. James focuses on the enacted love of neighbor, on *praxis*:

> What good is it, my brothers, if you say you have faith but do not have works? Can faith save you? If a brother or sister [James is here gender-inclusive] is naked and lacks daily food, and one of you says to them, "Go in peace; keep warm and eat your fill," and yet

you do not supply their bodily needs, what is the good of that? So faith by itself, if it has no works, is dead. (2:14-17)

James condemns the privileging of social status:

For if a person with gold rings and in fine clothes comes into your assembly, and if a poor person in dirty clothes also comes in, and if you take notice of the one wearing the fine clothes and say, "Have a seat here, please," while to the one who is poor you say, "Stand there," or, "Sit at my feet . . ." (2:2-3)

The term for "assembly" in Greek is *synagōgē*, or "synagogue"; ironically, the NRSV and NIV, which reads "meeting," both elide the letter's Jewish context.

James also condemns the rich, who "will disappear like a flower in the field" (1:10). In James, the rich—not imperial power, Satan, or false teachers—epitomize evil.

But you have dishonored the poor. Is it not the rich who oppress you? Is it not they who drag you into court? Is it not they who blaspheme the excellent name that was invoked over you? (2:6-7)

The author warns those who say, "Today or tomorrow we will go to such and such a town and spend a year there, doing business and making money" (4:13) that they really ought to be saying, "If the Lord wishes, we will live and do this or that" (4:15). Their fault—or "evil," as 4:16 names it—is their arrogance in assuming that they can secure their own lives without reference to God. James 5:4-5 catalogues their sins of praxis: they withhold the wages of the laborer (violating Lev 19:13; Deut 24:14) and they live in luxury, it seems, at the expense of the poor. In 5:6, James charges the rich with murder: "You have condemned and murdered the righteous [one], who does not resist you." Whether the author intended the "righteous" (*dikaion*) to refer to Jesus or to any righteous person or to both cannot be determined.

A possible framework for this understanding of socioeconomic oppression is evident in 4:4:

Adulterers! Do you not know that friendship with the world is enmity with God? Therefore whoever wishes to be a friend of the world becomes an enemy of God.

The "world" is often a negative term in James, a dangerous place whose structures of power and wealth threaten faithfulness to God (1:27). To be friends with the world inevitably means hostility to God, who favors the poor (2:5).

After delineating the oppressive system, Tamez turns to her second angle, that of hope. She observes that James consistently anticipates God's intervention to change the status quo. The opening verse provides the first indication. Tamez notes that in 1:1, the word normally translated "greetings" (Greek: *chairein*) literally means "rejoice." This common epistolary greeting anticipates subsequent expectations of God's intervention. Then, Tamez observes that James uses the term "blessed" (Greek: *makarios*) three times to express God's favor and blessing present in this oppressive situation. For example:

> Blessed is anyone who endures temptation. Such a one has stood the test and will receive the crown of life that the Lord has promised to those who love him. (1:12)

In 1:25 God's blessing belongs to those who observe the "royal law," which means loving one's neighbor (see 2:8). In 5:10-11 James declares Job and the prophets (who challenge the rich and powerful on behalf of the oppressed and weak) blessed because they endured difficult times faithfully. Finally, James provides a message of hope and a call for endurance: "Listen, my beloved brothers and sisters. [Here the Greek is gender-exclusive.] Has not God chosen the poor in the world to be rich in faith and to be heirs of the kingdom that he has promised to those who love him?" (2:5).

After detailing the context of oppression and the message of hope, Tamez turns to the actions or *praxis* that constitutes the faithful way of life. James's instruction assumes not isolated individuals but communal solidarity. The letter frequently uses the familial term "brothers" (Greek: *adelphoi*; 1:2, 16; 2:1). Plural verbs are common: "consider it nothing but joy" (1:2), "do not be deceived" (1:16), "be doers" (1:22). Often taking a dualistic perspective similar to that found in John's Gospel, James presents instruction in oppositional terms: look out for the rich (2:6-7); do not be friends with the world (4:4).

Tamez identifies three characteristics of the life of this new family of faith: militant patience, integrity, and effective prayer. By "militant patience" Tamez does not mean a passive attitude or a ready acceptance of suffering. This type of patience might be better understood as "endurance" (Greek: *hypomonē*, see 1:3-4), or actively resisting and overcoming trials. Job models this active endurance (see 5:11): he does not passively endure his suffering but struggles against it, refusing to accept it as normative or just. In the end, God vindicates him.

Similarly, James exhorts readers to "wait patiently" for the Lord's coming. The model is one of "patiently" awaiting the harvest (5:7-8). Farmers can do nothing to hasten the crop, but that does not mean they do nothing. They must "strengthen their hearts," expectantly waiting and not despairing (5:8). They are not to grumble against one another (5:9a). Instead, they are to follow the prophets' example in resisting oppression (5:10). Waiting patiently means actively pursuing a just way of life until "the Judge is standing at the doors" (5:9).

Central to this way of life is both personal and community "integrity" or consistency between theology and praxis. Because God is one (2:19), never changes (1:17), and displays a consistency of plan and performance (1:18), followers of God should be of singular intent and action, not double-minded. James spells out what the life of integrity looks like. It embraces poverty rather than wealth (1:9-11). It practices careful, not angry speech (1:19-21; also 1:26-27; 3:1-12). It not only hears the "perfect law, the law of liberty" but also does it (1:22-25). It cares for widows and orphans (1:26-27). It shows no partiality to the rich but honors the poor (2:1-7). It loves the neighbor (2:8-11) and practices justice, such as clothing the naked, feeding the hungry, and practicing hospitality (2:14-26; with echoes of Matt 25, the parable of the Sheep and the Goats).

Tamez identifies genuine prayer as a third act of praxis that accompanies militant patience and a life of integrity. Prayer plays a crucial role in the self-definition and functioning of the community. While the double-minded doubter engages in false prayer (1:6), as do those who covet and focus on pleasures (4:2-3), people committed to God's justice offer prayers of integrity. In 5:4, workers deprived of wages by landowners cry to God for justice.

James 5:13-16 exhorts those who suffer to pray, just as those who are cheerful are to sing songs of praise. James then turns to those who are suffering because of sickness. They are to summon the elders (Greek: *presybyteroi*), who are to pray over them and anoint them with oil. According to 5:15-16:

> The prayer of faith will save the sick, and the Lord will raise them up; and anyone who has committed sins will be forgiven. Therefore confess your sins to one another, and pray for one another, so that you may be healed. The prayer of the righteous is powerful and effective.

From a liberationist praxis, prayer becomes the means by which the sick person becomes a blessing and not a burden for the community. The sick person is the occasion for the community to unite, to confess sins, and to pray.

Tamez's reading highlights militant patience, integrity, and prayer in James. It is a reading situated in and especially attending to matters of economic justice, notably the exploitation and oppression of the poor. This example of a liberative reading raises some interesting questions. What might other readings of James in different contexts of injustice look like (for example, racial or gender or political injustice)? And would such readings identify aspects of James that might be understood to support oppressive structures and practices? And what might liberative readings of other NT texts look like?

CHAPTER 18

1 Peter

To frame our discussion of 1 Peter, this chapter employs a form of social-science criticism to look at the text's "social construction of reality." This construction comprises the worldview the text presents to assist its readers in understanding and legitimating their identity in their particular social circumstances. We begin by identifying the possible circumstances that the letter addresses. We then elaborate a dominant image in 1 Peter's construction of reality: its encouragement and affirmation that "Christians" (the term appears in 4:16) live as "aliens and exiles" within their Roman imperial environment (2:11).

Author and Audience

The letter begins by claiming Petrine authorship: "Peter, an apostle of Jesus Christ, to the exiles of the Dispersion in Pontus, Galatia, Cappadocia, Asia, and Bithynia" (1:1). In 5:1, the author presents himself as an elder (Greek: *presbyteros*) and witness (Greek: *martys*, "martyr") to Jesus, thereby legitimating his authority and solidifying his relationship with the readers:

> Now as an elder myself and a witness of the sufferings of Christ, as well as one who shares in the glory to be revealed, I exhort the elders among you.

This presentation is probably pseudonymous. The author employs Peter's name, reputation, and authority, just as the Pastorals use the name of Paul.

First, the high quality of the Greek belies authorship by a native Aramaic speaker from lower Galilee, an area that was not overly Hellenized, as we know from archaeological remains. There is little reason to presume that the apostle Peter had formal training in Greek rhetorical techniques. The claim that Peter dictated the letter to a scribe (an amanuensis), who translated the original Aramaic into elegant Greek, is compromised by the letter's consistent quotations from the Septuagint. To claim the scribe added biblical verses distances authorship even further from the apostle Peter.

A second argument against Petrine authorship is the letter's lack of references to Jesus' teachings. The author claims in 5:1 to be "a witness of the sufferings of Christ," which would be, at least as far as we know from the Gospels, at best an exaggerated claim. The Gospels do not present Peter as witnessing Jesus' sufferings: he sleeps at Gethsemane and flees from the cross. Rather, the verse is part of the letter's point that suffering is normal for Christians (for example, 2:21; 4:16) who share "Christ's sufferings" (4:13).

Third is the issue of the letter's date. Some early church tradition proposes that Peter, along with Paul, died in Nero's persecution of Jesus' followers in 64 C.E. Even were this not the case, the letter hints at a post-70 date, which would likely prohibit Petrine authorship. The term "Babylon" appears in 5:13 to identify the author's location. Babylon was the empire that destroyed the first Temple in Jerusalem in 587 B.C.E. and forced many of the city's inhabitants into exile. It comes to be identified with Rome after Roman troops destroyed Jerusalem and its temple in 70 C.E. (see *2 Baruch* 11:1; *4 Ezra* 3:1-3; *Sibylline Oracles* 5:143, 159; Rev 17:5, 18). The term not only links the destruction of the first and second temples; it also serves a subversive function. Just as God ensured that Babylon was destroyed (Isa 44:28–45:1), so the new Babylon, Rome, will also fall. In the context of 1 Peter, "Babylon" further functions to establish solidarity between author and audience. Babylon is the archetypal place of exile, so in locating himself in "Babylon," the author offers a construction of reality in which he shares the identity of "alien and exile" with the letter's recipients.

The recipients live in the Roman provinces of Pontus, Galatia, Cappadocia, Asia, and Bithynia—a diverse geographical region comprising almost 130,000 square miles (not quite as large as California, about twice the size of Florida). Rome had conquered Pontus in 63 B.C.E. (the same year the Roman general Pompey entered Jerusalem) and Galatia in 25 B.C.E. The other three areas came under Roman rule through diplomatic means (Asia 133 B.C.E.; Bithynia 74 B.C.E.; Cappadocia 17 C.E.), although they had little choice in the matter. Roman presence in the regions was uneven. As in Judea, Roman troops were based in urban rather than rural areas, and their primary task was to keep the peace, not roam the streets to intimidate locals. Most small villages went largely untouched by direct Roman presence, although the inevitable taxation and land confiscation made residents well aware of the empire's rule. The letter's agrarian images of grass (1:24) and shepherds (2:25; 5:4) are common in Israel's Scriptures and do not indicate that the audience consisted of farmers or rural dwellers.

The household code in 2:18–3:7, although conventional, indicates that the recipients likely included slaveholders and slaves. Some women appear to be married to Christians, and others to non-Christians (3:1). The numerous Septuagintal citations (for example, 1:24; 2:4-8) do not indicate the ethnicity of the recipients: the Septuagint was the "Bible" of the early church, and its Gentile members would be familiar with figures like Sarah and Abraham (3:5-6) and Noah (3:20), as well as with the Babylonian exile (1:1; 2:11; cf. 5:13). However, references to their former way of life marked by ignorance

(1:14), futility (2:18), immorality, and excessive idolatry (4:3-4) suggest an audience of Gentiles who now worship Israel's God.

Constructing Identity: The Chosen Race

Borrowing images from the biblical tradition, 1 Pet 2:9 declares the Christians to be "a chosen race, a royal priesthood, a holy nation, God's own people." The language echoes Deut 7:6:

> For you are a people holy to the LORD your God; the LORD your God has chosen you out of all the peoples on earth to be his people, his treasured possession." (See also Deut 10:15.)

The letter also evokes Exod 19:6a: "You shall be for me a priestly kingdom and a holy nation." Thus the author writes this Gentile community into the history of Israel: they can locate themselves in the national epic the Septuagint records, and simultaneously they can view themselves as treasured by God despite their present suffering.

The accompanying description of the Christian community as "chosen and destined by God the Father and sanctified by the Spirit to be obedient to Jesus Christ and to be sprinkled with his blood" (1:2) further defines the recipients' identity. First, the use of paternal language for God constructs the readers as members of God's family, as children of God the Father. Households were the basic societal structure of antiquity. One's membership in a particular household, and specifically one's relationship with a particular father/householder, whether prestigious or common, rich or poor, was basic to identity. Second, being "sprinkled with blood" evokes the language of Torah. This ritual anointed Aaron and his sons to the priesthood (Lev 8:30; see also the covenant ratification ceremony described in Exod 24:3-8). Such rituals were also known from various religious movements in the Gentile world, such as mystery cults (see the chapter on Colossians). The image suggested purification and so a distinction from the profane world. Such affirmations define the recipients' identity by connecting them both to Israel's story and to cross-cultural notions of sacrifice and purity.

Third, the language of "chosen" or "elect" and "destined" suggests privilege given by God the divine benefactor. The term "sanctified" means "set apart for divine service" and suggests privileged service. Jesus' death ("blood") identifies them and defines them as obedient to his purposes. Though "aliens and exiles" in the world, the recipients are the elect, chosen, sanctified, obedient children of God's household. God will protect them (1:5) as they await their "inheritance that is imperishable, undefiled, and unfading" (1:4).

The following verses reinforce the construction of Christian identity as distinct and special.

The prophets who prophesied of the grace that was to be yours made careful search and inquiry, inquiring about the person or time that the Spirit of Christ within them indicated when it testified in advance to the sufferings destined for Christ and the subsequent glory. It was revealed to them that they were serving not themselves but you, in regard to the things that have now been announced to you through those who brought you good news by the Holy Spirit sent from heaven—things into which angels long to look. (1:10-12)

The verses locate the recipients in the time of fulfillment of scriptural promises. Even the angels envy their privileged position. Although they are aliens and exiles, they are located at the climax of history, in the center of divine care, and within the household of God.

More expressions of their special identity follow in 1:23: "You have been born anew," using a compound form of the same verb that appears in John 3:7 when Jesus says to Nicodemus: "You must be born from above [or born again]." The image of rebirth reinforces the new kinship structure in which these Christians now locate themselves. Being "born anew" also means being "ransomed from the futile ways inherited from your ancestors" (1:18). The term "ransomed" appears, for example, in Mark 10:45 and Matt 20:28. Romans 3:24 and 1 Tim 2:6 (see the sidebar on p. 241) suggest that they required setting free from their previous existence. In Deut 7:8-9 the verb refers to God setting Israel free from slavery in Egypt. In Isa 43:14-15 it refers to God setting the exiles free from captivity in Babylon. Thus the Christians are set free from their old way of life. This language also suggests that their non-Christian neighbors are still in captivity, displaced from God and enslaved to sin. Without Christ, those who "do not believe" (2:7a) "stumble because they disobey the word" (2:8b) and are "not a people" (2:10).

Constructing Identity: Aliens and Exiles

Evoking the language of the Septuagint, the author adopts the recipients into the history of Israel and locates them as "chosen," "royal," and "holy." At the same time, the author constructs the recipients in terms of displacement and suffering. The address in 1 Peter to "the exiles of the Dispersion [Greek: *Diaspora*]" shares the term *Diaspora* with James (1:1), which addresses "the twelve tribes in the Dispersion." In James, the reference to "twelve tribes" suggests the heirs of Abraham, Isaac, and Jacob (for example, Gen 49:28; Exod 24:4; 28:21; Ezek 47:13; Sir 44:23; and even the gospel tradition: Matt 19:28//Luke 22:30). Although the term could be applied to any ethnic group that had relocated, whether by choice or force, for 1 Peter, in the context of other passages from the Septuagint, it also connotes the covenant community in exile. For example, Deut 30:4 reads:

> Even in your dispersion [Greek: *diaspora*] to the ends of the world, from there the LORD your God will gather you, and from there he will bring you back." (See also, for example, Ps 147:2; Jdt 5:19; 2 Macc 1:27.)

Thus the language of Diaspora connects the recipients again with biblical history.

And it does more. For 1 Peter, the "homeland" from which the recipients have been dispersed is not the land of Israel. It is the kingdom of heaven, or the realm of Christ. Thus 1 Peter adopts terms from Judaism's theological vocabulary and uses them to construct the identity of its Christian readers.

Co-opting Jewish Identity?

For some readers today, this social construction comprising a new identity for Christians creates a moral problem. In constructing Gentile followers of Jesus as heirs of and interpreters of Israel's Scriptures, 1 Peter claims for Christians an identity that Jews had already claimed. Further, the letter proclaims that God's purposes, known from Israel's Scriptures, find their fulfillment in Jesus. The effect of this proclamation is to read Jesus-followers into the story of Israel while reading Jews out. Put starkly, 1 Peter establishes Christian identity by dispossessing Jews.

What do readers do? Some, unaware of its exclusionary implications, accept the identity 1 Peter formulates. Other readers use canonical criticism to set this excluding construction alongside other New Testament texts (like Rom 3:1-4; 9:1-5; and 11:25-32) that express God's enduring faithfulness to the promises made to Abraham's children "according to the flesh." Other readers might choose to read 1 Peter generously and see it as both honoring the earlier biblical tradition and indicating a sharing rather than co-optation or replacement.

Consistent with the language of *Diaspora*, the author locates the recipients as "exiles" (1:1) and "aliens and exiles" (Greek: *paroikoi* and *parepidēmoi* [2:11]). The terms "aliens and exiles" suggest social, economic, or political marginalization and emphasize social distinctiveness. They commonly referred to "foreigners" or "strangers" who lacked local roots, often spoke a different language, observed different customs, and embraced different civic allegiances. Within the empire, such groups in some locations experienced restrictions on marriage, land ownership and inheritance by the next generation, voting, and participation

302

in trade or religious associations. They were also taxed at higher levels and experienced more severe legal penalties. In addition, their differences typically meant troubled interactions with local populations: disdain was rife, and suspicion, rumors, slander, and discrimination were common.

Whether those addressed by 1 Peter were an actual community of displaced "aliens or exiles" or whether the writer presents them as having this identity because they follow Jesus is not clear. It is possible that both are true.

Along with displacement, the author posits suffering as a significant part of the Christian identity: "For a little while you have had to suffer various trials" (1:6). How long is a "little while" is undetermined. Later comes the assurance that their suffering will end with God's direct intervention (5:10).

Some of the suffering results from verbal abuse. In 2:12 (also 3:16), the author notes that Jesus' followers are "maligned." The Greek term (*katalaleō*) literally means "to speak against," with connotations of "defame" or "slander." The content of this maligning is the charge that they are "doing evil," a term that can suggest engaging in mischief (as in 3:17) or even criminal action. The cognate noun in 4:15 is linked with murder and robbery. In 4:14 the author declares the recipients "blessed" when they are "reviled for the name of Christ."

Another potential source of conflict, and so an indicator of alienation from the prevailing society, emerges in 4:3-4:

> You have already spent enough time in doing what the Gentiles like to do, living in licentiousness, passions, drunkenness, revels, carousing, and lawless idolatry. They are surprised that you no longer join them in the same excesses of dissipation, and so they blaspheme.

Some Christians have stopped doing "what the Gentiles like to do," and distanced themselves from their former associates. The listing of "vices" is a stereotypical presentation of Gentile waywardness (see Wis 13–15; Rom 1:18-32); not every Gentile in antiquity lived a drunken, oversexed, and idolatrous existence. The vice list functions here to construct Christian identity as distinct from non-Christian norms. Ironically, even as 1 Peter expresses concern that the followers of Jesus are being maligned, the letter maligns those who do not follow Christ. Thus the text's social construction of reality reinforces the identity of its audience as suffering aliens and exiles and encourages them to remain separate from the dominant culture. At the same time, it constructs the identity of their former associates—that is, friends—as epitomizing evil. There is no call for the Christians to attempt to evangelize these former associates, or to call them away from behaviors the author finds abhorrent. The rhetoric is one of disgust, not of compassion.

Persecution?

There was no empire-wide persecution of Christians until 251 under the Emperor Decius. There were, though, a few sporadic, localized outbreaks. In 64–65, Nero took action against some Jesus-followers in Rome (Tacitus, *Annals* 15.44; Suetonius, *Nero* 16.2). In 110, Pliny, the governor of Pontus, acted against some Christians who had been reported to him (*Letters* 10.96). For the audience of 1 Peter, the conflicts likely comprised local verbal exchanges and social ostracism.

Should this separation from the dominant society, and the life of the alien and the exile lead to suffering, the author provides instruction: suffering serves to reinforce and promote the privileged role of Christians. Throughout the New Testament, remaining steadfast in the midst of suffering is a sign of honor, or what sociologists call "cultural capital." It manifests sincerity. It shows strength of conviction. Most important, it allows Christians to identify with Jesus. Just as the Christians are disdained and rejected, so Christ was "rejected by mortals yet chosen (cf. 1:2) and precious in God's sight" (2:4). The suffering of the Christians signifies that they, like Jesus, are at the center of the divine plan. They are redeemed by Christ, who "was destined before the foundation of the world, but was revealed at the end of the ages for your sake" (1:20).

1 Peter, Mark, and Suffering

The Johannine letters (1, 2, 3 John) show a connection with the Gospel of John, the Pastorals have much in common with Acts, James often echoes Matthew's Gospel, and 1 Peter evokes Mark's Gospel. One substantial echo concerns Mark's Christology: "For the Son of Man came not to be served but to serve, and to give his life a ransom for many" (10:45). In both Mark and 1 Peter, the suffering of disciples unites them with the suffering Christ. According to both authors, suffering is expected, steadfastness is encouraged, eschatological hope is proffered, and redemption is guaranteed. This link between 1 Peter and Mark's gospel might be supported by 1 Pet 5:13: "Your sister church in Babylon, chosen together with you, sends you greetings; and so does my son Mark."

Societal Participation

The opening section of the letter (1:2–2:10) constructs the distinct identity of the letter's recipients. Mixed in with descriptions of their special status as a chosen people living in a society that ridicules them for their beliefs are general exhortations about negotiating that identity. The recipients are to be distinguished from their former way of life (1:14), holy in imitating God (1:15-16), loving toward each other (1:22) and ridding themselves "of all malice, and all guile, insincerity, envy, and all slander" (2:1).

However, such generalities do not detail instruction for specific issues: How are "aliens and exiles" to relate to imperial power, what we today would call "civil religion," the ancient equivalents of saluting the flag, singing the national anthem, or celebrating Independence Day? Nor does the letter advise about regular social interaction: Can Christians engage in business relations with non-Christians? Dine at each other's homes? Maintain friendships?

Some interpreters have understood the letter to require Christians, as "aliens and exiles" from the dominant society, to adopt a sectarian existence. This would involve regarding the external world as evil, maintaining purity by social distance, showing complete commitment to other members of their group, and expecting reward (redemption, ransom) for their sacrifices, sufferings, and steadfastness. The negative descriptions of the Gentile world can support this interpretation; at the very least, Christians are not to be "doing what the Gentiles like to do" (4:3). This sectarian model is not, however, consistent with the letter's focus from 2:11 to the end. This section assumes the recipients' active involvement in the daily life of the Roman provinces. The central theme of their societal participation comprises "doing good works." Non-Christians will notice, and these actions will, according to the letter, lead them to an appropriate theological response at the Parousia:

> Conduct yourselves honorably among the Gentiles, so that, though they malign you as evildoers, they may see your honorable deeds and glorify God when he comes to judge. (2:12)

An important cluster of terms concerning "doing the good thing" recurs throughout the letter's instructions. According to 2:13-17, Christians are to "accept the authority of every human institution, whether of the emperor as supreme, or of governors." Roman power was paramount in the provinces that the letter addresses. The imperial cult—a key civic way of honoring the emperor through sacrifices, prayers, street parties, parades, games, and food distributions—was widely observed. Local elites typically promoted and financed these observations, and there were numerous opportunities for nonelite involvement. Although participation was not compulsory, it was expected, and there was much to be gained by it. The majority of the population participated by eating food, watching entertainment, witnessing sacrifices to images of gods and emperors, and by expecting that celebrations in honor of the gods and the empire secured the blessings and goodwill of both. Participation, even by the nonelite, gained social capital; nonparticipation was regarded as jeopardizing divine blessing and so endangering civic well-being.

Commentators usually interpret 2:17—"Honor the emperor"—to indicate limited participation. Christians are to adopt a respectful attitude to the emperor and Roman imperial power, but they are not to participate in imperial cult activity. That, like eating meat offered to idols, would compromise their identity.

There are at least three problems with this view. First, the letter does not in any way qualify the command to "honor the emperor." Second, the letter's strategy for Christians is announced immediately prior to this instruction, in 2:12. They are to do "honorable deeds" among the Gentiles so that Gentiles will glorify God. The "honorable deeds," elaborated in the following verses, include honoring the emperor. To refuse to participate in cultic celebrations, whether in civic festivals or in voluntary associations of tradespeople, would not be honorable. Worse, instead of prompting the glorifying of God, refusal to participate would create suspicion of and resentment toward Christians.

A third argument against understanding 2:17 as prohibiting participation in imperial civic rites is an argument from silence, but it is a strong one. First Peter commonly quotes from the Septuagint, but the writer does not quote a prohibition against idolatry. The closest such citation comes in 4:3: "You have already spent enough time in doing what the Gentiles like to do, living in licentiousness, passions, drunkenness, revels, carousing, and lawless idolatry."

This verse can be interpreted to mean Christians are no longer to participate in the "lawless idolatry" of imperial observances. But this conclusion misses the point of the verse. What 1 Peter condemns is not civic activity, but excessive or immodest behavior. It does not condemn all consumption of alcohol, all sexual acts, or all social interaction. It condemns what the next verse calls "the same excesses of dissipation."

Eating Meat Offered to Idols

Other New Testament passages indicate that the followers of Jesus debated how to negotiate the values and practices of Roman society. In 1 Cor 8–10, Paul appears to permit eating meat offered to idols, since followers of Jesus know that idols are not gods. Yet he advises against it lest weaker members of the congregation be led astray. Acts 15:28-29 presumes that Jews who follow Jesus would not consume such meat. The verses advise Gentile believers:

> For it has seemed good to the Holy Spirit and to us to impose on you no further burden than these essentials: that you abstain from what has been sacrificed to idols and from blood and from what is strangled and from fornication.

Instructions about abstaining from what has been sacrificed to idols would not be needed if everybody knew to do so. Revelation 2, addressed to churches in Asia, the same area 1 Peter addresses, attests a struggle between the writer and rival movements over eating food offered to idols. A group called the Nicolaitans and a prophetess nicknamed "Jezebel" advocate such participation. The writer of Revelation vigorously opposes it.

First Peter, then, not only advises but also requires Christians to participate in imperial rites. Perhaps the author knew of fellow Christians who had refused to conform to these social norms and had provoked verbal conflicts or something worse. Thus 2:15 insists, "For it is God's will that by doing right you should silence the ignorance of the foolish."

Yet while the letter commands its audience to "honor the emperor," it also reminds them constantly that they belong to Christ and God. In 3:15 the author instructs: "In your hearts sanctify [or reverence] Christ as Lord." While they publicly express loyalty to the empire, they are also to maintain their commitment to Christ. Attention to their inner commitment offers a strategy for coping with social pressures to participate in public rituals. This strategy continued among the followers of Jesus through the time of Constantine, when Christianity ceased to compete with the imperial cult and became the empire's religion. The third-century Christian writer Origen, commenting on the prohibition of images in Exod 20:5, distinguishes between "worship" involving "all one's soul" (see Deut 6:5) in an expression of genuine devotion, and "adoration," which involves pretending to worship because of social custom (*In Exodum Homilia* 8.4).

Household Codes

Conforming to social norms provides the context for the household code that follows (2:18–3:7). In our chapter on Ephesians, we outlined the form of household codes and various responses to it. Here we extend that discussion to focus on the contribution of the household code to 1 Peter's social construction of reality.

Every New Testament household code has a distinct concern. For example, unlike the code in Ephesians, 1 Peter offers no instruction to parents or children or even to Christian masters. Whereas Eph 5–6 is addressed to the followers of Jesus, 1 Peter's exhortations include an audience where church members are connected, through marriage (husband and wife) or ownership (slave and master), to non-Christians. For 1 Peter, the primary concern is the disruption in the household when someone other than the husband/master/father believes in Christ. The developed instruction to slaves and wives suggests that the disruption is created primarily by their new identity as Christians. The author, however, shows no concern for members of the household forcibly converted by the father/husband/master.

Like Ephesians, 1 Peter addresses slaves directly. Such direct address to slaves was rare in ancient literature. Stoic descriptions of household management were written to be read by slave owners, not by slaves. Both Ephesians and 1 Peter are, in this regard, departures from the cultural norm.

But they do not say exactly the same thing to slaves. Ephesians 6:5-8 instructs Christian slaves, "Obey your earthly masters with fear and trembling, in singleness of heart, as you obey Christ." They are to serve with "enthusiasm," and to remember that God will judge both slave and free. In 1 Pet 2:18-25, the exhortation to slaves demands more. The author adds that slaves must accept the authority of their masters "with all deference," and "not only those who are kind and gentle, but also those who are harsh" (2:18). The suffering that slaves routinely faced is made explicit in the next two verses:

> For it is a credit to you if, being aware of God, you endure pain while suffering unjustly. If you endure when you are beaten for doing wrong, what credit is that? But if you endure when you do right and suffer for it, you have God's approval. (2:19-20)

The letter not only sanctions slavery without hesitation, but worse, it provides divine warrant for the physical (including sexual) abuse of slaves.

The slaves 1 Peter addresses are likely to be urban (household) slaves rather than agricultural or mine workers or galley slaves. The term used for them is not the common word for "slave" (Greek: *doulos*) but a word that denotes a "household slave/servant" (Greek: *oiketēs*). The text does not distinguish between male and female slaves. For both, their bodies belonged to their masters. Masters could use those bodies for physical labor or sexual service, and they could subject those bodies to punishment (torture).

The next verses reinforce the exhortations to obedience and provide a christologically informed strategy for coping with abuse:

> Christ also suffered for you, leaving you an example, so that you should follow in his steps. . . .When he was abused, he did not return abuse; when he suffered, he did not threaten; but he entrusted himself to the one who judges justly. He himself bore our sins in his body on the cross, so that, free from sins, we might live for righteousness; by his wounds you have been healed. (2:21-23)

The author here draws on the image of the "suffering servant" depicted in Isa 53:5. This chapter, frequently quoted in Christian texts, is interpreted in several ways. For Matthew (8:17), the servant's suffering is related to Jesus' healings; in Acts 8, the conversation between Philip and the Ethiopian official, the emphasis is on fulfillment of prophecy; for 1 Peter, the emphasis is on Jesus' suffering in relation to the sufferings of his followers. Christian slaves can thereby see themselves connected not only to Jesus but also to biblical prophecy.

Just as the letter commends the Christian who suffers in steadfastness for the glory of God, here the slave epitomizes that *honorable* suffering. Yet the role accorded slaves is even more glorious. In Ephesians (5:23), the *husband* is linked with Christ: "The husband is the head of the wife just as Christ is the head of the church, the body of which he is the Savior." In 1 Peter, the *slave* is compared to Christ. By accepting suffering, slaves faithfully imitate Christ (2:19-21). The letter does not claim that the master who witnesses the slave's acceptance of abuse will come to repentance. Nor does it criticize such abuse.

In contrast to the submission of slaves, Christian wives have the potential to convert their husbands: "Even if some of them do not obey the word, they may be won over without a word by their wives' conduct" (3:1). This conduct consists of "purity and reverence" (3:2) and modesty (3:3). As in 1 Tim 2:9, so also here the author insists that the wife is not to draw attention to herself:

> Do not adorn yourselves outwardly by braiding your hair, and by wearing gold ornaments or fine clothing; rather, let your adornment be the inner self with the lasting beauty of a gentle and quiet spirit, which is very precious in God's sight. (3:3-4)

Although "aliens and exiles," the recipients apparently include women with access to gold jewelry and upscale garments. The reference could be primarily a rhetorical one to emphasize the point about modesty, but given the advice to engage in civic participation, which was especially important for people of some social status (or seeking that status), the former option seems more likely.

Whereas the author compares the ideal conduct of slaves to that of Christ, it compares the ideal conduct of wives to Abraham's wife, Sarah, and other women of the biblical tradition:

> It was in this way long ago that the holy women who hoped in God used to adorn themselves by accepting the authority of their husbands. Thus Sarah obeyed Abraham and called him lord." (3:5-6a)

On first reading, the instruction seems to set the husband in the role of Christ, who is also called "lord" (Greek: *kyrios*). Conversely, readers, then or now, who look closely at the Genesis story may find a possibly subversive message.

First, according to the Septuagintal reading of Gen 18:12, when the postmenopausal Sarah heard the prediction that she would bear a child, she "laughed to herself, saying, 'indeed, not yet has something like this happened until now, my lord [*kyrios*] being old [*presbyteros*].'" The Greek depicts Sarah referring to her husband as "lord," but the title appears in a context that suggests anything but obedience. Sarah's calling her husband "lord" here expresses doubts about his potency. Second, in the Masoretic or Hebrew version of Genesis, Sarah does not call Abraham "lord" or refer to him by that title. The verse simply states that Sarah "laughed to herself, saying, 'After I have grown old, and my husband is old, shall I have pleasure?'"

There may be additional hints of subversion. The text can be read as encouraging a countercultural ethos and instructing how to deal with the suffering such behavior provoked. For example, 4:1-6 insists that Christians avoid the dissipated behavior, including sexual behavior, that marks the Gentile lifestyle. Were slaves to follow this instruction, they might resist the sexual services they were expected to provide. Punishment (torture) would follow their disobedience. They suffer, then, because they did the right thing. First Peter commends them: "If you endure when you are beaten for doing wrong, what credit is that? But if you endure when you do right and suffer for it, you have God's approval" (2:20; see also 3:14, 17; 4:12-19).

The same point holds for Christian wives married to non-Christian men. Roman wives were expected to worship their husbands' gods, affiliate with those whom their husbands approved, and conform themselves fully to their husbands' desires. The wives 1 Peter addresses are out of compliance. They worship a God not sanctioned by their husbands. They affiliate with people of whom their husbands may not approve. They engage in beliefs and practices that their husbands would probably find inappropriate. And, as 1 Peter notes, they will suffer for their behavior. In turn, the more they suffer, the more they identify with Christ and his sufferings (4:13). Such "faithful" living brings honor from their fellow Christians. If their husbands were converted by witnessing their silent submission, so much the better.

The instructions to husbands are in one verse. Husbands are to "show consideration for your wives in your life together, paying honor to the woman as the weaker sex, since they too are also heirs of the gracious gift of life—so that nothing may hinder your prayers" (3:7). The presumption is, probably, that the wives will accept the Christian practices and beliefs as the husbands.

Household Codes, Commands to Suffer, and Contemporary Observance?

The social circumstances within which 1 Peter was composed provide a challenge for anyone trying to implement its instructions to wives (and slaves) today. Along with the canonical criticism we used in relation to the household code in

Ephesians, we can use social-scientific and ideological criticism to determine the extent, if any, that these texts should be applied in contemporary Christian contexts.

Some religious leaders still tell women in their churches that even in cases of domestic abuse, they must submit to their husbands. Often 1 Pet 3:1 is the proof-text: "Accept the authority of your husbands, so that, even if some of them do not obey the word, they may be won over without a word by their wives' conduct." However, wives are abused for a variety of reasons that have nothing to do with their proclamation of Christianity over and against their husbands' non-Christian observance. Today in most places in the world, women's profession of Christianity is not seen as alienating civic and imperial gods and thereby causing catastrophes that are interpreted as divine retaliations. Today, the husband who beats his wife is not seen, by most people, as asserting his spousal prerogative. He is breaking the law. Finally, today the image of a woman suffering abuse is not seen, either by most Christians or by the dominant culture, as heroic. It is seen as abusive. Her more honored position, outside of those who seek to impose first-century texts taken out of context on her behavior, is to stop the abuse, if possible and neces-sary, by getting herself and her children out of the household and into a shelter.

Some women feel they cannot extricate themselves from situations of abuse, whether because of economic need, psychological concern, fear for their children, or a host of other reasons. It is much easier to *advise* a battered woman to call the police or to flee than it is for the woman herself to *do* it. If a wife tolerates an abu-sive situation because of her understanding of 1 Peter, then it is the responsibility of a pastor and fellow Christians to protect her from abuse and to offer her a new construction of reality in which she is not identified by her suffering.

The extent to which 1 Peter speaks to women in areas where Christianity is the minority tradition, where it is suspect and even where it is illegal, is a related issue. In some cases, women are abused precisely because of their Christian claims. It would be inappropriate to presume that women in these areas have the same options as women in, for example, the United States. For such women, the letter's connection of the suffering of Jesus with their suffering may provide essential spiri-tual support. Our point is not to sanction abuse; it is rather to alert readers that all interpretations take place in a particular context, and that what seems unthinkable to one reader might be a lifeline to another.

Exhortations to do what is good, even if one would suffer for it, continue in 3:13-22. The opening rhetorical question seems naïve at best given the context: "Now who will harm you if you are eager to do what is good?" Among the numerous candidates already identified are masters and husbands, Roman society in general, or some loyal inhabitants in particular. The next verse, however, recognizes that suffering and doing what is good are related:

> But even if you do suffer for doing what is right, you are blessed. Do not fear what they fear, and do not be intimidated. (3:14)

Such blessings are guaranteed both through the association of the suffering but chosen Christian with the suffering Jesus and through additional evocations of the Septuagint. In 1 Peter, the story of Noah and his family (Gen 6–9)—displaced from their home and alienated from a society that is punished for its wickedness—serves at least two functions.

First, the flood story is introduced with a brief claim that Jesus "was put to death in the flesh, but made alive in the spirit, in which also he went and made a proclamation to the spirits in prison" (3:18-19).

Verse 20 indicates that these spirits were alive at the time of the flood. By making a link to Noah's time, the author shows that Jesus' suffering, death, and resurrection not only benefited his followers during his own lifetime and those addressed by 1 Peter ("to bring you to God," 3:18), but these salvific acts also impacted all people at all times, even those spirits who were waiting from ages past to receive redemption. The link with Noah locates 1 Peter's readers in a universal movement, encompassing all time and space, and vindicated by God. This scenario of Jesus preaching to these imprisoned spirits developed during the early Middle Ages into the "harrowing of hell," the belief that Jesus descended into hell to redeem the righteous people of antiquity. Verse 22 presents Jesus as victorious over "angels, authorities, and powers," indicating his great effectiveness.

Second, in a somewhat strained connection, the author reads the flood story as an anticipation of baptism. According to 3:20, "during the building of the ark . . . a few, that is, eight persons, were saved through water." Technically, floating on water in an ark differs significantly from being submerged in water in baptism, yet the author perseveres: "And baptism, which this prefigured, now saves you—not as a removal of dirt from the body, but as an appeal to God for a good conscience, through the resurrection of Jesus Christ" (3:21).

Through baptism, Christians encounter the benefits of salvation and can live faithfully in the midst of suffering.

Chapters 4 and 5 largely restate the emphases of the previous three chapters. They delineate what is good. They affirm that suffering is the norm for Christian existence. They declare that conversion distances the Christian from (stereotypical) "immoral" Gentile living. They reassure Christians of an eschatological destiny in which their suffering and endurance will be rewarded. They exhort support for one another in the present difficulties through prayer, love, hospitality, and using God's grace to serve one another. In 5:5, the author adds the command that the community submit to the "elders."

The letter concludes with final exhortations and greetings. The writer sends greetings from "Babylon" (5:13), likely referring to Rome. Perhaps that note offers a word of encouragement. Readers would know that the Babylonian empire fell and Israel returned to its land. They could thus be assured that Rome too will fall, and that their existence, constructed as "aliens and exiles," will end in the accomplishment of God's purposes.

And perhaps they would take one more hint of hopeful subversion. Most English translations read 5:13 as saying, "Your sister church in Babylon, chosen together with you, sends you greetings." However, the Greek does not use the term "church." It simply says, "She who is Babylon . . ." (NIV). While this "she" could be a church, for the Greek word for "church," *ekklēsia*, is feminine, the greeting could be from a woman, perhaps the leader of a house-church.

$\mathcal{2}$ Peter and Jude

2 Peter

Discerning genre—or the category of writing—influences how we interpret a text. We bring different expectations to a novel than to a historical study even though both use narrative, typically have heroes and villains, and tend to progress from one event to another. We read a law code differently from an advice column, yet both address proper behavior.

To determine genre, we use traits: title, author, publisher, vocabulary, style, content, and so on. Sometimes traits associated predominantly with one genre appear in a work primarily consisting of a different genre. Historical treatises might include poetry, novels might include social commentary, and cookbooks might include medical data. By combining genres, an author utilizes a wide range of literary techniques to influence readers.

Second Peter combines traits of at least three genres: a letter, the testament or farewell speech, and persuasive speeches. We begin by discussing the occasion of 2 Peter, as best as we can determine it from the contents. We look at how its three mixed genres contribute to its argument. Finally we jump to the short letter of Jude, which is the penultimate book of the New Testament. We do this because of the likelihood of a literary relationship between Jude and 2 Peter. We analyze how Jude's initial letter genre employs numerous references to biblical and Second Temple Jewish stories to make its argument against what may be the same teachers opposed by 2 Peter.

The Occasion of 2 Peter

We have already raised questions regarding the Pauline authorship of Colossians, Ephesians, the Pastoral Epistles, and 2 Thessalonians. Likewise we discussed the unlikely claim that Peter the Apostle wrote 1 Peter. The same questions apply to 2 Peter.

Doubts that this letter was written by the Galilean fisherman are not just modern. In the third century Origen (quoted in Eusebius, *Ecclesiastical History* 6.25.8) and in the fourth–fifth century Jerome (*De Viris Illustribus* 1) doubted Petrine authorship. Eusebius even indicates that 2 Peter does not belong to the canon (*Ecclesiastical History* 3.3.1).

Internal evidence also suggests Petrine authorship is unlikely. Second Peter uses numerous rare Greek words. Some 57 are *hapax legomena* (Greek: "something said once"), which means they do not appear elsewhere in the New Testament. Another 38 words appear only one or two other times. This vocabulary suggests not only a well-educated author but also one writing in the early decades of the second century when these terms become more frequent in Greek literature.

The letter's contents also strengthen this argument for a relatively late date. The author looks back on the apostolic period and distinguishes that time from the present, eschatological age: "That you should remember the words spoken in the past by the holy prophets, and the commandment of the Lord and Savior spoken through your apostles. . . . For ever since our ancestors died. . . ." (3:2-4).

The author presents Paul as a figure of the past whose legacy requires defense:

> Our beloved brother Paul wrote to you according to the wisdom given him, speaking of this as he does in all his letters. There are some things in them hard to understand, which the ignorant and unstable twist to their own destruction, as they do the other scriptures." (3:15-16)

This notice recollects the composition of Acts, also probably second century, which asserts Paul's fidelity to Jewish practice and harmony with Peter (contrast Gal 2). Consequently, 2 Peter likely belongs to the growing corpus written during the first few centuries in the apostle's name, including 1 Peter, the *Gospel of Peter*, *Acts of Peter*, and *Apocalypse of Peter*. Just as the Pastorals and the *Acts of Paul and Thecla* competed for the legacy of the Pauline tradition, so also the Petrine tradition became the locus of competition. Second Peter, like Acts, presents a harmonious relationship between Peter and Paul; Matthew's Gospel, with its emphasis on Torah observance and its "Great Commission" of Peter and his fellow Galilean disciples to evangelize "all the nations" (Matt 28:19), may represent an alternative to Pauline traditions; the second-century Pseudo-Clementine literature rejects Paul's teaching.

The situation 2 Peter addresses appears to be conflict involving competing teachers. From the writer's perspective, these other teachers are "false prophets" (2:1) and "scoffers" (3:3). It is possible they would have made the same claims about the author of 2 Peter. Even by the second century, the church had no formal orthodoxy or authority to declare a text or group orthodox or heretical. Despite the popular depiction of Jesus' followers all facing major persecution from the Roman Empire throughout the first three centuries, not only was persecution substantially limited, but also much of the New Testament focuses not on external pressure, but on internal dissension.

The author neither identifies these rival teachers nor outlines their teaching. The attack is by conventional polemic: name-calling ("animals" [2:12] and "children" [2:14]); accusations of sexual immorality (2:2, 14, 18); and charges of greed (2:2-3, 14). They are condemned for despising authority (2:10), which means they do not agree with the author. The author both anticipates and proclaims their apostasy: "They will deny the Master who bought them" (2:1) for they "have left the straight road and have gone astray" (2:15). Finally, come the expected warnings: their words are not to be trusted, for they mislead others (2:12, 18).

It is also possible that the opponents proclaimed a different eschatology from the one 2 Peter promotes, although any definitive reconstruction is limited by our lack of direct access to the opponents' position. The author, writing in the name of Peter (and so ostensibly in the mid-first century) predicts:

> In the last days, scoffers will come, scathing and indulging their own lusts and saying, "Where is the promise of his coming? For ever since our ancestors died, all things continue as they were from the beginning of creation!" (3:3-4)

For the setting the narrator creates, the recipients *are* living in those last days. Perhaps the (so-called) opponents were suggesting that Jesus will not return, and that he need not do so. They may have adopted a position of realized eschatology, such as we have seen in John's gospel, Colossians, and 1 Corinthians. Perhaps they believe that Jesus' work of salvation has already been completed.

Or perhaps their teaching was also influenced by the Epicurean view, growing in popularity in the early second century, that God was not closely involved in human matters and that humans were not accountable to any future judgment. The good are not ultimately rewarded, and the wicked do not suffer for the consequences of their actions. (See the discussion of Epicureans in the chapter on 1 Thess.)

Realized eschatology could easily result in forms of *antinomianism*, wherein individuals perceive themselves as free from any legal or moral constraints and so can do what they want. We observed that phenomenon in 1 Corinthians, and it may be in play here as well. As 2:19 warns:

> They promise them freedom, but they themselves are slaves of corruption; for people are slaves to whatever masters them.

For 2 Peter's author, Jesus' return is a key event in a cluster of eschatological events concerned with the final judgment. In arguing for God's fidelity and Jesus' certain return, the author makes several arguments. First is the reminder that teaching about eschatological matters is part of their tradition. It is not a new idea:

Therefore I intend to keep on reminding you of these things, though you know them already and are established in the truth that has come to you. (1:12)

Second, the author's credibility is based in eyewitness testimony and not invented story:

For we did not follow cleverly devised myths when we made known to you the power and coming of our Lord Jesus Christ, but we had been eyewitnesses of his majesty. (1:16)

The claim to eyewitness status asserts authority even as it reinforces the impression of Petrine authorship. The reference to "majesty" likely evokes the transfiguration. Here the author displays knowledge of a tradition also found in the Synoptics, "When that voice was conveyed to him by the Majestic Glory, saying, 'This is my Son, my Beloved, with whom I am well pleased.' We ourselves heard this voice come from heaven, while we were with him on the holy mountain" (2 Pet 1:17-18; see Matt 17; Mark 9; Luke 9).

The appeal to the Transfiguration serves to check the opponents' "myths," of whatever sort they might be. It also anticipates the coming of Jesus for the final judgment. Third, the author locates this teaching in a wider scriptural context. He insists: "No prophecy of scripture is a matter of one's own interpretation" (1:20). This "scripture" may refer to earlier Christian writings, such as the Gospels and a collection of Paul's letters. If so, it also suggests the relatively late date of 2 Peter. However, it may also refer to the Scriptures of Israel, likely in their Septuagintal form. Just as the followers of Jesus debated, and still debate, the legacy of Peter and Paul, so also they debated, internally as well as with Jews who did not follow Jesus, how to understand the texts that undergirded both traditions.

Fourth, the writer is certain the false prophets will be judged (2:1-3) both because a final judgment is part of the eschatological scenario and because God had judged others in the past. The author appeals to the condemnation of the rebellious angels (2:4), Noah's flood (2:5), the destruction of Sodom and Gomorrah (2:6), and the rescue of Abraham's nephew Lot (2:7-8) to remind readers that rescue of the righteous and judgment on "the unrighteous" are certain (2:9-10). Verses 11-22 catalogue their extensive unrighteousness. Fifth, the author reminds the readers of the conventional apocalyptic view that false prophets signal the nearness of the end time: "In the last days scoffers will come" (3:1-7). Finally comes the reassurance that nothing has gone amiss with the eschatological timetable. Doing some divine math, he asserts: "With the Lord one day is like a thousand years, and a thousand years are like one day" (3:8). God has not been unfaithful. "The Lord is not slow about his promise" but is working in the present to lead people to repentance (3:9). The author exhorts the readers to prepare for this certain but unknown "day" by living "lives of holiness and godliness."

Letter

The identification of the writing's genre as a letter shapes its interpretation. We expect it to address specific readers in particular circumstances. With the use, distribution, and collection of Paul's letters, Jesus-followers recognized the genre of letter as a legitimate and familiar form of communication.

Here we notice a difference with the Scriptures of Israel. While a few "letters" appear within larger documents (for example, 2 Sam 11:14-15; Ezra 4–5; Esth 9), these Scriptures contain no text that uses the letter genre except the Letter of Jeremiah (also known as the Epistle of Jeremy) found in the Greek Orthodox canon.

The letter called 2 Peter begins, predictably, with a salutation that identifies the sender as "Simeon Peter" and introduces him as "slave [Greek: *doulos*] and apostle of Jesus Christ" (1:1). The double name uses the Semitic form "Simeon" instead of "Simon" (see Acts 15:14). It presents the author as one to be honored and obeyed because of his association with Jesus.

"Slave and apostle" reinforce his authority. "Slave"—rendered in the NRSV and NIV as "servant"—anticipates and contrasts 2:19, where the author describes the opponents as "slaves [*douloi*] of corruption; for people are slaves to whatever masters them." "Apostle," with its literal meaning of "sent one" and its use in circles of Jesus' followers to denote individuals commissioned by Jesus, defines the writer as speaking authoritatively.

Why the letter appeals to Peter as its author, rather than, for example, Matthew or Mary Magdalene, is not clear. The text does not mention Jesus commissioning Peter for an ecclesial (Matt 16:13-20) or pastoral role (John 21:15-19). The only gospel reference is to Peter's place as an eyewitness to Jesus' Transfiguration (1:16-18). However, given that the recipients know of Paul's collected letters and quite likely know the gospel stories such that they would understand the allusion to the Transfiguration, it is likely that they are aware of Peter's role as the preeminent apostle and early leader of the Jerusalem community. Peter, in effect, outranks Matthew and Mary Magdalene. Moreover, having "Peter" endorse Paul's letters bolsters their credibility and undermines any suspicion that the two apostles were in competition or disagreement.

Verse 1:1b introduces the Epistle's recipients: "To those who have received a faith as precious as ours through the righteousness of our God and Savior Jesus Christ." Missing is a location, such as "in Corinth" or "in the Diaspora." No mention is made of a "church," or any previous relationship between author and audience. Instead, the author stresses their unity in belief: they have the same faith, granted by the same source. That their righteousness comes from God and Jesus "our savior" also furthers the themes of God's continual work and the soteriological role Jesus plays.

The greeting provides the third common feature of a letter's opening (1:2). The pairing of "grace and peace" occurs in most of Paul's letters (for example, Rom 1:7; 1 Cor 1:3). This echo strengthens the fictional construction of the author as Peter, an ally of and united with Paul (also 3:15-16). "Grace" (Greek: *charis*) conveys God's favor to them. "Peace" (Greek: *eirēnē*) comprises not simply an attitude but a sense of "wholeness" in the recipients' relationship with God. The following reference to the "knowledge of God" introduces a theme that will be developed subsequently. Second Peter refers numerous times to the knowledge (or experience) of God found in Jesus (1:3, 5, 6, 8; 2:20; 3:18). This "knowledge" is the realization that just as God was active in the past and at the time of Jesus, so God is active in the present and will be in the future. There is an implicit contrast with the opponents, a source of false knowledge.

Readers expect a thanksgiving to follow the greeting, but not so with this letter. While 1:3-4 describes, rather than gives thanks for, divine power and knowledge, verse 5 begins a speech that exhorts the recipients to adopt certain practices to secure their "entry into the eternal kingdom of our Lord and Savior Jesus Christ" (1:11). The letter genre of 1:1-2 is breaking down. The initial features of the letter genre—author, recipients, greeting—function to give the subsequent content credibility and authority.

Indications of the letter genre return at the end. New Testament letters typically end with three features: greetings (for example, 1 Cor 16:19-20; 2 Tim 4:19; 1 Pet 5:13-14), concluding comments (for example, 1 Cor 16:21-22; 2 Tim 4:20-21; 1 Pet 5:12), and doxologies (for example, 1 Cor 16:23-24; 2 Tim 4:22; 1 Pet 5:11, 14b). Second Peter lacks greetings, but there are concluding comments (3:17-18a), and the doxology directed toward "our Lord and Savior Jesus Christ" (3:18) recapitulates the greeting (1:2). The concluding exhortation to "grow in the grace and knowledge . . ." (3:18) echoes the greeting's prayer for "grace . . . in abundance in the knowledge of God" (1:2). And the doxology's declaration of glory to Jesus "both now and to the day of eternity" reinforces the document's focus on the certainty of God's activity in the present and future.

Testament or Farewell Speech

The genre of the "testament" or "farewell speech" is found in canonical materials such as Gen 49 (the testament of Jacob), Deut 31–33 (the testament of Moses), and the book of Tobit (an Old Testament Apocrypha/deuterocanonical book). It is also used in such pseudepigrapha as the *Testament of Abraham*, the *Testaments of the Twelve Patriarchs*, and the *Testament of Job*. The genre depicts an ancient distinguished figure, on his deathbed, offering his testament, usually comprised of ethical exhortations, blessings, and warnings about the future. That future predicted in the testament is the present as far as the audience is concerned. This interplay, which also appears in the "visions" recorded in apocalyptic literature, increases the writer's authority as one who could foresee the future and thereby guide his descendants.

Second Peter exhibits several features of this genre. The opening chapter sets the scene in terms of Peter's imminent death:

> I think it right, as long as I am in this body, to refresh your memory, since I know that my death will come soon, as indeed our Lord Jesus Christ has made clear to me. And I will make every effort so that after my departure you may be able to recall these things. (1:13-15)

Then, typical of a testament, the author reflects on the events of his life (1:16-19), including recalling the Transfiguration.

Next, "Simeon Peter" warns the recipients that there will be "false teachers among you" who will malign "the way of truth" (2:1-3). Using four biblical scenes of judgment and vindication, he foresees the demise of these false teachers in the final judgment (2:4-9). Their presence indicates that "the last days" have arrived (3:3). Here, instead of describing eschatological events as apocalyptic literature often does (for example, Mark 13; Rev), 2 Peter uses the testament genre to warn against opponents in the present and predict their imminent punishment.

To guarantee that judgment, the author adduces other examples of heavenly reckoning. First, "God did not spare the angels when they sinned, but cast them into hell and committed them to chains of deepest darkness to be kept until the judgment" (2:4). He refers to a legend, traceable to the third century B.C.E. and based in part on Gen 6:2-4, in which some angels rebelled. The war in heaven ended when God banished them and their leader (variously called Satan, Belial, Beliar, Mastema, and Asmodeus) to hell. According to *1 Enoch* (2:8; 69:8-11), these rebellious angels were responsible for teaching humankind how to make weapons of war, use cosmetics, and write.

The second guarantee of judgment consists of "a flood on a world of the ungodly" at the time of Noah (2:5).

The third is the destruction of Sodom and Gomorrah (2:6-10). For 2 Peter, the sin that prompted the destruction of these cities was "the licentiousness [or sensuality; Greek *aselgeia*) of the lawless" (2:7), "those who indulge their flesh in depraved lust, and who despise authority" (2:10). The writer does not refer explicitly to same-sex relationships. The earliest interpretation of Gen 19 appears in Ezek 16:49 and identifies the "guilt" of Sodom not as sexual or sensual depravity but as "pride, excess of food, and prosperous ease, but [the people] did not aid the poor and needy."

These major signs of divine punishment form the basis for the author's declaration of eschatological punishment. However the author anticipates a change in the means of punishment. Whereas God formed the earth "out of water" (3:5) and "deluged [it] with water" to destroy it (3:6), the "present heavens and earth have been reserved for fire, being kept until the day of judgment and destruction of the godless" (3:7). Thus the writer implicitly acknowledges the covenant with Noah: "Never again shall all flesh be cut off by the waters of a flood, and never again shall there be a flood to destroy the earth" (Gen 9:11). In the earlier assurance, nothing was said about destruction by fire. Using the traditional image of the eschaton and Jesus coming "like a thief" (1 Thess 5:2; Rev 3:3; 16:15), the author assures the readers:

> The heavens will pass away with a loud noise, and the elements will be dissolved with fire . . . [and] the heavens will be set ablaze and dissolved, and the elements will melt with fire. (3:10, 12)

The testament genre is finally evident in exhortations to righteousness in the midst of this eschatological wickedness. Ethical behavior combined with the sure belief in God's actions will save the recipients, just as Noah, "a herald of righteousness," and his family were saved from the flood (2:5), and Lot and his daughters were saved from Sodom's destruction (2:7-8). The letter's recipients are to lead "lives of holiness and godliness" (3:11). "In accordance with [God's] promise," they are to "wait for new heavens and a new earth, where righteousness is at home" (2:13). Here the author alludes to Isa 65:17 and 66:22.

Persuasive Speeches

In discussing 2 Corinthians, we employed rhetorical criticism, the ancient art of how to make a compelling argument. Central to rhetorical criticism is a concern with how speakers accomplish their purposes, whether informing, motivating, praising, discrediting, accusing, defending, or persuading. Along with genres of a letter and testament, the author of 2 Peter employs features of deliberative rhetoric, which seeks to persuade an audience.

Persuasive speeches constructed their argument in particular structures. The argument in 2 Peter proceeds through three main stages, called (using Latin names) the *Exordium*, the *Probatio*, and the *Peroratio*.

The *Exordium* (1:3-15) introduces the subject matter, ensures that the audience understands the seriousness of the material, and builds common ground with the audience. In terms of subject matter, the *Exordium* in this letter foregrounds God's blessings that enable escape from the world's corruption and participation in the divine nature (1:3-4). It exhorts the recipients to participate in God's purposes by developing characteristics consistent with their faith, such as goodness, knowledge, self-control, endurance, godliness, mutual affection, and love (1:5-9). By these means they will confirm their call and election, and they will enter into the kingdom of Jesus (1:10-11). The writer says his purpose is to remind the audience of things they know already (1:12) so they will remember them after his imminent death (1:12-15). That the audience will have regarded Peter as an authoritative speaker and likely will have known stories of his martyrdom enhances the likelihood of this reception. The *Exordium* seeks to secure their goodwill by recognizing their common faith (1:5), by contrasting them with what the writer presents as a common enemy (1:9), and by anticipating their eschatological destiny (1:4, 11).

The *Probatio* (1:16–3:13) presents the main arguments usually with a claim or proposition and then supporting material.

(A) 1:16-19, the first accusation and refutation. The "false teachers" claim that the Parousia is a "myth" in the sense of a false story. The author refutes this claim by appealing to apostolic, "eyewitness" testimony to the Transfiguration, which anticipates Jesus' return in glory. He also asserts that the Parousia is not a myth because it is confirmed by prophecy.

(B) 1:20-21, the second accusation and refutation. The "false teachers" dismiss the prophecy of "the power and coming" of Jesus (1:16) as the prophet's own interpretation. The author insists both that prophecy results from the activity of the Holy Spirit and that prophets (plural, and possibly referring to both men and women) speak not from themselves, but from God.

(C) 2:1-3a, a counteraccusation. Before two more accusations, the writer attacks the "false teachers." They have "destructive opinions," deny the Master, are immoral and greedy, and face "swift destruction." This discrediting attack further undercuts their two claims refuted in 1:6-21, and it prepares to refute their two additional claims in 2:3b–3:13.

(D) 2:3b-10, third accusation and refutation. The "false teachers," as part of their denial of the Parousia, reject the idea of divine judgment as "idle" and "asleep." The writer refutes this claim by citing examples of divine justice: the judgment of the angels, the flood, the destruction of Sodom and Gomorrah.

In 2:10b-22, the writer presents a digression (*digressio*) that expands the attack on the opposing teachers by elaborating their vices. They slander, behave immorally, have abandoned the faith, speak nonsense, and are surely condemned. This rhetorical move complements the refutations of their arguments. Not only are their claims in error; their character shows them to be unreliable.

(E) 3:3-13 fourth accusation and refutation. This follows a short transition in 3:1-2. The "false teachers" argue that the promised Parousia will not happen because those who should have witnessed it have died. The writer refutes the claim by reminding the recipients of the power of God's word (3:5-7), pointing out that God's perception of time is different from human perceptions (3:8), explaining that God patiently works for repentance (3:9), and exhorting the recipients to prepare for the "new heavens and a new earth" with "lives of holiness and godliness" (3:10-13).

The *Peroratio* (3:14-18) or closing summarizes the argument and makes a final appeal to the audience.

With these concerns, evident for what was likely an early second-century audience, we find issues that occupied the earliest followers of Jesus as well. The concern for the delay of the Parousia surfaces in the New Testament's earliest document, 1 Thessalonians. Exhortations to proper behavior pervade the canon, from Matthew to Revelation. Concern for avoiding false teachers (with "false" being determined by the author of each NT text) demonstrates the difficulty of establishing a normative Christology, theology, ecclesiology, and even praxis. Not only did Paul and Peter face opposition during their lifetimes; texts such as 2 Peter, as well as the Gospels and Acts and various letters, show the ongoing competition for their legacy. That competition continues to this day in both churches and classrooms.

Jude

The Letter of Jude argues against "certain intruders" who, the author contends, "pervert the grace of our God . . . and deny our only Master and Lord, Jesus Christ" (Jude 4). To address how the author makes his counterclaim, we attend to the letter's use of biblical texts and their afterlife in Jewish pseudepigraphical writings. First, however, we consider questions of authorship and relation of this short document with 2 Peter.

This last letter of the New Testament claims to be written by Jude (or Judas) "brother of James." The name "Judas," which would be in Hebrew "Yehudah," appears several times in the New Testament, but only Judas the brother of Jesus is known also to have a brother named James. According to Mark 3:6, Jesus had brothers named Judas and James. If the writer of Jude were Jesus' brother and identifies himself modestly here as the "brother of James" rather than of Jesus, the text would date to the mid-first century.

What's in a Name? Jude or Judas?

We can see in the translation of the name and so the title of the document as "Jude" rather than "Judas" certain ideological concerns at work. Because of "Judas Iscariot," the name "Judas" became associated with Jesus' betrayal. The Greek of the first verse, wherein the author identifies himself, reads "Judas," the same spelling as used elsewhere in the canonical literature. Translators, though, have sought to draw a distinction between this Judas and all the other men who bore his name by using Jude. A second, similar shift of translation also appears in the opening verse. The Greek for "James" is actually "Jacob"; the translations have Anglicized the name as James.

As with 2 Peter, a later date is more likely. The reference in Jude 17 to "the predictions of the apostles of our Lord Jesus Christ" suggests a period following the apostolic age. And, as with James and the Petrine letters, this letter provides very little detail about Jesus of Nazareth even while it shows extensive knowledge of Jewish sources.

Competition with Thomas Groups?

In the early second century, some Christian circles were associated with works such as the *Gospel of Thomas*, attributed to a figure named "Judas Didymus Thomas." "Didymus" is Greek for "twin," and "Thomas" is Aramaic for "twin," and consequently, the view began to develop that this "Judas," the brother of Jesus, was also his *twin* brother. Much like the legends of Castor and Pollux, or Clytemnestra and Helen, the twins were fraternal: one was divine, and the other human. Perhaps the author of this letter subtly appealed to Judas the brother of Jesus with the intent of reclaiming his authority from groups associated with the *Gospel of Thomas*. That scenario gains support from the letter's condemnation of those who "pervert the grace of our God into licentiousness" (4) and so, perhaps, saw themselves as already saved and not responsible for ethical action.

Jude and 2 Peter share a literary connection. Both texts speak of false teachers who "indulge the flesh" (2 Pet 2:10; Jude 8: "defile"), are like "irrational animals" (2 Pet 2:12; Jude 10) and "waterless" springs (2 Pet 2:17; Jude 12: "clouds"), and are "scoffers" (2 Pet 3:3; Jude 18). Both recount God's condemnation of the rebellious angels and of Sodom and Gomorrah (2 Pet 2:4-6; Jude 6-7). Both invoke the story of Balaam, the prophet originally hired to curse Israel but who blesses "the tents of Jacob" instead (2 Pet 2:15-16; Jude 11; see Num 22–23), and both exhort recipients to remember the apostles' words (2 Pet 3:2; Jude 17).

The style of the two writings, however, is substantially different, so it is unlikely they share the same author. To explain these extensive similarities, three configurations are possible. Either the texts share a common source, or 2 Peter was the source for Jude, or Jude was a source for 2 Peter. Early interpreters, regarding the Apostle Peter as superior to Jude, thought that Jude depended on 2 Peter. Questions of Petrine authorship as well as the observation that people in superior positions may well rely on the work of subordinates compromise this view.

Today, most scholars see 2 Peter as an edited version of Jude. This dependency emerges in 2 Peter's omission of references to the *Assumption of Moses* (Jude 9-10) and the quote from *1 Enoch* (Jude 14-16 citing *1 Enoch* 1:9), perhaps because they resembled the "myths" that the opposing teachers promoted.

Both 2 Peter and Jude reassure their recipients that God will punish the false teachers, just as evildoers have been punished in the past (Jude 5-16). The warnings reinforce their recipients' fidelity to the author's teaching (3) and distance them from the opposing teachers, "intruders" who are compared to ancient enemies (4).

Jude's first biblical allusion to judgment, which does not appear in 2 Peter, concerns the Exodus: "The Lord, who once for all saved a people out of the land of Egypt, afterward destroyed those who did not believe" (5). Here Pharaoh and the Egyptian army, drowned in their pursuit of Moses and the Israelites, are those who "did not believe," and the "belief" in question is the faith the author promotes.

The second reference to judgment is to a postbiblical legend. Jude 6 speaks of "the angels who did not keep their own position, but left their proper dwelling." These, says Jude, God "kept in eternal chains in deepest darkness for the judgment of the great Day."

The Pseudepigraphon *1 Enoch* interprets the story in Genesis (6:2) of the "sons of God" who "took wives for themselves" and whose activities immediately preceded the flood, as being about fallen angels. These "Watchers," as they came to be known, were supposed to protect humanity. Instead they led human beings into depravity. With this reference, the author demonizes the opponents and makes them part not simply of a contemporary religious debate, but of a cosmic battle. At the same time, the reference draws upon the apocalyptic aspects of *1 Enoch* to situate author and recipients in an eschatological context.

In Jude 7 a third reference links the "intruders" to judgment. The author mentions that just as the rebellious angels were punished,

> likewise, Sodom and Gomorrah and the surrounding cities, which, in the same manner
> as they, indulged in sexual immorality and pursued unnatural lust, serve as an example
> by undergoing a punishment of eternal fire.

The reference to "unnatural lust" (NRSV) reinforces the mention in verse 6 of the Watchers, since divine beings coupling with human beings was regarded as depraved. The Greek underlying the translation, *sarkos heteras,* literally means "other flesh," and indicates that the sin concerns intercourse with angels, not homosexuality. The writer also connects Gen 19 with the fall of the Watchers by referencing the punishment of the people of Sodom and Gomorrah. The destruction of two cities becomes an "eternal fire," a timeless damnation. For Jude, the people of Sodom and Gomorrah not only died in the destruction of their cities; their sufferings extend past their deaths into an afterlife of sorts. Finally, the reference to the destruction of the cities by fire finds a spark in 2 Peter's vision of eschatological conflagration.

Jude 9, the fourth reference, is an allusion to a second Pseudepigraphon, the *Assumption of Moses.* This document describes a dispute between the archangel Michael and the devil over Moses's corpse. Here the opponents are analogized to Satan. By extension, the recipients of Jude are the heirs of Moses. A cosmic battle is being fought over their bodies and their eschatological fates.

Jude 11 returns to the Torah (Pentateuch) for three more allusions to judgment. First, the author compares the false teachers to Cain (Gen 4:1-16; also 1 John 3:7). Not only was Cain known for his fratricide, but also by the second century C.E., if not earlier, Cain was also understood to be a child not of Adam, but of Satan. If this allusion, known from the *Gospel of Philip* and the relatively late rabbinic text *Pirke de-Rabbi Eliezer*, is in play, then Jude reinforces the demonic aspects of the opposing teachers.

Next, the author compares these opposing teachers to Balaam, the prophet who led Israel astray (Num 22, 31; see 2 Pet 2:15; Rev 2:14). The final reference is to Korah, who rebelled against Moses and who was, together with his associates, swallowed by the earth (Num 16). According to Jude 14-15, "it was also about these that Enoch" prophesied:

See, the Lord is coming with ten thousands of his holy ones, to execute judgment on all, and to convict everyone of all the deeds of ungodliness that they have committed in such an ungodly way, and of all the harsh things that ungodly sinners have spoken against him.

The reference is to *1 Enoch* 1:9. Again, biblical and pseudepigraphical materials are redefined with a cosmic context and compared to the situation of the recipients of Jude. The effect is to present the false teachers as evil, on the wrong side of a cosmic struggle, and under God's certain judgment.

Conversely, those who are loyal to the letter's teaching are assured of their righteousness and future vindication, as long as they follow the letter's closing exhortations to "build yourselves up in your most holy faith" (Jude 17-25).

Jude enacts a common strategy used in polemical situations and often found in apocalyptic literature. It divides the world into camps of the good (us) and the bad (them) and, using a range of texts, declares cosmic judgment in the name of God on the enemies. One might argue that this approach performs a useful function. It simplifies what seems to be a complex and contested situation, claims divine sanction for the division, declares that one's enemies will get their just rewards, and protects the community from a threat. But it does so by absolutizing the conflict in cosmic terms, removing the possibility of self-critique and responsibility and constructing God as the doer of destructive violence. In faith communities, for example, or in a global village where various faith traditions and claims coexist and are held with equal passion, are there more profitable ways of engaging conflict that might defuse it rather than ramp it up rhetorically to cosmic proportions?

1, 2, and 3 John

These three short writings, commonly called the Johannine letters, share common vocabulary and themes with both the Gospel of John and Revelation. Beyond that, their authorship, context, and even order of composition in relation to the other Johannine texts remain speculative. The first letter is anonymous; the second two are by an otherwise unknown person who calls himself the "elder" (Greek: *presbyteros*; see 2 John 1; 3 John 1). The scholarly consensus is that the "elder" authored all three texts in their canonical order, after the gospel. We will follow this consensus in this chapter.

To learn more about the circumstances that occasioned the three texts, we employ three approaches. The first is "mirror reading." This long-standing exegetical tool can, with careful use, play a role in historical reconstruction. The second is social-scientific criticism. The third, used in relation to the first two, is a form of rhetorical criticism that explores how the letters use specific rhetorical practices to establish group self-definition and maintain group loyalty. We begin, however, with consensus information about the letters.

Setting and Purpose

First John is not actually a letter; it begins not with salutation but with declaration:

> We declare to you what was from the beginning, what we have heard, what we have seen with our eyes, what we have looked at and touched with our hands, concerning the word of life. (1:1)

Second John addresses "the elect lady and her children" (v. 1). Traditionally, the "elect lady" has been understood to be a house-church, and "her children" its congregation. Another option is that the "elect lady" is a woman who leads a house-church and the "children" are members; a similar suggestion applies to the "co-elect" woman mentioned in 1 Pet 5:13. Third John is a personal letter to an otherwise unknown recipient named Gaius, probably the leader of a house-church.

None of the texts provides explicit clues concerning its date or location of either author or recipients. However, references to itinerant teachers suggest the recipients probably comprised several house-churches in a particular area: "Do not receive into the house or welcome anyone who comes to you and does not bring this teaching" (2 John 10). See also 3 John 7: "They began their journey for the sake of Christ, accepting no support from non-believers. Therefore we ought to support such people." Here we see a distinction from the missionary instructions in the Synoptic Gospels: there the disciples are sent to evangelize people *outside* the group. The situation in these letters appears to be one wherein insiders offer words of instruction and encouragement to other insiders.

Since Polycarp's *Letter to the Philippians* (written before ca. 140 C.E.) seems to indicate knowledge of 1 and 2 John, and since the style is closer to second-century patristic Greek than to earlier texts, we can approximate a date of about 110–130.

Mirror Reading

The occasion of the letters emerges from internal evidence. It appears a schism had occurred between groups of Jesus' followers. The elder explains:

> They went out from us, but they did not belong to us; for if they had belonged to us, they would have remained with us. But by going out they made it plain that none of them belongs to us. (1 John 2:19)

Three times the elder insists, "They did not belong to us." The Greek construction translated "from us" (*ex hymōn*) indicates origin and belonging, both of which were voided by their departure. Their departure, though, is not merely a social matter of a group division. The language of 2:19 expresses, in the context of Johannine literature, a cosmic judgment. In these texts, origin matters. One comes from, or is "of," or "belongs to," either God or Satan/the world (see 1 John 3:7-10; John 8:42-47). By leaving the community, the schismatics prove that they never truly belonged to it, or to God. Likely they would have said the same thing about the author.

It seems more than just one or two people left. In verses 7-8, 2 John states:

> Many deceivers have gone out into the world, those who do not confess that Jesus Christ has come in the flesh.

The term "many" may be hyperbole, but it does suggest more than a few. Perhaps the elder lost a substantial part of his house-church. He may feel under siege. He may fear that others will join his opponents.

To secure the loyalty of those who remain, the elder attacks the opponents. Thus we have to resort to mirror reading to reconstruct the views of the "other side" based on how the elder reflects them. The elder calls the schismatics "antichrists," people opposed to Christ. They are "deceivers" (2 John 7; Greek: *planoi*; the term suggests leading astray or wandering from the path). Their deception is a christological one, although what exactly the failure to confess that Jesus "has come in the flesh" means is not clear. It could refer to a denial of the incarnation, which is central to John's Gospel ("the Word became flesh" [John 1:14]). Or perhaps they did not identify Jesus of Nazareth as the Messiah:

> Who is the liar but the one who denies that Jesus is the Christ? This is the antichrist, the one who denies the Father and the Son. (1 John 2:22)

They may have thought of the Spirit as a divine being who temporarily sojourned in Jesus' human body, and then departed at the cross. Such a view is known from other early Christian writings. For example, some texts associated with the teacher Valentinus suggest, for example, that when Jesus uttered his "cry of dereliction" from the cross, "My God, my God, why have you forsaken me?" he was speaking as a human being who found himself bereft of the divine spirit that had been possessing him (*Excerpts of Theodotus* 61:6; see also the *Gospel of Philip* 68:26-28). Or perhaps they denied Jesus' physical resurrection, as did many so-called gnostic followers of Jesus.

Moreover, the elder condemns the opponents by locating them not only socially and christologically, but also in an eschatological timetable. Interpreting their departure as signaling the end times, the elder declares:

> Children, it is the last hour! As you have heard that antichrist is coming, so now many antichrists have come. From this we know that it is the last hour. (1 John 2:18-19)

Several apocalyptic texts suggest that as the present age draws to a close, opposition to divine purposes increases: the greater the evil, the closer the end. Various New Testament writers understand that with Jesus' resurrection the "last days" are under way already (Acts 2:17 and Pentecost; 1 Thess 4:13–5:11; Mark 13). They expected that in these days, opposition to God would increase, including teachings designed to lead the faithful astray. "False messiahs and false prophets" are to appear (Mark 13:22). "Paul" describes a "lawless one" whose "coming" is "apparent in the working of Satan, who uses all power, signs, lying wonders, and every kind of wicked deception for those who are perishing, because they refused to love the truth and so be saved" (2 Thess 2:3-12). In Revelation, two beasts "utter blasphemies against God" (13:6) and require worship (Rev 13:8, 15); one of these beasts is "a false prophet" (16:13).

In trying to reconstruct or even understand the conflict that precipitated these texts, we should remember that we do not have a version of events from these so-called deceivers or antichrists. Most likely they would not consider themselves to be "deceivers" or "antichrists." Nor is this description provided by a disinterested observer. Rather, 1 and 2 John offer polemic against people who have left. The texts are not written for *them* to read; they are not written to persuade *them* of their error or welcome them back. Rather the polemic is for the benefit of the letters' recipients. It is designed to discredit those who left, while securing the unity, beliefs, and practices of the writer's group. In polemical literature, caricature replaces careful description. Innuendo replaces integrity. Misleading and partial claims replace nuanced analysis.

When polemic appears in works considered sacred, the problem of mirror reading becomes exacerbated. Many readers of the Bible approach the texts as authoritative, and so they are predisposed to accept whatever the texts say. If the elder says that the schismatics are wrong, they are wrong. If the elder calls them liars (1 John 2:22), then liars they must be. Readers accept the perspective of the author. Missing from this reading strategy, though, is recognition that the text is perspectival and that in the late first century, categories of orthodoxy and heresy were not self-evident or fixed. A more historical approach would investigate the author's presentation and, without prejudging the opponents' views, attempt to reconstruct them as fairly as possible.

We have encountered this problem in several writings already. The Gospel of Luke, adopting a standard polemical trope, accuses Pharisees of being "lovers of money" (16:14; also 2 Tim 3:2). Conversely, polemicists charged early followers of Jesus with cannibalism and incest. These were standard attacks, perhaps prompted by (misunderstandings of) eucharistic language, the use of the kiss as a greeting, and reference to community members as "brothers and sisters."

Relying on the elder's descriptions of his opponents, we find comments on Christology, ethics, eschatology, and pneumatology, as we will elaborate in the next section. We might conclude that the dispute involved these matters in some way. But as we have seen in the reference to Jesus coming in the flesh, being specific is difficult. Social-scientific criticism may help in clarifying the details.

Social-Scientific Criticism

We have already presented several interpretive techniques associated with social-scientific criticism, including investigating concepts of honor and shame, the patronage system and euergetism, the construction of gender, the naturalization of slavery, and the social construction of reality. In mapping ancient cultural values, we have seen that social dynamics in antiquity can be alien to modern Western society, and so we are warned against anachronistically reading the ancient world according to twenty-first-century categories.

At the same time, we have also noted that certain cultural phenomena—households, living in a community, economic systems, division of the sacred from the profane—have cross-cultural functions. The discipline known as macrosociology investigates a common phenomenon in many different social contexts, whether fifth-century B.C.E. China or eleventh-century C.E. France. General parameters or models of these social structures can be formulated. The investigator then attempts to determine how they fit into or are modified by the specific context under investigation.

Models remain useful precisely because they are generalizing devices. Based on cross-cultural research, they can help identify some of the social dynamics at work related to particular social phenomena. Moreover, in alliance with work in classical studies, for example, models can perform a heuristic function. They can contextualize partial pieces of data or phenomena attested in a New Testament text in relation to more general patterns of social structures and dynamics. Models can link various data and fill in gaps not articulated in the text. They join the dots to provide a useful "map" of a situation, albeit at a somewhat generalized or abstracted level. Any model needs to be "tested" for commensurability in its use with a NT text.

From this more general outlining of social-science criticism, we turn to a particular area of social-scientific investigation that might provide insight into the Johannine letters: namely, study of schisms and formation of sectarian groups. Because schisms are common in religious communities across wide geographical areas and time periods, considerable data are available from which a generalized model can be constructed. Without expecting that every schism follows the same pattern, we can nevertheless use these models to sketch a possible setting for the Johannine letters.

One model[1] of a schism sees it develop through four stages. In diagram form, it looks like this:

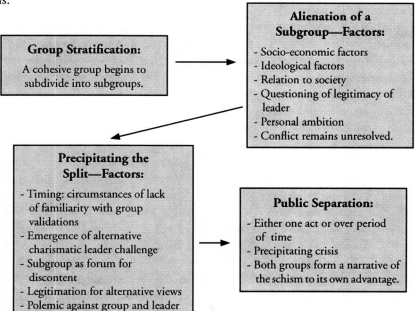

Group Stratification:

A cohesive group begins to subdivide into subgroups.

Alienation of a Subgroup—Factors:

- Socio-economic factors
- Ideological factors
- Relation to society
- Questioning of legitimacy of leader
- Personal ambition
- Conflict remains unresolved.

Precipitating the Split—Factors:

- Timing: circumstances of lack of familiarity with group validations
- Emergence of alternative charismatic leader challenge
- Subgroup as forum for discontent
- Legitimation for alternative views
- Polemic against group and leader

Public Separation:

- Either one act or over period of time
- Precipitating crisis
- Both groups form a narrative of the schism to its own advantage.

---

1. The model of schism used in this discussion of Johannine literature derives from Jason Merritt, *The Rhetoric of Religious Schism in 1 and 2 John* (PhD diss.; Brite Divinity School, TCU, Fort Worth), 57–126. Merritt develops the model largely from nineteenth- and twentieth-century US religious groups.

First, we explain the model and then use it to elaborate the circumstances of 1–2 John; next we will look at 3 John as a post-schism letter.

This model sees schism beginning with *group stratification.* A community divides into subgroups or cliques. This stratification becomes threatening when a subgroup becomes increasingly alienated. One factor prompting the alienation can be *socioeconomic disparity.* On the one hand, a subgroup from an elite context may determine that it no longer wants to be associated with artisans or peasants. On the other, the disadvantaged might resent the elite and accuse them of betraying the group's more countercultural or isolationist ethos.

The subgroup's alienation might also be grounded in *ideological* factors. Group principles may seem no longer convincing to some members or, conversely, some may think the group principles might have been compromised. Often *relation to society* is a source of contention among minority groups: one faction might be more assimilated than another; one might seek greater distinction from the surrounding world. *Personality* also impacts schismatic moves. Subgroups can develop among those with antipathy towards a group's leader or leadership, especially when that leadership is centralized, and when others with personal leadership ambitions emerge. Or again, one elite faction or even rich member may be competing with another for community leadership. The alienation increases if the conflict is not resolved.

The third phase concerns factors that precipitate the split. Schisms typically occur either early in a group's history, or after a leader's death, or after numerical growth. The key factor in the three situations concerns commitment to group principles. Early in a group's life, identity may not be clearly established or articulated. After a leader's death, different factions may come to support different leaders with differing visions. After significant growth, not all members are fully invested in the group's ideology; some will import new ideologies; some will seek influence or leadership roles. Other factors precipitating the schism can include the emergence of an alternative charismatic leader, the role of the subgroup as a forum for discontent and articulation of alternative views and practices, and polemic against the current group leader and other subgroups. Pressure from external forces can exacerbate all of these situations.

Finally, the separation occurs, either as a single act or over a period of time. After the separation, both the main group and the departed group formulate a narrative of the schism in which they frame the details to their own advantage. For instance, a voluntary departure will often come to be understood as an expulsion. That may be the case in John's Gospel, where the triple use of the unusual term *aposynagōgos* (to be "out-synagogued") may reflect not a formal process of expulsion, but a rewriting of the story by the group that left. The Greek term *ekklēsia,* usually translated "church," literally means "to be called out." This produces a much more positive self-definition than the possibly related situation in which the followers of Jesus found that their proclamations were not welcome in their earlier synagogues or other groups of affiliation. "Called out" sounds much better than "rejected." In the case of the Johannine letters, we have the perspective of the group that stayed.

This model provides possibilities for understanding the schism of 1–2 John. First, we can identify some factors that may well have contributed not only to group stratification but especially to the alienation of a subgroup. *Socioeconomic factors* may have been in play. First John 3:17 raises a concern with charitable care: "How does God's love abide in anyone who has the world's goods and sees a brother or sister in need and yet refuses help?"

One reading of this verse suggests that not sharing economic resources was a problem in the community. However, accusations of selfishness and lack of care for the poor are conventional invective.

If socioeconomic issues did contribute to the schism, then the elder's question will have rhetorical force regardless of the specific configuration of the two groups. If the group that left were those with greater resources, the verse expresses the elder's resentment at the schismatics' lack of charity. It would then have the rhetorical effect of telling the community, "Do not be like the schismatics." Conversely, the schismatics may have been among the poorer members of the community who left because they perceived their needs to have been ignored. If so, the verse has the rhetorical import of a rebuke, "Do not let this happen again."

Several other verses may clarify the situation. Second John 7 says, they "have gone out into the world." In 1 John 2:15-16, the elder disapproves of the world:

> Do not love the world or the things in the world. The love of the Father is not in those who love the world; for all that is in the world—the desire of the flesh, the desire of the eyes, the pride in riches—comes not from the Father but from the world.

The verses link riches and the world, into which the departed group has gone. Negative references to the world recur throughout (for example, "the world hates you" [1 John 3:13]; "the whole world lies under the power of the evil one" [1 John 5:19]). The letters, like John's Gospel and Revelation, display no interest in engaging, or evangelizing, "the world." Instead, the world welcomes those who separated: "They are from the world; therefore what they say is from the world, and the world listens to them" (1 John 4:5).

Taken together, these verses suggest that a group marked not only by being better off economically but also by more fully participating in and accommodating to their society, separated from the elder's group. The warning in 1 John 5:21 to avoid idols further supports such a scenario.

Another factor precipitating the schism may have involved new members concerned with *social mobility*. For example, individuals with economic resources (high income) but low social status might find new movements to be a fertile location for increasing their social capital as leaders or patrons. Perhaps the schismatics, resenting the elder's authority and having sufficient resources of their own, saw more opportunity in forming an alternative congregation.

A further factor that can contribute to the alienation of a subgroup is a dispute over ideology or theology. We have already noted that in 2 John 7, failing to confess that "Jesus Christ has come in the flesh" is part of the schism. The elder also charges the schismatics with denying that Jesus is the Christ, God's anointed one (2:22-23). The confessions of "his Son Jesus Christ" (3:23), and that "Jesus is the Son of God" (4:15; 5:5) and that "the Son of God has come and given us understanding" (5:20) are central to the elder's presentation. The subgroup may have denied these creedal statements in some way or understood them differently than the elder did.

The christological dispute might have also involved the reception and interpretation of John's Gospel. According to John 19:34, when the soldier pierces Jesus' side, "at once blood and water came out." The letters also pair blood and water: 1 John 5:6 proclaims:

> This is the one who came by water and blood, Jesus Christ, not with the water only but with the water and the blood. And the Spirit is the one that testifies, for the Spirit is the truth.

Perhaps the elder appeals to Jesus' crucifixion as *the* moment that revealed his identity as Christ and Son while the schismatic group devalued the crucifixion in favor of other soteriological options. Perhaps they held a more docetic Christology (the term comes from the Greek *dokeō*, which means "to seem" or "to appear") that denied the incarnation, the relationship of the Spirit to the human Jesus, and the saving power of Jesus' death. For followers of Jesus who adopted a docetic approach, Jesus only "appeared" to be human, and thus he was not actually "born" and did not "die."

Along with Christology, there seems to have been conflict over eschatology, soteriology, and ethics. A series of "If we say . . ." statements may refer to claims made by, or understood to be made by, those who left. Perhaps they claimed to have a relationship with God, but in the elder's opinion they did not live in a manner that reflects the relationship: "If we say that we have fellowship with him while we are walking in darkness, we lie and do not do what is true" (1 John 1:6). Perhaps they claimed perfection, which would fit within a realized eschatology, and saw no need for atonement, a final judgment, or a general resurrection: "If we say we have no sin, we deceive ourselves" (1 John 1:8) and "If we say that we have not sinned, we make him [God] a liar." (1 John 1:10). Perhaps, like some of Paul's opponents in Corinth, they claimed that they were *already* saved and that they did not sin. Given the likely influence of John's Gospel on the elder's community, claims of realized eschatology are not surprising. Verses such as John 5:24 could suggest that sin is no longer a factor in human life:

Very truly, I tell you, anyone who hears my word and believes him who sent me has eternal life, and does not come under judgment, but has passed from death to life.

The elder offers several reminders of the ongoing reality of sin even as he declares that Jesus' death "cleanses us from all sin" (1:7), that it was an "atoning sacrifice for our sins" (2:2; 4:10), and that he "was revealed to take away sins" (3:5).

The elder, like the author of the gospel, combines both realized and future eschatology. The former emphasis is evident in 1 John 5:11, "God gave us eternal life . . . in his Son." He insists that those who abide in Jesus have already "conquered the evil one" (2:13-14). The elder's complementary assertions of future eschatology counter the claims of a fully realized eschatology. He refers to the day of judgment (4:17), Jesus' return (2:28), and a future sinless state:

Beloved, we are God's children now; what we will be has not yet been revealed. What we do know is this: when he is revealed, we will be like him, for we will see him as he is. (3:2)

To ensure that his readers remain faithful to his version of the good news, the elder links the demand for ethical living with eschatological union with God (1 John 1:6-7), speaks of achieving perfection only through obedience (1 John 2:5), and insists that ethical living comprises preparation for eschatological events (1 John 2:28; 3.3). Indeed, 2 John 8 warns that one's blessings can be lost:

Be on your guard, so that you do not lose what we have worked for, but may receive a full reward.

Finally, the elder reframes the schism in terms of ethics. According to him, those who departed did not love other members of the group: "Whoever says, 'I am in the light,' while hating a brother, is still in the darkness" (1 John 2:9). The point is echoed in 4:20:

Those who say, "I love God," and hate their brothers or sisters, are liars; for those who do not love a brother or sister whom they have seen, cannot love God whom they have not seen.

This emphasis on loving members of the group continues from John's Gospel (13:34-35) and permeates the letters. It is also a love restricted to community members (also John's Gospel) and not offered to outsiders or enemies as in Matthew's Gospel: "Love your enemies and pray for those who persecute you" (5:44). The failure to love community members is epitomized by Cain, "who was from the evil one and murdered his brother" (1 John 3:12). Matthew again may offer a counterview in having Jesus teach, "So when you are offering your gift at the altar, if you remember that your brother or sister has something against you, leave your gift there before the altar and go; first be reconciled to your brother or sister, and then come and offer your gift" (5:23-24). The reference here, in the Sermon on the Mount, may well be an allusion to the story of Cain and Abel (Gen 4). According to the elder, the enemies are the children of the devil; for them there is no hope, and no compassion. He does not notice his own lack of love for those who departed. Likely they did not see much warmth and compassion stemming from him either.

Several factors, then, seem to have contributed to the formation of an increasingly alienated subgroup: socioeconomic inequalities with an openness to societal participation, and an alternative ideology or theology embracing christological, soteriological, ethical, and eschatological dimensions. Our model suggests we should expect conflict with the group's leader/s (here, the elder), which has not been resolved. Neither 1 nor 2 John, however, makes that explicit.

In terms of precipitating the split, the model directs our attention to matters of timing, the role of the alienated subgroup as a forum for discontent and for articulating an alternative worldview, the role of a charismatic leader, and polemic. Concerning alternative leaders, the elder speaks only in the plural terms of "false prophets," "deceivers," and "antichrists." Concerning timing, there is no mention of a death. The arrival of new members may be likely. Perhaps the alienated group, because of its openness to societal participation, attracted new members who questioned the group's leadership, and developed an alternative validation for the subgroup's beliefs. For the separating group, that alternative legitimation seems to be informed in part by interpretations of John's Gospel, particularly its realized eschatology.

Rhetorical Retrospection

In Classical Greek thought, rhetoric was understood to have three distinct albeit sometimes overlapping functions. *Judicial rhetoric* persuades an audience to make a judgment about events. *Deliberative rhetoric* persuades listeners to make a decision about the future. *Epideictic rhetoric* seeks to persuade listeners to affirm or denounce a point of view or quality. First and Second John, using primarily epideictic rhetoric, provide a retrospection or rehearsal of the schism from the perspective of the abandoned group—or, in the elder's view, the group that walks in the truth—and for the good of that group. The letters seek to have their readers affirm certain values and practices associated with a "true" understanding of the gospel, and to denounce those associated with the group that has left. The letters seek to unify and secure the loyalty of the group, affirm central truths, and discredit those who have left.

Rhetorically, the letters construct a strong division between "us" and "them." First John constructs "us" as those who have union with and belong to God while those who "went out" do not. "We" obey God's commandments and are "in him" (1 John 2:3-6; 5:2-3). "We" are from the Father (2:16), anointed with knowledge and knowing truth (2:21-22). "We" abide in the Father and Son (2:24), have eternal life (2:25; 5:11-13), are born of God (3:9; 4:7; 5:1, 18), are both from the truth (3:19) and from God (4:4-6). "We" love God (5:2) as God's children (5:19) who have received revelation from Jesus (5:20). The departed group would probably not agree that only the group that remained belonged to God. But we do not hear from them.

The elder translates these theological claims into terms of address that name the inside group's identity. Because they know the love of God (1:5; 4:7-12), the elder addresses them as "Beloved" (2:7; 3:2, 21; 4:1, 7). Because they are God's children (3:1-2), the elder addresses them with kinship or household language such as "little children" or "children" (2:1, 12, 18; 3:7, 18; 4:4). This language also presents the elder as the caring father. Because they have not "gone out," the elder seeks to secure their loyalty to him with more household language, addressing them as "brothers and sisters" (3:13; see also 2:9-11). This address subtly reminds them that brothers and sisters are to be faithful and loving and not act as Cain did.

This group or household is then placed rhetorically—and so, by goal, sociologically—over against "the world," which hates them and is under Satan's power (2:15-17; 3:13; 5:19b). Those who "love the world" do not know the love of God (2:15) and consequently do not belong to God. Those in the "world" and received by the "world" are the false, former community members: the liars, antichrists, and false prophets (2:18-22). The rhetorical situation is constructed in dualistic and cosmic terms: "we" are divinely sanctioned in union with God; "they" are children of the devil (3:8-10). Possibly 1 John works so hard to construct this dualism because while the alienated subgroup has departed, their threat has not, and those who are left remain vulnerable to it.

The structure of 1 John presents a second rhetorical strategy designed both to unify the group and to discredit those who have left. First John presents numerous pithy, repetitive statements rather than developed arguments. Repetition emphasizes a central point in circumstances where that point might be challenged. Amid the noise of competing claims, and the disruption and vulnerability of the schism, the elder hammers home his claims. The opening lines (1 John 1:1-3) set out the argument for the legitimacy of his views:

> We declare to you what was from the beginning, what we have heard, what we have seen with our eyes, what we have looked at and touched with our hands . . . we have seen it and testify to it . . . we declare to you what we have seen and heard.

337

Regular doctrinal statements underscore central claims: "The love of the Father is not in those who love the world" (1 John 2:15); "Jesus is the Christ" (2:22); "Everyone who confesses the Son has the Father also" (2:23); "He was revealed to take away sins, and in him there is no sin" (3:5).

A third rhetorical strategy involves the elder's appeal to tradition. This is especially evident in 1 John's opening four verses with its appeal to what has been heard, seen, and touched. This material sounds like eyewitness testimony, but the rhetorical form suggests an appeal to community tradition.

Finally, the elder solidifies the negative view of the opponents and the authority of his views by standard rhetorical forms still in use in community division and development today. He resorts to vilification via name-calling and guilt by association. First John refers to those who have gone out as liars (2:22) and "antichrists" (2:18, 22; 4:3; also "deceivers" in 2 John 7). The latter term, "antichrist," is a staple of Hollywood apocalyptic scenarios and associated in popular culture with the book of Revelation (which does not use the term). For 1 and 2 John, "antichrist" refers neither to a supernatural being nor a political figure. It describes the people (plural) who have left the group (2:19), deny Jesus is the Christ (2:22), and do not confess that "Jesus Christ has come in the flesh" (2 John 7). The term "antichrist" suggests those who are opposed to Christ.

Nevertheless, "antichrist" may have eschatological connotations. John states, "As you have heard that antichrist is coming, so now many antichrists have come" (1 John 2:18). This "knowledge" may be that of expectations associated with "the last days" or the "last hour" referred to in 2:18. The elder takes a somewhat general eschatological expectation and applies it to his social situation. He historicizes the expectation of an apocalyptic false teacher in terms of a group of people known to the congregation. The effect is to frame the schism as a sign of the end times.

Beyond eschatological vilification, the elder employs other polemic. Through allusion, the elder equates his opponents with two biblical figures of murderous evil. By describing their departure literally as "they went out" (2:19), the elder evokes John 13:30, where Judas leaves the Last Supper and "went out" (the same verb) into the darkness to betray Jesus. This allusion has three consequences. It presents those who "went out" as betrayers. It presents their action as of the devil, since "Satan entered into" Judas (John 13:27; see 13:2) and confirms their identity as children of the devil (1 John 3:8-10).

The elder further vilifies the opponents by linking them to Cain (Gen 4). The command to love one another and the expectation of sharing material possessions with those in need (3:11, 17) frame a section in which the elder insists that the congregation not be like Cain:

who was from the evil one and murdered his brother. And why did he murder him? Because his own deeds were evil and his brother's righteous. (3:12)

The opponents, like Cain, "went out" into the world. They refuse to share their possessions. They are betrayers, murderers, and children of the devil.

For the Johannine letters, the schism has consequences in terms of both social distinction and cosmic legitimation. The elder's highly dualistic presentation encourages his readers to affirm certain values and practices associated with a "true" understanding of the gospel and denounce those associated with the group that has left. It seeks to unify the group and secure their loyalty, while discrediting those who have left. For all the writing's talk of love, that love is confined to "one another" and does not extend to outsiders (cf. John 13:35).

The Effects of Schism: 3 John

1 and 2 John raise the question: Is it possible for religious communities to embrace diverse interpretations of their common tradition while extending love to all? The experience of schism in the Johannine letters (1 John 2:18) indicates that for the author of the letter, the answer is no.

Likely written in the aftermath of the schism, the 15 verses of 3 John evidence a league of house-churches among which there is considerable contact through traveling representatives. The elder, the author of the letter, appears to have some authority over other house-churches, for he sends emissaries, writes hortatory letters, and expects obedience (9). This authority may be more charismatic, or economic, than formal. No reference is made to his being a bishop or a deacon. Writing to a man named Gaius, likely the patron of a house-church, the elder begins with the happy observation:

I was overjoyed when some of the friends [the NRSV, attempting gender inclusivity, reads "friends"; the Greek *adelphoi* literally means "brothers"] arrived and testified to your faithfulness to the truth, namely how you walk in the truth. (v. 3)

He promotes the idea of welcoming itinerant missionaries who teach the gospel of which the elder approves: "Therefore we ought to support such people, so that we may become co-workers with the truth" (8).

Such itinerancy raises the important pragmatic question of how to discern faithful teachers from false ones. How does a group know that this itinerant teacher is not from the schismatic contingent? The elder had previously warned the "elect lady" about "many deceivers who have gone out into the world" yet do not confess that Jesus has come in the flesh and do "not abide in the teaching of Christ" (2 John 7-9). She is not to give them hospitality or receive them (2 John 10-11).

For 3 John, the question of extending hospitality concerns a particular conflictual situation. The elder notes that Diotrephes, another church leader, stands in opposition to his teaching:

> Diotrephes, who likes to put himself first, does not acknowledge our authority . . . [and is] spreading false charges against us. And not content with those charges, he refuses to welcome the friends, and even prevents those who want to do so and expels them from the church. (9-10)

His rejection of the elder's authority could be a personal power struggle, or Diotrephes could be among those who "went out."

The elder's harsh language about Diotrephes reflects a strong assertion of authority. The elder warns Gaius about Diotrephes's actions, and even threatens to come personally to condemn him:

> So if I come, I will call attention to what he is doing in spreading false charges against us. And not content with those charges, he refuses to welcome the friends, and even prevents those who want to do so and expels them from the church. (10)

Ironically, in encouraging Gaius not to imitate these evil ways exhibited by Diotrephes, the elder shows the same lack of hospitality of which he accuses his opponent.

The elder closes with the anticipation of a "face to face" meeting and exchange of greetings (13-15).

These Johannine letters demonstrate struggles among early Jesus-followers to define themselves in relation to other groups. Hospitality is an important value, much easier, though, to write about than to practice in contested situations. This longstanding struggle and challenge continue in the present day when missionaries or parachurch groups "compete" for influence in the same area, or when churches decide that other claimants to the name of "church" are not legitimate, or when "established" churches are less than welcoming to new "community" or "emergent" churches—and vice versa.

CHAPTER 21

$\mathscr{R}$evelation

This final book of the NT canon provides some of the most famous biblical images: Armageddon (16:16), the beast whose number is 666 (13:18), the four horsemen of the apocalypse (ch. 6), the whore of Babylon (17:5). Across two millennia, readers have attempted to understand these and other images, along with the whole document.

For some within the Christian community, Revelation is the center of faith, the focal point of God's plan for history. Correct interpretation both predicts and explains current politics, ecology, and human relations. For others, Revelation is an arcane, meaningless book that it is best left behind. George Bernard Shaw thought it was the "curious record of the visions of a drug addict." For some readers, Revelation provides the surety that despite evil, whether Roman imperial evil of antiquity or present-day nuclear threat, environment destruction, and economic exploitation, God's justice will prevail. For others, the book's sexual violence, militancy, and delight in bloodshed cannot be separated from its message. Despite its potential to provide hope and encouragement, they reject Revelation as counter to the good news of Jesus.

The book's name comes from its opening phrase, "The revelation of Jesus Christ." The Greek word translated "revelation" (*apo-calypsis*, English "apocalypse") comprises a prefix meaning "out of" or "from," and a noun meaning "conceal" or "hide." Literally the noun means "taking out of hiding," "uncovering," "un-concealing." The book could be called "Disclosure," or "Manifestation" as much as Revelation.

This name alerts us to an important question, "What does Revelation reveal?" The answers very much depend on a further question, "How do we read this book?"

In this chapter, we foreground the role that readers play in making meaning of a text. In this reader-response approach, we look at two major ways of reading Revelation and see the different meanings they produce. Seen as *prediction*, Revelation becomes a code that, with the right key, details the end of the world and the fates of those who follow or do not follow Jesus. Seen as *proclamation* (especially but not exclusively for first-century Jesus-followers), Revelation becomes the cry of the powerless against all opponents, whether the Roman Empire or any empire or rival ecclesial groups or people who reject Jesus or who behave in ways contrary to what the writer and reader consider to be the divine will. As proclamation, the book assures the righteous (the writer and those who agree with him) that they will enjoy paradise while the wicked (everyone else) will suffer eternal torment. Either interpretation can be both comforting and very dangerous.

We explain and evaluate these two ways of reading, consider how the book's three genres (letter, prophecy, apocalypse) contribute to this meaning-making, and look at some ways in which we might interpret the book's violence and hostility toward its opponents.

Revelation as Prediction

Readers who take literally John's opening claim to describe "what must soon take place" (1:1) understand Revelation to predict the future. They also usually understand the text as addressed to them, so they read the predictions in relation to their own circumstances and time. Revelation 1:3 states:

> Blessed is the one who reads aloud the words of the prophecy, and blessed are those who hear and who keep what is written in it; for the time is near.

This reading understands that time to be now.

Popular recent expressions of this view in the United States include Hal Lindsey's 1970 bestseller *The Late Great Planet Earth*, and the bestsellers of the first decade of the twenty-first century, the Left Behind series by Timothy LeHaye and Jerry B. Jenkins. Prediction readers not only seek to connect aspects of Revelation with world history; they also, typically, look forward to the final consummation when God destroys evil and when Jesus together with the saints reigns in victory for eternity. Hence, prediction readers are also millennialists in looking forward to this thousand-year reign. The term comes from Rev 20:4, which mentions the thousand-year reign of Christ together with his saints.

Prediction readings are not a modern phenomenon. In the early fourth century, Eusebius saw some of Revelation's "predictions" fulfilled in the conversion of the emperor Constantine. The twelfth-century monk Joachim of Flores concluded that the end would occur during his generation. In the sixteenth century, Martin Luther connected the beast of Rev 13 with the papacy. In the mid-nineteenth century, an upstate New York Baptist pastor named William Miller announced that Revelation (and other apocalyptic passages in the Bible) predicted the date when the world would end. His initial prediction of October 22, 1844, led his followers, called "Millerites," to prepare for their redemption when the "millennium," the thousand-year reign of Christ together with his saints, would begin.

One particular form of Millennialism, known as dispensationalism, began with the speculations of John Nelson Darby (1800–1882), one of the original Plymouth Brethren, an evangelical offshoot of Anglicanism that began in the early 1800s in Dublin. Darby divided history into seven eras, which he called "dispensations." He identified the present as the "church age" and anticipated that Jesus would return to reign for 1,000 years. After that millennium, there will be a final consummation. This theory gained popularity throughout the United States with the Scofield Reference Bible (originally published in 1909).

For prediction readers (dispensationalists and millennialists), the tribulation is a key event immediately prior to and leading into the millennium. This seven-year period, a time of ordeal for and testing of the faithful, is marked by the rise of an evil world ruler known as the *antichrist.* This term does not appear in Revelation. It comes from 1 John 2:18, 22; 4.3; 2 John 7, where the plural term refers to teachers who oppose Christ. Prediction readers import the term into their interpretations of Revelation and understand it in the singular, in relation to a world political, sometimes even supernatural, figure whom they regard as demonic.

Prediction readers also give much attention to perhaps Revelation's most famous symbol, the "beast whose number is six hundred sixty-six" (13:18). Revelation 13 actually describes two beasts. Of the first, John writes:

> One of its heads seemed to have received a death-blow, but its mortal wound had been healed. In amazement the whole earth followed the beast. (13:3)

First-century readers would recognize an allusion to the emperor Nero. He committed suicide in 68 but was rumored to have survived this "mortal wound," to have moved eastward to the Parthian empire, and to have been gathering an army to reconquer Rome. The text's initial readers, familiar with the Hebrew language, would also have recognized an allusion to Nero in the beast's number of 666. The allusion functions by means of a numerological technique known as *gematria.* In this system, every Hebrew letter has a numerical equivalent. The Hebrew letters that spell "Neron Caesar" add up to 666. The variant number in some early New Testament manuscripts, 616, also fits Nero. The letter *nun* (English n), which has the numerical equivalent of 60, and which in Neron serves as a case ending, can grammatically drop out.

Prediction readers, however, develop their own interpretations of the "mark of the beast." Although more Hollywood than holy word, the series called the "Omen" depicted the antichrist as having a 666 birthmark hidden by his hair. A former premier of the Soviet Union, Mikhail Gorbachev, had a birthmark on his forehead, which some prediction readers regarded as the mark of the beast. That the birthmark did not resemble a series of sixes proved irrelevant.

When Gorbachev facilitated the de-unification of the Soviet state, prediction readers recalculated. Ronald Wilson Reagan was a preferred candidate for some, given the six letters in each of his three names. Presidents Bush and Obama have been major candidates, as have been any secretary-general of the United Nations and any pope of the Roman Catholic Church. The identification matters for prediction readers since it indicates that the millennium is imminent.

Prediction readers also focus considerable attention on the reference to *Armageddon* in 16:16: "They assembled them at the place that in Hebrew is called Harmageddon." In English pronunciation, the "h" drops out. "Har" in "harmageddon" means "mountain" in Hebrew, and "mageddon" refers to Megiddo. Hence the original reference is to Mount Megiddo near Mount Carmel. The mountain had come to symbolize disaster since Judah's king Josiah was killed fighting the Egyptian army there in 609 B.C.E.

Prediction interpretations of *Armageddon* typically read the symbols in the text as having references in their own setting. Many interpret 16:16 to predict a final battle in Israel at Mount Megiddo. Hence such readers will scrutinize events in the Middle East for signs of war. The founding of the state of Israel in 1948 presaged for some readers the beginning of the end time. The reunification of Jerusalem after the Six-Day War of 1967 jump-started another bout of apocalyptic enthusiasm.

These interpretations are necessarily inconsistent. Prediction readers choose some symbols to import into the real world while ignoring others. For example, while Armageddon receives much attention, prediction readers do not require political candidates for the role of "the beast" or "antichrist" to have seven heads, even though 13:1 describes "a beast rising out of the sea having ten horns and seven heads." Yet when 17:9 notes that "the seven heads are seven mountains on which the woman is seated," some prediction readers attempt to locate a modern city built on seven hills. Among the contenders: Lynchburg, Virginia; Staten Island; Tehran; and Mecca. John's initial readers would have recognized the city on seven hills as Rome.

The prediction approach, despite the failure of calculations yet to come true, has much to commend it. For example, it takes seriously Revelation's theological and eschatological dimensions. It understands God to be involved in fulfilling biblical hopes and establishing justice, so that the prayer "Your kingdom come" (Matt 6:10//Luke 11:2) is finally answered. For those who are suffering, Revelation provides the surety that God is in control, that suffering can be mastered with steadfastness and faith, that evil will be punished and good rewarded. It also takes seriously Revelation's role as part of the sacred Scriptures of the church in speaking to the faithful.

Despite these contributions, the prediction approach remains problematic. First, its focus on the contemporary world and imminent future ignores the book's historical origins. Prediction readers ignore the import of Revelation's origin or choices about genre on its interpretation. As we have already noted, a text without a context can become a pretext for interpreting it any way one wants. If Revelation seeks to assure readers of both the end of their suffering and the promise of God's faithfulness, we might wonder how first-century readers would find good news in predictions that would not come to fruition for 2,000 years.

Second, the prediction reading understands "prophecy" (1:3) only in terms of predicting the future. It ignores biblical prophecy's address to the present, whether the first-century present or the reader's. It also ignores, or at least de-emphasizes, the Bible's consistent call for action in the present, such as care for the poor or love for neighbor. The goal of the prediction approach is to discover God's goals for the world and then to wait for God to accomplish these goals. Accompanying this view is the belief that the world is under Satan's power. The world is so corrupt that only God can fix it, and God will do so in the future by creating "a new heaven and a new earth; for the first heaven and the first earth had passed away, and the sea was no more" (21:1; see also 2 Pet for this imagery). Many prediction readers generally do not see themselves called to ameliorate this world, let alone to protect the environment. They are to endure faithfully within it until the end.

Although everyone who has read Revelation as predicting the imminent end of time has been in error, those who read Revelation as prediction are not dissuaded. That others have been wrong does not, in their view, preclude their calculations from being correct. Today there are websites, seminars, and sermons on the signs of the end, with every ecological disaster, medical epidemic, political shift, and international incident seen as confirming a prediction and bringing the end closer.

Revelation as Proclamation

Reading Revelation as proclamation (especially but not exclusively for first-century Jesus-followers) rather than as prediction begins with considering the text's historical origins and literary characteristics. This approach recognizes that the text had to have made sense to first-century Jesus-followers in the seven cities of Asia addressed in chapters 2–3: Ephesus, Smyrna, Pergamum, Thyatira, Sardis, Philadelphia, and Laodicea. This approach also understands Revelation as a mixture of at least three genres—apocalypse (1:1), prophecy (1:3), and letter (1:4)—and each provides clues to its meaning. Finally, like the prediction approach, proclamation readings find in Revelation a message about God's workings in the world and understand Revelation as saying something to contemporary Christian readers about belief and practice.

Not everything is clear about Revelation's circumstances of origin. The writer identifies himself as "John" (1:1, 4, 9; 22:8), but the name was common among Jews. Various NT figures named John have been proposed as the author: John the Baptist, John Mark, John son of Zebedee. The second-century church writer Justin Martyr (*Dialogue with Trypho* 81) identifies this John as "one of the apostles of Christ." His slightly later contemporary Irenaeus describes him as "the disciple of the Lord" who also wrote John's

Gospel (*Adv Haer* 3.11.1; 4.20.11). In the mid-third century, Dionysius of Alexandria argued on the basis of language and theological content that John's Gospel and Revelation had different authors. Thus the "John" who composed the text remains unknown.

Although the Greek of Revelation reads in part as if the author were thinking in a Semitic language such as Hebrew or Aramaic, it is unlikely that the author of Revelation was one of Jesus' disciples. The author does not mention this connection. Further, he seems to distance himself from the apostles when he remarks that the wall of the New Jerusalem "has twelve foundations, and on them are the twelve names of the twelve apostles of the Lamb" (21:14). The author simply describes himself as a "brother" (1:9), a familial term that underlines his solidarity with his readers. The letters to the seven churches in Rev 2 and 3 suggest he knows and is known by these congregations.

In terms of date, a long tradition locates Revelation circa 90 when Domitian was emperor. This link is based on the reference to seven kings, "of whom five have fallen, one is living, and the other has not yet come" (17:9-10). This verse was interpreted as pointing to Domitian. The five "fallen" emperors were Galba, Otho, Vitellius, Vespasian (d. 79), and Titus (d. 81), making Domitian the "living" one (81–96), with Nerva the emperor to come (96–98). During Domitian's reign, so the argument goes, followers of Jesus were persecuted for refusing to participate in the imperial cult. Proponents of this view see the writer as exiled to a penal colony on the island of Patmos (1:9) for his non-compliance. Supporting this claim is a reference in the church historian Eusebius that Domitian persecuted Christians because they would not worship him as "lord and god" (*Ecclesiastical History* 3.17-20; 4.26.9).

In recent decades, however, scholars have increasingly rejected this reconstruction. There is no evidence that Patmos was a place of exile or prison. Nor does John say that he had been exiled. Rather, he states that he is there "because of the word of God" (1:9). He may have been preaching, leading a congregation, or resting at home. Nor need 17:9-10 point to Domitian. If one begins counting from earlier rulers, such as Julius Caesar or Augustus, this eighth emperor would be the emperor Nero (54–68).

Even Eusebius's claim about Domitian's persecution lacks support. Eusebius (writing in the fourth century) cites Irenaeus (writing in the late second century) as his source for the claim that Domitian acted against Christians. However, Irenaeus only says that Revelation was written near the end of Domitian's reign. He says nothing about persecution. There is no evidence that Domitian aggressively promoted the imperial cult or demanded to be called Lord and God. Even if he had, participation in imperial cult activity was voluntary, not compulsory. Indeed, Revelation does not suggest a context of active persecution. John mentions only one martyr; writing to the church at Pergamon he states:

I know where you are living, where Satan's throne is. Yet you are holding fast to my name, and you did not deny your faith in me even in the days of Antipas my witness [Greek: *martys*; hence "martyr"], my faithful one, who was killed among you, where Satan lives. (2:13)

John sets Antipas's death in the past ("in the days of"), not the present. Far from being persecuted, chapters 2–3 suggest Jesus-believers were active participants in imperial society, and John is not happy about this situation.

Although a date circa 90 for Revelation is possible, a suggestion of the late 60s has increasing support. This was a tumultuous time marked by Nero's suicide, the chaos and civil war of the year of four emperors in 68–69, the Jewish revolt against Rome, and imminent destruction of the Jerusalem Temple (66–70). This dating sees John attempting to make sense of Rome's success against God's people, land, and Temple. A reference in 11:2 could reflect Rome's incursion into Jerusalem: the "court outside the temple . . . is given over to the nations, and they will trample over the holy city for forty-two months."

Whether dating Revelation to 69–70 or to Domitian's reign, the proclamation reading sees Revelation wrestling with Rome's power. John uses the term "Babylon" (16:19; 17:5; 18:2, 10), a code-term for Rome in several other post-70 Jewish apocalyptic writings (for example, *4 Ezra* 3:1-2, 28-31; *2 Baruch* 10:1-3; 11:1) and in 1 Pet 5:13. He signals this connection by describing Babylon, the "great whore" (17:1), as seated on "seven mountains" (17:9), a common description of the city of Rome. The name "Babylon" recalled the ancient empire that in the sixth century B.C.E. destroyed Jerusalem, burned Solomon's Temple, and took much of the population into exile. Israel's Scriptures depict Babylon's punishment in violent, sexualized terms (Isa 21, 47; Jer 51; Ezek 16:39; 23:10, 29; Nah 3:6; cf. Rev 17:16). The implication is that Rome, the new Babylon, too will fall.

Moreover, in John's view, Satan is at work through Rome's political and economic activities. John mentions a second beast, which "had two horns like a lamb and it spoke like a dragon" (13:11). This figure, who parodies the image of Jesus as a slain lamb (5:6), promotes both worship of the first beast/emperor (13:12) and the empire's economic activity.

And it [the second beast] causes all, both small and great, both rich and poor, both free and slave, to be marked on the right hand or the forehead so that no one can buy or sell who does not have the mark, that is, the name of the beast or the number of its name. (13:16-17)

This mark does not comprise, contrary to some prediction readings, the Universal Product Codes now found on most goods sold in the West, Social Security numbers, or a computer chip implanted in one's body. Rather, for John's original readers, the

347

symbolism was immediately recognizable. Slaves were branded, marked on their bodies. Thus John speaks of people being enslaved to Rome and its "divine" rulers. The chapter reveals that to participate in the daily activities of buying and selling is to serve the beast and the power "behind the throne." The second beast could be any of Rome's agents: provincial governors, imperial priests, or elite families who promoted the imperial cult in the seven cities.

John explains this slavery in cosmic terms. Those marked are slaves of the devil, since the two beasts are agents of the dragon, "the Devil and Satan, the deceiver of the whole world" (12:9). Devil and empire coalesce. Conversely, the followers of Jesus are marked with the Holy Spirit (7:2-3; 14:1): Jesus' followers are slaves to a different Lord.

Empire and worship also coalesce. John's rejection of Rome extends to those who befriend Rome. His dualistic worldview defines pure faith and praxis for the churches while demonizing and damning other church members who disagree with him. In 2:6, for example, he commends the Ephesian congregation for hating "the works of the Nicolaitans which I also hate." In 2:14-15, he excoriates the church at Pergamum for those "who hold to the teaching of Balaam, who taught Balak to put a stumbling block before the people of Israel, so that they would eat food sacrificed to idols and practice fornication. So you also have some who hold to the teaching of the Nicolaitans."

Balaam, a figure from Israel's wilderness trials (Num 22–24; Deut 23:4-5), came to epitomize the false prophet (see 2 Pet 2:15) who entices Israel to idolatry in the name of an enemy king. With this allusion to Balaam, John hides the name of his actual opponent and increases the opponent's evil by association with an arch-villain.

Similarly, to the church in Thyatira, John writes:

> You tolerate that woman Jezebel, who calls herself a prophet and is teaching and beguiling my servants to practice fornication and to eat food sacrificed to idols. (2:20)

"Jezebel" teaches that participation in imperial society does not compromise faithfulness. Again John links his opponent to an ancient figure: Jezebel was the Phoenician wife of King Ahab of Israel, opponent of Elijah the prophet, sponsor of the prophets of Baal, and murderer of the vineyard owner Naboth (1 Kgs 16–21; 2 Kgs 9). By labeling "Jezebel" a "deceiver," John associates her with three other deceivers: the "great dragon . . . that ancient serpent who is called the Devil and Satan, the *deceiver* of the whole earth" (12:9, emphasis added; see also 20:3, 10); the second beast, who "*deceives* the inhabitants of earth telling them to make an image for the beast" (13:14, emphasis added; see also 19:20); and Babylon/Rome, who "*deceived*" all the nations with her sorcery (18:23, emphasis added.) Figures that John hates overlap to increase each other's damnable essence.

John increases Jezebel's villainy by sexualizing her and her followers, and by cursing them with death:

She refuses to repent of her fornication. Beware, I am throwing her on a bed, and those who commit adultery with her I am throwing into great distress, unless they repent of her doings; and I will strike her children dead. (2:21b-23b)

Accusations of commiting "fornication" (*porneuō*; 2:14; 20) connect John to Israel's prophets, who also used sexualized terms to describe infidelity. In some cases, terms such as "adultery," "fornication," and "prostitute" serve as synonyms for "idolatry" (Hos 4:10-19; Ezek 16:15, 34). Psalm 106:35-39 describes how Israel "mingled with the nations and learned to do as they did. They served their idols . . . and prostituted themselves in their doings." Committing fornication is John's understanding of, and metaphor for, participation in Roman society (17:2; 18:3, 9). For example, the "kings of the earth [who] have committed fornication, and with the wine of whose fornication the inhabitants of the earth have become drunk" (17:2), are Rome's client kings who participate in the empire's economy through trade, taxes, tributes, and patronage.

By describing Rome as both idolatrous and adulterous, John conjoins anti-imperial and anti-sexual language. In Rev 17, he presents Rome as a "great whore" (*pornē megalē*) and a mother of whores. Conversely, he connects virginity with fidelity in describing the "one hundred forty-four thousand who have been redeemed from the earth . . . who have not defiled themselves with women, for they are virgins" (14:3-4).

Political purity and sexual purity blend together.

The reference to food sacrificed to idols could refer to meat that had been consecrated to various deities in the temples throughout the empire and then sold to the public or food consumed during a festival honoring Rome's gods and emperor. Such festivals took place in temples, like the altar of Zeus in Pergamum or temple of Artemis in Ephesus. They also were held in civic spaces such as squares, theaters, stadia, and gymnasia. In the cities John addresses, such celebrations were pervasive. The imperial cult was established in Pergamum in 29 B.C.E. (Dio Cassius 51.20.6-9). Smyrna became a center of observance in 23–26 C.E. (Tacitus, *Ann* 4.15), and Ephesus dedicated a temple to the Sebastoi, literally "the revered or exalted ones," referring to the emperors, in 89/90 C.E. The emperor and deities were also honored in association or guild meetings that provided social and economic interaction among artisans, merchants, and laborers.

To refuse to participate in such civic activities meant losing social, economic, and perhaps even familial connection. Withdrawal from society threatened one's livelihood and survival. Clearly Rev 2–3 indicates that some Jesus-followers saw no problem with societal and cultic participation. As our discussion of 1 Peter indicated, some Jesus-followers believed that such participation was necessary for survival, even while they acknowledged Christ in their hearts (1 Pet 2:17; 3:6).

John's view is much more hardline. He sees the Nicolaitans and followers of "Balaam" and "Jezebel" as having compromised their faith by participating in the broader culture, and he condemns them for it. His pastoral guidance comprises demand and threat:

Repent . . . If not, I will come and remove your lampstand from its place. (2:5)

Repent . . . If not, I will come to you soon and make war against them with the sword of my mouth. (2:16)

And I will strike her children dead. (2:23)

The letters to the churches mention one more enemy, this time related to synagogue affiliation rather than participation in the Roman economic and cultic systems. To the church in Smyrna, he says,

I know the slander on the part of those who say that they are Jews and are not, but are a synagogue of Satan. (2:9)

To the church in Philadelphia, he says,

I will make those of the synagogue of Satan who say that they are Jews and are not, but are lying—I will make them come and bow down before your feet. (3:9)

Many interpreters propose that John here reacts to the expulsion of Jesus' followers from local synagogues. However, this thesis follows from an unsustainable understanding of the origins of the Fourth Gospel (see the chapter on John's Gospel).

Another explanation has greater credibility. Perhaps we should take John at his word and see him as condemning Gentile followers of Jesus who claim to be Jews, but literally "are not." They are, instead, Gentiles who both follow Jesus and follow distinct Jewish markers such as circumcision and dietary regulations. Thus they would be comparable to the Galatians who sought circumcision and whom Paul condemned. In this scenario, John regards himself and his followers as the true "synagogue," the true Israel, the real Jews.

The rest of Revelation continues to reveal the dangers of cultural accommodation. Revelation 17–18 narrates and parodies a lament at the downfall of the "great whore" Babylon/Rome. Chapter 18 focuses on Rome's economic exploitation by and of client kings (18:9-10), merchants and traders (18:11-17a), and artisans and laborers such as shipmasters, seafarers, and sailors (18:17b-24). A voice from heaven cries out, "Come out of her, my people, so that you do not take part in her sins." (18:4). Jesus' followers are not to participate in Roman society, period.

Yet, ironically, they do. John's rhetoric of destruction and victory is not dissimilar to Rome's. As is typical of powerless groups overwhelmed by powerful force, John and his supporters mimic aspects of Roman rule in imagining the universal imposition of God's empire and destruction of God's enemies. John replaces the emperor's throne with the divine throne (4:1). The accolades showered upon God and the Lamb, "You are worthy" (4:11; 5:9), are the same as those showered on Rome's emperor. The 24 elders "cast their crowns" (4:10) before the heavenly throne, just as the Hellenistic kings and later Roman tributes did at the throne of the Roman ruler. Domitian had 24 lictors who would prostrate themselves before his throne. God has the same.

John's ultimate description of divine power emphasizes not the destruction of the nations but their inclusion in the new Jerusalem. They bring "their glory" to it (21:24). God's power, finally, is reconciling, not destructive. Yet this contrast should not be heard without caution. Imperial powers always present themselves as benign and well-intentioned.

Genre

Proclamation readings of Revelation take seriously the work's genres. Revelation employs three genres to make its proclamation then and now: apocalypse, prophecy, and letter. We discuss the contribution of each.

An apocalypse is most aptly defined as a type of revelatory literature: it discloses or reveals something, whether heavenly mysteries or eschatological scenarios. The revelation is usually mediated through a heavenly figure to a human being.

These features are evident in Revelation. It begins:

The revelation [Greek: *apocalypsis*] of Jesus Christ, which God gave him to show his servants what must soon take place; he made it known by sending his angel to his servant John. (1:1)

The revelation originates with God and is mediated through Jesus and an angel to a human figure, John, for disclosure. The opening genitive "of Jesus Christ" has both subjective and objective implications: it is both the revelation that Jesus gives to John (subjective) and a revelation about him and his eschatological roles (objective). In 4:1, Revelation employs another common apocalyptic feature, a tour of the heavens. For John, the tour reveals what true worship, not worship of imperial figures, looks like, and it demonstrates God's sovereign power (Rev 4–5).

The genre of apocalypses often emerges in situations of crisis or perceived crisis, and the texts tend to describe the situation in highly dualistic terms. For John, the crisis may well have been the entry of Rome into Judea and the threat its troops posed to the temple, but the crisis is not limited to this threat. For John, also critical is the participation of Jesus' followers in Rome's cultural world; they have, in John's view, become idolaters and "fornicators" in participating in Rome's world. They have not, therefore, been listening to John. Yet he is certain both that Rome and its allies will be condemned, and that those who remain faithful to (his understanding of) God will be saved. To secure his vision, John promotes a dualistic worldview in two ways. First, he contrasts the present era of cosmic and imperial evil with God's beneficent rule. Second, he contrasts the righteous few who will be saved with the unrighteous many, who will suffer eternal torment. Because God is in control of history, and because the battle being waged is cosmic, the righteous must remain steadfast. God will intervene to judge the wicked and vindicate the righteous.

The Origin of Apocalypses

The genre of apocalypses developed in Jewish circles circa 200 B.C.E. to 100 C.E. Daniel 7–12, an apocalypse, dates from circa 165 B.C.E., during the reign of the Seleucid king Antiochus Epiphanes, who attacked Jewish practices. In a series of three visions revealed through an angel, Daniel names a time of tribulation, announces God's intervention, and anticipates divine victory. Another apocalypse, *1 Enoch*, cited in Jude, describes economic exploitation and political oppression from sinful landowners and governors. God will intervene through a heavenly figure called both a Messiah and the Son of Man (not referring to Jesus!) who will execute judgment and vindicate the righteous. Two apocalypses, *4 Ezra* and *2 Baruch*, respond to the destruction of the Jerusalem Temple with assurance of God's ultimate punishments and rewards.

Responding to a crisis that shakes the community's understanding of its own identity, its communal "myth" (grounding story), and its eschatological anticipations, apocalyptic literature provides hope and encourages resistance. The hope is in the just God, who establishes justice; the resistance is fostered by the positing of a dualistic worldview that refashions the identity of who is "in" and who is "out."

The genre shows influences from Persian dualism in its tendency to oppose the righteous God and a satanic figure and its division of humanity into the saved and the damned. Apocalypses also draw upon various wisdom motifs, such as explanations of natural phenomena and a concern for the cosmos rather than just the people of Israel. The concern for natural phenomena suggests not only knowledge of but also power over the universe. The cosmic focus challenges political power by showing divine control of time and space from creation to eschaton, Jerusalem to Rome, heaven to hell.

The greatest influence on apocalyptic is likely to have been prophecy. Texts that could be considered apocalyptic appear in chapters from prophetic books, such as Ezek 40–48, Isa 24–27, 56–66, and Zech 9–14. Revelation draws upon Daniel's image of the "Son of Man" (1:13; 14:14; cf. Dan 7:14) as well upon the "Ancient One" (Dan 7:9, 13) in its description of this "Ancient One" as having hair "white as white wool, white as snow" (1:14). The Septuagint locates the book of Daniel after Isaiah, Jeremiah, and Ezekiel, and thus regards Daniel as the fourth great prophet. The compilers of the Septuagint recognized apocalyptic literature more as a form of prophecy than wisdom. The Tanakh, however, locates Daniel among the Writings (Ketuvim) and emphasizes the text's wisdom and historical elements while downplaying its apocalyptic passages.

Revelation 1:3 employs a beatitude to announce a blessing on "the one who reads aloud the words of the prophecy." The beatitude identifies that Revelation's second genre, prophecy, functions primarily as it does in Israel's Scriptures: not to predict the future, but to interpret and address the present in order to reveal how present actions determine future results. The visions in Rev 6, for example, disclose judgment that takes place now by means of imperial acts of conquest (6:1-2) and war (6:3-4).

Revelation reveals three cycles of judgment on Rome. The first comprises the opening of seven seals (6:1–8:5). The opening of the first four seals (6:1-8) releases the so-called four horsemen of the apocalypse, who represent conquering military power, violent unrest, economic exploitation resulting in famine, and disease and death. The fifth seal identifies those who suffer under imperial rule and seek God's revenge (6:9-11). The sixth releases cosmic and social collapse (6:12-17). The seventh, delayed by a vision of heavenly worship, signifies a time of silence and prayer (8:1-5).

The second cycle of seven judgment scenes follows in 8:5–9:21. Each trumpet blast unleashes consequences resembling the plagues that convinced Pharaoh to free the Israelites from slavery (Exod 7–12). The first four trumpets signal destruction but only(!) on one-third of the earth (8:6-12). The fifth blast sees locusts "like horses equipped for battle" released by the king of the underworld, Apollyon. They are allowed to destroy and torture for only(!) the limited period of "five months" (9:1-11). The sixth releases a cavalry from across the Euphrates. John's first readers would likely have heard a reference to Rome's rival empire, the Parthians (they would not have imagined helicopters, as some Predictive interpretations do). A seventh trumpet reveals the establishment of God's empire (11:15-19).

The purpose of this second cycle is named in 9:20-21. Ancient prophecy was designed to encourage repentance. Generally it suggested what would happen *if the nation did not repent*, rather than to describe a fixed future. Apocalyptic writers sometimes offer the possibility of averting destruction, though typically they see that option as unlikely. Rather than provoke people to repent, the plagues solidify the view that God's enemies are recalcitrant and deserve punishment. Those killed "did not repent of the works of their hands or give up worshiping demons and idols . . . And they did not repent of their murders or their sorceries or their fornication or their thefts" (9:20-21).

A third cycle of judgments is announced in chapter 16 as God's wrath pours out from seven bowls.

Revelation's third genre is that of the letter. John the sender (1:4a) identifies the recipients as the seven churches in Asia (1:4b), greets them ("grace to you and peace," 1:4), and gives thanks "to him who loves us" (1:5). As with the opening of Paul's letters, this formula anticipates themes that the rest of Revelation develops. These themes include God's omnipotent rule and Jesus as the suffering but resurrected one.

A modified letter format reappears in chapters 2–3. Seven letters elaborate the general address of 1:4 to "the seven churches that are in Asia." In words appropriate for each situation, John commends each church—except Smyrna (2:9-11)—for faithfulness and rebukes each church for the infidelity of cultural-imperial accommodation.

The letter format usefully frames Revelation's proclamation to the seven churches. But having established John's authority and the situation of the recipients in chapters 1–3, the format gives way to apocalyptic and prophetic material.

From Prediction to Proclamation to Praxis

Whether understood as prediction or proclamation, John insists that Jesus' followers must not accommodate to the empire. Sociocultural interaction, public ritual, and imperial values are rejected as satanic. Instead, followers are to remain steadfast and await the imminent end and the establishment of God's justice in the new Jerusalem. John calls six times for "endurance" or long-standing, faithful resistance (Greek: *hypomonē*), even to the point of death (2:2, 3, 19; 3:10; 13:10; 14:12).

How, exactly, John expects his readers to live is less clear. Revelation offers no program of sharing necessities, nor an alternative economy based in barter.

To reframe the question in the context of the United States today: How should twenty-first-century followers of Jesus live in and relate to a world constituted by a powerful cultural, economic, and military empire? Should they engage this world as reflecting God's blessing or as being under God's judgment or as a complex hybridity of blessing and challenge? Who or what makes the ultimate claim on their allegiance? Revelation makes clear that engaging such questions is not only difficult but also life-determining.

As we have noted, the Bible speaks to multiple contexts with multiple voices. Against John's insistence on withdrawing from society, the Bible provides numerous examples of individuals who are blessed by God for participating in societal structures and even serving as agents of foreign governments even while maintaining their own beliefs and practices. Joseph's rise to power and prominence in Egypt provides one example (Gen 37–50). Jeremiah's exhortation (29:4-7) to the exiles in Babylon to "build houses . . .

plant gardens . . . take wives . . . [and] seek the welfare of the city . . . for in its welfare you will find your welfare" offers a second. Esther, the queen of Persia, offers a third. There is biblical warrant for significant cultural participation.

Perhaps Jezebel in Thyatira appealed to these biblical characters. Perhaps like the Jewish writer Josephus, she saw God's blessing in Rome's ascendancy. Josephus attributes to King Agrippa II the quote, "[W]ithout God's aid so vast an empire could never have been built up" (*Jewish War* 2.360, 390-91; 5.367-68). Josephus, who like Agrippa came to view the revolt of 66–70 as politically suicidal, warns those who rebelled, "You are warring not against the Romans only, but also against God" (*Jewish War* 5.378; cf. 5.396, 412). If Rome's empire is deemed the locus of God's blessing, or at least is seen as having the potential to do good, active cultural participation is the best strategy.

John is having none of that. Likely aware of the futile revolt in Judea and even the Jerusalem Temple's destruction, he thinks that only God can redeem the imperial world. Faithful followers of Jesus should distance themselves from this world in the devil's power (chs. 12–14) and under God's judgment (chs. 6–11, 15–22) and wait for God's intervention.

As we have seen, this intervention is pictured as destructive. Along with the difficult question of cultural and political accommodation, Revelation raises the question of theological violence. John graphically imagines, indeed celebrates, both God's destruction of Rome (ch. 18) and the destruction of any, including church members, who participate in Rome's social and economic spheres (2:19-23). Scenarios of violent judgment and downfall, presented as visions (1:10-20; 9:17; 18:1), comprise a sustained theme throughout the Apocalypse.

Readers of Revelation, disturbed by John's fantasies of revenge, correctly note ways of mitigating these images. In keeping with Revelation's motif of the number seven, we offer seven qualifications of the volume's eschatological violence.

First, John's visions of Rome's violent downfall are qualified by the recognition that the empire brings about its own demise. The four seals described in 6:1-8 release conquest, war, economic exploitation, famine, and pestilence. While these disasters depict God's punishment, the destruction does not happen because God intervenes. Conquest, war, economic exploitation, and sometimes famine are commonly consequences of human endeavors. Military power was foundational to Rome's rule. Economic exploitation was the normal behavior of Rome's ruling elites. Thus Revelation indicates that God allows Rome to experience the consequences of its own rule.

There is, however, tragic fallout from God's nonaction. There is general suffering. The fifth seal depicts martyrs who cry out to God, "How long will it be before you judge and avenge our blood?" (6:9-11). Even here, however, readers can take a positive image: in the midst of suffering, the faithful have the right to call upon God for justice.

A second factor qualifies John's desire for vengeance. In 8:6-12, as each of the first four trumpets blow, disasters happen. A third of the earth is destroyed along with a mountain and a third of the rivers and of the sun, moon, and stars. The fifth trumpet releases a swarm of scorpion-like creatures that attack people, but do not kill them (9:1-11). The sixth trumpet produces an attack that kills a third of the population (9:13-19). Yet this violence, despite its devastation, is limited. Mercy tempers the destruction. Further, 9:20-21 makes clear that this violence is to be understood not as revenge or judgment but as a warning to bring about repentance. The final battle (16:12-16) occurs only after people have been given the chance to repent. The desire for punishment is modified by a chance for repentance. Yet it would be a rare apocalypse that depicted the repenting of the sinful. John is not Jonah.

A third qualification involves God's life-giving power. One of the elders invites John, "See, the Lion of the tribe of Judah, the Root of David" (5:5). In a remarkable juxtaposition, what John is invited to see differs greatly from what he actually sees. The powerful Lion turns out to be "the Lamb standing as if it has been slaughtered" (5:6). Rather than causing suffering by exerting power, the lamb appears to have suffered at the hands of power. Instead of slaughtering, it has been slaughtered. God has triumphed over Rome, not with an act of violence but by raising the slain lamb, Jesus, from the dead (see John 1:29, 36; 1 Cor 5:7; 1 Pet 1:19). This lamb does not draw blood; instead, John learns that those "who have come out of the great ordeal . . . have washed their robes and made them white in the blood of the Lamb" (7:14).

The lamb is one mitigation of the violent image of the Christ as warrior. John also qualifies the violent fantasy of the eschatological battle (19:11-21) by stating that the rider on the white horse fights not with literal weapons but with "the sword that came from his mouth" (19:21; see 19:15). He wears a robe "dipped in blood" (9:13). This blood is more likely his own blood, poured out for others (see 1:5; 5:9; 7:14; 12:11), than the blood of those he kills. This image of the eschatological warrior who conquers with the sword of his mouth may well derive from the *Psalms of Solomon* (17:35), a Jewish text written around the time Rome established control over Israel (63 B.C.E.).

A fourth qualification is the insistence that the violence is not arbitrary. Not only are the punishments inflicted on the earth designed to encourage repentance, but also an angel declares God's judgments are true and just and celebrates, "It is what they deserve" (16:5-7). One may, however, disagree with the view that people "deserve" devastation.

A "green reading" of Revelation provides the fifth qualification. Hail and fire, mixed with blood, are hurled at the earth and a third of the earth is burned, along with a third of the trees and all green grass (8:7). A star falls from heaven and poisons a third of the earth's water (8:10-11). Bioterrorism, climate disruption, global warming, food and water shortages, pollution, and the use of nonrenewable energy sources find their antecedents in John's visions.

Yet alongside the violence, John presents images of nature operating in harmony with God. In 4:6-9, John describes four "living creatures." They resemble, respectively, a lion, an ox, a human being, and an eagle, likely representing wild animals, domesticated animals, people, and birds. These living creatures "day and night without ceasing . . . sing, 'Holy, holy, holy, the Lord God the Almighty, who was and is and is to come'" (4:8).

The worship of God by "every creature in heaven and on earth and under the earth and in the sea" is again emphasized in 5:13.

Humanity, represented by the creature with the face of a human being, exists in unison with the animals. Humanity also exists in harmony with the earth and the heavenly bodies. Revelation 12 begins with the description of

> a great portent [that] appeared in heaven: a woman clothed with the sun, with the moon under her feet, and on her head a crown of twelve stars. (12:1)

When the "great red dragon, with seven heads and ten horns" (12:3) threatens the baby she is about to birth, she and her child are protected. The woman's newborn son is "taken to God and to his throne" (12:5), and she flees to a "wilderness where she has a place prepared by God, so that there she can be nourished for one thousand two hundred sixty days" (12:6). When the dragon pursues her, the woman then receives "the two wings of the great eagle" (12:14).

The woman is imaged first as a goddess attired with astral portents. She then becomes connected to the animal world by her wings. Finally, she is connected to the earth, itself personified: "The earth came to the help of the woman; it opened its mouth and swallowed the river that the dragon had poured from his mouth" (12:16). These images destabilize any limited association between the woman and the external world. She can be the church, Mary the "Queen of Heaven," the redeemed Israel, or any other symbol that brings together heaven and earth, humanity and nature, maternal protection and the need for others' support.

Sixth, at the end of the book, John speaks of healing, so that the final image is one of restoration and peace rather than violence and war. Even though the "nations" and the "kings of the earth" are destroyed (19:15, 19-21), they come to life by the light—that is, the saving presence—of God that shines from the new Jerusalem (21:24-25). John's vision ends with healing for the nations (22:2).

The seventh qualification of Revelation's violence is John's insistence that the followers of Jesus do not use violence. Followers of "the Lamb standing as if it had been slaughtered" (5:6) are to employ the same nonviolent means of resistance as the Lamb. They negotiate Rome's world by bearing "faithful witness" (1:5), refusing to compromise although their stance creates social and economic hardships and may lead to martyrdom. They are the ones who "come out" from Rome (18:4). These witnesses gain victory not by violence, but by faithfulness (7:14-17).

Committed to God's purposes manifested in Jesus, John's readers are to envision the day when their practice replaces Rome's oppressive system. They speak "truth about power" rather than "truth to power." In John's vision, only God has the power to destroy

Rome and bring the justice—including punishment—that those who choose to follow Satan deserve.

Afterword

Revelation cannot be neatly tidied at the end. Over millennia, readers have reacted in different ways to this writing.

The images of violence, including rejoicing at the destruction of opponents, prove too great for some readers. The message of God's triumph and vindication of the faithful does not compensate for the slaughter and vengeance. The medium of apocalypses, which includes these revelations of violence, becomes the message. Other readers can detach the message and the medium. Focusing on John's vision of divine justice, they read the violent images as "only" symbolic, or as explicable, understandable fantasies prompted by trauma.

For some readers, Revelation offers an image of gender dystopia. The saved are male virgins; women epitomize evil (the whore of Babylon), are silent and seemingly helpless (the woman clothed with the sun), or are turned into cities (the heavenly Jerusalem, which descends to earth "as a bride," [21:2, 9]). Yet other readers celebrate the chorus of the "Spirit and the bride," who both exhort, "Come" to those who are thirsty and seek the "water of life" (22:17). They do not take John's comments about male virgins literally, and they recognize that John does not talk about a "real" prostitute, but about the Roman Empire.

For some readers, John's insistence that "all nations will come and worship before" God is praiseworthy indeed (15:4). For others, John has replaced the Roman Empire with God and his Christ, who rules as emperor. The violence Rome used to conquer its colonies has been replaced by the violence God uses to conquer Rome and those whom John opposes (like "Jezebel"). For still other readers, the difference between Roman violence and divine violence is not only quantitative but also qualitative. The two simply cannot be compared. Rome is evil and God is just. Rome deserves its punishment and the gracious God and his sacrificial Christ deserve to reign. For some readers, "empire" is not the worst system in the world, or beyond it. For them, anarchy and chaos are worse than control.

These different interpretations have merits and limitations. At the end, Revelation's symbolism and message remain both compelling and mysterious. And at the end, Revelation cannot be read on its own. It belongs to the Christian canon and needs to be read in relation to these other texts and the reader's understanding of these texts.

$\mathcal{I}$ndex of Methods

CPSIA information can be obtained at www.ICGtesting.com
Printed in the USA
LVOW08s1801120116

470290LV00009B/910/P